PRAISE FOR *CHINA: THE BUBBLE THAT NEVER POPS*

"Orlik covers complex debates in crystal-clear prose, spiced up with anecdotes from his years on the ground in China. His book serves as a primer on China's modern economic history, but, most importantly, lays out a strong contrarian case for why it can avoid a future crisis."
—Simon Rabinovitch, Asia Economics Editor, *The Economist*

"No one is better equipped to help us understand and to prognosticate the outcome of China's debt problem than veteran analyst Tom Orlik. This book has a rare combination of intense focus on the details of this complex problem and a lucid style which makes it a fun and engaging read to the educated public. Readers should prepare themselves for a wild ride through the twists and turns of a potential Chinese financial crisis."
—Victor Shih, Ho Miu Lam Chair Associate Professor in China and Pacific Relations, UC San Diego

"Orlik plucks vivid examples from all over China to tell the story of the economy's remarkable rollercoaster ride. Beijing has defied the odds to survive four momentous economic cycles in forty years, Orlik explains. Aided by clear writing style and a healthy dose of good humour, he determines how China might reinvent its economy for a fifth time."
—Celia Hatton, Asia Pacific Editor, BBC

"Thomas Orlik's *China: The Bubble that Never Pops* provides a valuable historical overview of the build-up of debt in the world's second-largest economy over the last two decades. The author's deep knowledge and perceptive analysis make the book a timely contribution to our understanding of China's state-capitalist financial system and inefficient allocation of capital."—Minxin Pei, author of *China's Crony Capitalism*

"Orlik takes a dispassionate look at how, despite massive debt, non-performing loans, white elephant projects, and infamous ghost cities, China's economy has defied all the nay-sayers – at least for now. In *China: The Bubble that Never Pops*, Orlik offers an inventory of the policy tools – often unavailable to western central bankers and political leaders – that China's Party technocrats have used to manage the economy and prevent or forestall hard landings. Lucid and highly readable, this is one of those rare books that manage to be accessible to non-specialists while still offering ample detail and data to those steeped in the arcana of the Chinese economy."—Kaiser Kuo, host of *The Sinica Podcast* on SupChina.com

"Mr. Orlik does an excellent job of explaining why China's economy keeps confounding those who have predicted for years that it is a bubble about to pop. But he is no wide-eyed naif, rather he walks readers through all the issues and risks and help us understand how policymakers keep things together, while making clear that the risk of an eventual crisis is real."
—Bill Bishop, Publisher, *Sinocism*

"Orlik musters his deep knowledge (and dry wit) to explain the stresses building beneath China's remarkable growth. The author mines his experiences as journalist and analyst covering China and Asia to provide clear comparative examples – he deploys 1980s Japan, 1990s Korea, and the catastrophic sub-prime crisis in the US, to illuminate the decisions taken by Chinese policymakers. This book is an accessible primer for anyone who wishes to understand China's choices today."—Lucy Hornby, China correspondent, *Financial Times*

China

China

The Bubble that Never Pops

THOMAS ORLIK

Oxford University Press is a department of the University of Oxford. It furthers
the University's objective of excellence in research, scholarship, and education
by publishing worldwide. Oxford is a registered trade mark of Oxford University
Press in the UK and certain other countries.

Published in the United States of America by Oxford University Press
198 Madison Avenue, New York, NY 10016, United States of America.

CIP data is on file at the Library of Congress
ISBN 978–0–19–087740–8

1 3 5 7 9 8 6 4 2

Printed by LSC Communications, United States of America

For Josephine, Saul, and Faith

CONTENTS

ACKNOWLEDGMENTS

Writing a book is hard. Writing a book about China is harder. I couldn't have done it without support over the years from colleagues on the economics team at Bloomberg, in the *Wall Street Journal* newsroom, and the Stone & McCarthy office. At Bloomberg in Beijing, I worked closely with Fielding Chen, Qian Wan, Justin Jimenez, and Arran Scott, benefiting from their deep reserves of expertise, and even deeper reserves of good humor. Stephanie Flanders and Michael McDonough gave me flexibility to pursue a book project at the same time as my day job. At the *Wall Street Journal*, I was lucky to have Andy Browne as bureau chief, Bob Davis, Liyan Qi, Bill Kazer, Aaron Back, Esther Fung, and Dinny McMahon as collaborators on the economics beat, Duncan Mavin and Carlos Tejada as editors, the opportunity to write for Josh Chin's China Real Time blog, and research support from Lilian Lin. Working at Stone & McCarthy I benefited from the wisdom of Logan Wright and David Wilder, whose combination of enthusiasm and cynicism proved to be the correct attitude to sustain eleven years covering China's economy.

Everyone who follows the Chinese economy has benefited from the perceptive work and contrasting views of Nicholas Lardy and Barry Naughton. Their analytic chronicles of the reform era are required reading for all students of China, and significantly informed my thinking—as well as providing material for some of the historical sections of this book. Jason Bedford has dived deeper into the weeds of China's financial sector than most, and was generous enough to share some of his thinking. I learned from Jamie Rush and Chang Shu's work on the impact of a China crisis on the rest of the world, David Qu's expertise on China's approach to financial stability, and Dan Hanson's analysis on the impact of the trade war.

The International Monetary Fund does excellent work on China; I've benefited from reading a lot of it, and from speaking with some of the authors. Conversations with officials at the People's Bank of China, China Banking Regulatory Commission, China Securities Regulatory Commission, Chinese Academy of Social Science, and National Bureau of Statistics, gave me a window into the official perspective. Travel up and down the country, and meetings with local officials, bankers, businessmen, real estate developers, factory workers, and farmers added color and realism.

Weiyi Qiu provided professional research assistance, and Cecilia Chang contributed to sections on debt at state-owned enterprises. David Pervin at Oxford University Press gave wise counsel on the process and, together with Macey Fairchild, insightful comments on the draft. Bob Davis and Nicholas Lardy read through the near-final manuscript, saved me from some embarrassing errors, and made valuable suggestions that strengthened the text at key points. Damien Ma provided valuable feedback on the final chapter. This book would not have been possible without Zhang Ayi, who looked after our three children when my wife and I were working. My daughter Josephine wouldn't forgive me if I didn't acknowledge that she typed out the title.

I'd like to thank my father, Christopher Orlik, without whose constant questioning about when I was going to write another book I might never have written another book. I'd also like to thank my mother, Judith Moore, for never asking me if I was going to write another book, and refer my father to that as a model for future conduct. Finally, my biggest debt is to my wife, Helena, who knows far more about what's going on in China than I do, but has yet to be persuaded to write any of it down.

A Tree Cannot Grow to the Sky

"I know why you don't want to do it," says Xi Jinping, addressing a room packed with China's top cadres, "but if you can't control debt while maintaining social stability, I will question if you are up to the job." July 2017, Beijing is baking in the summer heat, and the National Financial Work Conference—a five-yearly gathering of China's policy elite—is in full swing. President Xi Jinping is in the chair, a white name card perched in front of his imposing bulk—as if anyone doesn't know who he is. Premier Li Keqiang, wearing the white short-sleeved shirt favored by Chinese officials, is studiously taking notes. In past administrations, the premier would be calling the shots on the financial system. This time it's different. Xi is playing an outsize role. Li has been edged aside. Rows of other officials—People's Bank of China governor Zhou Xiaochuan, party secretaries of provinces the size of European countries, chairmen of the world's biggest banks—listen attentively. Xi's tone is stern, his words explosive. The debt-fueled growth model that powered China through close to four decades of development now risks tipping the country into crisis. The lending feast is over. The deleveraging famine is about to begin.

"Financial stability is the basis of national stability," Xi says. "Deleveraging state-owned enterprises is the top of the top priorities." Xi ticks off the list of China's debts. Central government is on the hook for 40 percent of GDP. Adding local government, the level is 65 percent. For the country as a whole, government, corporate, and household debt is 260 percent of GDP, as high as the United States. That borrowing has kept the wheels of the economy turning, paying for an investment boom that offset the export bust from the 2008 financial crisis. Now it has run too far, leaving banks overexposed, state-owned enterprises and local government borrowers overstretched. Close to 4 out of every 10 yuan in national income are required for debt servicing. Even in the US on the cusp of the great financial crisis, debt costs didn't rise that high.

Xi puts a hard cap on local government borrowing, something like the US debt limit. To ensure compliance, a tough new regime is put in place. In the past, local officials were judged on their ability to produce growth. Now, on top of that, they will be judged on how much they borrow. And that record will follow them from post to post—an administrative albatross around their necks. In the past, long-term concerns about China's financial stability played second fiddle to social stability. Officials paid lip service to controlling lending. If there was a choice between higher unemployment and higher debt, they always opted for the latter. Now, Xi says, that game is over. Social stability can't be sacrificed, but debt has to come under control. Anyone who can't hit both objectives needs to look for a new job.

For Xi, sixty-four years old and marching inexorably toward his second term as general secretary of the Communist Party and president of China, financial policy is unfamiliar territory. China's most powerful leader since the great reformer Deng Xiaoping (some say since the great helmsman Mao Zedong) has made national renewal his rallying cry. At home, that meant a crackdown on corruption, with Xi's graft-busters going after gouging officials no matter what their status. Hundreds of top ranked "tigers" and thousands of more junior "flies" were caught in the dragnet—an attempt to make the Party's image as white as officials' short-sleeved shirts. Abroad, it meant muscular assertion of China's interests. Xi put his imprimatur on the Belt and Road Initiative—a massive investment program intended to extend China's strategic reach through Asia into Africa and Europe. For a man focused on the big picture, a "China dream" of state-planned prosperity to counter the American dream of rugged individualism, the nitty-gritty of the financial sector seems like an unwelcome distraction. Yet here Xi is, large and in charge, impassive and insistent.

Past Financial Work Conferences were important. At the 1997 meeting, then-premier Zhu Rongji laid the groundwork for a massive cleanup of the banking system. In 2007, the China Investment Corporation—the country's $940 billion sovereign wealth fund—was launched. In 2012, policymakers picked through the wreckage of the global financial crisis. The 2017 meeting is a watershed. China's number-one leader has delved into, and mastered, the complexities of the financial system. His speech is long, detailed, peppered with technical jargon. It's been written not by the People's Bank of China or the China Banking Regulatory Commission, but by the office of the Leading Small Group—an elite team reporting directly to Xi. It's as if President George W. Bush, before the storm clouds of the great financial crisis had started to gather, delivered a lengthy speech on the hidden dangers in mortgage-backed securities and collateralized debt obligations. For Xi, though, the new focus on financial stability is not a choice, it's a necessity.

In the years ahead of the great financial crisis—the Lehman shock that pushed the world's major economies into recession—China was already running off-balance. The combination of the one-child policy (which reduced the requirement for spending on children and increased the need for saving for old age) and an inadequate welfare state (which pushed families to self-insure against risk of unemployment and illness) drove the savings rate higher. A high savings rate meant consumption was weak. The economy leaned heavily on investment and exports as drivers of growth. As the crisis hammered global demand, exports evaporated and reliance on investment increased. A state-dominated banking system and industrial sector, combined with creaking government controls on how credit was allocated, meant lending and investment were groaningly inefficient. In the years before the 2008 crisis, 100 yuan of new lending generated almost 90 yuan of additional GDP. In the years after, that number fell below 30 yuan. More and more credit was required to produce less and less growth.

Years of breakneck expansion in borrowing placed China in a perilous position. Banks lent too much, stretching their balance sheets to the breaking point. From 2008 to 2016 the banking system quadrupled in size, adding 176.7 trillion yuan in assets. Shadow banks—lenders that dodge the regulations put in place to ensure the stability of the system—exploded onto the scene, extending credit at ruinous rates to firms locked out of access to regular loans. State-owned industrial giants went deep into debt, paying for new steel mills, coal mines, and cement kilns, adding to already burgeoning overcapacity. Real estate developers painted their balance sheets in red ink, borrowing to build ghost towns of unsold property. Local governments dodged the regulations intended to keep public debt under control, creating opaque investment vehicles to borrow off the books. In the best cases, they did so to pay for worthwhile but unprofitable public works. In the worst, they wasted funds on lavish new offices, or the money simply disappeared into foreign bank accounts. Neither the economy nor the financial system was on a sustainable trajectory. The clear and present danger, if China carried on down the same road, was a crisis.

China's Communist Party are keen observers of world history. Xi had seen how crises that start in runaway lending end with financial collapse, economic recession, social unrest, and political turmoil:

In Japan in 1989, excess lending resulted in a bubble in equity and real estate. The bursting of that bubble turned the land of the rising sun from a threat to US dominance to a stagnant also-ran in the global race and ended the decades-long reign of the Liberal Democratic Party.

In Asia in 1997, the combination of high foreign borrowing and crony–capitalist relations between banks and business tipped China's neighbors into crisis. Financial meltdown toppled leaders throughout the region, ending the thirty-one-year reign of Indonesia's Suharto and propelling a former dissident democracy activist into South Korea's Blue House.

In the United States in 2007, runaway mortgage lending and lax
financial regulation triggered the subprime mortgage crisis.
A painful recession and slow recovery resulted in a wrenching
shift in US politics—a wave of populist anger that swept Donald
Trump into the White House.

Taking a broader historical sweep, Xi's chief economic advisor Liu He has
written how financial crisis can kick-start transitions in the global balance
of power.[1] In the 1930s, the Great Depression heralded the shift from an
exhausted Europe to a vigorous United States. In the 2000s, in Liu's view,
the financial crisis accelerated the shift in the balance of power from the
United States to China.

Now, the alarm bells are ringing for China. "A tree cannot grow to the
sky," warned the *People's Daily*—the Communist Party's mouthpiece—in
a front-page article in May 2016. "High leverage will lead to high risk, if
not well controlled it will lead to systemic financial crisis and recession."[2]
The International Monetary Fund—high priests of the global economy—
were as alarmist as their sanitized intonation allowed. "International experience suggests that China's credit growth is on a dangerous trajectory,"
they warned, "with increasing risks of a disruptive adjustment."[3] On bare-
knuckle Wall Street, money managers saw no reason to pull their punches.
China was on a "treadmill to hell," warned short-seller Jim Chanos, famed
for his early call that energy trader Enron was a house of cards. What was
happening in China "eerily resembles what happened during the financial crisis in the U.S.," warned billionaire investor George Soros. Adding
weight to those warnings, almost two decades earlier Soros had been one

1. He Liu, *Overcoming the Great Recession: Lessons from China* (Cambridge, MA: John
F. Kennedy School of Government, Harvard University, 2014).

2. "Authoritative Person Talks about the Chinese Economy (权威人士谈当前中国经济),"
People's Daily, 9th May 2016.

3. Sally Chen and Joong Shik Kang, Credit Booms – Is China Different? (Washington,
DC: International Monetary Fund, January 2018).

of those who bet successfully against China's neighbors in the Asian financial crisis.

Could Xi pull China back from the brink? The conventional wisdom said no. Credit had expanded too fast and been allocated too inefficiently. Bottom-up estimates—based on parsing the balance sheets of listed companies—suggested that more than 10 percent of loans were already at risk of default. China's decades of double-digit growth, which had enabled it to outrun past financial problems, were receding into memory. Far-reaching reform of creaking state firms might shift the economy back onto an accelerated growth trajectory, and increase efficiency of credit allocation. The Xi administration, however, appeared more focused on strengthening the ramparts of the state than on tearing them down.

As Xi declared war on debt, most commentators saw two possibilities:

With the economy addicted to credit, aggressive pursuit of deleveraging would hammer growth. Businesses with falling profits and local governments with lagging land sales revenue would be forced into default. The deleveraging campaign would trigger the financial crisis it was launched to prevent.

If Xi moved more cautiously, modulating the campaign to ensure GDP stayed on target, deleveraging would be just another passing policy fad. Slogans would be enthusiastically repeated. Behaviour wouldn't change. China might enjoy a few more years of credit-inflated growth, but the day of reckoning would not be long in coming.

Put simply, Xi faced an unpalatable choice: crisis now or crisis later.

When it comes to China, however, the conventional wisdom doesn't always get it right. At the end of the 1970s, few expected Deng Xiaoping to extricate China from the ideological dysfunction of the Mao era, placing it on a path of rational development. In 1991, as the Soviet Union collapsed, it looked like red China was on the wrong side of history—facing a choice between democratic reforms or regime collapse. The Communist Party chose neither, and China continued to grow. In 1997, as the Asian financial crisis swept away crony–capitalist regimes from Indonesia to Korea, the days for China—with its in-cestuous state-owned family—looked numbered. Then-premier Zhu Rongji used the crisis as a catalyst for reform—closing loss-making business, recapitalizing the banks, and pushing for entry into the World Trade Organization. In the great financial crisis, the collapse in global demand hammered China's exports and threatened to tip the economy into recession. A decisive 4-trillion-yuan stimulus meant it did no such thing.

Xi's deleveraging campaign wouldn't be easy, but China still had impor-tant points in its favor:

A high domestic savings rate, combined with controls on households taking their funds offshore, meant the banks could count on a steady inflow of cheap domestic funding. Financial crises typically start when banks' funding dries up. In China, that was unlikely to happen.

Average incomes were scarcely a third of the level in the United States—meaning there was abundant space still to grow. No one expected a return to 10 percent annual GDP growth. Expansion at 6 to 7 percent was attainable, and would mean more profits for business, income for households, and tax revenue for government—all money that could be used to pay down debt.

A decade of reforms had shifted China from government-set to market-set interest rates, under-valued to market-priced currency, financial autarky to managed cross-border capital flows, and crude loan limits to a modern price-based monetary policy. All of those transitions promised to increase the efficiency of credit allocation, breaking the spiral of ever-increasing lending to pay for ever-decreasing growth.

In the real economy, rapid gains in household income, and the rise of the labor-intensive and capital-light services sector, held out the promise of a virtuous circle of rising consumption, higher employment, and less dependence on debt-fueled investment.

China's policymakers are not all-knowing or all-powerful. They do have an unusually extensive and powerful set of tools they can use to manage the economy and financial system, and experience dragging major banks back from the brink of crisis.

Those factors didn't guarantee success. As he launched the deleveraging campaign, Xi was betting they gave him a fighting chance.

China's Debt
Mountain: The Borrowers

In few places are China's inefficiencies and dysfunctions more evident than Liaoning—a province of 44 million in the rustbelt northeast of the country.

It is May 2016, and the meeting between Dongbei Special Steel Group—one of Liaoning's struggling state-owned enterprises—and its creditors is not going well. Perhaps the decision to create the Group by welding together three hundred-year-old steel plants was ill advised. Maybe management's decision to expand capacity into a saturated market was unwise. Whatever the reason, Dongbei has seen better days. In March 2016, Chairman Yang Hua was found hanged in his home—an apparent suicide. Days later, the firm defaulted on an 852-million-yuan bond payment—the first of a series of missed payments on bonds worth 7.2 billion yuan. Now the Liaoning government is trying to strong-arm Dongbei's creditors—an assortment of banks and bond holders—to agree to a deal, swapping their loans for an equity stake. Few want shares in a firm with no profits and little prospect of any. Despite proposing the deal, the government hasn't shown up to the meeting. Neither has Dongbei's new chairman, prompting a caustic query: "Is your new chairman dead too?"[1]

1. Yuzhe Zhang, "东北特钢失信样本," Caixin, 22nd July 2016.

Creditors, among them China's biggest banks, are understandably irked. Loans to state-owned industrial firms are meant to be the safest of the safe. If state firms can't make repayments from their revenue, they have assets that can be sold. If asset sales fall through, the local government stands behind the loan. Now both of those fail-safes had failed. Dongbei is in default. The creditors issue a statement, blaming the "inaction of the Liaoning provincial government" and calling for a boycott of bonds issued by the province. In a Chinese system where deals are cut behind closed doors and losers nurse their grievances in silence, that public outcry was unusual. It didn't do the creditors any good. In August 2017, a restructuring plan was approved. Creditors got 22 cents on the dollar, or fen on the yuan, in the Chinese context.

It is corporations like Dongbei Special that account for the lion's share of borrowing in China's economy. Based on Bank for International Settlements data, China's corporate debt at the end of 2016 was 118.5 trillion yuan, equal to 160.5 percent of GDP. Even that astronomical number likely understates the true level of borrowing:

> Starting around 2012, China's banks began aggressively moving loans off the balance sheet. Reclassifying loans as investment products enabled them to dodge regulatory controls on loan-to-capital ratios, as well as policy campaigns aimed at cutting off funds to firms operating with too much debt, or producing too much pollution. Poring through 2016 financial reports from 237 lenders, analysts at Swiss investment bank UBS found some 14.1 trillion yuan in shadow loans (equal to about 18.9% of GDP), up from less than a trillion yuan in 2011.[2]
>
> Tighter credit conditions have pushed cash-strapped firms into slower settlement of accounts—repaying loans from banks ahead of bills from suppliers. Accounts receivable for China's big industrial firms rose to about 12.7 trillion yuan in 2016 (17% of GDP), up from 7.1 trillion yuan in 2011.[3]

2. Alfred Liu, "These Are China's Shadow Banking Hotspots," Bloomberg, 6th September 2017.

3. *China Statistical Yearbook* (Beijing: National Bureau of Statistics, 2017).

Throw in a few trillion yuan in borrowing from informal lenders—a motley crew ranging from peer-to-peer lending platforms to loan sharks—and the actual level of corporate debt could be closer to 200 percent of GDP.

Even assuming the Bank for International Settlements number is correct, China's corporate debt rings alarm bells. As figure 2.1 shows, in international comparison it's a very high number—off the scale relative to both major developed and emerging economies. Corporate debt in the United States and Japan ended 2016 at 72 percent of GDP and 99.4 percent of GDP, respectively. Looking at other emerging markets, the average for Brazil, Russia, India, and South Africa—which together with China make up the BRICS—was just 44.4 percent of GDP.

Within China's 160.5 percent of GDP total for corporate debt, borrowing by state-owned firms like Dongbei Special accounts for an outsize share of the total. Based on National Bureau of Statistics data, as of 2016 total borrowing for state industrial firms was about 67 percent of GDP.[4] The International Monetary Fund put it at 74 percent of GDP.[5] The real total might be higher still. As the China experts at research firm Gavekal Dragonomics note, the bulk of accounts payable represents bills owed by state firms to their private-sector suppliers—a hidden debt pile for the state sector (and a hidden tax on private firms waiting to be paid for their work).

High debt for state firms is a problem. Given the special role they play in China's economy, it's not a surprise. State firms smooth the ups and downs of growth, drive the government's development strategy, and provide patronage opportunities for leaders.[6] In the first case, that means acting as the borrower of last resort, keeping the wheels of growth turning by breaking ground on new projects when private firms have turned cautious. In the second, it means borrowing to pay for the buildout of priority

---

4. *China Statistical Yearbook*, 2017.

5. Sally Chen and Joong Shik Kang., *Credit Booms—Is China Different?* (Washington, DC: International Monetary Fund, 2017).

6. Barry Naughton and Kellee Tsai, *State Capitalism, Institutional Adaptation, and the Chinese Miracle* (Cambridge: Cambridge University Press, 2015).

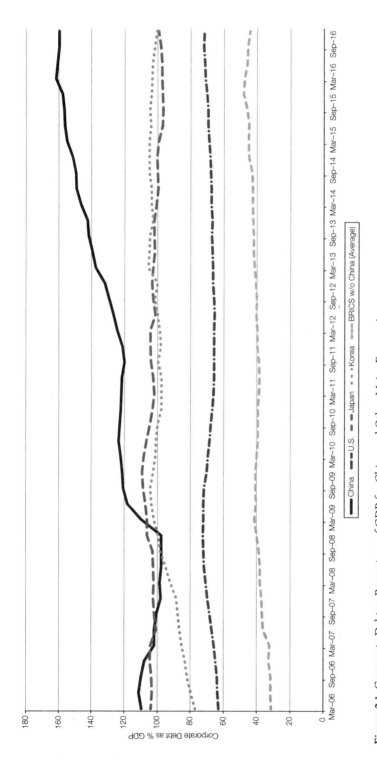

Figure 2.1 Corporate Debt as Percentage of GDP for China and Other Major Economies

SOURCE: Bank for International Settlements.

infrastructure and industrial capacity—steel mills, aluminum smelters, electricity and telecom networks, and the roads, rails, and ports necessary to take products to market. That buildout was capital-intensive, and so the state firms that took the lead role took on a heavy burden of debt.

That special role means state firms get loans to carry out priority projects—whether or not they will generate a profit. "We're state-owned," said the manager of a multibillion-yuan gas–power project in an industrial park near the northern metropolis of Tianjin, "so it doesn't matter if we make any money." If revenue isn't sufficient to cover repayments, loans get rolled over, or government backers provide additional support. Since April 2015, when power equipment producer Baoding Tianwei gained the dubious honor of first default by a state-owned firm, there has been a trickle of other missed payments—including the Dongbei debacle. Even so, from the perspective of the banks—almost all of which are also state-owned—loans to other parts of the family look like a safe bet.

If borrowing is required to drive development and manage the ups and downs of the economic cycle, concentrating the buildup of leverage in the corporate sector is the least bad option. When households borrow too much, as in the United States ahead of the great financial crisis, the result is McMansion-littered suburbia. If government borrows to fund consumption, as in Greece ahead of European debt crisis, the result is an unsupportable burden from public-sector wages and welfare payments. Sustaining growth with loans to businesses is—at least potentially—different. China's firms used their borrowing to fund investment in the capital stock—infrastructure and industrial capacity—expanding the economy's growth potential. China's capital stock in 2008 was about the same level as the United States in the 1950s.[7] Starting from a low base, China's corporates had a decent shot at making productive investments, generating returns that could be used to repay borrowing.

7. Fielding Chen, "Plenty of Room for Capital Spending in China," Bloomberg, 16th July 2014.

That's true in theory. In practice, it didn't work out that way. Indeed, the breakneck investment growth that began at the end of 2008, combined with the outsize share of credit directed to inefficient state firms, was bound to result in serious misallocation of capital. The cycle is a familiar one. Cheap credit drives aggressive investment. Aggressive investment results in excess capacity. Excess capacity means that prices and profits fall. Chief executives who enjoyed spending borrowed funds on the way up find that repayment is difficult on the way down. The problem of moral hazard—the assumption that deep-pocketed government backers will always repay loans to state-owned firms—compounds the difficulty. With the chances of default low, credit is priced too cheaply and allocated too carelessly.

The regional manager of one of China's more commercially oriented banks explained how lending decisions were made. "First we look at what the central government's plans are," he said, "then we work out which local projects fit into those plans—that's where we make our loans." That—offered as a straightforward explanation of operations rather than a confession of poor practice—shows how moral hazard permeates China's financial system. The loan assessment process had nothing to do with hard-nosed calculation of risk and return, everything to do with brown-nosed investigation of which projects had the backing of Beijing, and so would be immune from default.

Steel illustrates the corrosive impact of China's credit cycle. From 2007 to 2014, driven by firms like Dongbei Special, investment in steel production rose 80 percent. Demand managed a much smaller increase. The resulting overcapacity triggered a 70 percent drop in prices, turning profits into losses and pushing producers toward bankruptcy. According to the official data, bad loans stayed low. Using an alternative calculation, based on the share of debt taken on by firms without enough earnings to cover their interest payments, in 2015 the bad loan ratio for metals and other basic resources firms was 46 percent. Almost half of debt in the sector was with firms that didn't have enough earnings to cover interest payments on their loans, let alone repay principal.

The problem of torrid loan growth underpinned by pervasive moral hazard is not unique to China.

In Japan in the 1980s, major banks were at the center of "financial keiretsu," with cross-holdings of stocks and lending between bank and corporations. The interlocking network of cross-ownership and lending was thought to be a guarantee against default. In fact, while it did help smooth out bumps in the business cycle, it also encouraged loan officers to turn a blind eye to the risks, allowing lending to rise too fast and preventing banks from pulling the plug on failed projects.

In South Korea in the 1990s, massive conglomerates—known as *chaebols*—played a critical role in executing the government's industrial strategy. In return, they received an implicit guarantee against default, enabling them to tap loans at bargain rates. When financial deregulation eroded lending discipline, the result was a massive accumulation of debt, much of it wasted on vanity projects.

In the United States in the 2000s, mortgage lending rose too quickly, much of it channeled to households with limited capacity to repay—the NINJA loans to borrowers with "No Income, No Job, and No Assets." The foundation for that house of cards: government backing for giant mortgage financers Fannie Mae and Freddie Mac, which enabled them to borrow cheaply, stock up on high-risk loans, and operate with insufficient capital buffer.

It seldom ends well. The collapse of Japan's bubble economy in 1989, Korea's 1997 crisis, and the US subprime meltdown all found their origin in the twin problems of rapid loan growth and moral hazard. The difference in the case of China's state sector is that it's bigger. As figure 2.2 shows, revenue for China's state-owned firms is larger than the GDP of Germany.[8] If China's state-owned firms stumble beyond the ability of the government to support them, the consequences will be bigger, too.

8. *China Statistical Yearbook*, 2017.

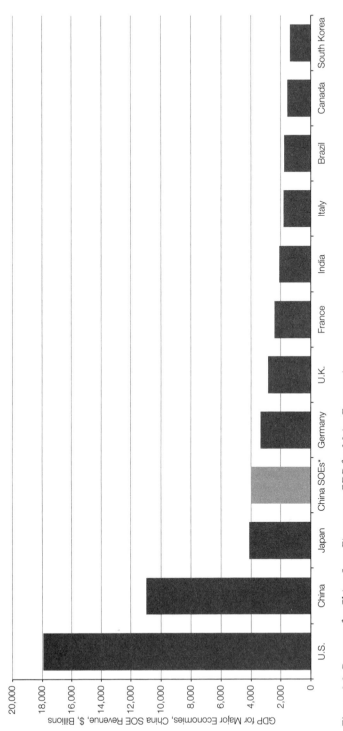

Figure 2.2 Revenue for China State Firms s vs. GDP for Major Economies

Total revenue of China's state-owned enterprises in 2014.

SOURCE: National Bureau of Statistics, IMF.

CHINA'S GREEK TRAGEDY—ADDING UP LOCAL GOVERNMENT DEBT

China's local governments, said an economist attached to the powerful National Development and Reform Commission, are like "lots of little Greeces." It's not clear if the reference was to Greece's high debt or to the fake budget numbers that tipped the European economy into crisis. In the case of Liaoning, both would be correct.

In Mao's time, Liaoning—which together with Jilin and Heilongjiang makes up China's northeastern rustbelt—was dubbed the "the eldest son of the republic," a reflection of its central role in efforts to accelerate industrialization. Fast-forward half a century and it looked more like an elderly relative. In 2016, the year of Dongbei Special's default, Liaoning's economy contracted 2.5 percent—the worst-performing province by a wide margin. Investment spending plunged 63.5 percent. Tax revenue—funds the government could have used to bail out its troubled enterprises—barely eked out an expansion. Even those dire numbers are open to question. China's auditors called out the Liaoning government for "rampant" exaggeration, including overstatement of fiscal revenue by at least 20 percent.[9]

For Liaoning's government finances, the beginning of the problem could be traced back to November 2008. It was then, responding to the collapse of Lehman Brothers and the start of the great financial crisis, that Premier Wen Jiabao promised a 4-trillion-yuan stimulus to keep China's growth on track. For Wen—who will be remembered for pinpointing China's economic problems but not nailing the needed solutions—it was his finest hour. The 4-trillion-yuan stimulus wowed the markets, saved the economy from recession, and reinforced the notion that China's authoritarian model was a viable alternative to the mess Western democracies found themselves in.

The trouble for Liaoning, and other provinces up and down the country, was that Wen only forked out 1.2 trillion yuan of the total. Local governments were on the hook for the rest. In Liaoning, borrowing

9. *People's Daily*, "辽宁省省长陈求发：我们顶着压力挤压水分," 17th January 2017

filled the gap. On a trip to the province in September 2009, Wen said the stimulus was aimed at solving China's short- and long-term problems—boosting demand and tackling the unbalanced reliance on credit-fueled investment."We have made vigorous efforts to stimulate consumption," he said, "[making] domestic demand, particularly consumer spending the primary driver of economic growth." The reality was rather different. Debt-financed buildout of infrastructure and industrial capacity kept the wheels of growth turning. There was little in Liaoning's stimulus that supported the needed rebalancing toward consumption. By 2016 the stimulus was over, returns on infrastructure projects were low, industrial firms (now producing more than they could sell) faced mounting losses, and the auditors were calling out provincial leaders for their fake data.

Already in 2010, the province's auditor found that 85 percent of local government financing vehicles—the shell companies through which stimulus funds were borrowed—had insufficient income to cover their debt payments.[10] By 2016, a trawl through bond prospectuses found that, on average, Liaoning's local government financing vehicles had return on assets of just 1 percent. A bottom-up look at corporate balance sheets found that about 10 percent of borrowers had insufficient income to cover interest payments on their loans.[11] Stimulus funds had buoyed growth through the downturn. They had not created enough revenue-generating assets to repay even the most heavily discounted loan.

How much debt does China's government have? According to the Ministry of Finance, total government debt at the end of 2016 was just 27 trillion yuan, or 37 percent of GDP. Public debt at that level looks manageable. Major developed economies like the United States (107 percent of GDP), Japan (236 percent), and Germany (68 percent) typically have a much larger burden, and considerably less scope to grow their way out

10. Judy Chen and Dingmin Zhang, "Liaoning Companies' Income Insufficient to Cover Debt Servicing," Bloomberg, September 9, 2011.

11. Tom Orlik and Justin Jimenez, "Bad Debts? That's a Flyover Province Problem," Bloomberg, April 12, 2017.

of difficulties. Major emerging markets like Brazil (78 percent) and India (69 percent) also compare unfavorably.

The question is, does 37 percent represent an accurate picture of China's government debt burden? It doesn't. The Ministry of Finance adopted a narrow definition of official borrowing including only central government debt, and the fraction of local government debt for which the central government has accepted responsibility. A complete accounting would include off-balance-sheet borrowing by local governments, and bond issuance by the government-owned policy banks that finance major infrastructure projects. Adding in borrowing by Dongbei Special and China's 19,272 other big state-owned enterprises, unfunded liabilities in the public pension system, and the potential cost of recapitalizing the banks would push the number higher still.

The explanation for the biggest chunk of hidden government debt—off-balance-sheet liabilities for local government—lies in an important dynamic in China's politics: the struggle for control between Beijing and provincial capitals. From the outside, it looks like President Xi Jinping, ensconced in his Zhongnanhai leadership compound, has a writ that runs down through province, county, and town to the smallest village. The reality, to quote a Chinese proverb, is that "the top has its measures, the bottom has its countermeasures." Chinese politics is not rigidly hierarchical; it is a struggle for control between the center and the provinces. Small wonder that then-president Hu Jintao's first anti-corruption scalp was the rebellious party boss of Shanghai, and that Xi's anti-corruption crackdown resulted in a new roster of loyalist party secretaries across the thirty-one provinces.

Central to that struggle between the center and the provinces: control of the budget. In 1994, fearing that China's reforms had stripped central government of the funds it needed to exercise effective control, then–vice premier Zhu Rongji realigned responsibility for taxing and spending. Local governments were left carrying the burden of paying for social services. Beijing grabbed the lion's share of the tax take. Caught between diminished revenue streams and expanding spending obligations, local cadres had to find a way to make ends meet. The beginning of a real estate boom, combined with a state monopoly on ownership of land, provided an ugly but effective solution. Land sales by the government to property developers became a major source of funds. At the same time, the creation of off-balance-sheet financing vehicles allowed local governments to evade controls on direct borrowing, tapping the banks for credit.

A typical structure for off-the-books borrowing looks something like this. Local governments inject land and other valuable assets into an off-balance-sheet financing vehicle and implicitly promise to stand behind any debt, enabling borrowing at below-market rates. Borrowed funds are used to pay for urban development projects—ranging from new roads and water treatment plants to tourist zones and affordable housing. If the projects go well, they generate revenue and the value of the other land on the balance sheet goes up, enabling repayment of borrowed funds. If they go badly, the local government has to step in with more support—injecting additional assets that can be sold to make repayments. That institutional framework had been in place since the 1990s, but it was not until the great financial crisis hit at the end of 2008 that local officials tested the limits of its potential.

For local government budgets, 2009 was close to a perfect storm. On the revenue side, the crisis hammered income from tax and land sales. On spending, local treasuries had to finance their share of Wen's 4-trillion-yuan stimulus, as well as increased social obligations. To fill the gap, they turned to borrowing. By the end of 2010, local government debt registered at 10.7 trillion yuan (26.1 percent of GDP), more than double its level two years earlier. By 2013, the last date for which comparable official data is available, the total had risen to 17.9 trillion yuan (29.9 percent of GDP). Even at that point, the official data—the results of an extensive trawl by the National Audit Office—likely understates the true debt level. In the years that followed, it definitely does.

In March 2016, then–minister of finance Lou Jiwei said that total local government debt at the end of 2015 was just 16 trillion yuan—some 1.9 trillion yuan lower than it had been two years earlier.[12] Given that both bond

---

12. Xiaoyi Shao, "China's Fin Min Says Risk of Local Government Debt Under Control," Reuters, March 6, 2016.

issuance by local financing vehicles and infrastructure spending financed by them had continued unabated, a drop in debt appears implausible. The likely explanation: under pressure to contain the problem without denting growth, officials had resorted to an accounting trick—reclassifying a chunk of local government debt as corporate debt. How high had debt actually risen? Diving into the balance sheets of local financing vehicles, a team of academics led by People's Bank of China advisor Bai Chong'en has a stab at the answer.[13] They estimate the stock of local government debt in 2015 at about 45 trillion yuan (64 percent of GDP).

Local debt isn't the only omission from China's government balance sheet. The policy banks—China Development Bank, Agricultural Development Bank, and China Export Import Bank—are immense, state-owned, and borrow extensively from the bond market to fund their operations. To get a complete picture of China's government debt, their borrowing has to be added to the total. At end 2016, China's three policy banks had liabilities of 21.7 trillion yuan, or 29 percent of GDP. Adding up central government debt, local government debt, and borrowing by the policy banks puts China's public debt at 130 percent of GDP in 2016. That's a troubling level. It places China's public debt in the range of major developed economies, and above most major emerging markets.

There's little consensus on the level at which government debt starts to be a problem. There is broad agreement on one point—higher is worse. Higher public debt means a heavier repayment burden. Funds that could have been used to pay for expanded provision of healthcare and education—a crucial underpinning of China's promised transition to a consumer-driven economy—have to be used for debt servicing. Banks that could be making more loans to entrepreneurial start-ups, catalyzing China's shift to a more dynamic, private-sector led growth model, find themselves using the funds to roll over loans to ailing government projects. In a downturn, financing a boost to growth from higher public spending or lower taxes is harder to do.

13. Chong-En Bai, Chang-Tai Hsieh, and Zheng Song, *The Long Shadow of China's Fiscal Expansion* (Washington, DC: Brookings Institution, 2016).

Worse, China's debt was increasing at a torrid pace. The official data put the 2016 budget deficit at 3.7 percent of GDP. As with the Ministry of Finance's take on the debt level, that reflects a strict definition of government borrowing. Taking account of off-balance-sheet borrowing, funds for infrastructure spending, and land sales, the International Monetary Fund calculated the "augmented deficit" at 10.4 percent of GDP. Deficit spending sustained at that pace would rapidly push China's public debt to vertiginous levels. In their seminal study of financial crises, Harvard economists Carmen Reinhart and Kenneth Rogoff found that the relationship between debt and crisis runs in both directions.[14] High debt causes crises, and crises result in higher debt. If China's hidden government borrowing does trigger a meltdown, the public finances would go in weak, and come out weaker.

GHOST TOWNS, REAL DEBTS: CHINA'S PROPERTY MARKET

China's state-owned enterprises and local governments are two legs of the rickety debt stool. The third is real estate.

The route along the high-speed rail from Zhengzhou, the capital of Henan province, to Luoyang, an industrial town ninety miles away, is crowded with property developments. Tower blocks rear out of the smog, in varying stages of undress. Some are little but a concrete shell, surrounded by scaffolding; others already have their skin of faux classical pillars and balustrades. They have one thing in common—little sign of life. Around the unfinished projects, there are no scurrying workers or clanking cranes. In the finished ones, no buyers throng the show rooms. That's not for want of trying on the part of developers: "Free car with every 15 percent down payment," proclaims the banner on one particularly forlorn-looking structure.

---

14. Carmen Reinhart and Kenneth Rogoff, *This Time Is Different: Eight Centuries of Financial Folly* (Princeton, NJ: Princeton University Press, 2011).

If buyers remain unenticed, there's good cause. In the great financial crisis and the years that followed, Luoyang's city government turned to property construction to buoy growth through the slump. With credit abundant and controls aimed at capping price rises stripped away, speculators drove demand higher. Sensing easy profits, developers started new projects. Industrial firms with no experience in property decided to get in on the action. The city government gave factories brownfield sites on the outskirts of town, encouraging them to vacate city-center plots to make way for new apartments and shopping malls. "You make a loan to an industrial firm to build a new factory, but the money ends up in real estate," said a loan officer from one of the main local banks.

Mr. Guo, the vice president of a local real estate developer, sensed the turnaround at the start of 2009. "Normally February and March are the off season for sales," he said. "This time, with supportive policies and government propaganda, buyers' confidence has increased."[15] Mr. Guo had a gift for understatement. As the US financial crisis hammered exports, booming real estate provided needed stimulus. Between 2010 and 2011, land sales doubled. The result, a few years down the line: a city swamped in oversupply. As of the end of 2016, Luoyang, a town of 6.7 million, had 33.7 million square meters of residential property under construction— five square meters for every man, woman, and child in the town. With the market flooded, the boom was over. In 2016, with prices falling, developers cut new project offerings by more than a third.

As with all bubbles, China's property bubble has a basis in fundamentals. Until the 1990s, there was no private housing market in China. Everyone from the Politburo Standing Committee in their leadership compound to the street cleaners in their dormitory lived in government housing. In the twenty years that followed the creation of the private market, the dilapidation of the public housing stock, millions of people per year migrating from the country to the city, and rapidly rising incomes for existing city dwellers drove huge demand. If construction had just kept pace, there

15. Zhang Yawu, "Spring for Real Estate Market Needs Common Care," *Luoyang Daily*, March 27, 2009.

would have been a major boom and no risk of a bust. The trouble is, even as demand was rising fast, supply rose faster.

From 2010 to 2017, looking at China as a whole, construction ran at about 10 million new apartments a year. As shown in figure 2.3, demand from rural migrants, natural growth in the urban population, and depreciation of the existing urban housing stock was less than eight million units a year. In the gap between those two numbers: ghost towns of empty property, uninhabited tower blocks ringing every city, and the Luoyang developer's desperate offer of a car with every down payment. In total, in 2016 there were about 12 million empty apartments in China—enough to house the entire population of Canada.

Two factors tipped China's housing market from urbanization boom into ghost-town bubble. First, for mom-and-pop investors, real estate was the only show in town. Bank deposits, with their below-inflation returns, looked unattractive. The rollercoaster stock market, lurching between huge gains and massive losses, was too volatile to act as a store of value. Wealth management products—retail investments with some of the safety of a bank deposit but markedly higher returns—could ultimately be a

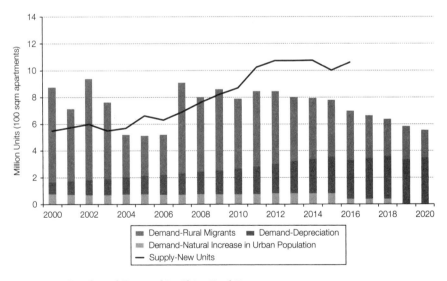

Figure 2.3 Supply and Demand in China Real Estate.
Source: Bloomberg Economics, National Bureau of Statistics

game-changer, but so far haven't slaked appetite for real estate. The result was intense speculative demand. According to the China Household Finance Survey—a large-scale national survey of saving and investment behavior—even as evidence of overbuilding grew, speculators accounted for about 30 percent of China home purchases.

Second, for China's government, real estate is the ballast that keeps the economic ship afloat. That's been true ever since the creation of the private housing market. In the late 1990s, China faced a twin challenge to growth. The Asian financial crisis hammered exports. Then-premier Zhu Rongji's root-and-branch reform of the state sector triggered a wave of factory bankruptcies and a sharp rise in unemployment. Investment in real estate, combined with a substantial slug of infrastructure spending, helped put a floor under growth. It remained true in the stimulus that followed the great financial crisis, when mortgage rates were cut, down-payment requirements lowered, and administrative controls lifted with an eye toward securing sufficient property construction to keep growth on track.

All of that construction has come at a price. Based on data from the National Bureau of Statistics, total debt for real estate developers came in at about 48.9 trillion yuan at the end of 2016, up from 10.5 trillion in 2008. Mortgage lending—including loans from a government fund for homebuyers—rose fast as well, climbing to 27.9 trillion yuan in 2016, up from about 4.5 trillion yuan in 2008. Putting those numbers together, total lending to the real estate sector rose to 76.8 trillion yuan (103 percent of GDP) in 2016 from 15 trillion yuan (47 percent of GDP) in 2008.

Even those numbers very likely understate the depths of the debt hole. On the developer side, government attempts to cool prices locked smaller builders out of access to conventional sources of credit. With the front door to the banks closed, many made use of the side entrance. "About 90 percent of our off-balance-sheet loans are to real estate developers," said one corporate loan officer at a major bank's Henan head office. For others, it means paying high rates—typically above 10 percent—to borrow from shadow banks. According to the China Trustee Association, at the end of 2016 shadow bank loans to real estate developers came in at 1.4 trillion yuan. A final group raised funds by issuing dollar bonds offshore—combining a higher cost of credit and exchange rate risk if the yuan depreciates.

Looking at developers' balance sheets, the signs of stress are clear. For China's most highly-levered home builders, debt is so high it would take more than ten years of earnings to pay it off. For the banks, risks are compounded by the critical role of real estate in the wider economy, and as collateral across their loan book. Real estate and construction account directly for 13 percent of China's GDP. Add in demand for steel, cement, home electronics, and furniture, and it's probably close to 20 percent. Weakness in real estate also hammers land sales—the main source of revenue for local government borrowers. And by reducing the value of collateral it triggers margin payments on loans—risking a downward spiral or falling prices, fire sales of inventory, and further price falls. A slump in real estate could have systemic consequences.

In the history of financial crisis, real estate plays a prominent role:

In 1989, at the height of Japan's property bubble, the land around the Imperial Palace was said to be more valuable than all of the real estate in California. Restrictions on bank loans to real estate developers were one of the catalysts for the bubble to burst, triggering a 72 percent drop in land prices and pushing Japan into a lost decade of stagnant growth and falling prices.

In 1997, with the Asian financial crisis poised to topple the region's economies like dominoes, Thailand's real estate bubble provided an early indication that something was amiss. Demand for office space in the capital, Bangkok, was running at less than half of construction.

In the United States in 2007, it was subprime mortgage lending that lit the fuse for the great financial crisis. Mortgage debt had risen to about 100 percent of GDP. "If you had a pulse, we gave you a loan," said an employee at Countrywide—a mortgage broker whose reckless lending helped bring on the crisis.

No surprise then that China's real estate sector has been a persistent focus of concern. "They can't afford to get off this heroin of property development," said Jim Chanos, the hedge fund manager who called the collapse of Enron back in 2001. "It's the only thing keeping the economic growth numbers growing."[16] Not to be rhetorically outdone by a foreigner, former Morgan Stanley economist Andy Xie chimed in. China's property investors were like "hairy crabs"—a Shanghai delicacy, best cooked in bamboo steamer baskets. "They will be cooked," said Xie, "they just don't know it yet."[17]

REASONS FOR RESILIENCE

There were plenty of reasons for concern about the health of China's borrowers. Getting less attention: the benefits of stimulus relative to the alternatives, the broader gains from infrastructure investment, and reforms that tilted the dial toward efficiency.

> There's a story, probably apocryphal, about a senior Chinese leader
> asked whether the short-term growth boost from stimulus
> was worth the long-term costs to the economy from increased
> reliance on credit-fueled investment. "A little bit more imbalance,"
> he is said to have responded, "is better than a lot of collapse."
> There is a high cost to recession and financial crisis. Workers
> who lose their jobs take a permanent step back as skills atrophy.
> Businesses that go bankrupt don't just spring back to life. The cost
> of failing banks, with their deep knowledge of what makes the
> local economy tick, is even higher—a point Ben Bernanke, chair
> of the Federal Reserve, made in his study of the Great Depression.

16. Shiyin Chen, "China on 'Treadmill to Hell' amid Bubble, Chanos Says," Bloomberg, April 8, 2010.

17. Andy Xie, "China Real-Estate Bust Is Morphing into a Slow Leak," Bloomberg, September 26, 2010.

China's stimulus was overdone. The alternative—inadequate
stimulus and recession—would have been worse.

With stimulus required, spending on investment was preferable to
spending on consumption. Yes, a lot of the funds were wasted,
but a lot were not. A study by the Chinese Academy of Social
Science found that China's government ended 2016 with net
assets of 120 trillion yuan (about 161 percent of GDP), including
its stake in state-owned enterprises. In a credit boom, asset
values are inflated. In a credit bust, financial assets lose value and
nonfinancial assets are difficult to sell. Still, a complete picture of
China's financial system has to consider the asset as well as the
liability side of the balance sheet. China's assets are probably not
worth as much as the Chinese Academy of Social Science says
they are. They are worth something, and taking that into account
makes the debt problem less daunting.

A bean counting approach to the value generated by investments
misses the larger social benefits. China's infrastructure generates
low returns, but then all infrastructure generates low returns.
That's because it's a public good—something that's provided at
low cost for the well-being of society. The state-owned firm that
builds a bridge or high-speed rail link or water treatment plant
might not generate much income. The firms and households
that use the new facilities do. Ultimately—China's government
hopes—that will result in enough tax revenue to make
everyone whole.

Finally, the defaults by Dongbei Special and others that signaled
weakness in China's financial system were also a step forward
on reform. It was moral hazard—the belief that all loans to state
firms had a no-default guarantee—that kept the credit flowing to
projects of dubious value. Losses for banks and bond investors
chipped away at moral hazard, encouraging more rational and
efficient allocation of credit. Defaults show cracks appearing
in China's financial system. Cracks, with apologies to Leonard
Cohen, are how the light gets in.

3

China's Debt Mountain: The Lenders

The year 2017 was not a good one for Anbang Insurance Group. China's third-largest insurer started the year boasting turbo-charged growth. A string of high-profile acquisitions, at home and abroad, included $1.95 billion for New York's storied Waldorf Astoria hotel. The firm had deep connections to the Communist Party elite—chairman Wu Xiaohui was married to a granddaughter of Deng Xiaoping. From the outside, Anbang looked like it was on an unstoppable roll.

Inside the system, though, alarm bells were starting to ring. In May, China's insurance regulator charged Anbang with "disrupting market order." A three-month ban on issuing new insurance products cut off a crucial source of premiums. In June, Wu fell into the clutches of the graft inspectors, part of an investigation into Anbang's overseas acquisitions, market manipulation, and "economic crimes." Then the final blow, with the banking regulator digging into the details of overseas bank loans to Anbang—along with giant conglomerates Fosun, HNA, and Dalian Wanda—suspicious of improprieties in its foreign acquisitions. For China's markets, that was big news. Shares in Fosun and Wanda—the only listed firms in the group—nose-dived.

Anbang's finances were opaque; the holding company was private and didn't disclose its assets or liabilities. But trawling through reports from major subsidiaries, analysts found total assets ended 2016 at about

2.5 trillion yuan—equal to more than 3 percent of China's GDP.[1] Anbang was a major investor in China Merchants Bank and Minsheng Bank—the eighth- and tenth-largest lenders in China, respectively (and the closest China has to big private-sector banks), and Chengdu Rural Commercial Bank, the largest local lender in Sichuan, a province of 87 million.

Banned from issuing new products, Anbang's sources of funding dried up. The risk, as China's regulators surely knew, was that as insurance policies matured, with no new funds coming in Anbang would be forced into a fire sale of assets in order to meet its obligations. If policy holders decided to cash in early, the pressure on Anbang to sell assets at bargain prices would be even greater. Anbang wasn't quite American International Group (AIG)—the giant insurer that threatened to topple the US financial system in 2008. AIG's trillion dollars in assets meant it was three times larger than Anbang in absolute size, and almost twice as big as a share of national GDP. Even so, the parallels went beyond the shared initials, and the risks were clear.

What pushed China's regulators to crack down so hard and so publicly on one of the mainland's biggest insurers? China's politics remained—as ever—opaque. The timing of the move so soon ahead of a leadership re-shuffle at the Party Congress expected in October 2017 raised suspicion of elite political infighting. The financial arguments for the clampdown, however, were clear. Anbang was gaming China's regulatory system, taking advantage of its status as an insurance firm to soak up cheap funding, and using that to go on an acquisition spree that appeared to have little commercial logic.

That's not how insurance firms—whose very purpose is to allow customers to manage risks—are meant to operate. On the liability side, insurers are expected to issue long-term policies that customers can cash in if they encounter illness or accidents. Anbang issued what looked like long-term policies, but with a low bar to cashing in early, the policies be-haved like short-term investments. An example of its liabilities: in 2015, Anbang raised 47.6 billion yuan with a product called Longevity Sure Win

1. Jason Bedford, *The Risks from Anbang and Other Platform Insurers* (Hong Kong, UBS, 2017).

No. 1. Investors could exit in 2017 with a tidy return of 4.7 percent. On the asset side of an insurer's balance sheet, it's normal to see ultra-safe and highly liquid bonds, generating a steady stream of income, and easy to sell if funds are needed. On Anbang's balance sheet were illiquid assets like the Waldorf Astoria hotel.

Anbang was an extreme example of this asset–liability mismatch, but it wasn't the only financial firm skirting the rules and growing faster than it could safely manage. What differentiated China's major banks from, for example, US investment banks on the eve of the great financial crisis is that they could count on a very stable funding base. That reflected a high national savings rate (China's households save about 30 percent of their income), a controlled capital account (making it hard to take savings off-shore), and a simple financial system (which means few places other than banks to park funds).

Industrial and Commercial Bank of China (ICBC)—the world's largest bank by assets—gets virtually all of its funding from domestic savers, many of whom put their funds in long-term deposits. Lehman Brothers—the US investment bank whose failure triggered the great financial crisis—got its funding from overnight borrowing in the money markets. ICBC's funding is cheap, and it's not going anywhere fast. Lehman Brothers' funding was cheap until the markets decided they didn't like its position in subprime mortgages; then it got expensive, then it disappeared. That's why Lehman Brothers collapsed. In the years following the financial crisis, one of the most troubling trends in China's banking sector was that the stability of the funding base started to erode. None of China's banks looked quite as bad as Lehman. A number followed the path of Anbang, relying on expensive and volatile short-term funding to supercharge their growth.

In particular, three forces began eroding the stability of banks' funding base and eating into net interest margins—the gap between the deposit and loan rates, which is the main source of profitability. Wealth management products (WMPs)—a new type of retail savings product—forced banks to compete for funds by offering higher returns to investors. Technology giants Alibaba (Amazon with Chinese characteristics) and Tencent (an online behemoth combining the features of WhatsApp, Twitter, and PayPal) launched massive online money market funds, sucking cash away from deposits. And the People's Bank of China (PBOC) made steady progress on liberalizing interest rates—taking banks from the cozy world of low-government set deposit rates and high-government set loan rates into a more competitive world where the cost of funds rose and interest margins narrowed.

In a Chinese market where *'financial repression'* kept deposit rates below the level of inflation, WMPs filled a gap - giving retail investors the safety and convenience of a deposit, but with markedly higher returns. Anbang's Longevity Sure Win No. 1—which, it turned out, provided neither longevity for the company nor a sure win for investors (though, in the end, no one lost their shirt)—is one example. Another comes from one of the banks in which Anbang was invested: China Merchants.

In 2017, China Merchants was offering savers a return of 4.9 percent on its Sunflower investment product, substantially higher than the 0.35 percent available on demand deposits or 1.5 percent for those willing to stash their funds away in one-year savings accounts. With inflation running at around 1.5 percent, only Sunflower offered savers a chance to increase their real wealth. "The deposit rate is very low," says Ms. Ye, a loan officer at the bank, explaining why she had invested more than 50,000 yuan (equal to almost her entire annual salary) in the products.

With most banks offering similar rates, and savers hungry for inflation-beating returns, the WMP market boomed. In 2010, WMPs accounted for an insignificant fraction of bank funding. By the end of 2016 there was 29.1 trillion yuan invested, equal to about 19 percent of bank deposits. Even that figure significantly understates banks' exposure to the new source of funding. With average maturities of just one or two months, WMPs had to be rolled over multiple times to keep banks in action. Over the course of 2016, banks issued 168 trillion yuan—more than the 150 trillion yuan in deposits outstanding.

Some banks were more exposed to the risk from short-term funding than others:

For the big state-owned banks, exposure was limited. ICBC, China Construction Bank, Agricultural Bank of China, and Bank of

China—collectively known as the big four—had already achieved sufficient scale, and could count on a too-big-to-fail national brand, and an extensive branch network, to continue soaking up deposits. WMPs accounted for just 9% of total liabilities.

For the next tier down—banks like China Merchants and China Minsheng, known as the joint stock commercial banks—it was a different story. China's second-tier banks combined commercial orientation, aggressive expansion plans, and a more limited branch footprint than their big-four rivals. That pushed a greater reliance on WMPs to fund expansion. For the group as a whole, WMPs at the end of 2016 equaled about 27 percent of total funding. For the most exposed, the total was above 40 percent

WMPs weren't the only threat chipping away at banks' cheap and stable funding base. In 2013, technology giants Alibaba and Tencent began offering online money market funds. With hundreds of millions of Chinese already using the firms' mobile payments apps, they rapidly gained scale. At the start of 2017, Alibaba's Yuebao—a name that translates as "leftover treasure"—became the world's largest money market funds, with 1.3 trillion yuan in assets under management. Those were funds that only a few years earlier, the banks would have counted as cheap deposits. Now they had to pay a premium to borrow them from Alibaba's asset managers.

Even as banks faced new threats to their deposit base, interest rate liberalization started to erode their margins. For decades, government-controlled deposit and lending rates had served China well. When the main priority was providing cheap funds for priority investments, policy-set rates did the job. Now the challenges for the economy were more complex. Government-set rates were too blunt an instrument to solve them. Higher rates were needed to shift more income to household savers and choke off credit to overcapacity industry. Market-set rates were needed so that credit could be allocated more efficiently. China's central bank progressively raised the cap on deposit rates and lowered the floor on loan rates, before ultimately removing them entirely in 2016. Competition for bank deposits was growing. Profit margins on the deposits that remained were narrowing.

Looking through the complexity, the emergence of WMPs and money market funds, and the shift from government-set to market-set interest rates, showed China following a pattern familiar from other countries going through a process of financial modernization. Banks were moving from a highly regulated system, where funding comes mostly from deposits and interest rates are set by the government, to a market-based system, where there is competition for funds and interest rates are set by the logic of supply and demand. There are positives to that evolution:

Banks are forced to provide higher returns to household savers, boosting their income and speeding China's transition to a consumer-driven economy. Given the difference in returns between WMPs and one-year deposits, in 2016 investors earned about an extra 870 billion yuan on their savings—equal to more than 1 percent of GDP. Over time, higher household income will catalyze China's rebalancing, reducing dependence on investment and exports as drivers of growth.

When banks pay competitive rates for funds, they have to charge competitive rates to borrowers. Efficient, productive firms will be able to pay; others will not. The result should be a process of creative destruction, where the strong survive and the weak are winnowed out. For the reformers at the PBOC, the hope is that interest rate liberalization will be the ratchet that engineers improvements in efficiency across the economy.

The sudden appearance of Alibaba and Tencent as dominant players in mobile payments, and small but growing players in the money management industry, could, over time, prove to be a game-changer. Payments data open a path to accurate credit scoring for business and households. In the right hands—perhaps because of a future joint venture between a major technology firm and a major bank—that could significantly increase the efficiency of credit allocation.

There were also risks. Increased reliance on expensive, short-term funding was a new and significant vulnerability for China's banks. Responding to the higher cost of funds, banks aiming to protect profit margins had to grasp for higher returns on their investments. In theory, market-set lending rates should drive efficiency gains across the economy. In practice, the reach for yield might push banks to take on too much risk.

A typical WMP promised to invest funds in a combination of bank deposits (completely safe), the money market (very safe), and bonds and loans (some safe, some less so). In 2017, three-year fixed-term deposits paid just 2.75 percent, money market instruments 4.7 percent, and three-year government bonds 3.6 percent. None of those would get returns up to the 4.9 percent return promised by products like Sunflower, let alone give banks a margin on top of it. To get to the required level of returns, asset managers would have to invest in high-yield corporate bonds and loans to low quality borrowers. Those investments certainly juice returns. Five-year corporate bonds with an A+ credit rating yielded 8.1 percent in the third quarter of 2017. Shadow loans could pay even more. The trouble is, they are long-term and illiquid, and carry a higher risk of default.

Back in December 2012, a rare default on a WMP issued by Huaxia Bank prompted one disgruntled investor to complain that "[this] is a state-owned bank, how can we trust the government and the Communist Party now that a state-owned bank refuses to pay our money back?"[2] In Beijing in 2016, scrolling LED displays above bank doorways warned would-be investors that higher returns come with higher risks. Despite that, most savers viewed WMPs to be just as safe as deposits and—beyond the neon banners—efforts to change that perception were limited. There have, undoubtedly, been multiple defaults on loans from the WMP pool. Banks absorb those losses in lower profitability, rather than passing them on to

2. Daniel Ren, "Huaxia Scandal Spotlights China's Ponzi Crisis," *South China Morning Post*, December 2012.

investors in lower returns. The benefit is that confidence remains high and funds continue to roll in. The cost is that the entire system is underpinned by moral hazard—the false belief that deep-pocketed, government-backed banks will always make investors whole.

In the cozy, tightly regulated world of the 1950s, US bankers operated on the 3-6-3 rule—borrow at 3 percent, lend at 6 percent and be on the golf course by 3pm. Till about 2010, that was also the world of China's bankers. With the sudden arrival of WMPs, money market funds, and market-set interest rates, for some the rule started to feel more like 5-8-9—borrow at 5 percent, lend at 8 percent, pray that the bank is still solvent tomorrow at 9am. What happens if those prayers go unanswered? What if higher funding costs, the reach for yield, and shrinking profits margins, push banks over the edge? The international experience is littered with examples of what can go wrong. The US savings and loan crisis—a 1980s precursor of the 2008 financial crisis—provides an illustration.

For a long time, savings and loans (S&Ls)—the type of local mortgage lender immortalized in Frank Capra's schmaltzy film classic *It's a Wonderful Life*—had a cozy existence. Depression-era regulations prohibited banks from paying interest on demand deposits, and capped rates that could be paid on savings. S&Ls could count on a steady stream of deposits, and in return provided homebuyers with affordable mortgages. In the 1970s and 1980s, that started to change. The S&Ls faced three challenges. First, interest rate liberalization meant higher costs and new competition for funds. Second, rampant inflation, and the decision by then–Federal Reserve chair Paul Volcker to choke off the money supply, added to funding costs and hammered demand for mortgages. Finally, the Reagan administration's ill-advised efforts at deregulation allowed owners to make reckless investments in an attempt to outgrow their problems.[3]

In the newly deregulated market, S&Ls could buy funding at any price and invest at any risk. Federal deposit insurance meant that if bets didn't

3. Martin Mayer, *The Greatest-Ever Bank Robbery: The Collapse of the Savings and Loan Industry* (New York: Scribner, 1990).

pay off, the taxpayer would bail out depositors. In the dash for growth, S&Ls went beyond their traditional focus on residential mortgages, investing in risky commercial real estate and even riskier junk bonds. When those investments failed, the S&Ls did too. Between 1986 and 1994, 1,043 of 3,234 S&Ls in the United States went bankrupt. According to the Congressional Budget Office, the cost of cleaning up the mess was $200 billion— about 3 percent of 1990 GDP.[4]

The parallels between the S&Ls and China's joint stock commercial banks are clear. Both responded to the deregulation of the financial sector by dashing for growth. Both expanded fast by turning away from safe, stable deposits toward higher-cost, more volatile sources of funds. Both tried to offset a higher cost of funds by reaching for higher returns with loans to risky projects. Both operated in an atmosphere steeped in moral hazard. The S&Ls had their federal deposit guarantee. Chinese households assumed that any funds invested in a product issued by a state-owned bank were backed by the government.

The difference: China's joint stock banks dwarf the US S&Ls in size. In 2016, joint stock banks had total assets of 96.8 trillion yuan—130 percent of GDP. Even at their peak, S&Ls assets never rose so nearly so high. China's banks continue to have important factors working in their favor. High inflation—one of the triggers for the US crisis—is conspicuous by its absence. China's banks are also better capitalized, giving them more capacity to absorb losses. The process of interest rate liberalization is being managed carefully, with the PBOC punishing small banks that try and suck up extra funds by offering unsustainably high rates. And in contrast to the Reagan administration, Xi's team has recognized and responded to the risks. If those fail-safes fail, though, the 3 percent of GDP losses the United States faced in the S&L crisis could be the tip of China's iceberg.

---

4. *The Economic Effects of the Savings and Loan Crisis* (Washington, DC: Congressional Budget Office, 1992).

WHERE ARE THE BAD LOANS? INSIDE CHINA'S SHADOW LOAN BOOK

Caofeidian—an industrial zone and port built on land reclaimed from the sea in the northeastern province of Hebei—was meant to kill two birds with one stone. The relocation of giant steel producer Shougang from Beijing aimed at reducing air pollution in China's capital, at the same time as breathing life into Hebei's lackluster economy. Beijing, the government's economic planners reasoned, had no shortage of jobs, but as the nation's capital—the venue for everything from the Olympic Games to G-20 summits—it would benefit from slightly less choking smog. Neighboring Hebei, with average incomes barely a third of the level in Beijing, could tolerate a few more bad-air days in exchange for a job-creating steel plant.

In 2010, work began on the new development. Seven years and 500 billion yuan later, Caofeidian was not a complete failure. Company buses ran blue-clad workers to and from the Shougang plant. With salaries around 6,000 yuan a month, locals considered it a good place to work. The gritty air bore witness to the fact that the furnaces were switched on, production underway. Even so, stationary cranes at a port ringed by abandoned real estate projects testified to expectations missed.

Perhaps a move out of the capital for Shougang—a firm whose name translates as "Capital Steel"—was always ill-omened. Competition from nearby Tianjin, which had its own busy port and industrial zone, didn't help. Neither did a 70 percent drop in the price of steel, from a 2008 peak to a 2015 trough. Shougang swung from a profit of 349 million yuan in 2010 to a loss of 1,138 million yuan in 2015. In the same year, output for Caofeidian fell 10.4 percent—a hard landing for the local economy. As for Beijing's smog, for a city powered by coal, ringed by hills, and in the path of winds from the industrial northeast, Shougang was only part of the problem. If there were any birds killed by the Caofeidian project, it was the result of pollution, as air quality in Hebei and Beijing continued to deteriorate.

If Caofeidian's slump had a cost for the banks, however, it was difficult to discern. At first sight, Bank of Tangshan, the biggest local lender, appeared a model of prudence. In 2016 it reported just 17 million yuan in nonperforming loans, equal to 0.05 percent of the loan book. Even in China, where an overall bad loan ratio of 1.7 percent reflected endemic underreporting, that was a strikingly low number. It's especially striking because Bank of Tangshan didn't have great material to work with. Tangshan—the city of which Caofeidian is a part—is most famous as the epicenter of the 1976 earthquake, which killed a quarter of a million people and, according to local superstition, heralded the death of Chairman Mao. In 2016, it was China's largest steel-producing city. How did a small city commercial bank, stuck in an aging industrial town and with its fortunes tied to an ailing megaproject, manage to keep its bad loan ratio so low?

For city banks like Tangshan, the answer to the mystery of the missing nonperforming loans lay in the rapid expansion of the shadow loan book. The term "shadow loans" evokes images of pawnbrokers, peer-to-peer lending platforms, and other shady operations. In fact, most of China's shadow loans originate with the banks. Here's how a typical loan is put together:

The bank has extended credit to a low-quality borrower, often an ailing industrial firm like Dongbei Steel, or local government financing vehicle borrowing to pay for an infrastructure project.

Regulatory requirements make it too expensive for the bank to maintain the front-door lending relationship. The borrower might be in danger of defaulting on its existing loans, and the bank loath to report an increase in nonperforming loans. Or they might be the target of a government campaign against high pollution or some other evil.

Cutting the borrower off entirely might push it into bankruptcy and trigger a default—not a desirable outcome. Instead of breaking the relationship, the bank finds a back-door workaround by inserting a shadow lender into the transaction. The shadow lender—typically a trust or asset manager— acts as a shell company, masking the true nature of the transaction.

The shadow lender provides a loan to the low-quality borrower. The
loan is then securitized, with the bank buying a security from the
shadow lender giving it a claim on the borrowers' repayment of
interest and principal.

In effect, the bank has made a loan. On the balance sheet, it appears as an
investment in a security issued by the shadow lender. In some cases, in a
final step, the shadow loan is included in the pool of WMP assets sold to
the bank's retail investors.

From the perspective of the individual transaction, everyone is a
winner. The low-quality borrower has the loan it needs. The bank has
retained the relationship, prevented the borrower from defaulting, and
hidden its exposure from regulators and shareholders. The shadow bank
has taken a small margin for its part in the transaction. From the perspective of systemic stability, everyone is a loser. The low-quality borrower is
paying more for access to credit, adding to its financial stress. The bank
has increased its exposure to a high-risk borrower, and without the increase in capital needed to offset the risk of default. The inclusion of the
shadow bank has lengthened the chain of transactions, adding cost and
complexity. The financial system has become more opaque, tougher to
regulate.

At the end of 2016, Bank of Tangshan had 110 billion yuan in shadow
loans sitting on its balance sheet. That was up 27 times from 3.9 billion
yuan three years earlier. It was equal to 54.5 percent of total assets—
meaning the bank had more shadow loans than it did normal loans. And
it handily outstripped the capital the bank had on hand to use as a cushion
against defaults.

Bank of Tangshan's situation isn't unique. At the start of 2010, bank loans
to other financial institutions, a proxy for shadow lending, were steady at
2.8 trillion yuan. By the end of 2016, they had risen to 27.2 trillion yuan.
As figure 3.1 shows, exposure varies across the sector. The highest risk is
concentrated in joint stock and city commercial banks—the second and
third tier of China's banking system. Looking at a sample of forty-one
banks, as of the end of 2016, shadow loans accounted for 17.2 percent of

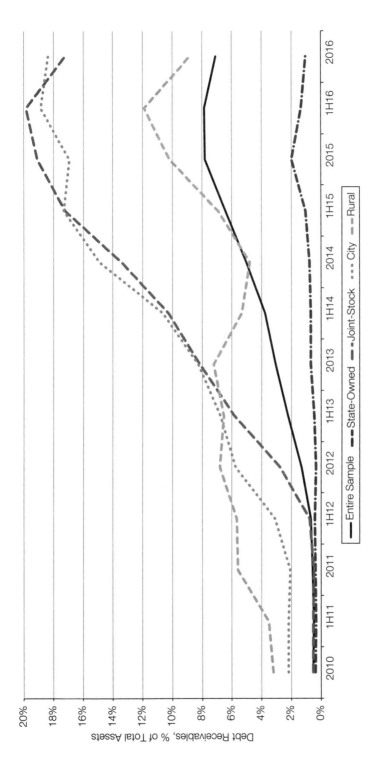

Figure 3.1 Banks' Shadow Loans as Percentage of Total Assets

Sample includes forty-one listed and nonlisted banks.

Created by the author using information from banks' financial statements.

assets at joint stock banks and 18.4 percent at city commercial banks like Bank of Tangshan. At top-tier banks like ICBC they accounted for just 1.1 percent of the total.

As with WMPs, different exposure to shadow loans reflected different starting points and ambitions. For the joint stock and city commercial banks, limited access to high-quality borrowers, a smaller deposit base, and higher cost of capital all made shadow lending attractive as a way to grow the business. For the city commercial banks, close control by growth-hungry local officials sharpened incentives and provided assurance that regulatory scrutiny would be limited. For the biggest banks, a Rolodex of the stateliest of the state-owned enterprises as borrowers, deposits hoovered up from branches on every corner, and low cost of capital all meant that growing the business through conventional lending was a more attractive option.

The history of financial crises is littered with examples of securitization gone wrong. In the United States in the run up to the great financial crisis, banks extended trillions of dollars in mortgages to low-income households. The claim on repayment was packaged and repackaged, sold and resold, bringing in fresh funds that extended the boom. By moving mortgages off balance sheet, banks dodged regulatory requirements on how much capital they had to hold, dashing for growth at the expense of stability for the system as a whole. A lengthening chain of transactions meant the final holder of the mortgage claim had no knowledge of the quality of the underlying borrower. The belief that the main participants were too-big-to-fail kept the funds flowing in, and meant the entire system was built on the shaky foundation of moral hazard.

All of those conditions were present in the case of China's shadow loans. The length of the financial chain was extended, with funding from a bank, loans originated by a shadow lender, and final claims—in some cases—sold on to retail investors in the form of WMPs. The low quality of the borrower was evident to the bank. To the retail investor that ended up owning the claim, it was invisible. Access to funds from issuing WMPs allowed joint stock and city commercial banks to expand at a dizzying pace. And by dodging regulations—hiding loans as investments—they were able to grow their assets without enough capital to absorb losses. For China's second- and third-tier banks, at the end of 2016, holdings of shadow loans were equal to 200 percent of the capital base, and for some the total was much higher.

Subprime mortgage origination in the United States rose from about $100 billion in 2000 to about $600 billion in 2006, taking the total over that period to about $2.4 trillion, or 17 percent of GDP.[5] In China, shadow bank lending rose from 420 billion yuan ($62.5 billion) in 2010 to 8.8 trillion yuan ($1.3 trillion) in 2016. The amount outstanding was 27.2 trillion yuan ($4 trillion), or about 36 percent of GDP. The US subprime crisis shook the world economy. A Chinese shadow banking crisis could break it.

HIRING THUGS AND DODGING DEBTS: SHADOW FINANCE WENZHOU STYLE

Mr. Hu is regretful. He made his money in Wenzhou, manufacturing shoes, lighters, and locks—whatever low-cost items could be sold at a profit to consumers in the United States and Europe. Wenzhou's location in coastal Zhejiang was once considered a curse. In the early days of the People's Republic, Chairman Mao feared arch-enemy Chiang Kai-shek would attempt to retake the mainland. If a Nationalist fleet landed from Taiwan, Wenzhou would lie directly on the path back to Chiang's hometown, Ningbo. That was enough to consign the region to oblivion in the eyes of Mao's economic planners—precious investment funds couldn't be risked on a city that might fall before an invading army.

The feared reinvasion never came. Chiang died in 1975. When Mao died a year later, and Deng Xiaoping began to lay the groundwork for China's reforms, Wenzhou's coastal location turned from a curse to a blessing. Over the next three decades, local entrepreneurs like Mr. Hu

---

5. *The Subprime Mortgage Market, National and 12th District Developments, Annual Report* (San Francisco: Federal Reserve Bank of San Francisco, 2007).

rode the wave of China's opening. Combining business know-how, cheap labor, and easy access to global markets, they grabbed the bottom link of the export value chain. The first wave of made-in-China goods—buttons, zippers, and tchotchkes that squeezed out low-end manufacturers in the West—was made in Wenzhou. Shadow finance played a crucial role. With state-owned banks still reluctant to lend, funds came from the informal market—that is, Mr. Hu and his friends lending to one another to pay for land, buildings, and capital equipment.

In 2008 the great financial crisis hit. Wenzhou's exporters were already feeling the pinch from higher wage costs, a stronger yuan, and stricter health and safety and environmental regulations. Now, with consumers in the West cutting up their credit cards, demand evaporated. Exports—growing more than 30 percent a year since China entered the World Trade Organization in 2001—collapsed, dropping more than 20 percent at the start of 2009. The government response was to tell the banks to ramp up lending. "Normally it was us asking the government officials for a favor; this time they called us," said Mr. Zhuan, the former head of a local bank. "They summoned all the local bank chiefs, told us not to call in any loans," he said. Then, at the start of 2009, the order came down from headquarters in Beijing: Lend! "We were issuing loans blindly," recalled Mr. Zhuan.

Wenzhou's old reliance on informal lending—networks of entrepreneurs providing credit to one another—supercharged the stimulus. Loans to firm A ended up as collateral for loans to firm B, which in turn was guaranteeing loans to firm C. With the export sector in the doldrums, factory owners didn't see any point in investing in their business. Instead, the credit flooded into real estate. In early 2010, Wenzhou property prices were up close to 22 percent from a year earlier—a rise that increased the value of collateral and enabled a fresh round of lending. Coachloads of Wenzhou speculators, traveling the country and snapping up new developments, became part of the folklore of China's property bubble. From the perspective of the individual bank officers, risks looked manageable. They were making a lot of loans, but they were all backed by collateral. From the perspective of the system as a whole, with the value of collateral artificially inflated, it was a house of cards.

According to Mr. Li, the head of one of Wenzhou's largest financial consultancies, it was the shuttering of an industrial park at the end of 2011 that triggered the crash. "The Party secretary had a strict attitude," said Li. "There were some heavy polluting businesses in the park; when they were shut down the value of the land fell, loans collateralized with that land were called in, the borrowers ran, and the crisis began." In the years that followed, credit expansion ground to a halt, house prices collapsed, and growth plunged. In 2007, the economy had expanded 14.2 percent from the previous year. In 2012, it grew just 6.6 percent. Even that massive drop in growth understates the magnitude of the slump. "The GDP data might have some issues," said a local official, wryly, "but it captures the trend." At least eighty executives declared bankruptcy, went into hiding, or committed suicide.

Mr. Hu, the exporter, counts himself among the losers. He guaranteed a 9-million-yuan loan for a friend who defaulted and fled to Vietnam, leaving Mr. Hu to pick up the bill. "I tracked him down but he was scraping a living washing motorcycles, so obviously couldn't repay," said Mr. Hu. "All I could do was hire some local thugs to beat him up; that made me feel better."

Another loser from the Wenzhou crisis: the city's growth model. Local entrepreneurs had grabbed the first link of the global manufacturing value chain. The next appeared out of reach. Hit by first the US subprime mortgage crisis, then the European sovereign debt crisis, and with rising wages and a stronger yuan eroding competitiveness, exports struggled to claw their way out of contraction. With no reason to plow more capital into their business, and the bitter experience of the real estate bust still fresh in their memory, Wenzhou's businesspeople needed a new place to put their funds to work. They found it in the city's informal banking industry.

"We started with about 200 million yuan, now we manage about 700 million," said Mr. Zhuan, who quit his job as bank manager to run a small loan company. "We have about ten investors—business owners that don't want to put more funds into their business." As of 2016, China's small loan shops managed close to a trillion yuan in assets. Mr. Zhuan's is one of about forty in Wenzhou, and among the largest. Investors get a return of about 8 percent, and borrowers pay an annualized rate of about 15 percent. "The banks only have loans for state-owned firms and government projects," says Mr. Zhuan. "We fill the gap." A growing proportion of loans are to consumers: covering the down payment on a house, the purchase of a car, even the startup costs of overseas education for an only child.

A few miles down the road from Mr. Zhuan's outfit is Dinxing Dai, a peer-to-peer lending platform that is providing credit on even more expensive terms. As figure 3.2 shows, annual rates were above 20 percent. Peer-to-peer lending ballooned in size, rising to over a trillion yuan in assets spread over 4,000 platforms in the middle of 2017, up from just 38 billion yuan at the start of 2014. Mr. Zhou, Dinxing Dai's chain-smoking chief executive, pauses from offering investment advice on one of several

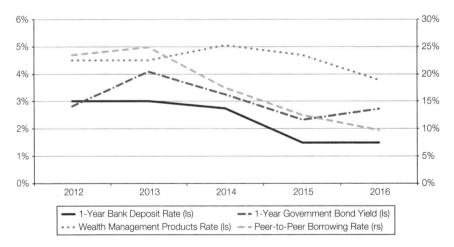

Figure 3.2 Returns for Investors in Banks and Shadow Banks
2012 data are estimated.
Created by the author using information from Bloomberg, ChinaBond, Diyi Wangdai
(第一网贷), and Yingcan (网贷之家).

mobile phones to provide assurance that risks are low. His platform teamed up with big data companies to manage the risk in their loans, he says. Locational data track borrowers. Those who spend too much time traveling around the country are considered higher risks and get charged more for credit.

In the best cases, big data might help minimize defaults. In others, this kind of high-tech hand-waving provides a cover for sharp practices. In December 2015, one of the biggest peer-to-peer lenders was exposed as a Ponzi scheme. Internet lender Ezubo is reported to have cheated its hundreds of thousands of investors out of about 50 billion yuan. Among the lurid details: nonexistent investment projects, a 12-million-yuan pink diamond ring purchased by the company's chief executive for his girlfriend, and a twenty-hour police dig to discover incriminating documents the company had buried.

In Wenzhou, it's tempting to say the economic model came full circle, riding out the great financial crisis and returning to the informal loan schemes that played such an important role in the city's original success. The reality is rather different. Wenzhou's shadow finance used to pay for the development of a world-beating export sector. After the financial crisis and real estate bust, it helped the remains of that export sector keep the lights on, and paid for the unaffordable consumer aspirations of a would-be middle class. The risks of shadow banking remained: regulation was light; borrowers were low-quality, capital buffers thin. The rewards for Wenzhou's economy were no longer there.

For China as a whole, the true shadow banks—not the trusts and asset managers that provide a deceptive cloak to obscure bank lending, but small loan shops and peer-to-peer platforms operating at the fringe of the system—were too small to cause a systemic crisis. At the same time, they appeared emblematic of a financial system that was running out of control. Lending grew too fast and was channeled to the riskiest borrowers. Funding was expensive and uncertain; capital buffers thin or nonexistent. Regulators appeared unable to get ahead of the problems. A crisis might not start today or tomorrow. Without reform, it wouldn't be too long coming.

SOURCE OF STABILITY

Reasons for concern about the lender side of China's financial system are
not hard to find. There are also sources of strength:

> Joint stock and city commercial banks were taking on a lot of risks,
> increasing reliance on expensive short-term funding and taking
> more and more chances on their asset allocation. The big state-
> owned banks at the heart of the system—ICBC and others—were
> not. They remained stable on funding, conservative on lending,
> well capitalized and profitable. China's high savings rate and
> controlled capital account meant funding for the system as a
> whole was not in doubt.

> China's shadow banking system expanded fast. In international
> comparison it doesn't look that scary. Based on data from global
> watchdog the Financial Stability Board, at the end of 2016,
> assets at China's "other financial institutions"—a euphemism for
> shadow banks—were equal to $9.6 trillion, or about 86 percent
> of GDP. The Euro area (270% of GDP), United Kingdom (263%),
> and United States (145%) were all at a considerably higher level.[6]
> That doesn't mean China's shadow banks aren't big enough
> to trigger a crisis. Clearly, they are. It does mean that, relative
> to their size, the amount of worry focused on them appears
> disproportionate.

> In many cases, stresses reflected growing pains from reform.
> WMPs, money market funds, and interest rate liberalization
> helped modernize the financial sector. They forced banks to
> operate in a more competitive market and sped the transition
> to a consumer economy, boosting income for household savers.
> Even the collapse of Ezubo and other shadow lenders —a gut
> punch for those who lost everything—sends a message that high

6. *Global Shadow Bank Monitoring Report 2017*, (Basel, Financial Stability Board, 2018).

returns come with high risks, and the government won't always come riding to the rescue.

Through all the stress, China's policymakers appeared relatively relaxed. Perhaps that was because a regulator panicking about financial risks is like the proverbial man shouting "fire" in a crowded theater—guaranteed to cause a stampede for the exit. Perhaps it's because they had seen it all before. In its forty years of reform, China had faced down problems worse than nonperforming loans.

4

China's First Two Cycles

The year 1989 was bad for China. On June 4, tanks rolling into Tiananmen Square began a bloody crackdown on pro-democracy protestors. The image of "tank man"—a loan protestor standing in the path of a phalanx of armored vehicles—was seared into the global consciousness. It was the closest that reform-era China came to regime collapse. The crackdown handed a bitter victory to conservative Party elders, closing the door to economic reform for years, and to political reform for generations. The proximate cause of the protests was the death of reformist former general secretary Hu Yaobang. In the background was a financial sector run out of control, rampant inflation, and a near-hard landing for the Chinese economy.

It was an early lesson on the relation between economic growth and so-cial stability, purchased at a high price. For future generations of leaders, from Jiang Zemin to Xi Jinping, it was a lesson that was impossible to forget.

The decade ended in tragedy. It started in hope. From 1949 to 1976, China had suffered privations and persecution—the worst of them self-inflicted. Under Chairman Mao Zedong, policy was set according to the dictates of ideological purity rather than evidence of what worked. The result was a series of disastrous mistakes. In the Great Leap Forward, Mao's ill-conceived and worst-executed attempt to accelerate the move from agriculture to industry, the forced-march pace required requisition of the grain harvest to provide funds for investment. With not enough left to feed the hungry population, the result was history's worst man-made famine. In the Cultural Revolution, fearing the creeping revival of bourgeois values, Mao turned workers against bosses, students against teachers, children against parents. A society turned on its head resulted in a decade of chaos and misery.

In 1976, Mao's death opened the door to the return of reason. The first response of China's new leaders, however, was not market reforms. Mao's short-tenured successor Hua Guofeng advocated what became known as the "two whatevers"—that is, to uphold whatever policy decisions Mao made, follow whatever instructions Mao gave. That was a misreading of the mood in post-Mao China. Millions had suffered humiliation under political campaigns. Tens of millions had suffered deprivation or worse under failed social policies. There was a hunger for a more complete re-appraisal. At a meeting in December 1978, Hua was quietly shuffled aside, saddled with the blame for the political and economic disappointments of the past two years. Deng Xiaoping emerged as China's paramount leader.[1]

China's central committee—the top tier of two hundred or so Communist Party cadres—is appointed for a five-year term. Each year, they convene for a meeting, known as a plenum, to set the direction of policy. The Third Plenum of the Eleventh Central Committee —the December 1978 meeting where Deng displaced Hua—marked a critical turning point. The success that followed reflected more a change in atti-tude from policymakers than any specific policies adopted. Hua's blindly faithful "two whatevers" was replaced by Deng's resolutely pragmatic "practice is the sole criterion of truth" as the guiding philosophy. In the new atmosphere, policymakers had a new freedom to experiment out-side of the narrow ideological confines of Maoism. Out of that freedom came the reform that did more than any other to accelerate China's early development: the end of agricultural collectives and the beginning of the "household responsibility" system, putting individual households back in control of farming.

1. Ezra Vogel, *Deng Xiaoping and the Transformation of China* (Cambridge, MA: The Belknap Press of Harvard University Press, 2013).

In theory, by bringing farmers together into larger work teams, collectives should have been a vehicle for modernizing China's farming. In practice, that's not how it worked. By separating effort from reward, the collective created massive incentives for shirking. Knowing that hard work and no work would both be rewarded with the same rice rations in the collective canteen, China's 800 million farmers collectively slacked off. Combined with national directives that ignored local conditions, and a reliance on quotas rather than prices to guide production, the result was decidedly unimpressive. In the three decades from the 1950s to the 1970s, despite being the focus of all-out efforts by policymakers, grain production only increased 5 percent.[2]

The household responsibility system overcame that problem. By restoring the link between effort and reward, it encouraged China's farmers to put their backs into it. The early signs were encouraging, with harvests rising. Initial experiments in Anhui and Sichuan provinces were rapidly rolled out nationwide. Zhao Ziyang—the Party secretary in Sichuan— would be tapped by Deng to serve as general secretary and spearhead a broader package of reforms. By 1984, 99 percent of rural households were participating in the system, up from 1 percent in 1979. The Third Plenum that marked the turning point in China's reforms had specifically banned the household responsibility system. But it wasn't the policy specifics that mattered, it was the change in philosophy. With Deng's focus on results rather than ideology, local farmers and officials had license to experiment, and whatever worked could be rapidly adopted on a larger scale.

Progress on the reform of industry was more halting, but the direction was the same. A series of policy documents on expanding enterprise autonomy aimed to do for factory managers what household responsibility had done for farmers—sharpen incentives by aligning effort and reward. In 1980, Deng promised to take the Party Committee out of day-to-day affairs in factories. Shougang—the steel giant that decades later would become a poster child for planners' overreach in the Caofeidian industrial zone—was at that time a beacon of reform, trialing new profit incentives for

2. Barry Naughton, *Growing Out of the Plan* (Cambridge: Cambridge University Press, 1995).

factory management. In 1982, price controls for buttons were eliminated. Eager entrepreneurs from Wenzhou began production, taking advantage of new freedom for local enterprises. The planned economy stayed in place, but for the first time enterprises were allowed to sell above-plan output and keep a share of the profits.

Special economic zones opened the door to global markets, giving local governments the flexibility to attract foreign capital, technology, and expertise. It was Xi Zhongxun—the Party secretary of Guangdong and the father of President Xi Jinping—who spearheaded the campaign for the first zone in Shenzhen. Inside the zone import and export tariffs were relaxed, and businesses could operate according to market principles, free of the constrictions of China's still-planned economy. It was a policy innovation that kick-started China's export industry and, as important, created a constituency calling for more market reforms. Firms outside the zone looked on enviously and demanded the same freedoms for themselves.

With the benefit of hindsight, China's early reform trajectory appears clear and policy choices consistent. For those in the trenches of 1980s policy debates, it was anything but. Reformers, headed by Deng, wanted rapid liberalization, seeing it as the path to rising living standards and national revival. Conservatives, headed by Party elder Chen Yun, advocated a more cautious approach, with a larger continued role for Soviet-style planning. Chen's "bird cage" theory captured the conservative philosophy. The economy, Chen said, is like a bird: "You can't just hold a bird in your hand or it will die. . . . You have to let it fly, but you can only let it fly in a cage. . . . Without a cage it will fly away." Keeping a caged bird healthy proved easier said than done.

In an irony that would not be lost on students of dialectical materialism, for both reformers and conservatives, success carried the seeds of its own destruction. Wins for the reformers would trigger overheating and inflation, allowing the conservatives to seize the reigns. Conservatives proved able to control prices only at the expense of hammering growth, opening space for the reformers to elbow their way back to the table.

In 1984, the political winds were blowing in favor of the reformers. Growth was strong and inflation low, reducing the argument for conservative caution. The household responsibility system had been a demonstrable success, delivering bumper harvests and strengthening the hand of market advocates. Deng seized the moment. The Third Plenum of the Twelfth Central Committee approved the Decision on Reform of the Economic Structure. The decision was a breakthrough. At the theoretical level, it affirmed that the difference between socialism and capitalism wasn't economic planning; it was public ownership. At the level of policy, it aimed at a reduced role for government-set prices and an expanded role for the market. Firms would be allowed to organize their own production in response to changing conditions, as signaled by market prices. As long as they were publicly owned—that was still socialism.

Separate from the decision, but equally consequential, the framework for a modern banking system was put in place. In the past, the People's Bank of China (PBOC) had functioned as both central and commercial bank, setting credit limits and determining who got loans. It was as if the Federal Reserve were the only bank in the United States, setting the money supply and allocating credit according to a government plan. Now, with the creation of Industrial and Commercial Bank of China, China Construction Bank, Agricultural Bank of China, and Bank of China—the big-four state-owned banks that would dominate the financial landscape for decades to come—central and commercial banking functions were separated. The PBOC would manage monetary policy. The new banks— still owned by the state but operating on something closer to a commercial model—would attract deposits and make loans.

Seizing the moment, the newly created commercial banks responded with a surfeit of enthusiasm. Credit growth in 1983 was already running at a respectable 13.7 percent annual pace. In 1984, it accelerated to a torrid 36.4 percent.[3] Lending expanding at such a rapid pace could only fuel overheating. That misstep by the reformers was the opening for which Chen and the conservative planners were waiting. They scrambled to reassert control. At a series of emergency meetings, provincial leaders were told to curtail major projects and cap bank lending. Chen used his post

3. Naughton, *Growing Out of the Plan.*

as head of the Central Commission on Discipline Inspection to reign in freewheeling cadres. Anticipating Beijing's later troubles containing ebullient local officials, those controls were only partially successful. With newfound influence over the banks, and more concerned about local growth than national overheating, local leaders paid lip service to Chen's concerns, but didn't substantially change course. In the three years from 1985 to 1987, annual credit growth never dropped below 20 percent.

A breakneck pace of economic expansion, torrid loan growth, and local leaders oblivious to central controls was already a combustible combination. The spark that triggered the blaze came in August 1988, when the Politburo endorsed Deng's plan for comprehensive removal of price controls.[4] The direction of travel was the right one. Market-set prices are a crucial underpinning of economic efficiency, signaling to firms where to produce more and where to cut back. China's dual-track pricing system— with state firms able to buy goods at a low government set price and sell them on at higher market prices—was a wellspring of corruption. The timing was disastrous. On August 19, the day after the Politburo meeting, the decision on price reform was announced in the *People's Daily*. Already struggling with high inflation, China's urban population rushed to the shops in a wave of panic buying. Stores emptied as households stockpiled ahead of an anticipated surge in prices. The official data showed retail prices for the second half of 1988 up 26 percent from a year earlier.

This was the setting for the Third Plenum of the Thirteenth Central Committee in September 1988. The Third Plenum of the Eleventh Central Committee in 1978 had launched the reform process. That of the Twelfth Central Committee in 1984 accelerated it. In 1988, the mood was different. Seizing the opportunity presented by spiraling inflation, Chen and the conservative planners redoubled their retrenchment policies. Investments were cut back, price controls reimposed, credit quotas strictly enforced. The result was a classic example of "operation successful, patient dead." Inflation was lowered, but only at the expense of hammering growth and

4. Vogel, *Deng Xiaoping and the Transformation of China.*

jobs. In 1988, GDP expanded 11.3 percent. In 1989, it plummeted to 4.2 percent.

The one-two punch—first high inflation hammering purchasing power, then slumping growth hitting wages and employment—proved disastrous. Public servants, already incensed at the corruption of senior officials and their families, saw soaring prices eroding the buying power of already meager salaries. Migrant workers, pulled into the big cities by the 1980s construction boom, found themselves jobless as investment projects were curtailed. It was in this atmosphere that the Tiananmen protestors' call for greater political freedom found an echo in wider social discontent, triggering first mass protests, then a draconian response from Deng and the Party elders.

For China's policymakers, two lessons stood out. First, big-bang reforms came with unacceptable risks attached. Deng's decision to pull off the plaster of government set prices in one swift movement had catastrophic consequences: spiraling inflation and social unrest. Second, an overheated economy had to be cooled down slowly, not doused in icy water. Chen's retrenchment policies, and the resulting drag on jobs and wages, had added to the atmosphere of unrest. In the years that followed, gradualism, on reform and on cooling an overheated economy, was the watchword for policymakers. That combination proved successful in preventing a repeat of the 1989 disaster. It also allowed problems—like excess loan growth—to run unchecked for too long. The price of delaying a day of reckoning could, ultimately, be that the day of reckoning would be too large to reckon with.

JIANG ZEMIN AND CHINA'S SECOND CYCLE

In 1998 China suffered something close to a financial crisis and economic hard landing. Credit growth plunged, crunching down from 23.8 percent at the start of 1997 to 13.4 percent in mid-1998, on its way to low single-digit growth in 2001. Bad loans surged. Guangdong International Trust and Investment Corporation, which had used its government backing to raise funds from investors at home and abroad, collapsed under $4.3

billion in debt, the money squandered on real estate, hotels, and securities trading.[5]

Based on the official data, GDP slowed to 7.8 percent growth from 9.2 percent—a sharp drop, and a fall below the 8 percent target. Even that 7.8 percent figure is widely suspected of exaggerating the reality. Premier Zhu spoke of a "wind of embellishment and falsification sweeping through the statistical system." Looking at everything from electricity output to air travel, Thomas Rawski, an expert on China's economy at the University of Pittsburgh, estimated that the true growth rate for the year could have been as low as 2.2 percent.[6]

The actual depth of the downturn will never be known. It's telling, however, that in response Premier Zhu launched a massive infrastructure stimulus—committing 1.5 trillion yuan over three years, the equivalent of 18.8 percent of 1997 GDP. Telling also that the bailout of the banks that started in 1999 had an initial price tag of 1.4 trillion yuan and continued to climb in the years that followed. If the downturn had not been severe, the reaction would not have been so big.

What had brought China to this extremity? Like the cycle that defined the 1980s, that of the 1990s began with Deng, and with a restoration of re-form momentum. In 1978, the defining event was the Third Plenum and the jettisoning of Maoist dogma in favor of pragmatic policymaking. In 1992, it was Deng's southern tour.

"My father," said Deng's son Deng Zhifang, speaking in late 1990, "thinks that Gorbachev is an idiot."[7] What had Mikhail Gorbachev, the General Secretary of the Soviet Union and the man who presided over its collapse, done to earn Deng's contempt? Gorbachev's mistake: attempting political and economic reform—glasnost and perestroika—at the same time. As a result, he lost control of the levers of power, losing both political control

5. Mark Landler, "Bankruptcy the Chinese Way; Foreign Bankers Are Shown to the End of the Line," *New York Times*, January 22, 1999.

6. Thomas Rawski, "What Is Happening to China's GDP Statistics?" *China Economic Review*, 12, 2001, 347–354.

7. Vogel, *Deng Xiaoping and the Transformation of China.*

and his ability to fix the economy. For China, Deng had chosen a different road, ensuring that the Communist Party maintained its monopoly on power and using that power to steer a path to a more efficient economy.

Even so, conservatives had always feared that economic reform would prove the thin end of the wedge, with rising wealth driving demand for increased political freedom, and an expanding role for the market eroding the legitimacy of Communist rule. The events of 1989, when economic instability and political discontent fused into social upheaval, appeared to confirm their darkest imaginings. Deng, now eighty-seven years old, found himself out of favor and—perhaps—out of time, unable to restart the reform process, unable even to get his views published in the *People's Daily*.

The conservative retrenchment policies introduced by Chen at the end of 1988 were kept in place. Zhao Ziyang, the architect of the 1980s economic reforms and the senior leader who had been most sympathetic to the Tiananmen protestors, was in jail. Jiang Zemin, his replacement as general secretary and now heir apparent to Deng, aligned with the conservative orthodoxy of the time. Western sanctions on trade with China dealt a blow to exporters in the new special economic zones, added to the us-against-them mentality, and stoked the anti-reform mood. The collapse of the Soviet Union at the end of 1991 confirmed the view of conservatives: further moves toward the market were not a good idea.

The forces aligned against reform were formidable. So was Deng. In January 1992, with little fanfare, he began his last foray into influence—a southern tour taking in the cities of Wuhan, Changsha, Shenzhen, and Zhuhai.[8] In Shenzhen, the site of China's first and most successful experiment in reform and opening, Deng said that "Shenzhen's development and experience prove that our policy of establishing the special economic zones was correct." In Zhuhai, the reform message was delivered again, and with a political edge. Deng attended a meeting with Qiao Shi, a member of the Standing Committee and a potential rival to Jiang as Deng's heir. "Whoever is opposed to reform must leave office," Deng said.

---

8. Vogel, *Deng Xiaoping and the Transformation of China.*

"Our leaders look like they're doing something, but they're not doing anything worthwhile."

The official press paid little attention to Deng's tour. A gaggle of reporters from Hong Kong and the freewheeling Guangdong newspapers were hanging on his every word, amplifying their impact, and turning Deng's tour into a national conversation about reform. In Beijing, the message was received loud and clear. By mid-February, even before Deng's return, Jiang was vocally supporting the call for accelerated opening. He arranged for Deng's speeches to be collected and circulated to senior leaders. The conservatives' success in containing inflation, and the easing of post-Tiananmen sanctions, would already have resulted in calls for loosening of economic controls. Now Deng's tour and Jiang's support redoubled the pressure.

In May, a swath of provincial capitals were granted the same economic privileges as the special economic zones, opening to foreign investment and trade. In Shanghai, development of Pudong—the district on the east of the river that would become China's financial center—moved off the drawing board into construction. It wasn't long before the results were evident in the data. With controls removed, local officials rushed to start a fresh round of industrial investment. Capital spending, languishing at 2 percent growth in 1990, rose 44 percent in 1992 and 62 percent in 1993. GDP growth accelerated from 3.9 percent in 1990 to 9.2 percent in 1991 and 14.3 percent in 1992. The Party Congress in 1992 became a celebration of Deng's reforms. His calls for accelerated efforts became Party policy.

Deng bequeathed Jiang with a restarted reform process, but also a problem to deal with. With investment running wild, the economy was once again overheating. By 1993, the consumer price index had broken above 10 percent. In 1994, it rose above 20 percent. Remembering what happened during China's last bout of high inflation, Jiang readied the riot police. This time, however, it wasn't Chen Yun leading the charge on retrenchment. Chen and other Party elders had stepped back from the front line of policymaking. Instead it was Zhu Rongji, the flinty-faced, no-nonsense vice premier, who found himself tasked with cooling an overheated economy.

In comparison with the retrenchment of 1988, and setting a pattern that would persist through the decades ahead, controls aimed at slowing lending and investment were applied gradually and with a light touch. "We are deeply aware," said Zhu, speaking to US magazine *Businessweek* at the start of 1994, "of the need to provide a soft landing for the Chinese people . . . if the growth rate were allowed to decline significantly, our social stability would be adversely affected, and if social stability were adversely affected, we would not be able to initiate reforms."[9]

With GDP growth in 1995 still at 11 percent and price increases still running in double digits, one might have wondered if Zhu's soft landing was actually no landing at all. Macroeconomic controls were tight enough, though, to prevent inflation spiraling higher. By the start of 1996, annual increases in the consumer price index were back in the single digits, tight enough also to end the rally in the infant stock market. Prefiguring later extreme boom–bust cycles, the Shanghai Composite Index rose from 393 in November 1992 to 1,536 in February 1993, before crashing back down to 339 in July 1994. Combining humor and resentment, stock pickers quipped that it wasn't a bear market or a bull market but a pig market—about as appealing to be in as a pig sty, and a pun on the similarity between Zhu's name and the Chinese word for pig, which is also pronounced "zhu."[10]

Zhu had gone one better than Chen, taming inflation without hammering growth. Left unaddressed, however, was an even larger task—cleaning up moribund state-owned industrial firms, and the overstretched state-owned banks that kept them afloat.

The Asian financial crisis strengthened incentives to accelerate reform. It was on July 2, 1997, that Thailand, under intense pressure from speculators, floated the baht. That was the start of a crisis that rolled across the region, toppling once-mighty banks and corporations, laying growth low and bringing governments to their knees. Japan, South Korea, Indonesia, Thailand, Hong Kong, Malaysia, Singapore, and the Philippines all slid into recession. In Indonesia, which saw a 13 percent contraction in output

9. Zhu Rongji, *Zhu Rongji Meets the Press* (Oxford: Oxford University Press, 2011).

10. Willy Wo-Lap Lam, *The Era of Jiang Zemin* (Upper Saddle River, NJ: Prentice Hall, 1999).

in 1998, the thirty-one-year reign of President Suharto came to an end. A photograph of International Monetary Fund managing director Michel Camdessus standing over Suharto as he signed up to stringent conditions for a rescue loan came to characterize the crisis, which many in Asia saw as caused by foreign investors and exacerbated by foreign governments.

The proximate cause of the crisis was speculative attacks by foreign speculators. Hedge funds like George Soros's Quantum Fund made big bets that Asian central banks wouldn't be able to maintain overvalued exchange rates, triggering a flood of hot money out of the region. The underlying cause was a crony capitalist system, with banks making loans based on political rather than commercial logic. For China, a closed capital account—with strict controls on any cross-border fund flows—meant immunity from speculative attacks. The charges of crony capitalism, however, hit uncomfortably close to home. If relations between banks, businesses, and government in Thailand, Indonesia, and Korea were too close for propriety, China's state-owned family was positively incestuous.

For Zhu, there were two questions: first, how to calibrate policy settings to ride out a crisis that threatened to hammer exports; and second, what structural changes would be needed to inoculate against a similar shock striking the mainland. On the first, China won plaudits for resisting the temptation to devalue the yuan—a move that would have bolstered exports, but exacerbated the crisis for the rest of Asia. A stable yuan provided an anchor for the region as currencies around it plunged. Instead, with hollowed-out exports laying bare industrial overcapacity, Zhu opted for a massive infrastructure stimulus—a 1.5-trillion-yuan splurge that anticipated the 4-trillion-yuan response to the great financial crisis a decade later.

On the second question, the lesson that China's policymakers drew was that reform needed to accelerate in some areas, and slow in others. State-owned firms needed to be cut off from life support, and operate on a commercial basis. Banks needed to make loans according to financial rather than political logic. On capital account opening, however—breaking down the barriers between China's financial markets and the rest of the world— caution was the watchword. "Asking a country to open its capital account prematurely," warned Zhu, "may even destroy the country's economy."[11] China's leaders had seen what happened to Suharto. They didn't want the same thing to happen to them.

Reform at the end of the 1970s was centered on a shift in mindset: Deng's "practice is the sole criterion of truth," an oblique but effective debunking of blind faith in Maoism. In the 1980s, the key win was the step away from the plan as the guide to production and prices. In the 1990s, it was public ownership that found itself in the reformers' sights. At the start of the reform era, state-owned enterprises were the engines of industrial development and a source of revenue for the government. By 1997, that was no longer the case. Profits for state-owned firms, equal to 15 percent of GDP in 1978, had fallen below 2 percent.[12] Even ahead of the Asian financial crisis, Zhu bemoaned a state sector that was riddled with overcapacity and burdened with debt, with three people employed to do the job of one.

At the Fifteenth Party Congress in September 1997, Jiang took aim at state ownership, calling for "removing the fetters of irrational ownership structure on the productive forces and bringing about a situation of multiple forms."[13] The word "privatization" was not uttered, but the direction of travel was clear. In the years that followed, Zhu presided over a root-and-branch reform of the state sector. Following a policy of "grasping the large and releasing the small," Zhu aimed to nurture a core of major state-owned enterprises, creating globally competitive firms that could go toe to toe with General Electric, Siemens, and Sony. Smaller firms faced privatization, merger, or bankruptcy. For many of their workers, this meant unemployment. In 1996, on the eve of ownership reforms, there were 142 million employed in the state sector, accounting for 72 percent of urban employment. By 2002, when Jiang and Zhu were preparing to pass

11. Zhu, *Zhu Rongji Meets the Press*.

12. Barry Naughton, *The Chinese Economy: Transitions and Growth* (Cambridge, MA: MIT Press, 2006).

13. Robert Lawrence Kuhn, *The Man Who Changed China: The Life and Legacy of Jiang Zemin* (New York: Crown, 2005).

the baton to the next generation of leaders, those numbers had fallen to 83 million and 33 percent.

The second target of Zhu's reform was the banks. In the early years of China's reform era, commercial banks did not exist. With a system of two hundred thousand employees across two thousand local branches, the PBOC allocated credit based on the priorities of state planners. Even after the big-four commercial banks were carved out in the mid-1980s, lending was driven more by political than commercial considerations. State firms investing in line with national development plans got credit, even if the projects had little chance of delivering a commercial return. Zombie firms with no viable business model but a crucial role in keeping unemployment low got credit, even if they had no chance of repaying it.

In such an environment, it was inevitable that banks would be plagued with low profits, high nonperforming loans, and an inadequate capital buffer. In 1998, the stock of bad loans was about 3.5 trillion yuan, equal to a third of GDP.[14]

The first challenge for Zhu was to deal with that legacy of troubled assets. In 1998 the government issued 270 billion yuan in bonds, with the proceeds used to recapitalize the banks. In 1999, the government established four asset management companies—one for each of the big banks. Operating on policy directives rather than commercial interests, they purchased 1.4 trillion yuan of bad loans from the banks, at face value. The second challenge was to instill in the banks a new commercial culture. That proved harder to do. In 2002, Jiang had a moment of nostalgia for the good old days when Shanghai bankers would take so much responsibility for bad lending decisions they would drown themselves in the Pu, the river that divides the east and west sides of the town. "How many bankers today have jumped in the Pu—or any other river—because of bad debts?" he asked.[15] Further government support would be contingent on banks putting their own house in order.

14. Naughton, *The Chinese Economy*.

15. Kuhn, *The Man Who Changed China*.

Even as banks moved closer to commercial operation and—a few years down the line—full-blown initial public offerings, nothing would dent the Party's control of their operations. Banks' role in managing China's development strategy, and smoothing the ups and downs of the growth cycle, was too important to allow them to become fully privately owned or market-oriented. "Like the People's Liberation Army," said one cadre during the 1998 reforms, "the banking system would remain a preserve of the Party and subject only to its control."[16]

Reform of the state-owned enterprises and the banks retooled China's economic engine. It was entry into the World Trade Organization (WTO) that provided the fuel to make it speed ahead. In 1986, when China first applied to join the General Agreement on Tariffs and Trade, it looked like an easy win. A government monopoly on trade—with all imports and exports channeled through state-owned Foreign Trade Corporations—was already on the way out. In the United States, the strategic calculation favored bringing China into the fold of global commerce as part of the counterbalance to the red menace of the Soviet Union. It turned out to be somewhat less straightforward than expected.

In China, fighting tooth-and-nail opposition from conservatives who feared Western influence and state firms that feared foreign competition, reformers worked to put in place the conditions for WTO membership. For the United States, however, the strategic calculation swung through 180 degrees. The collapse of the Soviet Union and end of the Cold War reduced the need for a close embrace with China. The horror of Tiananmen shifted the US focus on China away from its successful reforms toward its authoritarian government. Bill Clinton campaigned for the US presidency with a promise to get tough with the "butchers of Beijing"—tying WTO access to progress on human rights. US labor unions viewed China less as fellow travelers on the path to worker power and more as an unwelcome source of low-price competition.

If the obstacles were formidable, so too was the will to overcome them. For Zhu, WTO entry would not just allow China to tap global demand,

16. Lam, *The Era of Jiang Zemin.*

it would also be a catalyst for reform—attracting more foreign invest-ment and expertise, forcing strong Chinese firms to do better, pushing weak ones into bankruptcy. In the United States, the business lobby was salivating at the prospect of cheap workers and new markets. In April 1999, Zhu was embarrassed when an ill-fated trip to the United States failed to deliver the expected agreement. A few months later, the breakthrough was achieved. In 2001, at a meeting in Doha, fifteen years after China's appli-cation, the WTO welcomed China as its 143rd member. Hailing the deci-sion, Jiang promised China would "strike a carefully thought out balance between honoring its commitments and enjoying its rights." In the years that followed, as China's trade surplus with the rest of the world ballooned, it seemed the balance was more toward the latter.[17]

For China's leaders, the experience of the first half of the 1990s con-firmed the lesson they had learned at the end of the 1980s. The Chinese people must be provided with a soft landing; an overheated economy cooled slowly. The experience of the second half shows that they knew not to waste a good crisis. Asia's meltdown would provide the catalyst for root-and-branch reforms of state-owned enterprises, a recapitalization of the banks, and entry into the WTO. Those reforms, recalling the dynamism of the Deng era, would propel China's growth into the twenty-first century.

17. Kuhn, *The Man Who Changed China*.

China's Third Cycle and the Origins of the Great Financial Crisis

China's economy under Deng Xiaoping had been characterized by reform without losers. A few got rich first, most got richer, few were worse off. During the Jiang Zemin administration (running from 1989 to 2002), that was not the case. Progress on reform meant the shuttering of thousands of state-owned enterprises. Millions lost their jobs. The "iron rice bowl" of cradle-to-grave benefits was smashed. Even as the divide between winners and losers grew starker, Jiang moved away from Communist orthodoxy, enshrining the idea of merit-based rewards in the Party constitution. In 2002, Jiang's final Party Congress agreed on the principle that "labor, capital, technology, managerial expertise and other production factors should participate in the distribution of income in accordance with their contributions."[1] With that final jettisoning of Marx's "from each according to their ability, to each according to their need," the door to rising inequality was gaping wide.

Following Jiang, the first and most distinctive contribution of the Hu Jintao administration that started in 2002 was an attempted shift toward

---

1. Robert Lawrence Kuhn, *The Man Who Changed China: The Life and Legacy of Jiang Zemin* (New York: Crown, 2005).

a more inclusive model of development. Hu's first trip as Party secretary was to Hebei, visiting the last Communist headquarters in 1949 before they seized power in Beijing—a signal of return to the Party's orthodox and egalitarian roots. At the Third Plenum in October 2003 he staked out a more socially conscious vision of China's development, bemoaning the slow increase in rural incomes and the "prominent contradictions" that had left so many without jobs. One of Hu and his premier Wen Jiabao's first and most successful decisions was to reduce the burden of the agricultural tax, removing a drag on farmers' incomes.

In his ten years in office, Hu, himself from a humble background, maintained a steady focus on building a progressive social policy. He didn't get the job done, but he did make progress. In the old world, workers had enjoyed an "iron rice bowl" of cradle-to-grave welfare provided by state-owned enterprises. Housing, education, healthcare, and pension were all provided by the *danwei*, or work unit. In the new world most jobs were in private firms, and even for those that remained in the state sector, benefits were stripped back. Steadily increasing government spending on social services, and expanding coverage of health insurance, Hu didn't fully replace the iron rice bowl. He did at least provide the instant noodle cup of a rudimentary welfare state. Where Jiang's signature achievement was the "three represents"—bringing the capitalist entrepreneurs into the Communist Party fold, along with the workers and the farmers—Hu promised a "harmonious society" where the entrepreneurs didn't get rich at the expense of the workers and the farmers.

On financial reforms too, the early years of the Hu administration were a period of progress. With People's Bank of China (PBOC) governor Zhou Xiaochuan in the lead, China's technocrats set out a roadmap for recapitalizing, remodeling, and—ultimately—listing the banks. Carving out $45 billion from its foreign exchange reserves, the PBOC created Central Huijin, a state-owned investment vehicle that would use the funds to recapitalize the banks, plugging holes left by a decade's accumulation of nonperforming loans. At the end of 2003 Huijin injected $22.5 billion each into Bank of China and China Construction Bank, taking their capital base up to the 8 percent level required by international regulations.

The next step was introducing foreign strategic investors—needed not so much for their capital as for their expertise, and eager to gain a foothold in the Chinese market. HSBC took a 19.9 percent stake in Bank of Communications, China's fifth-largest bank. Bank of America and Temasek—Singapore's sovereign wealth fund—invested in China Construction Bank. Goldman Sachs took a 7 percent stake in Industrial and Commercial Bank of China (ICBC). Hank Paulson, at that time Goldman's chief executive, tells how the firm flew out senior executives to teach ICBC's cadres about risk management.[2] International standards on capital adequacy and strategic investments from foreign banks—both were a departure for a China suspicious of the destabilizing impact of global capital markets. Both were necessary, providing an international seal of approval as the banks prepared for listing on the global markets.

The final step was the initial public offering. Bank of Communications was the first to test international investors' appetite for a piece of China's financial story. Hong Kong, which combined global funds and standards with geographic proximity to the mainland and political alignment with its leaders, was chosen as the venue. Their June 2005 IPO raised $1.9 billion. On the first day of trading, the share price popped 13 percent. With the tone set, a positive reception for the other state banks was assured. Bank of China was next to market, raising $11.2 billion in June 2006. Seven months later in January 2007, the giant ICBC raised $21.9 billion—the world's biggest IPO.

China's reformers had attempted something rather ingenious—a bailout of the banks that was tied to the introduction of modern management and market incentives for improved risk management. "This is the last time," declared Lou Jiwei, then the vice minister of finance, reflecting hopes that this was the bailout to end all bailouts.

The listing of the state banks was a major step forward that left the reformers still significantly short of the goal of a modern, efficient financial system. On the achievement side of the ledger, taken together with the

2. Henry M. Paulson, *Dealing with China: An Insider Unmasks the New Economic Superpower* (New York: Twelve, 2015).

creation of the asset management companies in the late 1990s, the fancy footwork in deploying foreign exchange reserves cleaned up the banks' balance sheets. The nonperforming loan ratio for ICBC, for example, came down to 4 percent in 2006 from 24 percent in 2003. Foreign strategic investors—among them some of the world's leading commercial and investment banks—brought with them new technology and expertise. Stock market listings added market discipline to the incentives for good governance. Global investors' appraisal of the banks' performance was now reflected second by second in the ups and downs of share prices.

On the failure side, even after welcoming strategic investors and selling shares to the public, China's banks remained firmly under control of the state. Foreign investors had a seat at the table. Equity investors could signal their displeasure by selling the stock. But the majority of shares, and the entirety of control, remained in the hands of the government. As the prospectus for the ICBC IPO spells out, the bank's majority shareholders—the Ministry of Finance and Central Huijin—"have strong interests in the successful implementation of the economic or fiscal policies enacted by the State Council and/or the PBOC, which policies may not be . . . in the best interest of our other shareholders."

GOVERNOR ZHOU'S TRILEMMA

Entry into the World Trade Organization (WTO) was one of the defining economic policy successes of the Jiang administration. Failure to capitalize on the opportunity that presented to upgrade China's industrial structure, or to address imbalances in the drivers of growth it caused at home and abroad, came to define Hu's term.

Combining cheap domestic labor and advanced foreign technology produced impressive results. By 2005, China's annual exports were $763 billion, more than three times higher than in 2000, and rising rapidly. Chinese firms learned fast. Even as total exports rose, the share of domestic value added climbed to 68 percent in 2008, from 64 percent in 2000. National champions like Alibaba, the e-commerce giant that started life connecting Chinese firms with foreign buyers; Huawei, the telecom equipment firm and bête noire of US intelligence agencies; and Lenovo, one of the world's biggest producers of laptops, would not exist if China had not entered the WTO. For hundreds of millions of workers, life on the sweatshop production line was hard and sometimes bad for the health. But it provided a pathway out of hardscrabble rural poverty.

For China, WTO entry was a more or less unalloyed positive. What the rest of the world expected when they signed on the dotted line in Qatar, however, and what they actually got, were two different things. For many foreign firms, the door to the Chinese market remained closed. For others, the price of access was a joint venture with Chinese partners, with forced technology transfer eroding competitive advantage. In banking and financial services, behind-the-border restrictions—like strict controls on new branch openings—restricted foreign banks to tiny backwaters of the market.

More damaging than the foregone overseas gains were the manifest domestic losses. Wages in China were a fraction of the level in the United States and Europe. An exhaustive exercise by the US Bureau of Labor Statistics found that in 2005 China's factory workers earned—on average—about 83 cents an hour.[3] In the United States, the minimum wage was $5.15 and most earned more. An undervalued yuan, subsidized land, and cheap credit gave Chinese firms an additional competitiveness boost. Workers in the West found themselves first uncompetitive and then unemployed. An influential paper by a team headed by MIT professor Daron Acemoglu estimated that from 1999 to 2011, import competition from China led to US job losses in the range of 2 million to 2.4 million, with most concentrated in America's Rustbelt.[4]

3. Judith Banister, *China's Manufacturing Employment and Hourly Labor Compensation, 2002 to 2009*, (Washington DC, Bureau of Labor Statistics, 2013).

4. Daron Acemoglu, David Autor, David Dorn, Gordon H. Hanson and Brendan Price, Import Competition and the Great U.S. Employment Sag of the 2000s, National Bureau of Economic Research, August 2014.

In the 1970s and 1980s, Japan's rise had made it the job-stealing villain of the US economic morality tale. In 1985, in what became known as the Plaza Accord, Ronald Reagan's Treasury secretary James Baker strong-armed his Japanese counterpart into agreeing to a massive yen appreciation, aimed at restoring balance to bilateral trade. The results for Japan were disastrous: a slump in exports, a financial bubble, and a lost decade of stagnant growth. Fast-forward two decades, and it was China that posed the new threat to US jobs. The Treasury turned to the same playbook, calling for yuan appreciation to choke off China's exports and boost demand for US goods.

Faced with the same problem, it's no surprise that the United States would reach for the same solution. Learning from the Japanese experience, it's no surprise that China would resist. In May 2005, the US Treasury called China's exchange rate policies "highly distortionary."[5] They threatened to name Beijing a currency manipulator, opening the path to economic sanctions if the PBOC didn't loosen its grip on the currency. In the Senate, a bill called for across-the-board tariffs if the yuan didn't significantly strengthen against the dollar.

It was July 21, 2005, when the PBOC finally ended the yuan's ten-year peg to the dollar with a one-off 2 percent appreciation. It was, in a sense, a response to US pressure. The bigger picture, however, was that China had moved when it wanted, and by how much it wanted. Four years after entry into the WTO, exports were growing close to 30 percent a year. GDP was on track for another double-digit expansion. China, it was eminently clear, had been the major winner from the decision. A 2 percent yuan move, and a shift to a crawling peg against the dollar, was the blueprint designed by Governor Zhou. It was a move in the right direction, but nothing like the massive appreciation forced on Japan in the Plaza Accord, nor in any way big enough to narrow China's trade surplus. To do that, the number crunchers at the US Peterson Institute for International Economics said that a revaluation of more than 30 percent was required.[6]

5. *Report to Congress on International Economic and Exchange Rate Policies* (Washington, DC: US Treasury, May 2005).

6. William R. Cline and John Williamson, *New Estimates of Fundamental Equilibrium Exchange Rates* (Washington DC: Peterson Institute for International Economics, 2008).

For Zhou, China's lead financial technocrat, architect of many of its most important twenty-first-century reforms, the yuan strategy erred on the side of caution. Zhou did not want to repeat the mistakes of Deng's big-bang price deregulation, when a one-off move resulted in a chaos of inflation and social unrest. Neither did Beijing want to fall into the same trap as Tokyo—caving to demand for extreme appreciation, and crumpling the export-driven growth model.

Gradualism made sense, but it came at a cost. Zhou found himself, if not trapped, then at least severely confined by what economists call the "impossible trinity." The idea, which originates in 1960s work by Marcus Fleming and Robert Mundell, is that a country cannot simultaneously have a fixed exchange rate, free capital flows, and an independent monetary policy. That's because capital flows to where returns are highest, so countries with an open capital account must accept either interest rates in line with the global anchor—the Federal Reserve—or a floating exchange rate.

Many economies opt for independent monetary policy and a floating exchange rate. Independent monetary policy—the ability to set interest rates in accordance with national conditions—provides a crucial tool to manage the ups and downs of unemployment and inflation. A floating exchange rate helps keep trade in balance and provides a cushion against shocks, depreciating in the bad times and appreciating in the good. A few, like Hong Kong, have a fixed exchange rate but sacrifice independence of monetary policy (the Hong Kong dollar is pegged to the US dollar, and the Hong Kong Monetary Authority sets interest rates that mirror those of the Federal Reserve).

China, characteristically, tried to stake out a position slightly outside the established rules. Instead of having two of the impossible three, they opted for a little bit of each. The yuan was managed but also reflected market pressure; capital flows were restricted but not banned; the PBOC moved rates independently of the Federal Reserve, but had to keep its objective of yuan stability in mind. What that meant in practice is that in the early years of the yuan peg, in order to avoid surging capital inflows, interest rates were kept low—too low for an economy growing at China's pace.

As a rule of thumb, loan rates should be roughly in line with the pace of nominal GDP growth—a proxy for the expected return on investment. If they're too much higher, no one will borrow, hitting growth and employment. Too much lower and demand for credit will be too great, fueling inflation and asset bubbles. Deposit rates should be at least above the rate of inflation—otherwise, household savers don't get a fair return and consumption suffers. In China, the decision to manage the yuan meant that both of these rules were violated. Borrowers could tap funds at way below their expected return. Savers were penalized with below-inflation rates. China's economic structure was thrown off-balance, constantly at risk of runaway inflation and asset price bubbles, and with a worrying tilt away from consumption toward investment and exports.

Twice in the early years of the Hu administration, inflation pushed past the pain point for China's households—touching 5.3 percent in August 2004 and 8.7 percent in February 2008. Online jokers wondered if the real rate of price increases was even higher, asking satirically: "Do the statisticians buy vegetables?"

On the first occasion, interest rates didn't move at all. On the second, the PBOC raised the benchmark one-year deposit rate from 2.5 percent to 4.1 percent—still way below the level of inflation. Zhou found himself trapped on the horns of Fleming and Mundell's trilemma. Higher rates were necessary to choke off inflation. But despite China's closely managed capital account, higher rates would also attract hot money inflows. Speculators had multiple routes to bring funds into the country, from overinvoicing for exports to disguising portfolio flows as investment in factories and other bricks-and-mortar assets. Hot money inflows made it harder to manage the exchange rate and supercharged growth in the money supply—adding a fresh source of inflationary pressure.

With no easy options, the central bank allowed the pace of yuan appreciation to accelerate. A stronger yuan chokes off inflation by reducing demand for exports—increasing slack in the economy, and lowering import prices. As more rapid yuan appreciation drove more capital inflows, the central bank increased the share of deposits banks are required to hold in reserve, locking up the influx of funds before it could spill over into inflationary lending. The National Development and Reform Commission—the powerful economic planning agency—put a stop on any increases in government-set prices, and sent inspection teams out to twenty-six provinces to keep a lid on food prices.[7]

Concerted efforts by the central bank and the economic planners succeeded in bringing prices under control. China under Hu never suffered the vertiginous rise in inflation that pushed the economy, and social stability, to the brink in 1989. At the same time, the exchange rate, which sets the relative price of foreign and domestic goods, and the interest rate, which sets the price of money, are the most important levers for managing the economy. Holding them too low for too long, as China had done, introduced serious distortions. Inflation at 8.7 percent would not be the most serious challenge China had to deal with.

LAND GRABS AND ONLY CHILDREN: THE SOURCES OF UNBALANCED GROWTH

"This is where my farm was," says Mr. Fu, pulling his battered sedan alongside Golden Lakeshore, a collection of luxury villas on the outskirts of Chengdu, a city of 11 million in China's southwest. The villas are out of Mr. Fu's price range. When government-hired thugs drove him off the small plot where he ran a fish farm, local officials paid Mr. Fu just 9 yuan per square meter for it. The plot was quickly resold for 640 yuan per square meter to a developer, which built villas that sell for 6,900 yuan per square meter.[8]

Mr. Fu found himself unemployed, one among tens of thousands of former farmers who inhabited the impoverished fringes of Chengdu. He had no heart to start another business. "What's the point if the government can just destroy it?" he said. The problem of poverty was compounded by

7. Barry Naughton, "The Inflation Battle: Juggling Three Swords," *China Leadership Monitor*, Issue 25, 2008.

8. Tom Orlik, "Tensions Mount as China Snatches Farms for Homes," *Wall Street Journal*, February 14, 2013.

inability to access social benefits. Despite having his farm destroyed to make way for the expansion of the city, Mr. Fu was classified as a rural resident. Without an urban *hukou*—the residence permit which entitles locals to tap welfare payments and social services—he had no access to unemployment and pension benefits. His family, no right to public education and healthcare.

Mr. Fu is not alone. China's urbanization boom was built on land wrenched from tens of millions of farmers. Huang Qi, a land rights activist in Chengdu, heard stories like Mr. Fu's every day, thousands a year. Operating from his spartan apartment, Huang acted as a clearinghouse for information on land grabs, fielding a constant stream of calls on his mobile phone and posting the information on his website in the hopes negative publicity would stop the worst extremes. The authorities tolerated that act of constructive dissent for a while, then apparently decided it was too much trouble and locked him up for sharing "state secrets." The Chinese Academy of Social Science puts the number of landless farmers at 40 million to 50 million. A larger group of migrant workers, some 200 million, left the rural farm for the urban factory but can't access urban social insurance or services.

Mr. Fu didn't know it, but he—and the millions of other farmers displaced by the property boom—was the victim of a deep imbalance in China's economy: an excess of saving that threatened the sustainability of the growth model.

The problems start with the one-child policy. Introduced in 1979 as a way of controlling population growth, government-set limits on fertility were an egregious intrusion of the state into the private realm of the family. They would also have an outsize impact on China's economic structure. The need to beat the gender odds (in 2006 there were 106 boys for every 100 girls) and find a wife meant that families had to save to get their sons onto the property ladder. Fewer children to buy diapers, clothes, and food for meant lower consumption. Fewer children to rely on in old age meant more need for precautionary saving.

Other factors also drove saving higher. For farmers forced off their land, and those who left of their own accord to seek a better life in the city, China's welfare state provided scant protections. Survey work by Xin Meng, an academic at Australian National University, found that more than 80 percent had no coverage for illness, unemployment, or old age.[9] For urban workers, the situation wasn't much better. As state-owned enterprises were closed, the share of urban workers covered by health insurance tumbled. The average value of pension payments dropped from 80 percent of salary to 50 percent.[10] Those were wrenching withdrawals, stripping Chinese workers of the social protections on which they had come to rely, pushing them into precautionary saving against the risk of sickness and old age.

Higher inequality, in part the result of a real estate boom that immiserated some and enriched others, meant more wealth in the hands of the high-saving rich. A survey by Landesa, a nonprofit focused on rural affairs, found that on average compensation paid to farmers was just 2 percent of the value of land.[11] For unscrupulous local officials, the opportunity to gouge land from farmers at close to zero cost and flip it to real estate developers who could sell apartments and villas at a high price created massive opportunities for graft. "They all smoke Chunghwa," said a neighbor of Mr. Fu's, referring to local officials' taste for China's most expensive brand of cigarettes. Based on data from the China Household Finance Survey, the wealthiest 10 percent of China's households save 60 percent of their income and account for close to three-quarters of total saving.

An undervalued yuan and low government-set interest rates were also part of the picture. A made-in-China exchange rate meant exports were cheap and imports expensive. Factories up and down the east coast benefited as surging sales pushed profits higher. With higher profits,

9. Paul Mozur and Tom Orlik, "China's Workers Lingering in Cities," *Wall Street Journal*, December 30, 2012.

10. Longmei Zhang, *China's High Savings: Drivers, Prospects, and Policies* (Washington, DC: International Monetary Fund, 2017).

11. *Sixth 17-Province China Survey* (Beijing: Landesa, 2011).

corporate saving rose. Low interest rates reduced returns on saving. In theory, that should have meant reduced incentive to save. Empirical evidence is inconclusive, but in practice, with households saving for a defined objective (enough for a down payment on a house, for example), it may have increased the amount they needed to stash away.

In 2007, China saved 51 percent of its income. That was a remarkably high level. High in international comparison—the United States and Japan saved substantially less.[12] High also in historical comparison; in the early 1990s, China's savings rate was about 40 percent. It was also a problem. To support demand, preventing a slump in growth and employment, saving has to be recycled into spending. That can happen through investment. Or it can happen through exports—with savings loaned overseas and ending up as foreign demand. Expressed in the formal language of the economics textbook, savings minus investment equals the current account balance. Expressed in more straightforward terms, savings have to show up as either capital spending or overseas sales.

Turning 51 percent of GDP from saving to spending requires a lot of investment or a lot of exports. In China's case, it required a lot of both. In 2007, investment was 41 percent of GDP, and the current account surplus—the difference between exports and imports—was closing in on 10 percent. Once again, those were big numbers. During its period of intense industrialization in the 1970s, Japan's investment-to-GDP ratio peaked just above 40 percent of GDP. In 1986, at the height of concerns about made-in-Japan exports swamping US markets, Japan's current account surplus was just 4 percent of GDP. In 2001, the year it joined the WTO, China's capital spending was 36 percent of GDP, its current account surplus 1 percent.

In a developing economy, there are abundant opportunities for investment. China needed housing, office blocks, shopping malls, roads, railways, airports, power transmission, a telecom network, water

12. Saving rate (indicator), Organisation for Economic Co-operation and Development, OECD Library, doi: 10.1787/ff2e64d4-en (accessed April 24, 2019).

treatment plants, steel smelters, and shipyards. Even after funding all of these projects, saving at 51 percent of GDP meant there were too many yuan chasing too few investment opportunities. A major consequence of that was a housing bubble, with the price of property rising at a torrid pace. With developers scrambling to grab a share of the profits, and local governments hungry for land sales revenue, real estate construction rose from 450 million square meters in 1997 to 2,363 million square meters in 2007. Some got rich. Others were not so lucky. For Mr. Fu and other farmers who found themselves standing in the path of the savings-fueled real estate juggernaut, home, farm, and dignity were all crushed.

Property might have been the preferred investment option for China's high-saving households. It wasn't the only option. For many years, China's stock market had been moribund. In 2005, the stars were aligned for a change. A booming economy was driving soaring profits, with industrial firms reporting 42 percent gains in the first half of the year. A halt to new listings tilted the market from the chill of oversupply to the heat of excess-demand. The start of yuan appreciation added fuel to the fire, increasing the appeal of domestic assets and attracting hot money inflows from overseas.

In July 2005, just before the beginning of yuan appreciation, the Shanghai Composite Index touched a low of 1,011. It ended the year at 1,161, up 14.8 percent. In 2006 the market doubled, climbing 130 percent to end the year at 2,675. By the start of 2007, investors were in raging-bull mode. An honor roll of national champions—from ICBC to Air China—queued up to list. Millions of first-time punters piled in. Pensioner stock-pickers, staring transfixed at the flickering prices of the stock-trading screens, provided irresistible fodder for press photographers. The market roared to an October 16 peak of 6,092—up more than 500 percent from its 2005 trough. "Preventing asset bubbles is like preventing inflation, and it's the government's responsibility to ensure a fair, healthy and transparent stock market," said Premier Wen Jiabao, showcasing his signature combination of noble sentiment and missing action.

Oil major Petrochina's November 2007 initial public offering was timed to perfection, hitting the top of the market and briefly achieving a trillion-dollar market capitalization. If the Petrochina IPO captured the excitement of the China story in 2007, it also reflected the hype. A trillion-dollar price tag made it twice as valuable as Exxon Mobil, despite having barely half the revenue. A dual listing—with Petrochina traded in both Hong Kong and Shanghai—should have meant the same valuation in both markets. In fact, the two diverged, with the stock trading at 57 times earnings in Shanghai and 22 times in Hong Kong. The difference between the two reflected the speculative frenzy that gripped mainland investors—and, more than that, the massive store of savings trapped in the mainland market and looking for any investable assets.[13]

If Shanghai valuations looked too stretched to last, that's because they were. A combination of tighter monetary policy, an increased supply of shares as state-owned firms rushed to market, and hints of a "through-train" link to allow mainland funds to flow to Hong Kong proved too much for the market to handle. By the end of November, the index had tumbled to 4,871. After a brief revival in December and early January the rout resumed, taking the market down to 1,771 in October 2008.

The pension stock pickers—now impecunious—placed their heads in their hands for one last photo, the shutter clicked, and the story was complete. Trillions of yuan in paper wealth had been created, and then almost immediately destroyed. Many factors were at work. Surging industrial profits, optimism in the future, and the irrational exuberance of China's inexperienced investors all played a part. Behind it all, however, were the one-child policy, the destruction of the iron rice bowl of welfare benefits, government-set interest and exchange rates, and socialist inequality that would make a capitalist blush. The result: savings at 51 percent of GDP looking for a place to invest, and all the stolen land and speculative bubbles that brings.

13. Andrew Batson and Shai Oster, "How Big Is Petrochina?," *Wall Street Journal*, November 6, 2007.

The busted boom of China's stock market made for great headlines. For China's economy, however, it remained small news. Stocks were too insignificant as a source of corporate fundraising and store of household wealth to boost growth on the way up, or bludgeon it on the way down. The same could not be said of another consequence of China's high savings rate—the great financial crisis.

China's Economy in the Great Financial Crisis

September 15, 2008, was not a good day for the global economy. Lehman Brothers, the storied investment bank with a history stretching back to the middle of the nineteenth century, filed for bankruptcy. That news tipped the markets into freefall. The pass-through to the real economy was swift and severe. US output contracted, falling 8.4 percent in the fourth quarter of the year. Unemployment hit 10 percent. As financial contagion ripped through global banks and US consumers chopped up their credit cards, the crisis spread around the world. Europe and Japan followed the United States into recession. Recovery would be slow and painful. Even after the crisis was over, the United States and the world found themselves on a permanently lower growth trajectory. Faith in free markets, faith in globalization, and faith in establishment political parties was shaken to its core.

Success has many fathers; failure is an orphan. Many had theories on who else was to blame for the financial crisis. None wanted to claim it as their own. John Taylor, a professor at Stanford, blamed the Federal Reserve. Based on Taylor's own creation—the Taylor rule, which provides a rule-of-thumb guide to where the Federal Reserve should be aiming—rates had been "too low for too long." The result: a real estate bubble, and a stash of dodgy mortgage-backed securities on banks' balance sheets.[1] Ben Bernanke, a member of the Federal Reserve's Board of Governors during the time of the supposed "too low for too long" misjudgment, had his own explanation for what triggered the crisis: China.

In the years ahead of the crisis, Bernanke pointed out, the Federal Reserve had raised rates. It had done so cautiously, reflecting uncertainty about underlying economic conditions, but even incrementally executed the move from 1 percent in 2004 to 5.25 percent in 2006 was significant. Strangely, however, even as the Federal Reserve had moved short-term interest rates progressively higher, long-term rates—the price everyone from the government to homebuyers paid to borrow for major projects—stayed low. The yield on ten-year government bonds rose from about 4.7 percent at the start of the tightening process to 5.2 percent at the end. The reason, Bernanke said, was a "global savings glut," with most of the saving coming from China.[2]

China had learned from the rolling series of emerging market crises in the 1990s—from Mexico's "tequila crisis" in 1994 to the Asian financial crisis in 1997. These shared a common cause: a sudden exodus of foreign funding. Governments had followed the prescriptions of the Washington Consensus—opening to trade and capital flows. Instead of the promised accelerated development, however, they had suffered heightened instability. Observing events from a distance, it was natural for China to choose a different path. China would open to trade flows. It would not open its capital account or borrow from overseas. Instead, the People's Bank of China (PBOC) maintained close controls on cross-border capital flows, and built up a store of foreign exchange reserves.

As China's exports expanded faster than imports, a bulging trade surplus should have meant pressure for yuan appreciation. Instead, the PBOC intervened actively in the foreign exchange market, buying up

1. John B. Taylor, *Housing and Monetary Policy* (Cambridge, MA: National Bureau of Economic Research, 2007).

2. Ben Bernanke, *The Global Saving Glut and the U.S. Current Account Deficit* (Washington, DC: Federal Reserve Board, 2005).

trade-surplus dollars at a policy-determined rate. Those dollars drove the increase in foreign exchange reserves, which rose from $212 billion when China joined the World Trade Organization in 2001 to $1.9 trillion on the eve of the financial crisis. The lion's share of those reserves was invested in US Treasuries.

Put a different way, China saved 51 percent of its income. Much of that savings it used as investment at home—some going to worthwhile projects, some wasted on roads to nowhere or evaporated in speculative bubbles. What was left it lent to the US Treasury.

The consequence in the United States was bargain basement borrowing rates that fueled the real estate boom. With mortgage rates low, homebuyers took on more debt than they could manage. Investment banks, taking advantage of cheap funding, loaded their balance sheets with mortgage-backed securities. The increase in household wealth, or at least the illusion of it, reduced the US savings rate from low to nothing. Investment was channeled into equities and real estate rather than expanding productive capacity-capping growth in exports. With China in a self-reinforcing cycle of saving and trade surplus, and the United States in a self-reinforcing cycle of borrowing and trade deficit, the foundations of the financial crisis were laid. When the mortgage defaults began, the system toppled and then fell.

In the history of the great financial crisis, it is September 15, 2008— the day of the Lehman bankruptcy—that gets the most attention. It's November 9 that may end up having the larger long-term consequences. That's the day when a meeting of China's State Council, chaired by Premier Wen Jiabao, announced a 4-trillion-yuan stimulus package, a massive program of spending on infrastructure, affordable housing, and indus- trial upgrading aimed at keeping the wheels in the world's fastest-growing major economy turning. "Over the past two months, the global financial crisis has been intensifying daily," the State Council said. "In expanding investment, we must be fast and heavy-handed."

Details were lacking, but the signal was clear. The United States had faltered on its financial rescue and stumbled on its stimulus response. China would be decisive. US Treasury secretary Hank Paulson went down on one knee, a theatrical gesture to beg congressional leaders for stimulus funding. The Federal Reserve agonized over the legality of its rescue operations. In China, with its single-party state and subservient courts, there would be no such quibbling over democratic checks or legal balances. With demand in the United States and Europe poised to plummet, hammering exports, China opened its wallet to boost domestic demand. The 4-trillion-yuan stimulus was equivalent to 15 percent of GDP—close to the magnitude that Zhu Rongji had put to work in respond to the Asian financial crisis ten years earlier.

It was two weeks after Wen's November announcement before China's policymakers filled in the details of their stimulus plan. Spending on transport and power infrastructure would be the largest element, accounting for 1.8 trillion yuan of the 4 trillion. There was a trillion yuan for reconstruction following a massive earthquake in May 2008 in Wenchuan—a mountainous part of southwestern Sichuan province—that killed sixty-nine thousand and left 4.8 million homeless. Rural infrastructure, environmental investment, affordable housing, technology, and health and education filled out the total.

Wen committed 1.2 trillion yuan in central government funds. The balance, 2.8 trillion yuan, was to come from local governments and state-owned enterprises. If the same thing happened in the United States—a big-headline spending commitment, but with inadequate federal funds to back it up—the White House would be pilloried for running a fake stimulus. In China, given the growth-or-bust mentality of local officials, the concern was the reverse: local governments would not be too slow to spend; they'd be too fast. Within a month, eighteen provinces had piled in with proposals for projects with a total expenditure of 25 trillion yuan—more than 80 percent of GDP. In Sichuan, a local official apologized that capital spending in the first nine months of 2009 had come in at a mere 870 billion yuan. "We need more investment projects," he said.[3]

Funding was already moving into place. The PBOC had cut interest rates twice in quick succession, with one 27-basis-point cut at the start of

3. Lei Wang, "各地四季度加快投资建设 政府发文"囤项目," *Hexun*, 2009.

October 2008 and one at the end. Following the State Council announcement, they sent a decisive signal, cutting rates another 108 basis points—the equivalent of four rate cuts at once. Before the end of the year they would cut again. The interbank interest rate (the rate banks pay to borrow from each other) fell from a high of close to 4 percent in July to below 1 percent at the start of 2009. In parallel, the reserve requirement ratio (the share of deposits banks have to keep in reserve) was lowered, releasing more funds for lending. The 4-trillion-yuan stimulus provided the motive for banks to lend; bargain basement rates and a lower reserve requirement created the opportunity.

And lend they did. In the first quarter of 2009, banks made 4.6 trillion yuan in new loans, more than triple the level in the same period a year earlier. By the end of the year, there was 9.6 trillion yuan in new lending. That was a lot of money: close to double the total for the previous year, equal to about 30 percent of China's GDP, and double the dollar value of the US Troubled Asset Relief Program—the largest component of the US stimulus.

A lot of the new lending flowed to local government. In theory, local governments were barred from borrowing—a common-sense rule aimed at preventing local chiefs dashing for growth at the expense of blowing up the public debt. In practice, a workaround already existed, allowing local governments to set up off-balance-sheet vehicles to borrow. A shift in the rules made it easier for them to do so—a fateful move that solved the stimulus funding problem at the expense of opening a Pandora's box of financial risks. Local governments began a massive construction program. Investment in the transport network, already clocking 19.7 percent growth in 2008, accelerated to 48.3 percent growth in 2009.

Real estate boomed, a reflection not just of the surge in new lending but also of targeted efforts to ramp up property demand. China dropped a policy mandating punitively high borrowing costs for homebuyers—part of a precrisis attempt to cool the market. Homebuyers were enticed with rates at 70 percent of the benchmark. Taken together with the PBOC rate cuts, that meant mortgage rates fell from 8.2 percent in summer 2008 to

3.7 percent at the end of the year. Minimum down payments were reduced to 20 percent from 40 percent. The five years buyers were normally required to hold a home before they could flip it tax-free was reduced to two.

China's property speculators are not a group that needs much encouragement. Now, not to be outdone by local officials in their patriotic support for China in her hour of stimulus need, they responded with alacrity. Mortgage lending quintupled. In 2008, property sales fell 13.7 percent. In 2009, they roared back to 67 percent growth.

The industrial planners at the National Development and Reform Commission were also hard at work. "Long-range plans for adjustment and rejuvenation" aimed to seize the opportunity presented by the crisis to upgrade sectors from steel and shipbuilding to autos and electronics.[4] Autos also benefited from massive tax rebates, pushing sales from 4.2 percent year-on-year growth at the start of 2009 to 61.5 percent at the end. For hundreds of millions of rural residents, the government rolled out subsidies to buy home electronics—aiming to boost rural consumption and offset the impact of slumping foreign demand. Retail sales of home appliances accelerated to a peak of 62.3 percent annual growth at the start of 2010.

It worked.

In the first quarter of 2009, with exports contracting and stimulus yet to gain traction, growth shuddered to a halt. The official GDP gauge showed the economy slowing to 6.4 percent year-on-year, the weakest growth in almost two decades. China's GDP numbers come with caveats: the jagged edges of the economic cycle smoothed by the necessities of political message management. In the bad times, the official growth rate is almost certainly too high. In the good times, it is likely too low. In an unguarded moment, Li Keqiang—who in 2013 would follow Wen as China's premier—remarked that China's GDP data is "man-made." Li, at that time the Party secretary of Liaoning province, tracked bank loans, electricity output, and

---

4. Wang, "各地四季度加快投资建设 政府发文"囤项目.""

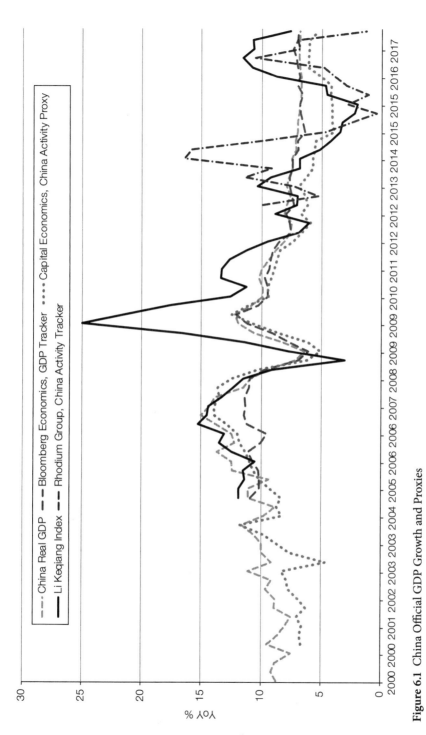

Figure 6.1 China Official GDP Growth and Proxies
Created by the author using information from Bloomberg, Capital Economics, China National Bureau of Statistics, and Rhodium Group.

rail freight as proxies for growth. As figure 6.1 shows, an index based on those inputs hit a trough of 2.6 percent growth at the end of 2008.[5]

Unemployment soared. A survey by Scott Rozelle, an academic at Stanford and an expert on China's rural economy, found that from September 2008 to April 2009 some 17 percent of migrant workers— 45 million of them—lost their job or delayed a move from the farm to the factory.[6] Journalists gleefully reported on Taiwanese bosses fleeing out of factory back doors, their suitcases full of cash, while mobs of unpaid workers protested at the front, angrily inquiring about missing salary payments. For a Chinese leadership focused, above all, on social stability, these were troubling signs.

By the second quarter stimulus had started to take hold, however, and by the second half of the year the economy was humming again. GDP reaccelerated, rising to 8.2 percent year-on-year growth in the second quarter on its way up to 11.9 percent at the end of the year. The Li Keqiang index pointed to an even more rapid recovery, hitting a peak of 26.8 percent growth at year end. The Shanghai market roared from 1,706 in November 2008 to 3,471 in August 2009, more than doubling in value. Workers who had lost their jobs in the export sweatshops found new work on the construction sites. Rozelle's survey found that by August 2009, the unemployment rates for migrant workers had fallen to 4.9 percent.

It would be eight years before unemployment in the United States returned to its precrisis level. Ten years on, the jobless still haunted the streets of capitals in Italy, Spain, and Greece. High unemployment and low wage gains had a wrenching impact on the body politic. Establishment parties were swept from power, replaced by populists who did a better job of identifying the problems but no better at finding solutions. In France, the National Front candidate made it into the last round of the presidential election. In the United Kingdom, 52 percent of the population voted

5. Simon Rabinovitch, "China's GDP Data Is 'Man Made,' Unreliable: Top Leader," Reuters, December 6, 2010.

6. Tom Orlik and Scott Rozelle, "How Many Unemployed Migrant Workers Are There?," *Far Eastern Economic Review*, 2009.

to exit the European Union. In the United States, Donald Trump won the presidency. In China, the recovery traced out a triumphant "V" shape and the specter of unemployment and social unrest was rapidly laid to rest; none challenged the Communist Party's grip on power. In the most straightforward terms, the 4-trillion-yuan stimulus was a success.

But even in the hurly-burly of 2009, as markets cheered the stimulus and world leaders lauded China's decisive action, doubts crept in. China's economic playing field was already tilted in favor of inefficient state-owned enterprises, against dynamic private firms. Investment was already running on steroids, at the expense of a stunted role for consumers. Now an unprecedented surge in credit was being channeled from state banks to state enterprises. A cement wave of capital spending crashed over the economy. The result could only be a system tipped further off-balance. Then there was the vexing question of how the borrowing would be repaid. Loans turned quickly into investment would buoy growth. Investment projects that were poorly chosen and sloppily executed would not generate sufficient revenue to repay the debt.

In the attainment of its immediate objective—securing growth and social stability—the stimulus announced on November 9, 2008, succeeded. As for the longer-term consequences, China's policymakers continue to wrestle with them.

TAKING AWAY THE PUNCHBOWL: THE FIRST EXIT FROM STIMULUS

"The Federal Reserve," said William McChesney Martin, who was chair from 1951 to 1970, "is in the position of the chaperone who has ordered the punchbowl removed just when the party was really warming up."[7] That was in 1955. Martin was speaking as the Federal Reserve sought to cool an overheated economy with a hike in interest rates. Approaching the

---

7. William McChesney Martin, "Address before the New York Group of the Investment Bankers of America," New York, October 19, 1955.

end of 2009, more than half a century later and half a world away, PBOC governor Zhou Xiaochuan was also eager to start removing the stimulus. Wen's 4-trillion-yuan investment program had succeeded. The economy had returned to double-digit growth. A rapid rise in house prices was a tell-tale sign of overheating. With the economy drunk on credit, Zhou wanted to take away the punch bowl.

For the local governments that did the borrowing and the banks that did the lending, it was a different story. To local officials, the stimulus presented a unique opportunity. Major investment projects were the path to an easy life—a source of growth, employment, and opportunities for graft. The only problem in normal times was a lack of funds and the need for regulatory approvals. Now the stimulus had turned local banks into ATMs for infrastructure spending, and virtually any project would get the green light. For banks, more loans meant more profits. And with lending ordered up by the highest level of leadership, there was an implicit guarantee that the government would backstop any bad debts.

From June 2009, without making a formal move on interest rates, the PBOC quietly began withdrawing funds from the market. The China Banking Regulatory Commission, under the leadership of veteran financial reformer Liu Mingkang, insisted banks build up their capital buffer, and made an initial accounting of loans to high-risk local government lending platforms. In January 2010, reacting to a surge in new lending in the first weeks of the year, the central bank raised the reserve requirement ratio, requiring banks to lock up a larger volume of their deposits rather than lending them out. As banks' cost of funds started to edge higher, Beijing's money mandarins hoped, they would transmit higher rates to borrowers, taking the edge off demand for loans.

It wasn't until April 2010 that policy decisively turned toward tightening. On April 17, the State Council published its Ten New Articles plan to curb the runaway property market. All of the apparatus of control on the real estate sector—normally deployed in careful and measured sequence— was suddenly rolled out simultaneously. Taking aim at the speculators that accounted for about a third of the market, the new policy raised down-payment requirements and mortgage rates. Developers suspected of holding back project launches to benefit from rising prices would have their access to finance cut off. The supply of new land for housing would more than double, with a high proportion allocated to affordable homes. A real estate tax—necessary to punish speculators for holding empty property—would be trialed.[8]

The impact on the markets was immediate. Home sales plunged, dropping 70 percent in Beijing and Shanghai, according to reports from local analysts.[9] With real estate developers looming large among listed firms, the fortunes of everyone from steel firms to banks closely tied to the property cycle, and investors already nervous following hints of tightening from the PBOC, the equity market wasn't far behind. The Shanghai Composite Index fell from a peak of 3,166 before the announcement to a trough of 2,363 in July 2010, losing 25 percent of its value.

When there are bubbles in the real estate sector, China's central bankers typically turn to targeted policies to take aim at speculators and developers. They raise down-payment requirements for homebuyers, rather than hiking interest rates for the whole economy. By the final months of 2010, it was clear that rocketing property prices were a symptom of wider overheating. Credit growth, which dipped in the second quarter following the State Council announcement of the Ten New Articles, was accelerating again. The resumption of yuan appreciation—with the crisis-era peg to the dollar broken in June 2010—was a contractionary policy (denting exports), but it also added to price pressure (attracting hot money inflows). Inflation was moving out of the government's comfort zone. It was time to move from targeted controls toward a comprehensive tightening of policy.

In October 2010 the PBOC raised interest rates 25 basis points, the first of a series of moves that took the one-year deposit rate from an all-out stimulus low of 2.25 percent to a higher but still pro-growth 3.5 percent in July 2011. It wasn't enough. By the time the National People's Congress rolled round in March 2011, the consumer price index was pushing past

8. Barry Naughton, "The Turning Point in Housing", *China Leadership Monitor*, 2010

9. Jing Jin and Stephanie Wong, "China's May Property Sales Drop in Beijing, Shanghai," Bloomberg, June 1, 2010.

5 percent—the danger line at which inflation stops being a concern for the policy wonks and starts raising fears of social instability. "Inflation is like a tiger," warned Premier Wen. "Once it gets free it's difficult to get back in its cage."[10]

A sign that the fight against inflation was swinging into mass-line campaign mode: the National Development and Reform Commission (NDRC)—the government's powerful economic planner—got in on the action. The NDRC imposed price controls on coal and banned exports of fertilizer (an attempt to contain costs for food producers). In April, inspection teams were dispatched from Beijing to the provinces, aiming to strengthen the wavering resolve of local officials in the battle against real estate speculators. With indirect controls on mortgage rates and down-payment requirements ineffective in checking the expansion of the bubble, the inspection teams added a new performance metric to the report cards for local cadres: controlling property prices. Local officials who failed to cap increases in home prices could kiss their hopes of promotion goodbye.

The public mood also shifted. In July 2011 in Wenzhou—China's entrepreneurial hub—two high-speed trains collided on a viaduct. Forty were killed and 192 injured. The story of Xiang Weiyi, a two-year-old girl who survived the crash but lost both her parents, tugged at the nation's heartstrings. The government came under fire for secretive and insensitive handling of the aftermath. Millions of netizens on Weibo—at the time a raucous and freewheeling Chinese version of Twitter—looked on aghast as videos showed the cleanup operation, massive cranes pawing mechanically at the smashed carriages. The *Economic Observer,* a hard-hitting newspaper with a social conscience, defied the instructions of the propaganda ministry. In a "Letter to Yiyi" (a familiar name for Xiang Weiyi, doubling the last syllable) they published a special report calling out the "hypocrisy, arrogance, rashness and cruelty behind this tragic story."[11]

The Wenzhou crash came hard on the heels of a corruption scandal, with Minister of Railways Liu Zhijun hauled off by the investigators.

10. Xin Zhiming, "Wen Calls Inflation a 'Tiger,'" *China Daily*, March 15, 2011.

11. Josh Chin, "A Letter to Yiyi," *Wall Street Journal*, July 31, 2011.

Among other blots on his official record, Liu was reported to have kept eighteen mistresses, a state of affairs more easily explained by his stash of 800 million yuan in bribes than by his diminutive stature or stringy comb-over. At stake for the government was the prestige of a project that had a totemic significance for China's stimulus. Since the start of the financial crisis, close to 1.5 trillion yuan had been sunk into expansion of the high-speed rail network. The aim was to shorten travel time between China's provinces and to give Chinese firms a leg up on replicating the Japanese, French, and Canadian technology behind the trains. Coming amid a period of national soul-searching on the costs of high growth, the Wenzhou crash prompted a rethink. In 2009, in the first flush of stimulus, railway investment grew 69 percent. In 2011, it contracted.

DRINKING POISON TO CURE THIRST: THE DIFFICULTY OF EXITING STIMULUS

It was in Wenzhou, too, that the first consequences of the withdrawal of stimulus were felt. The combination of reliance on shadow finance (prone to dry up fast when the liquidity taps are turned off), heavy investment in real estate (a market now frozen by the government's tightening campaign), and the European sovereign debt crisis (prolonging the slump in exports) proved too much to handle. In the summer of 2011, the press was so full of lurid stories that it appeared Wenzhou's 9.1 million residents were having to pick their way cautiously through the streets between the bodies of suicide victims and fleeing factory owners toting suitcases stuffed with cash. Growth plummeted.

At the start of October, Premier Wen flew in, promising Wenzhou's shadow banking crisis would be resolved within a month. As an indication of seriousness, with him he brought central bank chief Zhou Xiaochuan and Minister of Finance Xie Xueren. A 100-billion-yuan government bailout fund (more than 25 percent of GDP for the city), strong-arming creditors to give debtors some breathing space, and permission for Bank of Wenzhou to go beyond normal limits in lending to local entrepreneurs, succeeded in restoring a semblance of order. (Strikingly, Wen did not condemn Wenzhou's informal financial system—the shadow banks that local entrepreneurs relied on to finance their business—as part of the problem. Instead, Wen identified it as an important innovation, a way of allowing private firms to tap credit and something the rest of country could learn from.)

The Wenzhou crisis was an attention-grabbing indicator of the stresses that accompany withdrawal of stimulus. It was not the beginning of a larger meltdown. For all its centrality to the local growth story, Wenzhou's network of informal lenders was too small to threaten contagion on a wider scale. Industrial and Commercial Bank of China, with its 15 trillion yuan in assets—more than forty times larger than the entire economy of Wenzhou—was not going to be knocked over by a bankruptcy at a button factory, or the collapse of a small loan shop with a few hundred million yuan in assets. After Wen's trip there were no more steps to tighten, but there wasn't a substantial move in the direction of loosening, either.

In April 2012, that changed. The Wenzhou crisis wasn't a trigger for contagion. It was a leading indicator of the stresses that accompany withdrawal of stimulus. The combined weight of tighter credit conditions, sustained real estate controls, and now a European sovereign debt crisis in full swing showed up in the national data. Factory output, consumer spending, and investment all slowed. Sales to crisis-stricken Europe contracted, dragging overall exports down to low-single-digit growth. The reserve requirement ratio had already been cut, freeing up more funds for the banks to lend. Now the PBOC moved on interest rates. A 25-basis-point cut in June and another in July took the deposit rate back down from 3.5 percent to 3 percent, reversing a substantial portion of the poststimulus tightening.

The central bank gave the move a reformist twist. Loan and deposit rates remained set by the government. But now the PBOC lowered the floor on what banks could charge for loans and raised the ceiling on what they could pay on deposits, giving the markets a larger role in setting the price of money. In addition, loan rates were cut slightly more than deposits—a signal that the central bank wanted to reduce banks' hugely profitable net interest margins, preserving income for household savers. Those were important steps toward more market-based interest rates, edging toward removing one of the major distortions in China's economy. They didn't hide the direction of policy: a return to stimulus.

There was no official about-face on the real estate sector. The central bank proclaimed loudly that policies aimed at controlling bubble-high house prices remained in place. But with the focus now swinging back to supporting growth, the signal was clear. Speculators rushed back into the market and sales reaccelerated. Credit growth, slowing continually from its peak at the end of 2009, now ran faster. On a visit to Jiangsu province in July 2012, Wen promised to "stabilize investment"—an ambiguous phrase, but in the context a clear indication that the government was moving into pro-growth mode. Rummaging around in their store of aphorisms, economists warned that another round of stimulus would be like "drinking poison to cure thirst." By then, however, it was too late. The first attempt to curb the excesses of the 4-trillion-yuan stimulus was over, and the market had learned something about China's policymakers' appetite for the pains of credit withdrawal: it was limited.[12]

Why was Wen so trigger-happy on a second burst of stimulus? One reason was concern about the impact of the European sovereign debt crisis. Central banks around the world were cutting rates and expanding balance sheets. The Bank of England moved into a second round of quantitative easing. The Federal Reserve would follow at the end of the year. China, too, faced a blow from weaker European demand, and that accounts for part of the shift back toward pro-growth policies. A second reason was the unfortunate fact that withdrawing stimulus created a drag on growth. As China's leaders would discover repeatedly, and in myriad different ways, in the years ahead, getting off the stimulus tiger was harder than getting on.

There were also other factors at work. China doesn't have elections. It does have political cycles, and 2012 was a crucial year. After ten years at

12. Barry Naughton, "The Political Consequences of Economic Challenges," *China Leadership Monitor*, Issue 39, 2012.

the helm, Hu's time behind the big desk in Zhongnanhai was drawing to an end. A Party Congress in November would begin the transition to a new generation of leadership. Xi Jinping was widely expected to take Hu's place as general secretary of the Communist Party. Li Keqiang was favored to take over from Wen as premier—a consolation prize after Hu Jintao failed to secure the top job for his preferred successor.

China's leadership transitions lack the public drama of a US election. They are still fraught affairs, with candidates and kingmakers maneuvering for support behind the scenes. This time around, the Bo Xilai affair exposed cracks in the façade of Party unity. Bo was Party secretary of Chongqing (a metropolis in southwestern China), a Politburo member, and a dark-horse contender for a position in the Standing Committee. Like Xi, he was Communist royalty, the son of Party elder Bo Yibo, who had fought alongside Mao in the civil war and served as the first minister of finance after the People's Republic of China was formed. Bo the younger had won adulation and approbation in equal measure for a populist style, including a massive social housing program, a strike-hard campaign against local gangsters, and the revival of Cultural Revolution–era Communist culture, complete with singalongs of revolutionary songs.

Wen was not a fan. The premier used his press conference at the National People's Congress in March 2012 to launch a thinly veiled attack on comrades who had not learned the lessons of history—an oblique reference to the dark days of the Cultural Revolution when the cult of personality around Mao had disastrous consequences. Days later, Bo was out of a job and under investigation, the beginning of a process that would see him expelled from the Communist Party and jailed for life. The catalyst for his downfall was a scoop from the *Wall Street Journal* on the murder of a British businessman by Bo's wife, Gu Kailai.[13] Behind the scenes, however, was a Communist Party closing ranks against a charismatic maverick who threatened the orderliness of the leadership transition and, ultimately, the rules- and consensus-based approach to governance painstakingly developed as a check against return to the chaos of the Mao era.

13. Jeremy Page, "Fearful Final Hours for Briton in China," *Wall Street Journal*, April 12, 2012.

Perhaps with the situation in Europe deteriorating, Wen didn't need additional reason to add to the stimulus. If he did, the need to prevent the Bo scandal from generating instability ahead of the leadership transition provided it.

History has not been kind to the Hu Jintao era. There were some definite successes. After the growth-at-all-costs approach of Jiang Zemin, the shift in emphasis toward a more people-centered development model was a step in the right direction. There was some concrete progress: reducing the tax burden on hundreds of millions of farmers and moving the rudiments of a national welfare system into place. In the financial sector, shares in the big state-owned banks were sold in Hong Kong and Shanghai, the yuan moved off its dollar peg and started the long march toward fair value, and interest rates began their move away from government control toward determination by the market. In its response to the great financial crisis, China won plaudits for its swift and decisive action, keeping the wheels of growth turning at home, and playing a major part in propping up global demand.

Even as Hu eked out modest progress, the question is why he didn't achieve more. There was certainly no extension of Zhu's root-and-branch reform of the state sector, or the farsighted triumph over the narrow interests of state firms and local officials evident in entry to the World Trade Organization. Indeed, a combination of activist industrial policy, with a starring role for state-owned enterprises, and the 4-trillion-yuan stimulus channeled from state banks to state firms, meant movement was in the wrong direction. Even on his home turf of social policy, Hu failed to deliver on his early promise. Farmers were still without land rights. The creaking *hukou* system—which tied access to social benefits to place of birth—meant millions of migrant workers were second-class citizens in the cities where they lived and worked. Worst of all, the price of securing growth through the financial crisis had been an unsustainable surge in credit.

One reason Hu didn't achieve more was a leadership style that supporters lauded as consensus-based and procedurally thorough, but critics panned as weak and ineffective. Under Xi, that would be the first thing to go.

Xi Jinping and the Start of China's Fourth Cycle

The Xi Jinping era, it was clear from the beginning, was going to be different. Contrasts between the new general secretary—in power from November 2012—and his predecessor were quick to emerge and sharply drawn. Hu Jintao was the son of a small business owner and a teacher. Xi was the princeling son of Xi Zhongxun, who fought in the revolutionary war and played a starring role in Deng Xiaoping's early reform and opening, steering the creation of the special economic zones in Guangdong. Hu rose through diligence and ability. So did Xi, but combined with that was the confidence and connections that come from birth into one of Communist China's ruling families.

Despite being handpicked by Deng, Hu had started his first term from a position of weakness. The Standing Committee was expanded from seven to nine members, making consensus harder to reach, and packed with supporters of retiring general secretary Jiang Zemin, making it harder for Hu to steer his preferred policies through. Jiang retained his position as chair of the military commission. Hu was denied the designation as core of the leadership—a term that signified something more than first among equals, and which had been applied to Mao, Deng, and Jiang.

Xi entered from a position of strength. The Standing Committee was reduced from nine back to seven members. Hu failed to pack the committee with his supporters, and relinquished chairmanship of the military commission. Xi wasn't immediately designated as the core of the leadership, but that would come before too long.

On policy too, Xi was quick to stake out a different direction of travel. Hu's first trip had been to Hebei, visiting the last Communist Party headquarters in 1949 before they seized power in Beijing—a signal of return to the Party's orthodox and egalitarian roots. Xi's first trip was to Guangdong, following in the footsteps of the 1992 southern tour that Deng had used to restart the reform process. "Empty talk endangers the nation," said Xi in one of his first remarks as Party secretary. "Only hard work achieves national revival." When Deng said something similar on his southern tour, it was read as an implicit criticism of the stalled reform process under Jiang Zemin. Now Xi was echoing those remarks, implicitly criticizing the wasted opportunities of the last ten years.[1]

Despite the symbolism of the Guangdong visit, Xi's first flexing of muscles was not on economics, but politics. Corruption, he warned the Politburo a few days after taking office, could end the Party and the state. He promised a crackdown, targeting both "tigers and flies"—high-ranking officials and lowly local bureaucrats. As a sign of seriousness, Wang Qishan, recently elevated to the Standing Committee and one of the Communist Party's most effective fixers, was placed in charge of the graft-busting Central Commission for Discipline Inspection.

The crackdown defined the first years of the Xi presidency. Tens of thousands of officials, from once-mighty members of the Politburo Standing Committee to humble local administrators, were caught in the investigators' dragnet. For China watchers, controversy centered on two questions: First, was this a genuine attempt to restore clean governance or a power play by Xi, ousting his rivals and installing his allies? Second, for all the undoubted benefits of reducing corruption, was the fear-driven campaign throwing government into disarray and hurting the economy?

1. Barry Naughton, "Signaling Change, New Leaders Begin Quest for Economic Reform," *China Leadership Monitor*, Issue 40, 2013.

On the first question, the answer was straightforward: it was both. Weeding out corrupt officials was good policy. It also instilled respect for Xi among officials who remained, and allowed him to quickly move his supporters into key jobs, making it easier to consolidate power and push forward his agenda.

On the second, the answer is more complex. The received wisdom, underpinned by a wealth of anecdotes, is that the campaign threw a wrench into the machinery of government and hurt the economy. Big-ticket construction projects, the story goes, were put on hold. Lavish official banquets were replaced with more modest affairs, emulating Xi's call for officials to be content with "four dishes and a soup." GDP growth slowed from an average of 9.3 percent in the three years before the crackdown to 7.3 percent as Wang's investigators spanned out across the country.

A careful look at the data, however, points to a different conclusion. Looking at corruption investigations on a provincial basis, and cross-referencing that against shifts in growth and economic structure, reveals that there is no consistent relationship between the number of officials investigated in a particular province and what happened to its growth rate. Indeed, the evidence points in the opposite direction. Ahead of Xi's crackdown, provinces that had a more significant problem with corruption grew more slowly. Corruption wasn't a growth accelerator; it was a growth depressor. That is consistent with the global experience of graft as a drag on development, and suggests that lower levels of corruption—if that's the result of the campaign—will be a long-term positive for China's growth.[2]

Deng had favored leaders who were "tough with both fists"—willing to wield the big stick on social order, and with the technical competence needed to push through complex economic reforms. Xi fitted the model. As the anti-corruption campaign swung into action, work was also underway on a comprehensive blueprint for economic reforms.

2. Tom Orlik and Fielding Chen, China Anti-Graft Campaign Not a Drag on Growth, Bloomberg, June 13, 2016.

The World Bank, working with the State Council's Development Research Center, had already delivered *China 2030*—a major report on steps needed to sustain China's growth out to 2030.[3] The main message: reduce government controls on capital, labor, energy, and other factors of production, allowing the efficiency of the market to produce superior growth performance. Xi's top economist, Liu He, was marshalling inputs from the 50 Economists Forum, a group of distinguished, reform-minded Chinese policy wonks.[4] Both groups were providing input into a larger reconsideration of China's economic policy. It had been at the Third Plenum of the Eleventh Central Committee in 1978 that Deng had begun the reform and opening process. Xi wanted the Third Plenum of the Eighteenth Central Committee at the end of 2013 to be the launchpad for his economic program.

Before he could get there, there was another problem to deal with: a meltdown in China's money market. The money market is where banks and other financial firms tap funds to finance their operations. In China, that typically means big banks, which have a surplus of deposits, lending to small banks, which have a deficit. Back in 2013, the People's Bank of China (PBOC) was attempting to shift monetary policy away from crude volume-based controls (telling banks how much to lend) toward more sophisticated price-based tools (using interest rates to match credit supply and demand). That gave the money market additional significance as a channel for transmitting policy—higher rates to choke inflation, lower to buoy growth.

In general, money market rates were managed in line with the benchmark deposit rates set by the central bank. In mid-2013, that was 3 percent. On June 2013 the money market rate hit 28 percent, a nosebleed-inducing high that sparked a panicked global reaction. Rumors of a default by a major bank swirled across trading desks, adding to the unease. With

---

3. *China 2030: Building a Modern, Harmonious and Creative Society* (Washington, DC: World Bank, 2013).

4. Barry Naughton, "Leadership Transition and 'Top-Level Design' of Economic Policy," *China Leadership Monitor*, 37, 2012.

investors scrambling for cash, the bond market sold off. The Shanghai Composite Index tumbled, falling 5.3 percent on a single day. In the United States, markets were already having nightmares about Federal Reserve tapering, after Chairman Ben Bernanke told Congress the central bank might cut the pace of bond purchases. Waking up to what looked like a "Lehman moment" in China—with the credit markets freezing and solvency of major banks at risk—the S&P 500 registered its biggest one-day drop since the Greek sovereign debt crisis in 2011, falling 2.5 percent.

The strange thing about the money market meltdown was that it reflected a deliberate policy action—or rather inaction—from the PBOC. The main concern for the central bank was that low and stable funding costs were enabling an unsustainable buildup of financial risks. That was evident in surging debt levels, with economy-wide borrowing rising from 162 percent of GDP in 2008 to 205 percent in 2012. It was evident also in a growing maturity mismatch, with banks and shadow banks financing long-term assets using short-term liabilities. One gauge of that: turnover in the money market rose from 56 trillion yuan in 2008 to 136 trillion yuan in 2012, equal to more than 250 percent of GDP for the year.

If all that sounds similar to the combination of helter-skelter loan growth and reliance on short-term funding that triggered the US financial crisis, that's because it was. When the banking system faced a seasonal liquidity squeeze, the PBOC saw an opportunity to send a message. June is typically a time of stress for China's money markets. Tax season and a holiday at the start of the month add to demand for funds. Big banks hoard funds ahead of mid-year reports, ensuring they meet regulatory requirements on the ratio of loans to deposits. This time around, there was an additional challenge. Bernanke's attempt to signal a slowdown in the Federal Reserve's quantitative easing triggered the "taper tantrum." Funds flowed out of emerging markets. China, despite maintaining close control on its capital account, wasn't immune.

Under normal circumstances, the PBOC would smooth out the problems, injecting funds to make up the shortfall in the market. This time, aiming to teach lenders that reliance on short-term funding was a risky business, they did not. Interest rates rose. As it became clear that the central bank didn't intend to fill the funding gap, they rose higher. With panic setting in, even banks that did have funds hoarded them rather than lending them out. Borrowing costs spiraled up. Chinese and global equity markets chased each other down.

Perhaps deciding they had made their point, possibly concerned about the consequences for the real economy, and maybe under pressure from higher levels of government, the PBOC relented. Even as money market rates touched 28 percent on June 20, the central bank was already quietly intervening, providing discounted funds to the banks that needed them most. Reporters for Bloomberg noticed a spate of transactions at the end of the day at rates far below the prevailing level in the market—a sign that policymakers were injecting discounted funds.

A few days later, the crisis was over. Ling Tao, the deputy head of the central bank's Shanghai branch, made a first and last appearance in the glare of the media, promising the bank would "strengthen communications with market institutions, stabilize expectations and guide market interest rates within reasonable ranges."[5] The money market rate headed down to less palpitation-inducing levels, reaching 3.8 percent by the first week of July. The crisis was over. The PBOC had given the borrow-short, lend-long cowboys in the shadow banking system a bloody nose, forcing them to reckon with higher financing costs and plunging asset prices. The cost for doing so—a moment of panic that had spilled from Chinese to global markets—had been high.

"Must we accept parenthood for every economic development in the country?" asked Benjamin Strong, the first head of the Federal Reserve Bank of New York. "We would have a large family of children. . . . Every time any one of them misbehaved, we might have to spank them all." The problem Strong identified is that "there is no selective process in credit operations."[6] Raising or lowering rates for one borrower means raising or lowering them for all.

5. Bloomberg News, "PBOC Says It Will Ensure Stability of China's Money Market," Bloomberg, June 25, 2013.

6. David Wheelock, *Conducting Monetary Policy without Government Debt: The Fed's Early Years* (St. Louis: Federal Reserve Bank of St. Louis, 2002).

That was in 1925. Almost ninety years on, the PBOC had discovered the same thing. They had a specific problem: shadow banks abusing access to cheap funding to grow their loan books too quickly. They tried to use a general instrument—very high interest rates—to solve it. By spanking all the children for the misbehavior of one, they almost brought the financial system crashing down.

Compounding the problem was that communication from beginning to end had been somewhere between inadequate and nonexistent, culminating in the appearance of an unknown third-tier bureaucrat as the public face of a system-shaking crisis. The threat to financial stability the PBOC had identified was real. The instruments they had to tackle it were inadequate. As stability was restored, attention turned toward the Third Plenum in November 2013—and hopes for a comprehensive solution to China's economic woes.

THE THIRD PLENUM AND XI'S REFORMS

In the 1990s and early 2000s, Yantian—a factory town in southeastern China—was a poster child for the country's economic rise. By 2013, it had become a symbol of the struggle to avoid a new mediocre of social fracture and slowing growth.[7]

In the early days of the reform era, bargain-basement wages, an open door to global markets, and a business-savvy leadership transformed Yantian from a sleepy farming hamlet to a humming factory town with a population close to 150,000. On the eve of China's 2001 entry into the World Trade Organization, there were more than four hundred foreign firms in the town producing cheap electronics, toys, and other goods for export.[8] A 27-hole golf course catered to the Hong Kong and Japanese factory bosses. "If every village in China were like Yantian," a visiting

---

7. Tom Orlik, "How China Lost Its Mojo: One Town's Story," *Wall Street Journal*, October 1, 2013.

8. Tony Saich and Biliang Hu, *Chinese Village, Global Market*, (Basingstoke, UK: Palgrave Macmillan, 2012).

Communist Party dignitary said, "we would already have overtaken the US."

By 2013, the number of foreign firms in town had fallen to 150. Higher labor costs, a dearth of available land, and weaker export demand in the wake of the great financial crisis drove some into bankruptcy; others to cheaper locations. The number of migrant workers—human engines of Yantian's development—halved. "The export sector doesn't have a long future," said Deng Zerong, Yantian's Communist Party secretary, and—according to local folklore—a distant relation of China's great reformer, Deng Xiaoping.

The city is a cluster of factories, bordered at one end by the golf course. A bust of Deng gazes down benignly from a family shrine on a hill overlooking the town. Centuries ago, the Yantian Dengs and China's great reformer shared a common ancestor. When China's reform and opening began in the 1980s, the city was ideally placed to seize the opportunity. A location an hour from Hong Kong and next door to Shenzhen—site of the first special economic zone—meant perfect conditions for an export boom. "It was like finding a hill made of gold right outside the door," Mr. Deng says.

The risks attached to overreliance on exports started to become evident as early as the late 1990s, when the Asian financial crisis swept some Yantian firms into bankruptcy. The financial crisis of 2008 pushed others into the red. More than two hundred failed, or moved to other locations where labor and other costs were cheaper.

The factories that remained faced lower profitability. Rising wages and a Chinese currency that had gained more than 30 percent since the PBOC broke the peg to the dollar in 2005 took a toll. At Dongguan Shinano Motors, a Japanese firm that employed four thousand workers in the town, wages rose 40 percent from 2007 to 2013, withering profit margins. Aiming to cut costs, the parent company opened another factory seven hundred miles inland, where wages were lower. The next move might be to Southeast Asia, the factory boss said.

In miniature, Yantian's growing pains were China's growing pains. On the demand side, the great financial crisis cratered exports. Then, as factories struggled to get back on their feet, Europe's sovereign debt melt-down prolonged and extended the downturn. On the supply side, Yantian's factories could compete on price but struggled to differentiate on quality. "There are too many people making the same things," said Mr. Deng.

As the pool of workers dwindled and the yuan rose, even competing on price became harder to do. China's working-age population shrank in 2012, breaking a rising trend that stretched over the reform era. In large part, that reflected the impact of the one-child policy. According to United Nations' projections, from 2010 to 2030 China's labor force is expected to shrink by 67 million workers—more than the entire population of France. As the supply of workers falls, wages rise and competitiveness is eroded.

Like other local leaders faced with slowing exports, Yantian's chiefs turned to real estate to bolster the economy. In summer 2013, three major residential projects were underway on the town's main drag, with scaf-folding and cranes already up. Mr. Deng wanted to see more. "All of this needs to go," he said, with a sweeping gesture, taking in the swath of higgledy-piggledy low-rise buildings that covered the rest of the town. Local leaders also shifted into financial services, investing the town's funds in a loan guarantee company.

At the largest real estate project, a 270,000-square-meter villa develop-ment called Blue Mountain, yellow golf carts ferry potential buyers from nearby Shenzhen around the compound's man-made lake. In a neigh-boring project, the town has taken a majority stake. Sharply rising prop-erty prices suggested a bubble in the making. Home prices in the town doubled from 2007 to 2012 as developers offered buyers incentives from Apple computers to gold bars. Many of the locals own two or more homes, an indication that speculation rather than genuine demand is driving the market.

More sustainable growth in Yantian required a more hospitable ap-proach to migrant workers, allowing them to make the town their long-term home. Despite providing the muscle that powers the export and construction boom, China's hundreds of millions of migrant workers find themselves locked out of full participation in the benefits. The *hukou* system ties access to social benefits to place of birth. Rural migrants can leave home to work. But when their own children need to enter the school system, or they need support through unemployment, illness, or old age, they have to return home. By their mid-twenties, 37 percent of China's rural residents move to work in cities. By the time they get to their mid-thirties, just 18 percent are still away from home.

Yantian is more hospitable to its eighty-thousand-odd migrants than most towns in China. Basic schooling, subsidized by local taxpayers, is available to some children. Eligibility is decided based on a scoring system that takes into account payment of social insurance, homeownership, and compliance with China's single-child policy. Factories also expanded coverage of health insurance to more workers—a requirement that is more strictly enforced in Yantian than some other parts of the country. But the conditions to qualify for basic schooling, for instance, are too onerous for many migrants, most of whom are too poor to buy a home.

Many still think like Ms. Lei, a thirty-year-old woman from inland Hubei province. She says she is in Yantian "only temporarily." With no local health coverage and no place for her thirteen-month-old son when he gets to school age, Ms. Lei and her husband planned to move back to their hometown. "We really need migrants," says Deng Manchang, the second in command in Yantian's local government, "but we cast them out."

In November 2013, as the 376 members of the Communist Party's Central Committee gathered in a freezing Beijing for the Third Plenum, it was problems like those of Yantian that they were attempting to solve. Expectations were high. Back in 1978, the Third Plenum marked a fundamental change in China's economic policy—the beginning of reform and opening. Deng Xiaoping's far-sighted decision to throw off the dogma of the Mao era and make "experience the sole criterion of truth" began a process that transformed China from an impoverished basket case to a global powerhouse.

Thirty-five years on, the old drivers of growth were running out of steam. A crisis-battered global economy could not absorb ever-increasing quantities of Chinese exports. China's households could only buy so many houses (after extensive research, economists have concluded that one each is about right). The *hukou* system was a self-inflicted wound, compounding the impact of China's demographic drag by locking hundreds of millions of rural workers out of long-term life in the city. Not visible in Yantian with its entrepreneurial hustle, but farther inland and in the industrial north, a moribund state sector was a drain on resources and drag on growth.

At first, it seemed the Third Plenum had fumbled. As the meeting ended on November 12, a flimsy communique mouthed familiar reform platitudes but provided little substance. The financial press piled in with derisive commentary. "This not a blueprint for reform," concluded one hapless economist, summing up the disappointed mood. They spoke too soon. At plenum feasts, the communique is just the appetizer. The main course comes in the more substantial decision.

When it arrived on November 16, the Decision on Major Issues Concerning Comprehensively Deepening Reform was, as the name suggested, comprehensive. China's leaders set out a framework for reshaping not just the economy and financial markets, but also the legal system, foreign policy, even Chinese culture. Xi Jinping, it was made clear, had held the pen—a departure from the past pattern where management of the economy had been the domain of the premier, and an early sign of Xi's expansive role.

The market should play the "decisive" role in resource allocation, the decision said. At first sight that looked like a victory for the reformers, a commitment to the market in line with the suggestion from the World Bank in its *China 2030* report. In almost the same breath, however, there was reassurance for conservatives: the state should remain "dominant." To some, that looked like a drafting fudge, a form of words aimed at appeasing both market reformers and socialist hardliners. Maybe. But it also represented continuity with policy stretching back to Deng's view on Gorbachev's failures—a strong state being not a barrier to market reforms, but a prerequisite for them.

The most striking immediate change—a relaxation of the one-child policy—exemplified the challenges and limitations of the reform program.

China's families had been restricted to one child since 1979. The initial motivation was fear of overpopulation and resource scarcity. By a happy accident, the policy also primed China's economy for growth—minimizing the time prime-working-age parents were focused on childcare, and so maximizing participation in the labor force.

The costs were enormous. The one-child policy represented an intrusion of the state into the most intimate realm of the family, often brutally enforced. Apart from the initial boost from reducing working time lost to child care, the economics didn't make sense. Families with only one child spent less (fewer mouths to feed) and saved more (fewer children to take care of them in old age). That was a significant contributor to China's high savings rate—the original sin in its unbalanced growth model. As demographic destiny played out, China faced a shrinking working-age population and a burgeoning old-age dependency ratio, with every young person working to support two retired parents.

Change was overdue, and the Third Plenum decision was a move in the right direction. At the same time, the new policy demonstrated the challenges facing China's reformers. The shift was incremental, not absolute—the one-child policy was not abolished, just relaxed for families where both parents were only children. Worse, for many young couples, the one-child policy was no longer the binding constraint on fertility. More years spent in education, high-pressure jobs, and the high cost of housing, childcare, and education meant that many now voluntarily chose to have just one child.

The difficulties confronting reformers on the one-child policy encapsulated the challenges that bedeviled the broader Third Plenum agenda. Getting agreement on anything beyond incremental reforms was difficult, and incremental reforms might be insufficient given the magnitude of the challenges China faced. No surprise then that after the initial blaze of pro-reform propaganda, progress was hard to come by. On the critical questions facing China—what to do about the *hukou* for migrants like Ms. Lei in Yantian, what to do about land rights for farmers like Mr. Fu in Chengdu, what to do about ailing state-owned enterprises like Dongbei

Special in rust-belt Liaoning—the decision set out sensible if unspectacular proposals:

> On land, local governments' monopoly control of the rural land sales was to be broken, allowing farmers to sell at market price.
>
> On *hukous*, rural residents were to be encouraged to move to small towns, but steered away from big cities.
>
> On state-owned enterprises, an essential core of strategic firms like Petrochina and Industrial and Commercial Bank of China would stay under state control. Commercial firms—local steel or coal producers, for example—would be subject to market forces.[9]

The details, however, were disappointing. The New National Urbanization Plan, released in March 2014, mapped a path to urban *hukou* status for 100 million migrants by 2020—still leaving a floating population of 150 million. Reforms were targeted, with a policy of "opening small cities and controlling big cities." The problem with that approach was that opportunities are in the biggest cities. In the United States, no one dreams of leaving their small town for life in Fort Smith, Arkansas.[10] They dream of New York or Los Angeles. In China, no one dreams of life in Hefei, the benighted capital of Anhui province. Everyone wants to go to Beijing or Shanghai. Under the new plan, that path was blocked.

Reform of the state sector was never going to be easy. Taken as a group, China's state-owned enterprises have revenue as big as the GDP of Germany. Leaders of major firms have the equivalent of vice-minister status on the government's totem pole. At a local level, state firms are deeply embedded in the political system, the main instrument for managing the ups and downs of the economic cycle, and a critical provider

---

9. Dan Rosen, *Avoiding the Blind Alley: China's Economic Overhaul and Its Global Implications* (New York: Asia Society, 2014).

10. Samuel Stebbins and Evan Comen, "These Are the Worst Cities to Live in Based on Quality of Life," *USA Today*, June 13, 2018.

of employment and social services. It was no surprise that the proposals contained in the decision went nowhere. In the aftermath of the Third Plenum, the only eye-catching initiative to emerge was a cap on pay for top managers—a gimmicky attempt to signal action against inequality, not the kind of far-sighted policy required to shift incentives across the sector.

In May 2014, attempting to frame the narrative on a period of slower but hopefully more sustainable growth, Xi adopted the phrase "new normal." Noting that much about China's development was copied from overseas, cynics were unsurprised to discover that Xi's was not an original formulation. Richard Miller, an economics correspondent with Bloomberg, coined the term to characterize the sluggish rebound in the United States and other developed economies after the financial crisis. In the China context, Xi was putting a more positive spin on it, suggesting that annual expansion in the 7 percent to 8 percent range, combined with energetic attempts to ameliorate imbalances, was preferable to a stimulus-supported return to the double-digit growth of the precrisis era.

Not to be left out of the "new + adjective" competition, International Monetary Fund managing director Christine Lagarde warned that the world was slipping into a "new mediocre," and for China that was what it felt like. GDP growth had already decelerated from 10 percent in mid-2011 to 7.5 percent in mid-2014. With pressure from demographics and debt, and no prospect of a return to the export boom that drove pre–financial crisis growth, few expected it to linger there for long. Most foresaw a continued decline.

SHANGHAI'S BUSTED BOOM

The exception to the rule on lackluster reform came from the financial sector. Since 2007, there had been talk of a "through train," punching a hole in the normal controls on cross-border capital flows to allow mainland investors to buy stocks in Hong Kong, and Hong Kong investors to buy stocks in Shanghai. Now those plans were coming to fruition. In April

2014, at the Boao Forum in Hainan—one of China's more high-profile talking shops, where foreign CEOs hobnob with Communist cadres— Li Keqiang announced plans to connect the Hong Kong and Shanghai markets.

In theory, the price of a stock should be the same no matter where it is traded—a share in Petrochina in Hong Kong represents the same owner-ship of the company that one in Shanghai does. In reality, China's controlled capital account meant that Shanghai and Hong Kong markets are moved by different forces. Investment options are different, with a more limited range of financial assets on the mainland. Supply of funds moves in different directions—mainland China's driven by the pace of loan growth, Hong Kong's by global capital flows. Sentiment can vary, with Shanghai investors marching to the beat of a national drum and Hong Kong more in tune with the international mood. As a result, share prices in dual-listed companies can diverge widely.

Announcement of the coming Shanghai–Hong Kong connection suggested cross-border flows would soon arbitrage away the differences. In April 2014, when Li's announcement was made, Shanghai stocks were slightly cheaper than their equivalents in Hong Kong. By November, when the scheme went live, they were trading at a slight premium. With both markets rising, by the end of the year Shanghai had gained close to 50 per-cent, making it the best-performing market in the world by a wide margin. This wasn't China's first equity boom. The market had surged in 1992 and again in 2007. It was to be its most dangerous.

At the beginning, a rise in Shanghai stock prices on expectations the new connection with Hong Kong would drive an influx of foreign funds had made sense. As 2014 ended and 2015 began, a rational response to an arbitrage op-portunity turned into a speculative frenzy. Top leaders, from Premier Li on down, cheered the market higher, with their words echoed and reechoed in the state press. The talk was of a "reform dividend"—with markets suppos-edly pricing in the coming gains as Third Plenum policies fired the next stage of China's development.

Novice investors, with more enthusiasm than experience, piled in. A survey by the China Household Finance Survey found that two-thirds of new investors lacked a high-school education—an echo of the famous story about the shoeshine boy sharing stock tips with millionaire Joe Kennedy ahead of the 1929 US stock market crash.[11] Margin trading—investors using borrowed funds to bet on ever-increasing gains—pushed the market into overdrive. Investing in stocks with borrowed funds was a risky business; a slight downturn in the market could wipe out an inexperienced investor.

On June 12 the Shanghai market hit a peak of 5,166, the highest level since the 2007 boom–bust cycle. In July 2015 the tipping point arrived. The China Securities Regulatory Commission—missing in action as the market was on the way up—decided that now was the moment to make its presence felt. A new policy threatened to cap funds that equity brokers could lend to investors. Fearing a reduction in the inflow of margin finance that had driven the market higher, traders pulled back.

As the market began to fall, China's investors discovered that margin calls could accelerate the way down just as much as leveraged bets did the way up. In three short weeks, the Shanghai index fell by a third. More than 11 trillion yuan ($1.6 trillion) of wealth was wiped out—greater than the entire annual output of the Canadian economy.

"We can close it down and reopen it later," said China's great reformer Deng Xiaoping, calming communist fears on the launch of a capitalist innovation—that is, the stock market. That was in 1992. Close to a quarter-century later, Deng's successors discovered that was easier said than done.

On July 4, 2015, Xiao Gang—China's top securities regulator—summoned executives of the twenty-one biggest brokerages to his headquarters at Focus Plaza. His objective was simple: corral the reluctant big shots into committing funds to a market rescue plan.[12] It was a tense ninety minutes. The brokers were fierce competitors, not used to working together or to giving over control of their investment decisions to the government. In the end, grumbling, they promised to put 120 billion

11. Tom Orlik, "China's High School Dropout Equity Rally," Bloomberg, March 31, 2015.

12. Enda Curran and Keith Zhai, "China's Journey from New Normal to Stock Market Crisis Epicenter," Bloomberg, August 25, 2015.

yuan—some 15 percent of their net assets—to work in a market rescue fund. A statement issued after the meeting glossed over the differences. The brokers "have confidence in the development of the country's capital market, and agreed to resolutely maintain the stable development of the stock market," it said.[13]

For a while, it looked like it was enough. July 4 was a Saturday. When trading opened on Monday, the markets rose, and in the weeks ahead traced out a choppy upward path. Then the second shoe dropped.

For many months, China's foreign exchange market—still closely controlled by the government even as the forces of supply and demand played an expanded role—had been out of balance. Traders' view on the yuan had diverged from that of the PBOC. Traders thought the yuan should be weaker, reflecting pressure from falling exports and outflows through an increasingly porous capital account. Policymakers resisted. Every day traders would sell the yuan down, only to see the PBOC reverse those losses the very next morning—setting a new rate for the currency that ignored the market signals.

That tug of war had continued since the start of the year, but it wasn't a sustainable solution and the PBOC knew it. For one thing, the PBOC's intervention made nonsense of China's claim that the exchange rate was market-determined. For another, the International Monetary Fund wanted the gap between the PBOC and market view eliminated as a condition of awarding the yuan reserve currency status—a long-cherished goal for Beijing.

With the equity markets apparently stable, PBOC governor Zhou Xiaochuan decided it was time to act.

At 9.15 a.m. on August 11, the PBOC announced its yuan fixing—the rate it wanted the currency to trade against the dollar for the next twenty-four hours. On a typical day, the fixing would be set a fraction of a percent up or down from the previous day. That day's fixing was 6.2298, a drop of 1.8 percent from August 10. The PBOC had moved its fixing into line with

13. Curran and Zhai, "China's Journey from New Normal to Stock Market Crisis Epicenter."

the yuan's market price, a move they saw as a minor technical adjustment. That wasn't how the market saw it.

The fragile calm that followed the July 4 equity market rescue was shattered. A 1.8 percent drop was the largest single-day yuan depreciation ever. Far from interpreting the PBOC's move as a minor technical adjustment, the markets believed it signaled a major strategic shift. China's exports had been languishing, falling in all but two of the first seven months of 2015. That was a drag on growth, a threat to factory profits and, ultimately—if unemployment rose—to social stability. In the mind of the markets, China was now bowing to the inevitable by restoring export competitiveness with a yuan devaluation.

The 1.8 percent drop, investors assumed, was just the beginning. Traders recalibrated their expectations, pricing in a rapid yuan fall in the months ahead. PBOC deputy governor Yi Gang attempted to undo the damage with a press conference calling for calm. By then, it was too late. The central bank's surprise move had shifted market expectations toward a devaluation, maybe a rapid one—with the yuan falling from its new 6.4 handle to below 7 to the dollar.

Worse, the PBOC's yuan move seemed to confirm the darkest suspicions about China's real growth rate. Skeptical investors had long believed that China's GDP data was massaged upward for political reasons. Unwittingly, the central bank had lent credibility to that argument. After all, if growth was really robust at the 7 percent reported by the National Bureau of Statistics, why would the PBOC need to try a Hail Mary depreciation play?

Fearing further depreciation, investors scrambled for the exits and capital cascaded out of the country; about $540 billion left before the year was out. The plummet in the equity markets resumed, and this time there was no stopping it. By the time the rout was over, at the end of January 2016, the Shanghai index was down close to 50 percent from its peak and 18.8 trillion yuan in wealth had evaporated—more, if the drop in the Shenzhen and Hong Kong markets is added to the total. The contagion ripped around the world. "Heightened concerns about growth in China . . . have led to notable volatility in financial markets," said Federal Reserve chair Janet Yellen, her trademark technical language betraying a hint of alarm.

The Federal Reserve had been planning four rate hikes in 2016. With the fallout from China hitting growth and markets, they only managed one.

More by luck than judgment, the worst for China's wider economy and financial system was avoided. China's equity market generates a lot of headlines. But as a store of wealth for households and a source of investment capital for businesses, it plays a limited role. Even during the boom—which saw novice investors piling in—the vast majority of Chinese households held no stocks. For those that did dabble, equity holdings were typically dwarfed by property and bank deposits. Businesses funded their capital spending mainly with loans from the bank and, to a lesser extent, borrowing from the bond market. Even at the height of the market boom, equity issuance accounted for just 5 percent of fundraising. The collapse of the markets would have only a limited impact on spending on roads, real estate, and factories.

As a result, the pass-through from market meltdown to how much consumers spent or businesses invested was limited. High-end eateries in Shanghai's Liujiazui financial district—the closest China has to Wall Street—might have sold less hairy crab (a local delicacy) and *baijiu* (the fiery liquor drunk at Chinese banquets). But in general, the economy weathered the storm. The financial system, too, was bowed but unbroken. Equity brokers bore the brunt of the crisis, but bankruptcies were in the main avoided. China's banks, the backbone of the financial system, were left holding the tab for unpaid margin loans. But even that 2.3-trillion-yuan price tag seemed to leave barely a ripple on their balance sheets.

China's reputation, however, was in tatters. Thirty years of rapid growth had built a lot of credibility. A decisive response to first the Asian financial crisis and then the great financial crisis had added even more. Now all that had been sacrificed. China's maladroit reaction to the equity meltdown had pulled back the curtain, revealing regulators that were no better equipped to deal with a crisis than their counterparts in the United States had been in 2008. China's policy team had shown themselves to be behind the curve, unable to grasp the complexities and interlinkages at work. The biggest funds and brokers in the market were state-owned. So were the majority of listed firms. But that hadn't made it any easier to restore

stability. The tools of state control and ability to plan for the long term—
which were supposed to set China apart from the free-market United
States—proved illusory or ineffective.

Compounding the blow, a heavy-handed response had called into question China's commitment to market opening and reform. Some thirteen
hundred stocks—close to 45 percent of the total—were suspended from
trading. Hordes of investors were stuck holding positions that they didn't
want. Foreign analysts and investors—minor players in an overwhelmingly
domestic drama—were vilified in the state press as the evil masterminds
of the market's collapse. To stem the tide of capital outflows, the central
bank had imposed oppressive controls. Individual banks were required to
be in balance on the foreign exchange transactions at the end of each day,
so there were no more funds going out than there were coming in.

To prevent the market slide, the government had effectively done what
Deng had suggested twenty-three years earlier. With trading in close
to half the stocks suspended, the chill of the government intervention
permeating the rest, and cross-border capital flows blocked, the market
had been turned off.

Around the world, central banks and investment funds were taking
careful note. The equity market might be little more than an entertaining
sideshow. But the crisis there seemed to foreshadow what might happen
if China faced a genuine system-shaking shock. The results were not
reassuring.

Deleveraging
without Self-Detonating

From Wall Street's traders to the International Monetary Fund's PhDs, China's equity market meltdown and yuan devaluation trauma were confirmation of what many had long assumed to be the case. What looked like glittering success was in fact the iridescent patina on a rapidly expanding bubble. It might not have burst today, it might not burst tomorrow, but it would burst, and probably sooner rather than later. For China's leadership, the same events contained a different lesson—it was time to tackle risks to financial stability.

In 2016, when deleveraging was hoisted near the top of the government's list of priorities, the conventional wisdom was that policymakers faced an impossible choice. They could allow credit to run unconstrained, propping up growth for a few more years but inflating the bubble even further and making the ultimate day of reckoning even worse. Or they could slow the expansion of credit, hitting corporate profits, local government revenue, and household income, and making it harder for borrowers to repay their loans. By hammering confidence and triggering a wave of defaults, the attempt to deflate the bubble could bring about the crisis it was intended to avoid.

The conventional wisdom was wrong. Two years into the deleveraging campaign, China's policymakers had achieved faster growth, a steady debt-to-GDP ratio, and a shrinking shadow banking sector. How did they do it? The answer lies in a combination of the underlying resilience of the economy and financial system, the underappreciated ingenuity of policymakers, and the unusual resources of an authoritarian state.

The beginning of effective action came in January 2016, with a front-page article in the Communist Party's mouthpiece *People's Daily*. An "authoritative person"—widely believed to be Liu He, the chief economic advisor to President Xi Jinping—issued a clarion call for a new approach to sustaining growth. China's economy, the authoritative person said, reflecting the official penchant for numerical formulations, was suffering from "four downs and one up . . . growth is down, industrial prices are down, business profits are down, fiscal revenue is down, economic risks are up."

The solution wasn't just another round of stimulus. After all, "with global growth weak, using stimulus to use up excess capacity is like preparing food for two when there's only one guest; they could eat as much as they could and it still wouldn't all be gone." The only choice, the authoritative person said, was a new approach to economic policy: supply-side reform.

Supply-side reform is a term familiar in the West as the tagline for policies pursued by US president Ronald Reagan and British prime minister Margaret Thatcher in the 1980s. In China, it took on a different meaning. Following the precepts of pro-market thinkers like Friedrich Hayek, Western leaders aimed to boost growth by lowering taxes and reducing regulation—moves they hoped would liberate the dynamism of the private sector. In China, the end goal of a stronger economy was the same, but the path there was very different. Instead of reducing government intervention in the economy, China's supply-side reform agenda would significantly increase it.

China's policymakers had always found themselves caught between the imperative to support growth and the urgency of progressing reforms. Growth, employment, and social stability had to be maintained, even when that required stimulus that exacerbated the economy's imbalance toward excess investment and increased the burden of debt. Equally, there was a pressing need to restore balance and reduce debt, but it was thought that could only happen at a cost to growth. The grand vision of supply-side reform was that supporting growth and reforming the economy were objectives that could be pursued at the same time.

The authoritative person set out five objectives: reduce overcapacity in industry, reduce inventory in real estate, deleverage the economy, reduce costs from administrative approvals, and in case there was anything left out—fill in weak spots. "There's an arithmetic relationship among the five elements," the authoritative person explained. "Reducing housing stocks has an 'additive effect,' offsetting the 'subtractive effect' of cutting excess capacity."

With President Xi throwing his personal weight behind the policy, and much at stake with a leadership reshuffle on the cards at the Nineteenth Party Congress, provincial leaders rushed to get in line. Guizhou—an impoverished province in southwest China, its development impeded by a landlocked and mountainous geography—was near the front of the queue.[1]

In February 2016 Guizhou's government published a plan targeting the closure of 510 coal mines, a move that would shutter tens of millions of tons of capacity. Zombie firms would be dealt with by mergers, restructuring, or bankruptcy. Competitive firms would get subsidies to help them upgrade technology. Guizhou's governor—second in command after the Party secretary—would take charge. In 2016, 121 coal mines were closed, reducing capacity by 21 million tons. In 2017 the target was to close another 120 coal mines and shutter 15 million tons more in capacity.

In Jinsha, a coal-mining town of seven hundred thousand that is a two-hour drive from provincial capital Guiyang, it was Mr. Wan who made it happen. On loan to the local government from a major coal mining firm, and charged with managing the program of closures, he was a busy man. Ensconced in a spartan office—an electric heater whose top doubled as a tea table taking the edge off the mountain's foggy winter chill—he explained how it happened. "National targets are allocated out to the provinces," he

1. Qian Wan and Tom Orlik, "Is Supply-Side Momentum Ebbing? View from Guizhou," Bloomberg, February 11, 2018.

said, "then provinces divide those targets up between prefectures, and so on down to counties and towns."

Under his supervision, Jinsha closed 44 coal mines in 2016 and 2017, cutting 5.5 million tons of capacity from a total of 16.8 million. It wasn't easy. Mr. Wan had to manage compensation payments for mine owners, coal shortages for power generators, and in one case backstop debts owed by a mine owner to shadow lenders. Unemployment, however, remained under control. Most of the workers in the small private mines targeted for closure were casual laborers who moved on to other opportunities.

The risk, as officials shuttered operations in the province's pillar industry, was that growth would take a hit. To prevent that, Guizhou opened the stimulus taps. Public–private partnerships—a financing innovation that shifted the initial cost of a project off the government's balance sheet and onto that of the construction company—were the main channel for support. From 2015 to 2017 infrastructure investment financed through the new partnerships came in at 305 billion yuan, equal to 22.5 percent of GDP. To help pay their share, local government financing vehicles issued a net 226 billion yuan in bonds. An even larger amount issued by the provincial government helped refinance existing borrowing at favorable rates. The result was a surge in infrastructure spending that connected every city in the province to the highway system, boring tunnels through the mountainous landscape. Capital spending surged, propping up GDP growth above 10 percent.

With those efforts replicated on a national level, 2016 and 2017 were a period of renewed energy on structural reform, and stabilization on growth. Taken together, efforts to close redundant plants and mines, and a drop in new capital spending, chipped away at excess capacity. In steel, the government cut about 65 million tons in capacity from the 1.1-billion-ton total in 2016, and roughly the same amount again in 2017. In coal, 400 million tons were cut in 2016 and 2017. Capital spending on steel production fell 10 percent in 2017. In coal mining, it fell 12.3 percent.

The government took aim at the problem of fragmented industrial organization, driving consolidation around the larger firms and forcing smaller ones to merge or close. That wasn't pretty to watch.

Mega-mergers—like the welding together of steel giants Baosteel and Wuhan Steel in October 2016—were dismissed by China analysts as mergers in name only. In most cases, the firms were already so large that scope for additional economies of scale was limited. Nicholas Lardy, an expert on China at the Peterson Institute of International Economics, argued that the track record of mergers between state firms is not impressive. In the period of consolidation ahead of the great financial crisis, even as the number of firms fell and the size increased, performance continued to deteriorate.[2]

This time there was a more positive dynamic at work. Merging firms changes the way they think about future expansion. As separate firms, Baosteel and Wuhan Steel might decide they both need to grab more market share with a new blast furnace. The result would be overcapacity. Operating as a single entity, they should plan capacity expansion more closely in line with the needs of the market.

A massive fiscal boost kept the wheels of growth turning. Taken together, the on- and off-balance-sheet fiscal deficit for 2016 and 2017 ran deeper than 10 percent of GDP. That's a very significant stimulus— equivalent to the amount the US government was shelling out to support growth in the depths of the great financial crisis, or the Greek government in its sovereign debt crisis. In China, it paid for a sustained high in infrastructure spending, which expanded 19 percent in 2017, offsetting the drag as capacity in steel, coal, and other heavy industry was shuttered.

EXORCISING THE GHOST TOWNS: HOW CHINA TURNED THE REAL ESTATE LIGHTS ON

Efforts to achieve Liu's second supply-side reform objective—reducing inventory in real estate—were no less energetic. Property oversupply was a major talking point for China market bears and a headache for

---

2. Nicholas Lardy, *China's SOE Reform—The Wrong Path* (Washington DC: Peterson Institute of International Economics, 2016).

policymakers. From 2011 to 2016, China built more than 10 million apartments a year. Demand averaged less than 8 million units. In the gap between those two numbers: ghost towns of empty property, cement shells of skyscrapers ringing the edge of major cities, and finished developments with no lights on at night. Zhu Min, at the time the deputy managing director of the International Monetary Fund and a former senior official in the People's Bank of China (PBOC), said in 2015 there were a billion square meters of empty property.

The consequence, if the market had been left to its own devices, would have to be a significant contraction in supply and fall in prices, as excess capacity was absorbed. Balance would be restored, but only at the expense of a crunching correction in GDP. That's why short-seller Jim Chanos called China "Dubai times 1,000"—referring to the overbuilding that triggered a 50 percent drop in property prices in the desert kingdom in 2009 and 2010. Happily for China's economy, and the commodity producers from Australia to Brazil that relied on demand from the property boom, the market was not left to its own devices.

In Guiyang, the capital of Guizhou province, the effort to reduce real estate inventory reshaped the urban landscape. Old properties were torn down, part of a massive program of slum clearance. As excavators clawed the old low-rise developments into rubble, cranes added stories to gleaming new skyscrapers. In 2017 the central government tasked Guizhou with clearing 429,800 slum properties—the second-largest number of any of China's thirty-one provinces. With an urban population of 15.7 million, that is equivalent to tearing down about 5 percent of the housing stock.[3]

With compensation from the government, slum residents could afford to move into one of the new skyscrapers. To lock in that process, compensation—typically about 3,000 yuan per square meter—wasn't paid directly to the residents. Instead it was placed in an escrow account, then paid directly to the developer once residents decided which apartment they wanted to occupy. That wasn't the end of efforts to boost demand.

3. Qian Wan and Tom Orlik, "How Slum Clearance Exorcised Fear of Ghost Towns," Bloomberg, April 2, 2018.

Anyone who bought a house got a local *hukou*—guaranteeing access to local welfare benefits and increasing the incentive for out-of-towners to buy.

It worked. Outside the showroom of Official Residence No. 1—an expansive new development of high-rises, villas, schools, and shopping malls—golf carts decked out as Rolls Royce waited to shuttle buyers back and forth. Attendants, clad in brown felt uniforms with chunky gold brocade—someone's idea of an old-time chauffeur, shivered ill-tempered in the cold. Inside, Mr. Zheng, the project manager, was more cheerful. He brandished a laser pointer—stock in trade for China's property impresarios—using it to pick out different parts of a scale model of the development. "Sales are going well," he said, grinning.

Strong sales and rising prices buoyed profits for real estate developers. Prices in the capital Guiyang rose 10.4 percent in 2017. Land sales were also buoyant, rising 27.9 percent, supporting revenue for the local government. Local residents say even that understates the actual pace of price gains. With ensuring housing affordability one of the performance metrics for local officials, most are unwilling to let new developments come to market at rising prices. To get around that, but also keep the market humming, developers report a low price to the government for the shell apartment. Buyers pay a substantially higher cost, with the increment recorded as a separate payment for decorations and furnishings.

Guizhou is an extreme case, but the same pattern was replicated across the country. The Ministry of Housing and Urban Rural Development set ambitious targets for slum clearance—6 million units a year from 2015 to 2017, and 5 million a year from 2018 to 2020. China Development Bank—the massive state-owned policy bank—provided funding, tapping cheap credit from the PBOC to do so. From mid-2015 through the end of 2017 the PBOC made about 2 trillion yuan in loans earmarked for slum clearance. Commercial banks, often owned by local governments, chipped in additional funds.

There's a "helicopter money" feeling to the process: the central bank printing money to cover the losses of real estate developers. At the same time, even if slum clearance started with the whirring of the PBOC's printing press, it ended with repayment of the borrowed funds. Local governments clear away slum houses, paying the former residents with borrowed funds and gaining ownership of the land. Residents whose slum homes are cleared use the funds toward the purchase of a new apartment. That absorbs excess inventory, pushing real estate developers' profits higher. With stronger profits and anticipating higher demand, developers buy more land from local governments. With the revenue they get from land sales, local governments repay the money they've borrowed, closing the loop.

Slum clearances might have been the most striking, but it wasn't the only measure used to bolster real estate demand. Mortgage lending also soared. Bank loans to households rose 21.4 percent over the course of 2017. PBOC governor Zhou Xiaochuan gave the nod of approval. At his annual press conference at the National People's Congress in March that year, he said mortgage loans supported an entire ecosystem of real estate developers, construction firms, and commodity producers. The implication: mortgage lending is a valuable contribution to society, and the regulators would take a positive view of banks that did more of it.

Administrative controls on who can buy a home were hardened or softened, depending on where excess inventory was greatest. In major cities like Beijing, where demand outstripped supply, there were strict controls on who could buy. For out-of-towners with no Beijing *hukou*, it was tough to find a rung on the property ladder. Even for locals, mortgages were hard to come by—especially for second- and third-homebuyers. In Guiyang, in contrast, it was a free-for-all, with no paper trail of tax receipts or residence documents required of buyers and banks eager to lend. "Home loans are the safest type of loans," said the manager of a Guiyang branch of one of the big-four banks, explaining why he made so many of them.

ELIXIR FOR ZOMBIES: HOW SUPPLY-SIDE REFORM
TACKLED THE PROBLEM OF DEBT

The most highly indebted sectors of China's economy are heavy industry, real estate, and local government. The official data doesn't provide a breakdown of debt on a sector-by-sector basis. Using financial reports from listed companies gets around that problem. In 2015, at the height of concerns about a financial crisis, average debt for China's 181 listed real estate developers was 18.3 times annual income. With debt at 17.9 times annual income, iron and steel firms were not far behind. For some local government financing vehicles the problem was even more severe—with no regular income, they depended on land sales to repay their borrowing.

Those averages obscure more extreme levels of stress at the bottom end of the spectrum. The rustiest steel firms had debt equal to a hundred years of income. In Liaoning province, local government financing vehicles that had borrowed at rates of 8 percent or above were generating return on assets of 1 percent or below—making repayment a near impossibility.

Debt crises don't start with average borrowers; they start with the weakest borrowers. Their defaults trigger a reassessment of risk, lenders pull back, and higher-quality borrowers run into trouble. Based on the debt levels of the weakest industrials, real estate developers, and local government financing vehicles, in 2015 China was in a lot of trouble.

How has supply-side reform managed to turn that situation around? Stripping through the complexity of capacity closure targets and slum-clearance financing, the aim of supply-side reform was rather simple: make debt repayment easier by reflating the economy. For students of financial crises, reflation is a familiar tactic. The twist in the Chinese context, and evidence of the sophistication of the tools that Beijing could bring to bear in addressing the problem, was that reflation was targeted at the parts of the economy that had the highest debt.

From 2012 to 2015 the industrial sector was mired in deflation and profits sank. Industrial firms were fighting a losing battle, attempting to repay a fixed pile of debt with a shrinking income. Firms with the highest debt faced the biggest drop in prices and profitability. By closing down excess capacity and ramping up demand, supply-side reform turned that situation around. From 2016—coinciding with Liu He's launch of supply-side reform—prices rose and profits climbed. By the start of 2017, industrial profits were up 31.5 percent from a year earlier.

From 2013 to 2015 real estate was plagued by overcapacity. Home sales first decelerated and then contracted. Prices dropped with them, hitting profits for developers. New construction also contracted, dealing a blow to demand across the industrial sector and taking a chunk out of growth. By tearing down slum dwellings and relocating the residents to new developments, policymakers turned that problem around. By the end of 2016, property sales were up 22 percent and prices had climbed 10 percent. With profits rebounding, developers started to break ground on new projects.

What was good for real estate developers' profits was also good for local government finances. In some provinces, revenue from land sales accounts for more than a quarter of income. In 2015, with real estate sales slumping and developers swamped in overcapacity, land sales plummeted 23.9 percent. Local government finance vehicles, which relied on land sales to repay their borrowing, faced default and bankruptcy. By the end of 2017, with land sales roaring back to 49.4 percent growth, they were flush with cash.

Credit policy also worked to alleviate stress. Finance for slum clearance was provided by the PBOC, with more than 2 trillion yuan in low-interest-rate loans. An explosion in mortgage lending drove property demand to renewed heights, adding to debt for lightly leveraged households, and sparing the balance sheet of highly leveraged developers. Infrastructure spending was financed through public–private partnerships, with the up-front cost paid by the builder rather than requiring local governments to borrow more money.

In contrast to efforts decades earlier in the United States and United Kingdom, China's supply-side reform agenda didn't make the economy more efficient. Indeed, by inserting the hand of the state so forcefully into so many aspects of economic life, it almost certainly made it less efficient. There was more than a touch of accounting sleight of hand, reducing local government borrowing by requiring local-government-owned construction firms to borrow for them. On the key objective of lowering financial risks, however, by shifting so large a share of national income to the most highly stressed borrowers, it was brutally effective.

A TREE CANNOT GROW TO THE SKY: THE DELEVERAGING AGENDA

Deleveraging—a fancy word for reducing debt as a percentage of income— was already one of the objectives of supply-side reform when it was set out in January 2016. Such was the importance of that aspect of the plan that it got an additional boost. In May 2016 the authoritative person reappeared, once again on the front page of *People's Daily*, this time proclaiming the end of China's debt-driven development model. "A tree cannot grow to the sky," the authoritative person said, "high leverage must bring with it high risks." The message was clear: financial risks were rising. The current course could only end in crisis. Preventing that from happening was one of the major tasks facing the government.

With the *People's Daily* article, financial risk moved from a fringe concern of a few pointy heads at the PBOC to the top of everyone's list of things to do. Supply-side reform addressed financial risks obliquely, by raising income for the most highly indebted borrowers. Now, alongside it, there was the deleveraging agenda, tackling financial risk directly by taking aim at the most overstretched parts of the financial system.

Some of the moving parts were already in place. As the guardians of the financial system—the smartest guys in the room, and the most international in orientation—the PBOC had long been vigilant on risks of a credit crisis. At the start of 2010, with the 4-trillion-yuan stimulus still in full swing, it was the PBOC that first attempted to edge policy back toward normalcy. In 2013 they fired a shot across the bows of financial buccaneers in the shadow banking industry, engineering a precipitate increase in short-term borrowing costs to choke off their source of finance.

In 2016 they were ready with a more comprehensive and subtle approach to addressing the problem: the macro-prudential assessment.

A rather opaque term, "macro-prudential" actually means something quite straightforward. 'Prudential' regulation aims to secure the stability of individual financial firms—for example by requiring them to hold enough capital to cover potential losses. 'Macro-prudential' regulation attempts to do the same thing for the financial system as a whole.

In a meeting room at a bank in Zhengzhou, the capital of Henan province, the risk management department had no misunderstanding on the meaning or the importance of the PBOC's new tool. "We got a 'B,'" said the official charged with managing the process. "If we got a 'C' the PBOC would limit our business." Under the macro-prudential assessment, the Henan lender, like all banks in China, provided a quarterly report to the PBOC on its assets, liabilities, capital buffer, and interest rates. Across all of those dimensions, the central bank checked to see if they were crossing regulatory red lines. Too many loans to high-risk industries? Too much dependence on short-term sources of funding? Offering irrationally high interest rates to lure deposits? Inadequate capital buffer to absorb losses? All resulted in a lower score.

Banks that score high, with an "A" on the PBOC's metrics, get rewarded with higher rates on their reserve deposits (all of China's banks have to keep a substantial chunk of deposits on reserve at the PBOC; receiving higher rates on them would directly contribute to higher income). They also get more flexibility to expand their business. For banks that score a "B," like the one in Henan, it's business as usual. Banks unfortunate enough to come out with a "C" get punished with lower rates on their reserve deposits and a regulatory clampdown that makes it harder for them to grow their business.

The PBOC was not the first central bank to deploy macro-prudential tools to manage risks to financial stability. In the wake of the great financial crisis there was a global surge in activity, as policymakers developed new instruments to disentangle management of monetary policy from regulation of the financial sector. The Financial Stability Oversight Council in the United States, the European Systemic Risk Board, and the Bank of England's Financial Policy Committee were all established earlier. The PBOC was the first to develop such a comprehensive toolkit, to implement it so actively and with such fine differentiation on a bank-by-bank basis, and to use it to tackle such an extreme risk to financial stability.

The macro-prudential assessment solved two critical problems for the PBOC. First, it got the bank past Benjamin Strong's dilemma about spanking all the children when only one had misbehaved. As the PBOC had learned back in the June 2013 money market shock, pushing up borrowing costs enough to deter shadow banks also chokes off funds for responsible lenders, and deals a blow to the real economy. Using macro-prudential tools, the PBOC could separate financial regulation from monetary policy. Interest rates could be used to manage growth and inflation. Macro-prudential tools could be used to manage risks to stability. The system the PBOC put in place allowed for management on a bank-by-bank basis. Banks that stepped out of line could be punished. Banks that toed the line were rewarded.

Second, China's attempts to clamp down on financial risks were often derided as a game of whack-a-mole. Regulators would clamp down on one area of sharp practice, only to see a new dodge spring up elsewhere. Barred from making loans to high-debt real estate developers, for example, banks instead made investments in shadow banks, and the shadow banks loaned the funds to the same end borrowers. By taking a comprehensive view of banks' balance sheets, the macro-prudential assessment solved the problem. With multiple mallets and a bright light shining on all the holes, the PBOC was now positioned to whack all the moles, some of the moles, or none of the moles—as it saw fit.

The macro-prudential assessment wasn't the only show in town. The China Banking Regulatory Commission (CBRC) got a heavyweight new chief, Guo Shuqing. Guo, a former deputy governor of the PBOC and acolyte of pro-market reformer Zhou Xiaochuan, came out swinging against risks to financial stability. A series of new regulations made it harder for banks to dodge controls on expanding their loan book through complex arrangements with shadow banks. In June 2017 some of China's biggest corporations—titans like real estate developer Dalian Wanda and insurance conglomerate Anbang—were shaken by news that the CBRC was investigating their overseas borrowing, aiming to head off risks from capital flight.

The China Securities Regulatory Commission, embarrassed by its mishandling of the equity market boom and bust, also got a new face at the top. Liu Shiyu, another former deputy governor at the PBOC, quickly proved a more muscular presence than his predecessor, Xiao Gang. In December 2016 he took aim at "barbarian" insurance firms using leveraged finance to launch hostile takeovers of listed firms. The head of the China Insurance Regulatory Commission, who had turned a blind eye to such sharp practices, soon found himself out of a job and under investigation for corruption.

For local government loans—perhaps the biggest headache for the banks—a massive debt swap dialed down the stress levels. The program started at the beginning of 2015 with the promise of a trillion yuan in debt swaps. It expanded rapidly to 3.8 trillion yuan at the end of the year. By the end of 2016, 9.9 trillion yuan had been swapped, and at the end of 2017 the total reached 14.2 trillion yuan—equal to almost a quarter of GDP. Local governments were the big winners. Most had borrowed short-term at market rates, typically with a one-year loan at a rate of 6 percent or above. With those funds going to pay for public infrastructure projects that would generate no returns while under construction and only low returns after that, the financing structure made little sense. Now they were refinancing by issuing five-year bonds at 3 percent. The long-term, low-cost financing was more closely aligned with their long-term, low-return assets. And the immediate stress of debt servicing was substantially reduced.

Banks were pushed to divest themselves of bad loans and raise more capital. Many did both. Back in Zhengzhou, the government pushed through the merger of thirteen local lenders to form Zhongyuan Bank. Along the way, they sold off bad loans and injected fresh capital. The aim, according to the prospectus, as shares in Zhongyuan were marketed to investors in Hong Kong: to create a bank with "a higher capital base" and "stronger capability to withstand potential risks." In an initial public offering in July 2017, the bank raised a billion dollars. On a small scale,

Henan's provincial government had replicated the cleanup and listing that had taken Industrial and Commercial Bank of China and other giants to market in the mid-2000s—writing off bad loans, injecting capital, promising revamped operations, then tapping the market for funds.

They weren't alone. As figure 8.1 shows, from 2015 to 2017, the volume of bad loans written off accelerated at a rapid pace. Trawling through the balance sheets of forty-one listed banks, from 2015 to the first half of 2017, 1.3 trillion yuan in bad loans were sold or written off. That was up from a total of just 400 billion yuan in the previous three years, and equivalent to about 1 percent of banks' total loan book. With every province in China setting up its own asset management company to buy bad debts from the banks, demand was strong. "We used to be able to buy bad loans at an 80 percent to 90 percent discount to face value," complained Mr. Li from the Wenzhou financial advisory. "Now demand is so strong the discount is sometimes just 30 percent."

The results were impressive. There are various ways of tracking growth in China's credit. The PBOC publishes a series on "aggregate finance," which includes bank loans, bond issuance, equity fundraising, and shadow

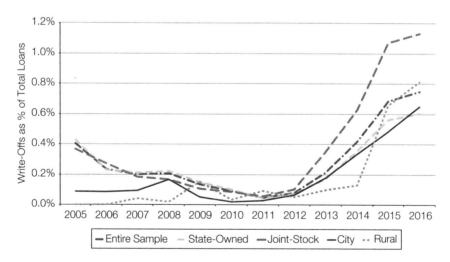

Figure 8.1 Loan Transfers and Write-Offs
Sample includes forty-one banks.
Created by the author using information from Bloomberg .

bank activity. Netting out equity finance provides a high-frequency read on the pace of credit growth. In early 2016, that was expanding at 12.5 percent a year. By mid-2018 it had slowed to 9.9 percent. A more comprehensive read comes from the CBRC's series on total bank assets. That captures banks' on-balance-sheet lending activity, and their off-balance-sheet investment in shadow banking products. It shows an even sharper drop, from 16.5 percent annual expansion at the end of 2016 to 7.4 percent in the first quarter of 2018.

The slowdown in lending came almost entirely from the riskiest parts of China's financial system: shadow bank loans. Bank claims on other financial sectors—a series from the PBOC that captures bank loans to shadow banks—peaked at 73.7 percent annual growth in February 2016. By mid-2018 it was contracting. On the liability side, too, there was a shift away from risky short-term funding from the issuance of wealth management products back toward safe and boring deposits. At the end of 2015 bank funding from wealth management products was up 56.5 percent from a year earlier. In 2017, it didn't expand at all.

Focusing the slowdown on shadow banking didn't just lower financial risks, it also preserved growth in the real economy. Bank loans and bond issuance fund real activity: investment in factories, infrastructure, and real estate. Shadow banks—providing the equivalent of payday loans for cash-strapped private businesses, or funds for speculation in the property or equity markets—do not. Put simply: bank loans make the economy grow, shadow bank loans don't. By keeping the former turned on, and turning the latter off, China's policymakers could partially square the deleveraging–growth circle, slowing lending without cratering growth.

I AIN'T AFRAID OF NO GHOST TOWN: HOW CHINA DEFIED THE DOUBTERS

With the supply-side reform and deleveraging agendas, China had a working strategy in place to slow the debt machine. Supply-side reform stabilized growth and reflated the economy. Real growth held steady at around

7 percent. Nominal growth accelerated from a low of 6.4 percent year-on-year at the end of 2015 to 10.7 percent at the end of 2017. That acceleration in nominal growth is important. Steel smelters, real estate developers, and local government financing vehicles don't repay debt with earnings after adjustment for inflation. They repay debt with nominal earnings. Deflation—which means lower nominal earnings—makes debt repayment harder. Inflation—which means higher earnings—makes debt repayment easier. The deleveraging agenda slowed the pace of credit growth.

Put the two pieces together, and the combination of faster GDP growth and slower credit expansion started to bring China's leverage ratio under control. Based on data from the Bank for International Settlements, from 2008 to 2016 China's debt-to-GDP ratio rose from 142 percent to 250 percent. In 2017 and 2018, it levelled off, ending 2018 at 254 percent. Calculations by the McKinsey Global Institute show the same trend—with a marked slowdown in the pace of debt accumulation. China wasn't deleveraging. But it had stopped adding leverage, and done so without hammering growth. Relative to expectations—that was a major achievement.

In a German bar nestled incongruously under a giant illuminated corncob in Zhengzhou's newly built central business district, business is brisk. Young professionals in the Henan capital are enjoying ice-cold glasses of Weissbier and listening, slightly perplexed, to a British–Russian cover band belting out a passable version of "Angel," a turn-of-the-century hit by Jamaican pop star Shaggy. It's the kind of bizarre, engaging cultural mishmash on display by virtue of China's sudden arrival on the world stage. All the participants—band, patrons, bar staff—seem slightly unsure why they are there. It's also evidence of how successful China has been at turning around what many saw as a hopeless situation.

Back in 2013 a visit by cable news channel CNN to Zhengzhou's new central business district found buildings empty and property agents hustling to make sales. The CNN broadcast became part of the "ghost town" narrative that shaped the global understanding of China and reinforced the negative perception of investors. Fast-forward to 2017 and the new district is full to capacity—complete with illuminated corncob and German bar. Town planners are working on an additional new district to absorb the excess demand. "Where's the ghost town?" asks Mr. Zhao, a manager at the local government financing vehicle that paid for development of the new district. "Back in 2013 I couldn't get a taxi because there were none around," he added. "Now I can't get one because there's too many other people trying to get one."

At the Bank of Zhengzhou—one of the biggest local lenders—the government's deleveraging efforts are in full force. The shadow loan book crunched down from 82 percent growth in 2016 to 1 percent contraction in 2017. Funds raised from wealth management products swung from rapid expansion to mild contraction. Delving into corporate balance sheets for Henan's listed firms, the share of loans to zombie firms dropped sharply. Through it all, GDP growth for the province held steady at 8 percent a year.

A ghost town that turned into a thriving business hub, a runaway banking system brought to heel, and zombie firms that lurched back to life, all with the economy clocking steady growth: back in 2015, for Henan and for China, that Goldilocks scenario was beyond the imagination of the bears. By the end of 2017 it was an outcome that had—at least for the moment—been achieved. For Henan, there was another important factor at work: the upgrading of the industrial structure. In 2010, attracted by lower wage costs, strong transport connections, and a raft of government incentives, Taiwanese electronics giant Hon Hai Precision Industry moved an iPhone assembly plant to the province. Other manufacturers followed, setting up shop in the same industrial park. In 2016, Henan produced 258 million mobile phones.

That move up the value chain, driving an export boom that raised incomes across the province, was an important part of Henan's turnaround story. In charge at the start of the process was Li Keqiang, who served as Party secretary for the province up to 2004. Now ensconced as premier in Beijing, Li and his team wondered if a similar trick could be pulled off on a national level.

Technology Transfer and Trade Tariffs

At 3 p.m. on October 16, 1964, China exploded an atom bomb, joining the United States, the Union of Soviet Socialist Republics, the United Kingdom, and France in an elite club of nuclear powers. Chairman Mao was pleased. "This is a major achievement of the Chinese people in their struggle to increase their national defense capability and oppose the US imperialist policy of nuclear blackmail and nuclear threats," read the official statement. It was a hard-won achievement. Awestruck and terrified by the destruction of Hiroshima and Nagasaki by the United States in World War II, China's rulers scrambled to develop their own nuclear capability—the threat of mutual destruction seen as the only guarantee against the threat of US imperialism.

At first, they found a willing partner in the Soviet Union. Moscow had successfully tested its own nuclear device in 1949 and, in a spirit of communist brotherhood, was open to sharing its technology. That cooperation came to an end in 1959, part of a broader deterioration of relations as Soviet leader Nikita Khrushchev denounced his predecessor Joseph Stalin and pursued a policy of peaceful coexistence with the West. Chairman Mao's nonchalant attitude to nuclear war didn't help either. "Let us imagine how many people would die if war breaks out," Mao mused. "There are 2.7 billion people in the world. . . . I say that if the worst came to the worst and one-half dies, there will still be one-half left, but . . . the whole world would become socialist."

For Khrushchev, even making the perfect socialist omelet didn't justify breaking that many eggs. As the transfer of technology ended and Soviet advisors returned home, China's ambition of a rapid march toward nuclear status was frustrated. "The Soviet side's stranglehold on us on the crucial issue of key technology is really infuriating," wrote Nie Rongzhen, Mao's point man on the nuclear project, in 1960.

The end of Soviet assistance, however, was not the end of the project. "Maybe," Nie continued, "this kind of pressure will instead become the impetus for developing our science and technology so we strive even more resolutely for independence." Drawing on what they had already learned from some fourteen hundred Russian advisors, gleaning further insights from scientific publications in the United States and Europe, and peeking in on other countries' weapons tests, China completed the march toward nuclear status, detonating a twenty-two-kiloton device in Lop Nur, in the deserts of Xinjiang in the northwest of the country. The next step was to develop a mode of delivery. That was accomplished just eight months after the first test, with a nuclear bomb dropped from an aircraft. A year later, China was able to fit nuclear warheads onto medium-range missiles.

They would not match the size of the US or Soviet arsenal, but China's achievement of nuclear status was a watershed moment in modern history. With China a nuclear power, its southwestern neighbor—and potential challenger as Asian hegemon, India—was sure to follow. When India followed, so did Pakistan. President Richard Nixon's 1972 visit to China, and the alignment with the United States against the Soviet Union that followed, would have been impossible had China not achieved nuclear parity with the dueling Cold War rivals. Technology transfer, combined with China's determination, changed the world. It may do so again.

Fast-forward half a century, and China's fourth-generation leader—Hu Jintao, in power from March 2003—was casting around for a policy agenda. Hu had inherited an economy primed for growth. Entry into the World Trade Organization (WTO), closure of thousands of state-owned enterprises, and a cleanup of bad loans in the banking system were all significant positives bequeathed to him. It wasn't enough. Exports were booming, but even as annual growth in overseas sales topped 40 percent, the contribution of Chinese firms remained limited. High-tech inputs came from Japan, Korea, and Taiwan. Intellectual property and brands were owned by US and European multinationals. Multinationals did their research and development in their home country, leaving China in the dark on how new products and technologies were developed. Chinese firms and workers were confined to the low-value, low-wage task of snapping the pieces together. If China was going to move up the value chain—critical to sustaining its rise toward high-income status—something had to be done.

The first iteration of an answer came in 2006, with the snappily titled National Program for the Development of Science and Technology in the Medium- and Long-Term. At the center of the plan, and catching the attention of foreign governments and multinationals, was a commitment to "indigenous innovation." That opaque term—the original Chinese is close to "self-directed innovation"—actually means something rather simple: China wanted control of the technologies that were necessary to the next stage of its development. As a first step, the plan identified sixteen mega-projects spanning microchips, broadband, alternative and nuclear energy, aerospace, and healthcare. R&D investment would be increased to 2.5 percent of GDP in 2020, up from 1.4 percent in 2006. Given the size of the Chinese economy, and expectations of continued rapid growth, that was an eye-catching commitment.

Also eye-catching were the similarities between the approach taken by China's fourth generation of leaders and that of its first generation. Western countries, with some notable exceptions for national priorities like nuclear weapons or the moon landing, followed a bottom-up innovation model. Academics select their own lines of inquiry, and corporate labs compete to spin theoretical insight into market application. China, with its weak science and technology base and pressing need to catch up with global leaders, would make the exception into the rule. The state would direct academic, military, and corporate research with a view to hitting specific objectives by a specific time. That was true when Nie led the nuclear project. It would be true again when Hu set the indigenous innovation engine in motion. Elder researchers, some of them involved in China's atom bomb and ballistic missile programs, were consulted on early drafts of the Medium- and Long-Term Plan—a signal of continuity.

The great financial crisis threw industrial planning into higher gear. The 4-trillion-yuan stimulus funded nine sector programs, ranging from steel and shipbuilding to autos and electronics. Programs under consideration for years but not given the green light by the State Council were rushed into operation. The sixteen mega-projects originally planned for implementation over fifteen years from 2006 to 2020 were accelerated. In October 2010 the efforts of the Hu administration culminated with identification of seven strategic emerging industries, ranging from environmental technology to information technology and new energy vehicles, seen as essential if China was to achieve advanced-economy status.

Industrial planners were conflicted. On the one hand, their programs were now funded and operational. On the other, the farsighted objective of increasing efficiency and advancing toward the technology frontier was overwhelmed by the pressing short-term need to fire up investment, protecting growth above 8 percent through the global downturn. Ultimately, the wave of funding and top-level support worked in the planners' favor, setting in motion a long-term program where they pulled the levers and China's top leaders had a vested interest in success. In the early 2000s, following Zhu Rongji's "grasp the large, let go the small" reform of the state sector, the private sector advanced and the market played an expanded role in allocating resources. Now that swung into reverse; "the state advances, the private sector retreats" was the spirit of the time.

Ascending to the presidency in 2013, Xi Jinping inherited an economy that was already tilting back toward industrial planning and an expanded role for the state in directing China's technology catch-up. Once in power, he pushed even further in that direction. The place where it all came together was in a blueprint for long-term industrial development called Made in China 2025. Published in May 2015 the China 2025 plan is based on the idea that the manufacturing sector is in the midst of a fourth revolution. The first came in the eighteenth-century with the invention of steam power, the second with electricity in the nineteenth century, the third with computers in the twentieth. The fourth will combine industrial robots, artificial intelligence, big data and cloud computing, resulting in a manufacturing sector that marries automation and efficiency with customization and a dynamic response to a changing market.

The focus was on ten sectors: information technology, robotics, aerospace, maritime equipment and ships, trains, new energy vehicles, power, agriculture, new materials, and pharmaceuticals and medical instruments. In some cases, the aim was to develop end products like airplanes or ships. More important, however, were technologies that would underpin leading-edge production across the economy, such as artificial intelligence and industrial robotics. Like the nuclear pioneers learning from Russian advisors, the aim was not to reinvent foreign technologies, but to reverse-engineer and replicate them.

What had changed from earlier plans was the scale of ambition. The 2010 plan aimed at innovation as an end in itself. The 2015 plan aimed at innovation as a way to reform the entire manufacturing system. The main China 2025 report was somewhat vague about objectives. In accompanying documents, the government set out specific targets. For sectors identified in the plan, China wanted domestic firms to produce 40 percent of key components by 2020. By 2025, China wanted the domestic share up to 70 percent.

To get there, China's industrial planners deployed a formidable arsenal of policy instruments and natural advantages. Those can be grouped under three headings.

Activist policymakers. China had a plan for industrial development and the determination to carry it out. Strategic direction came from the Leading Small Group for Building an Advanced Manufacturing Industry, chaired by Xi's economics tsar Liu He. Implementation came from the Ministry of Industry and Information Technology. Provincial governments rolled out their own versions of the plan. State-owned enterprises targeted acquisition of the requisite technology from foreign firms, with funding provided by state banks. Coordination between those groups was far from perfect. There were gaps, overlaps, missteps, and bureaucratic turf wars. But no other major government had thought so long or so hard about technological development, and none had taken such far-reaching steps to achieve its objectives.

Massive resources. In 2017 China spent $444 billion on research and development (R&D). Only the United States—with R&D at $483 billion—spent more. The entire European Union spent $366 billion. In addition to spending on R&D, China was forking out billions to buy foreign technologies. Among the jewels in the crown: home appliance maker Midea's $4 billion acquisition of the German robotics firm Kuka. Accompanying the spending power: an ever-increasing supply of brain power. In 2017 China had more than two million research students, and 600,000 studying overseas.

A huge domestic market. Whether it's to tap the low-cost, integrated supply chain or to access the market of 1.3 billion customers, multinationals have to be in China. China's policymakers are masters at using that to their advantage, steering foreign firms into joint ventures, or requiring them to hand over valuable technology, as the price of market entry. Competitive dynamics between multinationals operating in the same sector, and between foreign governments attempting to promote their national champions, makes it hard for any individual firm to refuse.

Local governments piled in. A year after China 2025 was published, at least seventy provinces, cities, and county-level administrations had followed up with their own plans. Looking just at robotics, there was a flurry of local initiatives as officials rushed to align with national priorities and grab a piece of the industry of the future. In Guangdong province— China's manufacturing hub—capital Guangzhou offered a 20 percent subsidy to firms buying locally made robots. Dongguan, a grim expanse of factory towns whose migrant population made its name synonymous with prostitution,[1] promised 200 million yuan in support, and cheap loans for firms investing in automation. Not to be outdone, Zhejiang province offered 280 million yuan in subsidies. Ganyao—a town of forty thousand whose name means "makes kilns"—decided to reinvent itself as an advanced manufacturing hub, aiming to attract thirty robotics firms by 2023. "It was like building something from nothing," the Party secretary said.[2]

There are well-founded doubts about the value of input data as a gauge of the quality of science and technology outcomes. R&D funding can be wasted or misappropriated. Postgraduate students can lose themselves in the library rather than adding value in the laboratory. On outcome metrics too, however, China registered steady progress.

There were more inventions. The number of triadic patents—patents deemed valuable enough to register in the United States, Europe, and Japan—by Chinese inventors rose from 87 in 2000 to 3,890 in 2016. That's still considerably behind 14,220 for the United States, but the acceleration is impressive. A look at patents on an industry-by-industry basis shows that it's in priority sectors targeted in the China 2025 plan where the most progress has been made.

There were more innovative businesses. In 2008, the Chinese firm with the biggest market cap was Petrochina, a state-owned energy giant focused on the necessary but uninspiring business of pumping oil. In 2018 it was Tencent, started by technology entrepreneur Pony Ma, boasting the WeChat super-app that combines messaging with social network and payments, and investments in everything from leading-edge healthcare firm iCarbonX to Uber-slaying ride-hailing app Didi Chuxing.

Global rankings were up. The Global Innovation Index—a joint report by Cornell University, INSEAD, and the World Intellectual Property Organization—is the most comprehensive

1. In Chinese, the phrase "Going to Dongguan" is slang for visiting a prostitute.

2. Yan Jie, *Firing Up Robotics in Small-Town Zhejiang*, Sixth Tone, October 16, 2017.

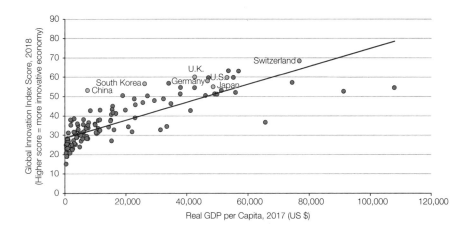

Figure 9.1 Innovation Score and GDP per Capita
Created by the author using information from the World Bank, Cornell University,
INSEAD, and the World Intellectual Property Organization.

effort to grade countries on their innovation capacity. In 2010
China ranked forty-third. In 2019 it had risen to fourteenth—the
highest-ranked middle-income country, and one spot ahead of
Japan. As figure 9.1 shows, relative to its income level, China is
already an innovative economy.

WORKERS ARE COSTS, MACHINES ARE ASSETS: WINNERS AND LOSERS FROM CHINA 2025

What happens if China realizes its 2025 ambitions? For China, control
of the commanding heights of industry would be a new growth driver.
Chinese firms would claim a bigger piece of the pie in the home market,
expand sales abroad, and account for a larger share of the value-added
in finished products—displacing imported components from Japan,
Korea, and Taiwan. Global demand for products targeted as part of China
2025 is measured in trillions of dollars. Claiming a progressively larger
share of that market could buoy China's annual growth above 5 percent

through 2025 and beyond. Assuming nominal growth of 8 percent and a US economy expanding at about 4 percent a year, that would put China on course to overtake the United States as the world's largest economy by the end of the decade.

A transition from heavy industry to advanced manufacturing and services would help tackle China's structural woes. In particular, a more innovative economy would be less dependent on debt. Capital intensity levels across China 2025 sectors vary. Building ships and airplanes is far more capital-intensive than researching new medicines. In general, however, China's industries of the future are less capital-intensive than its industries of the past. As a result, borrowing needs are reduced. If the China 2025 plan succeeds, corporations would be less dependent on debt and deleveraging will be easier to do.

A more innovative economy would be more environmentally sustainable. Advanced manufacturing and services firms are markedly less energy-intensive than traditional industry. Keeping growth on target by building a lot of infrastructure requires a lot of steel, which means burning a lot of coal. Keeping growth on target by enjoying the flow of income from intellectual property rights in new pharmaceuticals doesn't burn any coal at all. If the China 2025 plan succeeds, China should be able to continue growing at a rapid clip and achieve modest improvements in air quality and other measures of environmental sustainability.

Innovation would offset the drag from a shrinking workforce. Output per worker is markedly higher in advanced industries than it is in traditional industries. In 2017 Petrochina had 812,861 employees and 313 billion yuan in earnings—about 385,000 yuan per employee. Tencent had 38,775 employees and 96 billion yuan in earnings. More than 2 million yuan in earnings per worker makes Tencent five times more productive than Petrochina. As China's working-age population shrinks, technologies that boost productivity will be increasingly important.

For China as a whole, the benefits will be significant. Among the ranks of individual workers, however, there will be losers as well as winners. At Han Ma Electronic Technology, a smartphone screen producer in

Dongguan, robots are the future. "Wage costs are rising," explains Mr. Gao, the chief financial officer. "So, we moved from Shenzhen to Dongguan and spent 8 million yuan to automate the factory." As of 2017 the company had just 130 workers, compared with 250 in 2014. Downsizing might not be good news for the workers, but from the manager's point of view, the advantages are clear. "Workers are costs," Gao says. "Machines are assets."

Economists have a way of thinking about what jobs are likely to be replaced by machines— exposure to routinization. The more a job can be broken down into routine and precisely defined tasks, the more easily it can be automated. In China, with hundreds of millions of middle-skill workers employed on the factory production line, exposure to routinization is high. None of the sectors targeted for accelerated development in the China 2025 plan are labor-intensive. All of them have production processes that operate with a high degree of automation. Two—robotics and artificial intelligence—explicitly aim at replacing workers with machines.

The risk of robot takeover is high enough to have Arnold Schwarzenegger saddling up for a final reboot of the *Terminator* franchise. It is also high enough to spark concerns about a sharp rise in inequality. The experience across Western societies is that advances in technology come hand in hand with a widening gap between rich and poor, often with wrenching consequences for social harmony and political order. Automation displaces workers. The shift from an organized workforce to casual employment managed through platforms like Uber (or its Chinese rival, Didi) erodes workers' bargaining power. Economies of scale and network effects concentrate the benefits of advances on a few superstar firms. Amazon in the United States and Alibaba in China are doing very well; smaller brick-and-mortar rivals are not.

Taken together with globalization - which further erodes workers' bargaining power - in advanced economies those forces have contributed to a decline in labor's share of national income and an increase in inequality. In the United States, in the fifteen years from China entering the WTO in 2001 to 2016, real income for the bottom 40 percent of earners was flat, and for the middle 20 percent it barely increased. Almost all the gains went to the top few percent, with the top 5 percent seeing income rise 10 percent. Labor's share in national income fell from 65 percent in 2001 to 60 percent in 2014.

In China, so far, that hasn't happened. Wage growth remains rapid. Low- and medium-skilled workers most at risk from displacement by technology are seeing some of the most rapid gains. That's because for China's blue-collar class, the gains from globalization have so far outweighed the costs from automation. US manufacturing workers didn't just get replaced by robots, they got replaced by cheaper Chinese workers too. Just as US workers suffered the costs of that transition; Chinese workers enjoyed the benefits. That state of affairs won't persist forever, or even for long.

There are already signs that China's robot army is advancing at the expense of its human workers, and at a larger scale than at Mr. Gao's Han Ma Electronic. At Hon Hai Precision Industry, the electronics giant that snaps together Apple iPhones, Chairman Terry Goh said back in 2011 that the firm planned to employ a million robots within three years. In the years that followed, the firm's workforce shrank from a peak of 1.3 million in 2012 to 987,000 in 2017—a drop of 24 percent. With revenue over the same period expanding 20 percent, it seemed like human hands were passing their work to more dexterous mechanical fingers. JD.com, the challenger to Alibaba for China's e-commerce crown, is moving toward automation of its warehouses. In one of its laboratories, a robot can sort thirty-six hundred objects an hour, four times more than a person.[3]

Inequality is not just a moral and a social problem; it is also an economic one. Economists going back to John Maynard Keynes recognized that concentration of wealth in the hands of the few erodes the spending power that keeps the economy at full employment. "In so far as millionaires find their satisfaction in building mighty mansions to contain their bodies when alive and pyramids to shelter them after death," Keynes wrote, "the

3. Dexter Roberts, "Resistance is Futile: China's Conquest Plan for Robot Industry," Bloomberg, April 24, 2017.

day when abundance of capital will interfere with abundance of output may be postponed."[4] In less florid language: rich people spend a lower share of their income and save a higher share. As a result, assuming no offset from spending on mansions or pyramids, the larger the share of national income that goes to the rich, the lower the level of consumption, and the weaker growth.

China is already one of the most unequal societies in the world. In 2015 the Gini coefficient was 0.5, putting China among the ranks of extremely unequal African and Latin American countries. China's new rich are certainly trying to spend their money. That's how LVMH—owner of the Louis Vuitton brand beloved of fresh-minted millionaires—grew its Asia ex-Japan sales from $3.3 billion in 2006 to $16 billion in 2018. It's how Mercedes quadrupled its average monthly China sales from 2011 to 2018. The trouble is, even with LV-monogrammed everything and luxury SUVs parked two-deep at every intersection in Beijing's business district, China's new rich can't spend enough to lower their savings rate.

The risk from China's 2025 agenda is that even as advances in technology continue to expand supply, by reducing households' share of total income and tilting what is left even more toward the richest households, the same advances in technology will reduce demand. The result will be a Chinese economy that looms even larger as a share of global GDP—rising from 16 percent of the total in 2018 to a projected 20 percent in 2025—but is an even bigger source of imbalance and instability. With consumption insufficient to fuel the economic engine, China would have to continue relying on debt-financed investment at home and protectionism-inducing exports abroad to keep growth on track. Trade partners would lose jobs— this time not to Chinese workers, but to Chinese robots.

For the rest of the world, then, the China 2025 agenda presents three interconnected risks. Most obviously, the risk confronting advanced economies is that China will eat their lunch. As Chinese firms gain market share in new-energy vehicles, industrial robots, and batteries, that will

---

4. John Maynard Keynes, *The General Theory of Employment, Interest and Money* (New York: Palgrave Macmillan, 1936).

come at the expense of losses for foreign firms. A look at exports of China 2025 products on a country-by-country basis shows who has the most at stake. Germany, South Korea, and Taiwan stand out as the most exposed. German automobiles; South Korean electronics, autos, and shipping; and Taiwan's semiconductors all face a new competitive threat. Strangely, given how President Donald Trump led the charge in opposing China's industrial ambitions, the United States has less to lose—at least in terms of export market share. That's a reflection of the low share of exports in GDP, and relatively limited presence in advanced manufacturing.

The challenge for countries like the Philippines, Vietnam, and Bangladesh that aim to follow China up the development ladder is that mastery of a new generation of automated production processes may enable China to retain its low-cost advantage. As figure 9.2 shows, years of rapid wage increases mean China's workers are no longer cheap. In Guangdong in 2016, the average factory worker could expect to make about $800 a month. In a factory in Bangladesh, workers earned just $147. Migration of low-value-added manufacturing out of China to new low-cost locations is already underway. That process is not inevitable. In the past, firms looking to dodge rising costs on China's coast could leave, or they could look for cheaper workers inland. Now they have a third choice: follow Han Ma's Mr. Gao or Hon Hai's Mr. Gou with an investment in labor-saving automation.

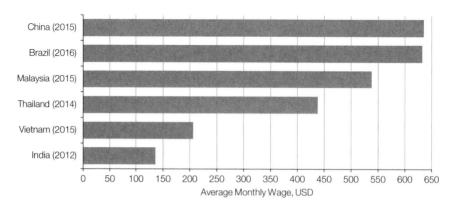

Figure 9.2 Wages for China and Other Emerging Markets
Created by the author using information from Wuhan University.

China's technological gains won't end the migration of labor-intensive employment to Southeast Asia. But it could significantly reduce its scope.

Finally, if increased automation boosts production capacity at the expense of greater inequality, a China tilted further toward saving and away from spending, and toward exporting and away from importing, would be a drag on demand and a source of imbalance for the rest of the world. Measured as a share of GDP, China's trade surplus won't balloon back to the elevated levels seen before the great financial crisis. It's easy to imagine a situation where it plateaus and then rebounds a little higher. Given China's greater weight in the global economy, a trade surplus of 2 percent of GDP in 2025 would represent a bigger drain on demand from the rest of the world than a 10 percent surplus did back in 2007.

DONALD TRUMP AND CHINA'S NEW COLD WAR

To his more impassioned detractors, Donald Trump bears more than a passing resemblance to his disgraced predecessor Richard Nixon. Trump's dog-whistle appeal to the grievances of white working-class voters finds its origins in Nixon's Southern strategy, which tapped simmering resentment over the end of segregation. His disregard for legal niceties—critics say—echoes the indiscretions that ended with Nixon's impeachment. When it comes to China, the similarity ends. Nixon opened China up. Trump tried to close it down.

Nixon called his 1972 trip to China "the week that changed the world." That's no exaggeration. Nixon's meeting with Chairman Mao ended more than two decades of hostility between the two sides, and restored normal diplomatic relations. Mao died in 1976. In 1978, when Deng Xiaoping launched the reform and opening process, friendly relations with the United States provided the crucial underpinning. The path for Chinese goods to enter global markets was open. So too was the door for Western capital, technology, and expertise to enter China. Without the Nixon visit, China's reform and opening would have been a more faltering process.

On June 16, 2015, Trump announced his bid for the US presidency. After descending the elevator into the lobby of New York's Trump Tower, the real estate mogul gave a forty-five-minute speech to the assembled throng of journalists and supporters. It was his accusation that Mexican immigrants to the United States are rapists that hit the headlines. Nestled among promises to build a "great, great wall on our southern border," repeal the "big lie, Obama-care," and an accountant's report on his net worth, was a promise to get tough with China. "Our country is in serious trouble," Trump said. "When was the last time anybody saw us beating, let's say, China in a trade deal?" Under a Trump presidency, he suggested, that situation would change. "I beat China all the time," he said. "all the time."

There's nothing particularly surprising about candidates talking campaign-trail tough about China. In 1992, Bill Clinton inveighed against the "butchers of Beijing." George W. Bush labeled China a "competitor" instead of a "strategic partner." Courting the support of the unions, Barack Obama said China's trade surplus came directly from manipulation of its currency. Once installed in the Oval Office, and despite sitting behind the Resolute desk, successive presidents found their toughness wavering. Clinton welcomed China into the WTO. Bush needed China's support in the war on terror. Obama, preoccupied with the financial crisis, never followed through on his threat to call China out for its undervalued currency.

This time it looked like things could be different. Maybe it was because of the impact of China's rise on Trump's core supporters—blue-collar workers in the American Rustbelt. Maybe because US businesses, until now the chief cheerleaders for closer US–China ties, had turned sour on the relationship - irked by forced technology transfer and a playing field tilted in favor of domestic rivals. Maybe because China had overplayed its hand, Xi Jinping's muscular assertion of China's global interests—a departure from Deng Xiaoping's "bide our time, hide our strength" doctrine—was coming too early. Maybe it was Trump's long-standing antipathy to China. "You motherfuckers," he said in a 2011 speech. "We're going to tax you 25 percent." Whatever the reason, for Trump, China-bashing was more than just a campaign-trail talking point.

That was clear early from his appointments. As United States trade representative, he tapped Robert Lighthizer—a veteran of the Ronald Reagan administration and a longtime opponent of China's entry into the WTO. As economic advisor he appointed Peter Navarro, a professor at University of California Irvine and author of a book titled *Death by China*. Behind the scenes was the man credited with the successful strategy of the Trump campaign, Steve Bannon. Bannon saw the threat from China as similar to that posed by the "hyper-nationalist" rise of Nazi Germany in the 1930s. "China is everything," he said. "We don't get China right, we don't get anything right."[5]

It wasn't too long before Trump's China policy became clear from his actions. In January 2018, tariffs were introduced on solar panels and washing machines—a warning shot. Then, in March, tariffs on steel and aluminum were added, aimed at blocking China's efforts to export its overcapacity. In April, there were sanctions on Chinese telecom equipment firm ZTE. A ban on ZTE buying components from US firms threatened to put the Chinese firm out of business. If all of that added up to little more than small-arms fire, in July the heavy artillery boomed into action. Tariffs on $50 billion in Chinese imports sparked an immediate retaliation. In September, tariffs were imposed on a further $200 billion. A December meeting between Xi and Trump at the G-20 in Buenos Aires resulted in a temporary truce. In May 2019 the truce broke down and the artillery boomed back to life. Tariff rates were raised, telecoms giant Huawei—a much bigger fish than ZTE—faced sanctions, and Trump threatened that was just the beginning.

China had long accused the United States of a Cold War mentality aimed at blocking its rise. As successive presidents held the door to the global economy open for them, those accusations rang hollow. Under Trump, for the first time, they had the ring of truth.

Tariffs imposed through May 2019 were already significant enough to move the dial on China's immediate growth prospects. Tariffs at 25 percent on $250 billion in exports threatened to knock a percentage point off 2019

5. Michael Wolf, *Fire and Fury: Inside the Trump White House* (New York: Henry Holt, 2018).

GDP growth What concerned China's policymakers more was the direction of travel. Trump warned that tariffs could be levied on the entirety of China's $505 billion in exports to the United States. Tariffs at that level would reduce growth by 1.5 percentage point taking the expansion of GDP for 2019 down from an already lackluster forecast of 6.2 percent to a disastrous 4.7 percent.

Lower exports would be a direct blow to demand (though the impact would be partially diffused among Japan, Korea, Taiwan, and other suppliers of components snapped together in China's electronics assembly shops). With exports weaker, there would be less incentive to expand manufacturing capacity, so investment would fall. Higher costs for imported goods—the result of reciprocal tariffs imposed on US imports—would dent household's spending power. As the same dynamic played out in the United States, growth there would slow and demand fall, triggering a second-round impact on China's exports. Plunging equity markets could compound the blow, denting business and household confidence.

The new barriers Trump threw in the path of technology transfer were a serious risk to China's long-term development. From that first nuclear test back in 1964 China relied on overseas technology to accelerate its development. Khrushchev's decision to pull support almost stopped the program in its tracks. Fast-forward to the Trump presidency, and sanctions on ZTE and Huawei highlighted China's continued vulnerability. The two firms might not have been the absolute pinnacle of China's technological achievements. But as telecom equipment producers that beat back US and European rivals for global market share, they weren't far off. US sanctions, if fully implemented, would have pushed ZTE into bankruptcy, and placed Huawei in a precarious position. There was simply no Chinese capacity to produce the advanced US semiconductors that were essential inputs into their products. The threat of sanctions was a reminder that for all its impressive progress and overvaulting ambitions, China wasn't ready to go it alone.

There would, of course, be a cost to the United States for slamming the door. US firms that sold high-tech products to China—like chip-producer Qualcomm, which counted ZTE among its customers—would lose revenue. US firms that produced in China, such as Apple, could find themselves with missing links in their supply chain. US universities that counted on revenue from Chinese students—there were 340,000 Chinese students in the United States in 2018—would lose out on lucrative fees. Perhaps that's why the United States hesitated on the brink of across-the-board tariffs. At the same time, with the United States now viewing the China relationship through the lens of geopolitical rivalry, and technology one of the main battlefields, many feared the fall of an economic iron curtain dividing the world's two great powers.[6]

Other countries moved in the same direction. In the United Kingdom, successive governments cited a tradition of openness as justification for a relaxed attitude to Chinese investments. Huawei provided the pipes for parts of the telecom network. China General Nuclear Power—a state-owned enterprise—got the green light for investment in a nuclear power plant. But in 2018 the United Kingdom joined the United States in sanctioning ZTE as a risk to national security and considered removing Huawei equipment from its telecom network. Australia, Canada, and New Zealand—which together with the United States and United Kingdom make up the "five eyes" intelligence-sharing alliance—all moved in the same direction.

Perhaps there's no need for China's industrial planners to be overly concerned. The relationship between China and other major powers is like that captured in game theory's "stag hunt." The hounds—United States, Japan, Germany, and other major economies—can capture the stag (China), but only if they work together and don't get distracted. Unfortunately for foreign countries and corporations, each is easily distracted by the individual gains China dangles. As a result, cooperation breaks down and China wins. The lesson of the last few decades is that China is a very skillful stag, and other major economies are comically maladroit hounds. A German car company doesn't want to share its technology with a Chinese joint venture partner? No problem—we'll see if a Japanese car company would like more market access, providing of course they are willing to disclose

---

6. Hank Paulson, "Remarks by Henry M. Paulson Jr. on the United States and China at a Crossroads," Paulson Institute, November 6, 2018.

what's under the hood. France's president wants to raise human rights issues? Very well; the next leaders' trip to Europe will skip Paris and bring
deals to Berlin and London instead.

The bigger point is that China—for all its dysfunctions—can, when
it needs to, move with unity of purpose. Market access, big orders from
Chinese firms, regulatory approvals, and CEO invitations to an audience
with the premier can all be turned off or on to achieve a desired end. For
the West, that is not the case. Competition between nations means the
United States, Japan, Korea, Germany, and other major economies find
it hard to coordinate their actions. Competition between corporations
is even more cutthroat, making cooperative outcomes even harder to
achieve.

"Donald might not be Nixon in China," said Roger Ailes, the founder
of Fox News and (before his death in 2017) confidant of the president,
suggesting that Trump might not have the same transformative global vision as his predecessor.[7] Perhaps, but a destructive vision can be equally
powerful. For a China poised for growth at the end of the Mao era, Nixon's
visit came at exactly the right time. For a China struggling with debt in the
middle of the Xi era, Trump's darker view of China's rise may have come
at exactly the wrong one.

7. Wolf, *Fire and Fury*.

This Time Is Different?

"There is a particular pattern by which a crisis developed," wrote Liu He, chief economic advisor to President Xi Jinping. At first sight, "it seems that a crisis . . . is full of surprises caused by low-probability events and luck . . . but actually this is not true." With a team plucked from the People's Bank of China, China Banking Regulatory Commission, and Development Research Center of the State Council—the elite of China's financial policymakers—Liu delved into the history of the Great Depression of the 1930s and the great financial crisis of 2008, aiming to discover the underlying patterns at work. "The primary purpose of the study," he wrote, "is to predict what changes may happen in the future by understanding past events."[1]

Liu wasn't the first to examine past financial crises for clues on how to avoid a repeat. The classic theoretical treatment of the boom–bust dynamic inherent in financial capitalism comes from US economist Hyman Minsky in his book *Stabilizing an Unstable Economy*. "Stability leads to instability," Minsky wrote. "The more stable things become and the longer things are stable, the more unstable they will be when the crisis hits." In *Manias, Panics, and Crashes: A History of Financial Crises*, economic historians Charles Kindleberger and Robert Aliber populated Minsky's abstractions with a lively relation of the details of crashes from the South Sea Bubble to

---

1. Liu He, *Overcoming the Great Recession: Lessons from China*, John F. Kennedy School of Government, Harvard University, July 2014.

the Bernie Madoff Ponzi scheme. "Historians view each event as unique," they wrote. "In contrast economists search for the patterns in the data, and the systematic relationships between an event and its antecedents."

It starts with a genuine innovation. In 1720 the South Sea Bubble—one of the first examples of a speculative frenzy gripping the British market—was inflated with prospects of high profits from trade with richly endowed colonies in the New World.[2] In the 1840s, railways raised the prospect of drastically reducing transport times, prompting an investment frenzy. In the twentieth century, automobiles and electrification were the catalyst for America's Roaring Twenties. In the 1990s the Internet revolution promised to radically reduce communication costs. For those that move early and with determination, control of those technologies holds out the promise of massive profits.

In China there have been multiple mini-bubbles that started with hopes for game-changing innovation and ended in disaster for investors. Everything from hopes of a "reform dividend" boosting corporate profits, to a caterpillar fungus with aphrodisiac properties, has triggered investment manias. The larger picture, however, is that China itself is the innovation. A developmental state that combines cheap domestic labor with advanced foreign technology drove thirty years of 10 percent annual growth. A 457-billion-yuan economy in 1980 had by 2018 become an 88.7-trillion-yuan economy. Everyone wanted a piece of the action.

Hoping to seize the opportunity, businesses borrow money to invest. There's a powerful pro-cyclical dynamic at work. An influx of funds pays for an initial wave of capital spending. With higher investment providing a boost, growth accelerates, profits rise, asset prices inflate, and confidence in the value of the innovation that initiated the boom is reinforced. John Maynard Keynes, the father of modern economics, spoke of "animal spirits"—that indefinable feeling of confidence that propels business and investment decisions. With animal spirits quickening, entrepreneurs

2. James Narron and David Skeie, *The South Sea Bubble of 1720: Repackaging Debt and the Current Reach for Yield* (New York: Federal Reserve Bank of New York, 2013).

become more eager to borrow, and banks and investors more willing to provide funds.

In 1846, at the height of Britain's railway mania, proposed routes totaled ninety-five hundred miles—enough to stretch from the tip of Scotland to the toe of Cornwall eleven times over. Stock markets, at that time a recent innovation, provided the funds to pay for construction. As more investors piled in, stock prices rose, reinforcing belief in the value of the railway companies' plans.[3] In the United States, ahead of the 2007 real estate meltdown, extending credit to low-quality borrowers pushed demand for property higher. Prices rose, collateral seemed adequate, and profits healthy. Even the experts were lulled into a false sense of security. "We've never had a decline in housing prices on a nationwide basis," said Ben Bernanke.

In China, the 2015 equity bubble provides an example of credit extending the boom. As the Shanghai market rose, investors borrowed funds to buy more stocks. Speculation with borrowed funds rose from 400 billion yuan in mid-2014 to 2.1 trillion yuan in mid-2015. As credit poured in, stocks rose higher, conviction that rising markets reflected economic success was reinforced, and the incentive to invest was redoubled. The same dynamic has played out, over a longer period of time and with less extreme ups and downs, in real estate. Credit-boosted demand meant that house prices—and profits for real estate developers—spiraled higher, reinforcing the incentive to invest.

As excitement mounts and asset prices rise, the focus for investors flips from expectations of future profits to expectations of capital gains. Put another way, the basis for the investment decision shifts from "Will the asset I am investing in generate high returns?" to "Will I be able to find someone to buy this asset from me at a higher price?" At the start of 1720, shares in the South Sea Company traded at £128. By June they had risen to £1,100. In the dot.com bubble, the Nasdaq gained 255 percent from 1998 to 2000. The common refrain from the market bulls, and the title of Carmen Reinhart and Kenneth Rogoff's classic treatment of financial crises: "this

3. James Narron and Don Morgan, *Railway Mania, the Hungry Forties, and the Commercial Crisis of 1847* (New York: Federal Reserve Bank of New York, 2013).

time is different." Sure, past booms have been followed by an inevitable bust. This time, the innovation is genuine, the price gains sustainable, and wise investors set to enjoy outsized returns.

In China, evidence of investors speculating on capital gains rather than calculating on increased profits is not hard to find. From July 2014 to July 2015 the Shanghai Composite Index rose more than 150 percent. Over only a slightly longer period of time, the price of property in Shenzhen rose from 22,900 yuan to 60,700 yuan per square meter—close to tripling. The vast herd of tech unicorns (startups with a valuation of more than a billion dollars) frolicking around Shenzhen points to a venture capital bubble. Investors are not buying a share of future profits; they are chasing expectations of outsize speculative gains.

Information asymmetries allow valuations to run further out of line with fundamentals. The gap between the knowledge of wily insiders and gullible outsiders can be wide. In 1825 Scottish adventurer Gregor MacGregor was able to float a bond on the London market on the promise of outsize profits from investment in Poyais, a Central American principality. The only catch was that —outside of MacGregor's outsize imagination—Poyais didn't exist.[4] In the great financial crisis, complex derivative products enabled investment banks to shift risks off their own balance sheets onto those of their unsuspecting customers. "The whole building is about to collapse anytime now," bragged Goldman trader Fabrice Tourre, and "the only potential survivor, the fabulous Fab."[5]

In China, information asymmetries are not an unfortunate bug in an otherwise transparent system, they are a pervasive feature. "They have no idea what they're buying," said one of the financial engineers behind the 29-trillion-yuan wealth management product market, referring to retail investors ignorant of the risks they were taking on. The quality of assets on banks' 27-trillion-yuan shadow loan book is invisible to everybody but the

4. Don Morgan and James Narron, *The Panic of 1825 and the Most Fantastic Financial Swindle of All Time* (New York: Federal Reserve Bank of New York, 2013).

5. Matt Wirz, "Goldman Mortgage Trader Convicted of Fraud Pursuing New Career in Academia," *Wall Street Journal*, July 2, 2018.

banks. In the equity market, insiders have access not just to confidential company information but also to government data and policy decisions before they are announced. "I can get any document I want," bragged one equity strategist at a leading Chinese bank.

Moral hazard—belief by investors that a deep-pocketed government will prevent defaults—extends the boom. Ahead of the great financial crisis, Fannie Mae and Freddie Mac, the giant financing companies that were the final buyers of subprime mortgages, were seen as too official to fail. Lehman Brothers—with its $639 billion in assets—was too big to fail. Since the market-friendly chairmanship of Alan Greenspan, the Federal Reserve had a reputation for riding to the rescue in periods of turbulence. The erroneous belief in those multiple no-fail guarantees drove speculative imbalances past the point of no return.

In China the problem of moral hazard is even more entrenched. State ownership of the banks and borrowers fosters the belief that default is a distant prospect. Even in parts of the economy that operate more on market principles, China's stability-focused policymakers frequently intervene to put a floor under losses. The "national team" of state-backed investors buys into the stock market to prevent sharp drops. The central bank intervenes in the currency market to steady the yuan. At the economy-wide level, the government's commitment to its annual growth target acts like a giant put option—assuring investors that if things get really bad, stimulus support won't be long in arriving.

As valuations become increasingly stretched, financial distress sets in. Signs that borrowers are unable to service their debts make sellers more anxious and buyers less eager. Finally, the failure of a few highly leveraged borrowers triggers a rush for the exit. In Germany, they have a word for it: *Torschlusspanik*, or the rush to get to the door before it shuts.[6] In 1873, the US railway bubble ended when Jay Cooke & Co., one of the major banks financing construction, suspended deposit withdrawals, which triggered a panicked run on any banks linked to railway finance. In September 2008

6. Robert Aliber and Charles Kindleberger, *Manias, Panics, and Crashes: A History of Financial Crises* (New York: Palgrave Macmillan, 2011).

Lehman Brothers' announcement of a $3.9 billion loss was the trigger for a pullback of lenders, making it impossible for the investment bank to roll over its borrowing.

China has never experienced an economy-wide door-shut panic. It has experienced it in particular markets. In June 2013, as rumors of default by a major bank swirled, all the lenders disappeared from the money market. In July 2015 the door slammed in the equity market. As leveraged bets unwound and share prices plummeted, there were no buyers to be found. In 2018, the trillion-yuan peer-to-peer lending market imploded. There was a flood of investors attempting to exit, but no new funds coming in.

The pro-cyclicality of credit works on the way down as well as the way up. In the financial markets, as asset prices fall, speculators who had borrowed to fund their investments face margin calls, forcing them to liquidate their positions. With the number of sellers increasing, asset prices fall further. In the real economy, lenders pull back and credit conditions tighten. That results in weaker demand, pushing businesses from profit to loss and turning households from confident to cautious. Seeing the deterioration in economic conditions they anticipated, lenders double down on caution and the supply of credit shrinks again.

In the Great Depression, the stock market crash triggered a run on the banks. As the financial system imploded, businesses and farmers dependent on credit went belly-up, defaulting on their loans. Deteriorating conditions triggered a further contraction in lending. Locked in a deathly embrace, the real economy and financial system spiraled down. Unemployment in early 1933 hit 25 percent. Eleven thousand of America's twenty-five thousand banks went under.

In China, the closest equivalent was the pullback of banks from the rustbelt northeast in 2015 and 2016—a dearth of credit compounding the problems of debt-burdened industrial firms and exacerbating the downturn. Premier Li Keqiang was alive to the dangers. "There's a saying that investors shouldn't go to the northeast," he said. "We can't let that become the reality."

If crises have a certain regular pattern, unchanged from the South Sea Bubble in 1720 to the great financial crisis in 2008, they also have important differences. The modern banking system, with its unlimited ability to create credit, is a different beast from the gold-hobbled lenders of the seventeenth and eighteenth centuries. A United States where the Federal Reserve can act as lender of last resort—preventing the failure of systemically important firms—is different from the United States of the nineteenth and early twentieth centuries, before the Federal Reserve existed or had realized the extent of its powers. A crisis in the United States, which can fund borrowing in its own currency, is different from a crisis in a Latin American or Asian country, where foreign funds exit at the first sign of trouble.

To gauge China's position in the cycle of leverage and deleverage, and the magnitude of the risks it faces, it's useful to place it in the context of recent crises with which it shares common features. Japan's yen appreciation, real estate boom and bust, and prolonged battle with deflation have more than a passing similarity to China's experience. South Korea's crony–capitalist ties between banks and corporations mirror the incestuous links between banks and businesses in China's state-owned family.

LESSONS FROM A LOST DECADE: JAPAN'S BUBBLE ECONOMY

December 1989 was the peak for Japan. On December 29 the Nikkei 225 stock index hit 38,915. Investors valued Japanese firms four times higher than their US peers. Stockbrokers feasted on foie gras sprinkled with gold leaf. Golf club memberships changed hands for tens of millions of yen. The land surrounding the Imperial Palace in Tokyo was said to be worth more than all the real estate in the state of California.

It was policymakers that spoiled the party. The Bank of Japan was concerned about the "dry wood" of rising asset prices—tinder for inflation—created by loose money supply. Public anger at the property bubble, which made millionaires out of lucky landowners but took the dream of home ownership out of reach for everyone else, prodded the government into action. Both groups were betting they could take the air out of the bubble without denting Japan's development trajectory. They were wrong.[7]

On December 25 Yasushi Mieno, the Bank of Japan's hawkish new governor, proved to be more Grinch than St. Nicholas when he jacked interest rates from 3.75 percent up to 4.25 percent. Two more rate hikes in March and August would take them to 6 percent. New property controls required bank loans to real estate to expand no more quickly than total credit. Given that real estate loans were growing about 15 percent a year and manufacturing loans were not growing at all, that was a significant new constraint. The legislative diet passed a land tax. Implementation wouldn't come until 1992, but combined with higher borrowing costs and lower loan growth, the expectation of higher taxes was enough to spoil the party.

Markets went into freefall. The Nikkei hit its low point for the year at the start of October, touching 20,221, down close to 50 percent and with trillions of yen in wealth evaporated. In the years ahead it would continue its fall, ending in October 1998 down 67 percent from its 1989 peak. Land prices fell more gradually, but in the end fell further, with a 72 percent decline from peak to trough. In the unlikely event that the Imperial Palace found itself on the auctioneer's block, the emperor would find himself reduced from California to merely Ohio real estate asking price.

With policymakers making a deliberate pre-emptive move to prick the bubble before it burst, and no immediate signs of a downturn in growth, the stimulus was slow to arrive. In 1991 contagion from plunging markets to the real economy swung the Bank of Japan back into easing mode. By then, it was too late. Japan's economic miracle was over. Its lost decade had begun.

Like all bubbles, Japan's had a basis in fundamentals. The era of supercharged industrialization, which saw annual growth above 10 percent

---

7. Shigenori Shiratsuka, *Asset Price Bubble in Japan in the 1980s: Lessons for Financial and Macroeconomic Stability* (Tokyo: Bank of Japan, 2003).

in the 1960s, was over. But the economy continued to clock enviable growth rates, averaging 4.5 percent a year in the 1980s. The industrial planners at the Ministry of Economy, Trade and Industry remained sure-footed in their development strategy, directing the assault of Japan's corporates on the few remaining bastions of US competitive advantage. A novel based on their exploits, enticingly titled *Summer of the Bureaucrats*, was popular enough to be made into a TV drama.[8]

The Sony Walkman, Toyota cars, Panasonic videos, Seiko watches, Casio calculators, and Nikon cameras were demolishing their rivals. Fueled by their success, Japan Inc.'s share of global exports rose from 6.7 percent at the start of the decade to a peak of 9.5 percent in 1987—quite an achievement for a country home to only 2.5 percent of the world's population. Japanese corporates went on a buying spree, snapping up iconic assets like New York's Rockefeller Center and Hollywood's Columbia Pictures. A 1980 broadcast by NBC captured the hand-wringing mood of corporate America: "If Japan Can . . . Why Can't We?" In politics, the view among Japan's elite was that the United States was in a tailspin of debt dependence and decline. Japan was preparing for a future G-2, a world in which the United States would provide the security muscle and the innovation flair, Japan the manufacturing backbone.[9]

Such was the worldview that informed the thinking of investors in Japan's markets, and such was the environment in which the bubble was inflated. Five factors tipped a rational response to positive fundamentals into the irrational exuberance of a bubble economy.

Massive yen appreciation dealt a blow to the competitiveness of Japan's exports. With protectionist legislation rumbling through Congress, in 1985 US Treasury secretary James Baker summoned his counterparts from Japan, West Germany, France, and the United Kingdom to a meeting in New York's Plaza Hotel. In

---

8. Chalmers Johnson, *MITI and the Japanese Economic Miracle* (Palo Alto, CA: Stanford University Press, 1982).

9. Andrew Gordon, *A History of Modern Japan* (New York: Oxford University Press, 2013).

what became known as the Plaza Accord, the five agreed to
coordinated action to weaken the dollar. For Japan, the effect
was immediate, lasting, and disastrous. The yen strengthened
from 242 to the dollar in September 1985 to 121 in January 1998,
doubling in value. Exports, the main engine of Japan's growth,
swung from 21 percent annual growth in late 1984 to 21 percent
contraction in summer 1986.

The Bank of Japan cut rates, taking them from 5 percent when
the Plaza Accord was signed to 2.5 percent in 1987. That too
was a concession to the United States, which demanded not
only a stronger yen but also a stronger Japanese economy to
boost demand for US products. The hope was that cheaper
funds would drive a wave of productive investment. The
reality was that credit growth accelerated, but with Japan Inc.
already lumbered with excess capacity, investment went mainly
into unproductive assets. Real estate speculation boomed;
manufacturing investment slumped. Outstanding loans to
corporates and households rose from 143 percent of GDP at the
start of the decade all the way up to 210 percent of GDP in 1990.

The banking sector was deregulated but not reformed—a problem
that would resurface in Korea's crisis a decade later, and in China
after the great financial crisis. With the rise of the corporate
bond market in the 1980s, banks lost their most creditworthy
customers. They turned to new lines of business: mortgage
lending to households and loans to small businesses. Lack
of experience in screening credit risks meant an explosion
in collateral-based lending. In real estate, the result was a
vicious circle of rising credit, high land prices, higher values
for collateral, and further increases in lending—the classic
destabilizing credit cycle that Minsky warned of.

The banking system remained governed by an antiquated set of
regulatory and ownership arrangements. The "convoy system"
meant that all banks were under the guidance of the Ministry
of Finance, which directed lending toward national priorities

in return for protection against the consequences of bad loans. Oversight was tight at the top, but progressively laxer for small banks and shadow banks, which found loopholes to work around the rules. Major banks like Sumitomo and Mitsubishi were the center of a "financial *keiretsu*," with cross-holdings of stocks and lending between a main bank and firms in other industries. In the good times, those close relations helped smooth out the bumps in the business cycle. In the bad times, they encouraged banks to keep zombie firms alive for too long.[10]

Japan didn't have as much development space as it thought. By 1989, Japan's households were about 80 percent as well off as those in the United States—an indication that the world's second-largest economy had all but closed the gap with the first. The main drivers of growth were close to used up. An urbanization rate of 77 percent meant property construction was no longer a powerful engine of demand. Japan's corporates were dominating electronics and making major inroads into autos, touching the outer limits of the technology frontier and grabbing a politically troubling share of global markets. Scope to grow by producing ever more advanced goods for export was depleted. With debt high and investment running at about a third of GDP, ramping up lending to pay for a wave of capital spending didn't look like an attractive option.

The bubble burst in slow motion. In the years following the market crash, policymakers did enough to stave off a financial system meltdown and outright recession, but not enough to put the economy on the path to recovery. Two parallel—and unhelpful—dynamics were at work.

First, continued belief in the no-bank-failure guarantee of the Ministry of Finance's convoy system, close relations between bank lenders and

10. Etsuro Shioji, "The Bubble Bust and Stagnation of Japan," in *The Routledge Handbook of Major Events in Economic History*, edited by Randall Parker and Robert Whaples (New York: Routledge, 2013).

corporate borrowers, and accounting rules that permitted the banks to exaggerate their capital buffer and conceal their losses all allowed the wounded banking system to limp on. The day of reckoning on bad loans was delayed, at a cost to the vitality of the economy. Banks were locked into unproductive lending to zombie firms with little hope of a return to profitability.

Second, with land and equity prices collapsing, even viable firms found themselves technically insolvent, saddled with liabilities worth more than assets. The result was what Nomura Research Institute economist Richard Koo called a "balance sheet recession."[11] As a result, instead of investing in new machinery or workers, businesses used any profits they had to pay down their debt. That might have made sense for individual firms, but with everyone doing it at the same time, the result was a disaster, triggering a downward spiral of inadequate demand, falling prices, shrinking profits and wages, and further erosion of demand.

The obvious solution proved impossible to deliver. Regulators should have waded into the markets, separating the viable banks from the failures, recapitalizing the former and pushing the latter into restructuring or bankruptcy. That was easy in principle, but difficult in practice. Public hostility to a bank bailout—seen as slush funds for a corrupt nexus of politicians and financiers—was high. There was no legal framework for managing a bank bankruptcy. In an interconnected financial system, ring-fencing healthy banks as others failed might be impossible to do. Growth had slowed, but unemployment below 4 percent in the mid-1990s remained inside the comfort zone—meaning there was little sense of urgency to deal with the problems.

It wasn't until 1997 that the failure of Sanyo Securities, a mid-size brokerage, triggered a renewed crisis and a decisive response from policymakers. By that time the damage had been done. GDP growth, which had averaged 4.5 percent in the 1980s, fell to 1.6 percent in the 1990s. Japan ended the decade in contraction. Unemployment had ended

---

11. Richard Koo, *The Holy Grail of Macroeconomics: Lessons from Japan's Great Recession* (New York: Wiley, 2009).

the 1980s at 2.3 percent. It ended the 1990s at 4.7 percent and still climbing. Even that low number reflected Japan's unique labor market institutions, with workers accepting flat or falling wages as an alternative to unemployment. With banks locked into lending to zombie firms, and viable firms focused on debt repayment rather than expansionary borrowing, rate cuts by the Bank of Japan were unable to kick-start growth. That left the job of boosting demand to the Ministry of Finance. Government debt, a modest 67 percent of GDP in 1990, climbed to 132 percent in 1999.

Political stability crumbled. From the collapse of the bubble in 1989 to the beginnings of a turnaround under Prime Minister Junichiro Koizumi in 2001, Japan had eight different prime ministers—two of them in office for less than a year. After more than three decades in power, the Liberal Democratic Party was ousted by a series of unstable coalitions headed by breakaway members of their own party. Worst of all, Japan lost its leadership position in Asia. In 1989, Japan's economy was six times larger than China's. By 2010, as a lost decade segued into a lost generation, China had taken the lead. Japan, the country that had once dominated Asia militarily, then through its economic might and technological prowess, now watched in agonized and self-inflicted stagnation as China usurped its role as regional hegemon.

The parallels between Japan's bubble economy and lost decade, and China in the post–financial crisis period, are striking. That's not a surprise. China consciously followed Japan's development model, paving its path to prosperity with a combination of industrial planning, state-directed credit, and an undervalued currency. As a result, China suffered from many of the same distortions. Mercantilist policies aimed at grabbing export market share, stoking protectionist sentiment in the United States: check. Wasteful public investment resulting in a landscape littered with roads to nowhere: check. Government direction of the banks resulting in massive misallocation of credit: check. Pervasive moral hazard, behind-the-scenes deals to stave off bankruptcies, and an industrial landscape stalked by zombie firms: check, check, and check.

Even Western concern about China's rise echoes that about the land of the rising sun three decades earlier. Books like *When China Rules the*

World by British scholar Martin Jacques, the evocatively titled *Becoming China's Bitch* by US author Peter Kiernan, or the ominous-sounding *The Coming China Wars* by Peter Navarro, the US academic who went on to serve as economic advisor to President Donald Trump—all channeled fears about the rise of the red star over China. Consciously or not, they were tapping the same sentiment that motivated books like Ezra Vogel's *Japan as Number One*, published in 1979. In China itself, hubris about the middle kingdom's manifest destiny also mirrored that of Japan's elites in the 1980s. Xi Jinping's call for a "new model of great power relations" was an echo of Japan's aspiration for a G-2 relationship with the United States.

China's equivalent of the Plaza Accord came in July 2005, when—under pressure from the United States—the People's Bank of China began the process of yuan appreciation. Learning the lesson from Japan's disastrous experience, China constrained its currency to strengthen at a much more moderate pace. From 1985 to 1988, the yen doubled in value against the dollar. From 2005 to 2008, the yuan gained a comparatively modest 20 percent—a blow to export competitiveness, but not the hammer blow suffered by Japan's firms. In the end, yuan appreciation wasn't needed to crush exports. The great financial crisis came alone and did the job.

When exports crunched down, contracting 16 percent in 2009, China, like Japan, turned to a massive monetary stimulus. Indeed, China's stimulus was significantly larger. From 1985 to 1989, Japan's private-sector credit-to-GDP ratio rose 42 percentage points. From 2008 to 2017, China's rose 96 percentage points. In China, like Japan, that resulted in distortions in two directions: overinvestment in industry and bubbles in stocks and real estate. Overinvestment left China's firms, like Japan's firms before them, burdened with excess capacity, falling prices, weak profits, and trouble servicing their debt. The situations are so similar that the models economists use to track zombie firms in China are borrowed from earlier analysis of Japan.

China's stock bubble burst in 2015, an event that had less serious consequences than Japan's implosion because of the smaller role the stock market plays in China's financial system. The real estate bubble continues to expand. The land around the Forbidden City—the closest thing China has to an Imperial Palace—isn't worth quite as much as all the real estate in California, but property is still plenty expensive. Shanghai, Shenzhen, and Beijing all rank among the most expensive ten cities in the world to buy a home.

There are also important differences. Back in 1989, Japan's GDP per capita was already closing in on that of the United States. Space for catching up with the global leader was all but used up. In 2018 China's GDP per capita was just 29 percent of that in the United States. It should have decades of rapid growth still to come as it closes the gap. Back in 1989, Japan was 77 percent urbanized. In China in 2017, that number was just 58 percent. Real estate won't return to its role as all-conquering growth driver, but neither is construction about to grind to a halt. Japan, with its 120 million population, has a big domestic market. China, with its 1.3 billion population, has a vast domestic market, making it more straightforward to transition away from exports as a source of demand, and easier for firms to achieve world-beating economies of scale.

On the policy response, too, the approach of Beijing has been different—and better—from that taken by Tokyo. In Japan in 1990, the year after the bubble collapsed, the Ministry of Finance ran a small fiscal surplus, adding to the problem by acting as a drag on growth. It was only in 1998, with the financial system melting down and the Asian financial crisis in full swing, that they ran an aggressive stimulus, with the fiscal deficit touching 10 percent of GDP. Even that was steadily managed down in the years that followed. Zombie firms were kept on life support, draining vitality from the system. In China, by contrast, the combination of demand-boosting fiscal stimulus and zombie-slaying supply-side reform gave the economy a shot at growing through its problems.

China didn't just learn the lessons from Japan's success on the way up; it also learned the lessons from Japan's missteps on the way down. The result: Japan suffered a lost decade that segued into a lost generation; China, so far, has not.

DE-CONTROL WITHOUT DE-PROTECTION: SOUTH
KOREA AND THE PERILS OF FINANCIAL LIBERALIZATION

For Korea, the Asian financial crisis was slow to arrive. Throughout the summer of 1997 and into the fall, it seemed the speculative attacks that laid low first Thailand, then Indonesia, Malaysia, and the Philippines, would be a problem confined to Southeast Asia. Thailand's real estate bubble—with demand for office space in capital Bangkok running at less than half of construction—might be ready for a correction. In Indonesia, President Suharto's crony–capitalist regime, including among other things a monopoly on clove distribution for his son, hid a multitude of financial sins. But Korea was the poster child for development. Following in the footsteps of Japan, the population had been lifted from poverty in the wake of the Korean War to GDP per capita of $13,100—more than two-fifths of the level in the United States—in 1996.

A swath of indicators pointed to responsible economic policy and strong growth prospects. The government had been living within its means, running year after year of budget surplus. The Bank of Korea had kept a lid on inflation. Exports were notching double-digit growth and expected to continue to do so. In a report that was quietly shelved after the crisis broke, the IMF opined that "the situation in Korea is quite different to that in Southeast Asia, and our assessment is that the weaknesses in the financial sector are manageable if dealt with promptly."[12]

Korea's fundamentals, it turned out, were not as rock-solid as they appeared. The problem, according to Joon-Ho Hahm, who helped direct Korea's response to the crisis before going on to serve on the Monetary Policy Board of the central bank, was an explosive combination of "de-control without de-protection."[13] The government had liberalized the financial sector, but it had not put in place the regulations necessary for a

---

12. Paul Blustein, *The Chastening: Inside the Crisis That Rocked the Global Financial System and Humbled the IMF* (New York: PublicAffairs, 2003).

13. Wonhyuk Lim and Joon-Ho Hahm, *Turning a Crisis into an Opportunity: The Political Economy of Korea's Financial Sector Reform* (Washington, DC: Brookings Institution, 2006).

market-based system to thrive, or shaken investors' belief in the implicit no-default guarantee enjoyed by the giant conglomerates—known as *chaebols*—that dominated the corporate landscape.

The consequence: *chaebols* were able to take on mind-boggling levels of leverage, with little oversight from lenders. For some of the largest, debt-to-equity ratios of 500 percent meant the slightest decline in their debt-servicing ability would push them into bankruptcy.[14] As Paul Blustein, a journalist who chronicled the Asian financial crisis, notes, three factors made the high debt levels especially problematic:

> Financial deregulation led to a mushrooming of shadow banks, often the captive financing arms of major *chaebols*. Continued belief in the blanket no-default guarantee meant they were able to offer savers higher rates than mainstream banks, rapidly expanding their market share.
>
> Funds were used for empire building and vanity projects that contributed little to the *chaebols'* bottom line. SsangYong Group and Samsung piled into autos, a market already dominated by Hyundai, Daewoo, and Kia. The Halla Group invested in a world-class shipyard, apparently motivated by sibling rivalry between its owner and his older brother, the owner of Hyundai.
>
> Reliance on short-term foreign funding was high. From 1994 to 1996, Korea's debts to the rest of the world rose by more than $45 billion.[15]

Put the pieces together and the result was a financial system stuffed with nonperforming loans, and reliant on the rollover of short-term foreign finance to stay afloat. According to Hahm's estimate, bad loans added up to 28 percent of GDP in 1998. It was a system set for collapse. When the

---

14. Chan-Hyun Sohn, *Korea's Corporate Restructuring since the Financial Crisis* (Seoul: Korea Institute for International Economic Policy, 2002).

15. Blustein, *The Chastening*.

Asian financial crisis triggered a reappraisal of risks across the region, that's exactly what it did.

The crisis played out in two stages. In the first, with Asian economies toppling like dominos, foreign investors started paying attention to Korean risks. When they did, borrowers that had looked rock-solid started to look shaky. Foreign reserves that had appeared ample started to appear inadequate. All at once, the foreign funds that had seemed like an inexhaustible flood slowed to a trickle, and then dried up completely. In November 1998, six months after speculators first started asking questions about the Thai baht, Korea called the IMF to ask for a loan.

For a country with a bitter history of colonization, and fiercely proud of its recent rise, it was a moment of shame. The headlines in the next day's newspapers told the story: "National Bankruptcy," said one; "Humiliating International Trusteeship," ran another. That's not too far off. Encamped at Seoul's Hilton Hotel, the IMF and US Treasury held out the promise of rescue, but only at a price. Korea got $55 billion to cover its foreign debts and fend off default. In return, it was forced to accept tough new policy settings, sweeping structural reforms, and market openings at a moment when a battered won guaranteed foreign buyers a bargain price.[16]

Short-term interest rates were raised to 25 percent from 12.5 percent—a move the IMF said was necessary to bring foreign funds back in. Necessary or not, elevated rates hammered the highly indebted *chaebols*, exacerbating the crisis. Caps on foreign ownership were removed, a measure demanded by the US Treasury. The principled argument was that greater competition in the financial sector was required to break the incestuous relations between local lenders and borrowers. This was true, but it certainly didn't hurt that US firms would be able to come in and snap up bargains.

Even worse, the rescue package didn't work. After a respite of a few days, the second stage of the crisis began. Funds resumed their exodus and the won resumed its plunge, dropping by the 10 percent limit for five consecutive days. The United States blamed Korean politics. With an election looming, all the candidates had signed off on the IMF rescue package.

16. Blustein, *The Chastening*.

Then Kim Dae-jung—a former pro-democracy dissident, then head of the pro-worker opposition party and the leading candidate—broke ranks, striking a populist chord with a promise to get better terms for Korea if he was elected.

Politics aside, the rescue package sums didn't add up. Korea's foreign-exchange reserves had depleted to $6 billion. In 1998 there was $116 billion in foreign debt falling due. There were also questions about the real size of the IMF's $55 billion package, with a $20 billion tranche pledged by the US Treasury seeming to flicker in and out of view. When leading Korean newspaper *Chosun Ilbo* published the debt and reserve numbers, apparently from a leaked IMF report, the game was up. Realizing that even after the rescue Korea still lacked funds to cover its debts, foreign investors resumed their exodus.[17]

Facing an imminent default by the world's eleventh largest economy, the IMF and US Treasury had no easy options. The outcome of the election—with a victory for Kim—helped tip policy makers toward attempting one last stand. The election result removed the overhang of political uncertainty. Despite outsider status, and his pre-election wobble, Kim signaled a willingness to implement tough pro-market reforms. On December 22, the Federal Reserve Bank of New York called in representatives of the six biggest banks to ask them to participate in a bail-in, rolling over their loans to Korea. Their response: why didn't you ask us sooner?[18]

A frenetic end to the year, with policymakers across the United States, Europe, and Japan working the phones to reach the biggest banks, brought the crisis to an end. For Korea, however, the pain was just beginning. Financial chaos on its own would already have dealt a severe blow to growth. Combined with higher interest rates and bone-crunching reforms imposed as conditions of their rescue, it plunged the economy into recession. In 1995 the economy had grown 9.6 percent. In 1998 it contracted 5.5 percent. Workers accustomed to a job for life faced wage cuts and—in many cases—redundancy. Unemployment rose from 2 percent in 1997 to

17. Blustein, *The Chastening.*
18. Blustein, *The Chastening.*

7 percent in 1998. The ultimate cost of the bailout rose to 160.4 trillion won, about 21 percent of 1997 GDP.

For China's leaders, the parallels were clear. China, like Korea, relied on exports as a major driver of demand—placing them in the row of Asian dominos that could be knocked over if one country faltered. China, like Korea, managed rapid industrialization through a nexus of closely controlled banks and corporates—a crony–capitalist system that accelerated development but allowed problems to build behind the scenes. China, like Korea, had banks stuffed with nonperforming loans, estimated at about a third of GDP in 1998.

Korea had plunged into recession, the government forced to go cap-in-hand to the IMF. US officials had dictated terms, forcing through a market opening in which Korea's prized corporate assets sold for a song. The political order had been shaken, with a former dissident pro-democracy protestor winning the presidency. None of that could be allowed to happen in China. The Korean experience was a catalyst for Premier Zhu Rongji's purge of the state-owned enterprises and reform of the big banks, ending with a massive write-off of bad loans and listing on Hong Kong's public markets. Korea's experience with foreign lenders pulling the plug was also a reason for China to go slow on capital account opening.

Two decades on, the Korea crisis remains a useful point of comparison for China. Beijing has taken tentative steps to solve the problem of moral hazard, including carefully managed defaults by small-scale borrowers. Despite that, the belief that the government stands behind the debts of major state-owned firms, and the investment products sold by state-owned banks, remains pervasive. The rise of China's shadow banking system mirrors the experience in Korea—liberalization of finance running ahead of necessary regulations or removal of the no-default guarantee. Bottom-up calculations, based on the share of loans to firms without enough earnings to cover their interest payments, put bad loans in mid-2016 at about 13 percent of GDP. That's not quite as high as Korea's 28 percent, or the 30 percent estimate for China back in 1998. Given the massively increased size of China's economy, the dollar amount is much larger: about as large, coincidentally, as Korea's GDP.

The differences are also important, and in the end may prove to be decisive. Korea was behind the curve in responding to its problems. China has been ahead of it. Korea's *chaebol* chiefs were allowed to run wild, investing in vanity projects that resulted in massive misallocation of capital. In China, wayward executives have been brought to heel, with some falling into the clutches of the corruption investigators. In Korea, growth in shadow banking ran unchecked until the crisis hit. In China, from 2016, the government moved aggressively against the shadow banks—bringing asset growth for the sector down to zero. Perhaps most important, China is a lender to the rest of the world, not a borrower from it. Learning from Korea's experience, China allows foreign funds to play only a limited role in the economy. "Big financial crocodiles"—as foreign speculators are known in China—might have been allowed to gobble up Seoul. They would not be able to so much as nibble Shanghai.

11

War-Gaming a China Crisis

China Dream, a novel by exiled storyteller Ma Jian, tells the story of Ma Daode, a local official with a plan to wipe out uncomfortable memories—his own and everyone else's—with a new, high-tech "China Dream device." Ma, whose name translates as "morality," finds his grip on reality slipping away. Land is needed for an industrial park to develop his dream-killing brain implant. To make way for construction, Ma oversees the destruction of the village where he stayed as a youth during the Cultural Revolution. The return to the home of his past rekindles memories of the suicide of his parents, following persecution that he instigated. His phone rings constantly as rival cadres, self-serving subordinates, and demanding mistresses jostle for attention. The action ends with Ma leaping from the balcony of his mistress's apartment. In his mind he's taking a great leap into a "glorious future." In reality, like a depressing number of Chinese officials, he's committing suicide. The China Dream device, needless to say, never gets off the drawing board.[1]

In Liu Cixin's science fiction fantasy *The Dark Forest*, the universe is a dangerous place where predators stalk and the best hope for planetary survival is to hide. When a Chinese scientist, thrown into despair by the extremities of the Cultural Revolution, sends out an intergalactic signal, the earth's location is discovered and a fleet of alien colonizers sets out to take possession. In a trilogy that spans the early days of the People's

1. Jian Ma, *China Dream* (Berkeley, CA: Counterpoint, 2019).

Republic of China to humanity's fight for survival hundreds of years in the future, Chinese scientists, detectives, and entrepreneurs are the leaders of the global resistance. Chinese, melded with English, is the lingua franca. When one of the characters goes into hibernation and awakes in the distant future for the final battle against the aliens, they find their bank account at Industrial and Commercial Bank of China still open, and—more wonderful still—with significant accumulated interest, an early vote of confidence in the long-term benefits of Liu He's deleveraging campaign.[2]

Which vision of China's future is correct? Is it Ma Jian's dystopian rhapsody in which a society is trapped by its failure to come to terms with its past, where officials spend more time in the brothel than planning the next stage of development, and technology is an instrument of control rather than a lever for growth? Or is it Liu Cixin's vision of a China that is effortlessly part of global political, economic, and technological leadership, its centuries-old banks making a mockery of the Cassandras of collapse? It's possible to make a powerful case for both. In the end, the latter is more likely to be true. First, let's take a look at the former.

At the start of 2019, according to calculations from the Bank for International Settlements, China's debt was equal to 259.4 percent of GDP. Calculations by Bloomberg Economics come in around the same level: 276.2 percent of GDP. Most calculations of China's debt focus on the borrower side, adding up loans to business, households, and government. Using an alternative approach that focuses on lenders, University of California San Diego professor Victor Shih gets to 328 percent of GDP in mid-2017.[3] A straight look at bank assets puts outstanding borrowing at 312 percent of GDP, suggesting that Shih's higher estimates are not out of the ballpark.

Even using the lower end of those estimates, debt at 259.4 percent of GDP presents China with two serious problems.

2. Cixin Liu, *Dark Forest* (New York: Tor Books, 2015).

3. Victor Shih, *Financial Instability in China: Possible Pathways and Their Likelihood*, (Berlin: Mercator Institute for China Studies, October 2017).

First, as figure 11.1 shows, China has advanced-economy debt levels but emerging-market income levels. Based on the same Bank for International Settlements metrics, in early-2019 the United States had debt at 249.3 percent of GDP, slightly lower than China. US GDP per capita, however, was $56,500, more than three times higher than China. Looking at major emerging-market economies, GDP per capita was closer to China's $17,000. Debt levels were markedly lower. In mid-2018 the average debt for Brazil, Russia, India, and South Africa—which together with China make up the emerging-market BRICS club—was 123.3 percent of GDP.

China's combination of advanced-economy debt levels and emerging-market income levels is a unique disadvantage. Along with exports, credit is the fuel that powers the development engine. Borrowing pays for upgrades to industry and to infrastructure. China's income level should mean it has years of catch-up growth ahead. By maxing out on debt at a middling level of development, China has made it more difficult to close the gap with high-income countries.

Second, the pace of debt accumulation rings an alarm bell on the risk of crisis. In the four years from 2004 to 2008, outstanding borrowing in China's economy was steady at about 150 percent of GDP. Buoyed by exports, the economy grew without increasing its dependence on

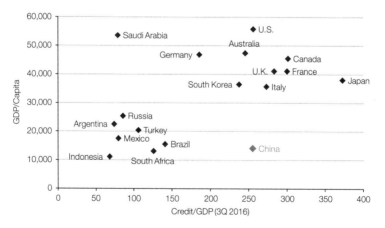

Figure 11.1 Debt to GDP and GDP per Capita for Major Economies
Created by the author using information from the Bank for International Settlements and the International Monetary Fund.

borrowed funds. In the decade from 2009 to 2018, debt rose to 254 percent of GDP, an increase of more than 100 percentage points. It's hard to find examples of other major economies that have taken on debt at a similar pace. It's easy to find examples of those that have taken on less, and still faced a crisis.

In the United States, outstanding borrowing rose to 229 percent of GDP in 2007, from 190 percent in 2001. That 39 percentage point increase came ahead of the biggest financial crisis since the Great Depression. In Greece, debt rose to 244 percent of GDP in 2010 from 171 percent in 2001—a 73 percentage point increase that anticipated the plunge of Greece, and the eurozone, into a rolling five-year crisis. Closer to home, in the eight years ahead of the Asian financial crisis, Korea's debt-to-GDP ratio rose only 44 percentage points. The International Monetary Fund (IMF) counted forty-three countries where the debt-to-GDP ratio had increased more than 30 percentage points over a five-year period. Among them, only five ended without a major growth slowdown or financial crisis. Narrowing the sample to look only at countries that started with debt above 100 percent of GDP, as China did, reveals that none escaped a crisis.[4]

The peculiar features of China's financial system add to the risks.

On the borrower side, the outsize role that state-owned enterprises like Dongbei Special play in the economy, and the implicit guarantee that government stands behind their debts, tilted credit allocation in their favor. The same was true of local government investment platforms, the off-balance-sheet vehicles city cadres use to raise funds for infrastructure spending. It is China's private-sector firms that show the highest return on assets: 9.5 percent in 2017. Based on the official data, the return on assets for state-sector firms was just 4 percent. Taking account of subsidies state firms receive in the form of cheap access to credit and land, even that overstates actual performance.[5] Local government investment vehicles,

4. Sally Chen and Joong Shik Kang., *Credit Booms—Is China Different?* (Washington, DC: International Monetary Fund, 2017).

5. Nicholas Lardy, *The State Strikes Back* (Washington, DC: Peterson Institute of International Economics, 2019).

many of which have no income except from selling their endowments of land, do even worse. By concentrating credit on the least efficient borrowers, China's banks added to the problems innate in a rapid rise in lending.

On the lender side, China's major banks moved closer to the market and made attempts to improve efficiency. At root, they were still state-owned and operated on a logic dictated as much by policy as by profit. In the early stages of development, directing lending to priority projects makes sense. It's easy to see that a road from the factory to the port would increase efficiency, obvious that a larger steel plant would generate economies of scale. At a later stage, when the economy is more complex and development depends on innovation rather than infrastructure, policy-directed lending is unlikely to do the job. Banks end up funding projects like Caofeidian, the failed port development in Hebei. Lending based on the orders of bureaucrats rather than the logic of the market, they are more likely to end up with an unsupportable stash of nonperforming loans.

Adding further to the risks is a creaking system of macro-economic controls. For much of the period in which debt was building, the central bank kept a tight rein on interest rates and the yuan. The price of money and the price of domestic versus foreign goods are key instruments for control of the economy. Set by the market, they drive efficient allocation of resources. Set by the government, they do not. In China's case, an artificially weak yuan encouraged businesses to focus on capital-intensive manufacturing for exports, not capital-light services for domestic consumption. Artificially low interest rates made it cheap to borrow, providing funds for projects that had little commercial rationale. Both contributed to the rapid increase, and inefficient allocation, of credit.

The rise of the shadow banks compounded the problems. Shadow lenders, with inadequate capital to absorb losses, an expensive and unstable funding base, and exposure to the riskiest borrowers, played a larger role in the financial system. Mainstream banks—especially joint stock and city commercial banks like the Bank of Tangshan—increased their reliance on short-term, high-cost funding and ratcheted up their exposure to opaque shadow loans. In summer 2019, the failure of Baoshang Bank—a small lender operating out of Inner Mongolia, showed the cracks starting to appear.

Evidence of stress is not hard to find. The incremental capital output ratio—a measure of how much capital spending is required to buy an additional unit of GDP growth—rose from 3.5 in 2007 to 6.5 in 2017, the highest level in the reform era.[6] The additional GDP generated by each new 100 yuan of credit fell to 32 yuan in 2018, down from 95 yuan in 2005. According to the Bank for International Settlements, close to 20 percent of GDP has to be used to service debt—higher than the United States on the eve of the great financial crisis. The picture that emerges is of a Chinese economy where an ever-increasing volume of debt-fueled investment is required to fuel an ever-decreasing volume of growth. The consequence is an unsupportable burden of repayment and a burgeoning stash of hidden bad loans.

In the past, China was able to outrun its problems. At the end of the 1990s, China's bad loans were close to a third of GDP—a seemingly insurmountable burden. After a decade of double-digit growth, the same bundle of bad loans was a forgotten footnote in the history of China's rise. The same trick will be difficult to pull off again.

At the end of the 1990s, China had a young and growing population. Zhu Rongji's root-and-branch reforms of the state sector retooled the economy for growth. Entry to the World Trade Organization opened the door to an untapped global market. The ratio of bad loans to total lending was high, but overall debt levels were low, making recapitalization of the banks relatively affordable. In 2018, all those factors were reversed. The working-age population was aging and shrinking. What looked like a far-reaching commitment to pro-market reform at the Third Plenum in 2013 petered out, with Xi Jinping calling for "bigger, better, stronger" state-owned enterprises. The world was no longer an untapped market. With China's biggest trade partner—the United States—swinging toward a protectionist stance, it looked like it might be tapped out. Recapitalizing

---

6. Yiping Huang, *2018 Jingshan Report*, (Beijing: China Finance 40 Forum, 2018).

the biggest banking system in the world would be neither cheap nor straightforward.

Attempts at innovation and entrepreneurial endeavor are ineffective within a controlling, state-dominated system. On innovation, a torrent of funding has created the sheeny veneer of success. Critics say the reality behind it is mediocrity and asset price inflation. Firms that succeed often benefit from massive government subsidies, protection from foreign competition, and what friends call technology transfer and rivals technology theft. By flooding target industries with investment, government planners don't generate the scale they need to succeed; they do generate a rush of new entrants and rampant overcapacity. The result—evident in China's robotics sector—is firms struggling just to stay afloat, cutthroat competition on price, and no one spending on research and development. "I think the future is bright," said one robotics entrepreneur, speaking in 2018. "I just hope we get there."[7]

For private firms, the story is equally uninspiring. After falling consistently throughout the reform era, the share of the state sector in industrial assets steadied in 2014 and then rose slightly. Supply-side-reform mastermind Liu He insists his program is not anti–private sector. The reality on the ground is that it's mainly private firms facing closure, and state firms enjoying expanded market share and higher profits. Since the start of the supply-side reform campaign, state investment has outpaced spending by the private sector—often by a wide margin. Superstar technology firms faced a Communist Party determined to prevent threats to social stability, even if it meant wading into their affairs and data. Foreign firms marking up the organization chart for their China venture found they had to include a place for a Communist Party committee.

Finally, if a crisis does occur, the lesson of the 2015 equity meltdown is that the government would be ill-equipped to respond. As the Shanghai Composite Index halved in value, wiping out trillions of yuan in wealth, policymakers tried repeatedly to arrest the decline.

7. Qian Wan and Tom Orlik, "Anti-Reagan Industrial Policy: The Subsidy Cycle," Bloomberg, August 8, 2018.

State-owned investment houses were instructed to put together a rescue fund. The state-owned press was told to shore up sentiment by focusing on good news. The People's Bank of China (PBOC) slashed interest rates. Ultimately, it was only when more than a thousand shares were suspended from trading—effectively turning the market off—that the fall ended. China's policymakers are celebrated for their far-sighted approach to economic planning, a marked contrast with the short-termism and partisan bickering that too often characterizes the United States. In the face of a fast-moving crisis, the curtain was pulled back and they were revealed as no better able to manage than governments anywhere else in the world.

That, more or less, is the lens through which most economists and investors view China. The economy has too much debt, taken on too quickly, and allocated by a deeply flawed financial system. Bad loans, unrecognized in the official data, are already high enough to pose a threat to stability. A shrinking working-age population, state-encrusted corporate sector, and wrong-headed policy agenda mean the chances of outrunning the problems are slight. If a crisis does break out, China's policymakers will prove unequal to the task of ending it. Viewed from that perspective, the question on China's financial crisis is not if but when, and how bad it might be.

THE PAST IS PROLOGUE: IMAGINING A CHINA CRISIS

What could trigger a crisis? China's own recent history provides abundant examples:

In 1989, following years of runaway loan growth, there was a misstep on reform—moving too quickly from government- to market-set prices. And there was a misjudgment in how to deal with an overheating economy—slamming on the brakes and bringing growth screeching to a halt. GDP growth for the year fell to 4.2 percent, and social unrest shook the regime to its core.

In 1998 the Asian financial crisis hammered exports, at the same
time as profitability for industrial firms was slumping and banks
were struggling with nonperforming loans. The official data
shows growth for the year resilient at 7.8 percent. Academic
estimates based on tracking electricity, airline passengers, and
other proxies put it at 2.2 percent or below.[8]

In 2008 the great financial crisis hammered exports again—and this
time with more at stake, as overseas sales had become a more
significant driver of growth. The official data showed growth
sliding to 6.4 percent. The reading from the Li Keqiang index—
the proxy gauges used by China's premier back when he headed
Liaoning province—suggest it may have actually dropped as low
as 2.4 percent.

In 2012, in Wenzhou, a combination of the European sovereign debt
crisis pounding exports and tighter policy whacking shadow
lenders and real estate speculators brought the local economy to
its knees. Plunging property prices, fleeing factory owners, and
an emergency visit by Premier Wen Jiabao painted a picture of a
city on the brink.

In the 2013 money market crisis, the PBOC's maladroit attempt to
contain shadow banking by jacking up borrowing costs froze
the financial system. With rumors swirling of default by a major
bank, lenders pulled back, money market rates soared, and the
world feared that China was facing a Lehman moment.

In 2015 the equity market crash threatened a wider blow to
confidence, and mishandling of yuan depreciation triggered
a wave of destabilizing capital outflows. The government was
forced to halt trading on the equity market, and erect barriers to
capital outflows, to prevent a systemic crisis.

In the same period, in Liaoning and other northeastern provinces,
the end of the stimulus exposed a creaking industrial structure,

8. Thomas Rawski, "What's Happening to China's GDP Statistics," *China Economic Review*, 12, 2001, 347–354.

triggering a plunge in growth and leaving many firms unable
to service their debts. A 5.4-trillion-yuan regional economy—
equivalent to Turkey in size—faced a slide into recession and
bankruptcy.

That brief history of national-level near misses and local-level direct hits
should convince that China is not crisis-proof. It also provides a checklist
of potential triggers. A slump in exports, a plunge in real estate, overly ambitious reform, draconian tightening, market meltdown, capital outflows,
or simply the inertial weight of zombie firms all have the potential to push
China into crisis.

In the past, when problems occurred, China always had the growth momentum, policy space, and political determination to manage through,
fending off a hard landing. That won't always be the case. Flip the calendar
forward to 2024 and consider a pessimistic but plausible scenario for what
China's economy might look like:

A shrinking working-age population, stalled reform of the state
sector, and unending trade war have put a cap on growth . Based
on projections from the IMF, growth will have slowed toward
5 percent. On a more pessimistic scenario, it could already be in the
low single digits. Reviewing a swath of historical evidence, Harvard
economists Lant Pritchett and Larry Summers conclude that
China's annual growth is on a path down to 2 percent.[9] Capacity to
grow through problems is much depleted.
Successive rounds of credit-fueled stimulus have pushed debt to
vertiginous heights. Taking account of projections on growth,
credit intensity, and bad loan write-offs, economist Fielding
Chen projected that by 2024 China's debt will have risen toward

9. Lant Pritchett and Lawrence Summers, *Asiaphoria Meets Regression to the Mean* (Cambridge,
MA: National Bureau of Economic Research, 2014).

330 percent of GDP.[10] Within that, government debt approaching 100 percent of GDP (even on the conservative official measure) would limit space for infrastructure stimulus. Higher household debt would make it harder to ramp demand by leveraging mortgage borrowing. Policy space to respond to the crisis would be used up.

Xi Jinping has broken through the two-term limit that would have seen him step down in 2022. Seventy-one years old and in power for twelve years, Xi faces a challenge familiar to other long-serving leaders—policy ideas that looked fresh in 2012 are now looking stale, wise counsel is harder to find, potential successors are jostling for position. The policy imagination and unity of purpose that enabled China to ride through past challenges might be harder to find.

Checks and balances that could have provided a corrective against policy mistakes have disintegrated. The freewheeling press that turned Deng Xiaoping's southern tour into a national conversation on reform has been silenced. The space for constructive dissent—where activists like Huang Qi, the Chengdu land-rights advocate, call out bad practice without challenging Communist Party rule—has narrowed to the point of nonexistence.

In the past, a blow to growth from crumbling real estate or exports, a mis-step on reform, a market meltdown, or capital outflows were triggers for a decisive and ultimately successful response from the government. In the future, that might not be the case.

If China does slide into crisis, what would happen to the economy? A look at the international experience provides a window into thinking about the problem. In 1997, when the Asian financial crisis was just a glint in a hedge fund manager's eye, Korea's economy expanded 5.9 percent.

---

10. Fielding Chen, "Debt on Pace for 327% of GDP by 2022, Model Shows," Bloomberg, November 20, 2017.

In 1998, with the crisis in full swing, it contracted 5.5 percent. Closer to the epicenter of the crisis, Indonesia suffered an even more extreme blow, with its economy swinging from 4.7 percent expansion to 13.1 percent contraction. The United States slid from a 3.5 percent expansion in its pre–financial crisis boom to a 2.5 percent contraction in its financial crisis bust. Before the European sovereign debt crisis, Greece was clocking a 5.6 percent growth rate. In the depths of the crisis, its economy contracted 9.1 percent.

Carmen Reinhart and Kenneth Rogoff's seminal work *This Time Is Different* cuts through a thicket of historical evidence, emerging on the other side with calculations on the average impact of major banking crises on asset prices, growth, unemployment, and government debt:

> Asset prices collapse, with an average 35 percent drop in real house prices stretched over six years, and equity prices falling 56 percent.
>
> Output falls more than 9 percent, with a recession lasting on average two years. The unemployment rate rises an average of 7 percentage points, with the increase stretching over four years.
>
> Government debt increases 86 percent, as the state takes on the burden of financing the recovery and recapitalizing the banks.

Those are not encouraging numbers. More troubling, given that the extent of the financial imbalances that have built up in China are larger than those in almost any other country, the cost if imbalances unwind in a disorderly way would very likely be higher.

CORRIDORS OF CONTAGION: TRACKING GLOBAL RISKS FROM A CHINA CRISIS

Call it "Sinophrenia": the simultaneous belief that China is about to collapse and about to take over the world. Reading the news headlines, and listening to commentary on China's economy and foreign policy, it seems both are true. On the one hand, debt is too high, the property bubble too big, and the shadows of the financial sector too dark for the economy to steer clear of crisis for much longer. On the other, China has a master plan for taking over the technologies of the future, a muscular diplomacy that is extending influence around the world, and an economy poised to challenge the United States for global leadership.

In few places are the contradictions so evident as in thinking about the Belt and Road Initiative—Xi's signature attempt to lift China's geopolitical heft into line with its economic might. It was in September 2013, on a visit to Kazakhstan, that Xi announced plans for the silk road economic belt—stretching from China, through central Asia, the Middle East, and Europe. A month later, in Indonesia, he set out plans for the maritime silk road, spanning Southeast Asia, Oceania, and Africa. The names were fancy but the plan was straightforward: leverage China's financing and expertise to strengthen infrastructure links with the rest of the world. More construction would provide an immediate boost to growth, and use up some of China's spare industrial capacity. Better trade links would boost exports and support longer-term development. Dangling major investment projects would give growth-hungry foreign governments reason to think twice before stepping out of line with Beijing.

For some it was a masterful power play, evidence of China's enormous resources and long-term vision. As Washington, DC—still reeling from the great financial crisis—began retreating from its international commitments, the contrast between a China on the advance and a United States on the decline was sharply drawn. The Philippines, a key player in the disputed South China Sea and a bellwether for sentiment in Southeast Asia, was quick to switch sides. President Roderigo Duterte called President Barack Obama a "son of a bitch" and headed to Beijing to see what goodies Xi was handing out. The unfortunately acronymed Belt and Road Forum drew twenty-nine heads of state to Beijing. They listened politely to Xi promise a "new type of international relations featuring win-win cooperation," but were probably more interested in the 540 billion yuan in funding that was up for grabs.

For others, it showed that Beijing's reach continued to exceed its grasp. The initiative was long on ambition and publicity, short on actual investment. In 2016, with controls on capital outflows hardened following the yuan meltdown, China's outbound investment actually fell. Foreign exchange reserves, once seen as an undepletable hoard that China could use to buy overseas assets and influence, suddenly appeared barely adequate to ensure currency stability. Chinese provinces that were meant to benefit from improved infrastructure links did no better—and in many cases worse—than the rest of the country. In 2018 the incoming government of Malaysia—another Southeast Asian bellwether—cancelled Chinese-sponsored projects, and warned that the Belt and Road Initiative represented a "new colonialism."

As ever, in cases of acute Sinophrenia, it turns out that both sides have a point but neither are entirely right. Belt bulls missed the dysfunctions, missteps, overlaps, and overreach that characterized the early stage of the initiative. Belt bears couldn't see the wood for the trees. Pointing gleefully at project-level failures, they missed the bigger picture as China began steadily pouring more concrete and stealthily pulling more strings across Asia, the Middle East, and Europe.

One thing all sides could agree on: the Belt and Road Initiative showed that China's global influence had increased. As of 2018, China's economy was the second-biggest in the world, accounting for close to 16 percent of total output. It was the world's second-biggest importer, receiving $2.1 trillion in shipments. Metal producers from iron ore majors in Australia and Brazil to copper mines in Chile count China as their biggest customer. China ranks second behind the United States in terms of oil consumption. Everyone from Apple to Walmart depends on Chinese factories as a critical link in their supply chain. China's stock market is the second-largest in the world (behind only the United States) and its bond market is the third-largest (behind the United States and Japan). Linkages between China's markets and the rest of the world are small, but growing at a rapid pace.

As long as China's growth remains on track, those avenues of influence remain a positive for the rest of the world. In a crisis, they would become corridors of contagion.

To its trading partners, China is a combination of competitor, partner in production, and customer. In a crisis, a collapse in exports as factories failed might benefit some competitors. The dominant impact, however, would be a drag on growth as the main link in Asia's manufacturing supply chain breaks and China's demand for imports collapses. Asian economies, integrated in the global production chain with China, would be especially hard hit.

China's limited capital market ties with the rest of the world mean the direct impact through financial channels would be small. As the experience of China's 2015 equity market plunge demonstrates, the indirect impact from a collapse in confidence could be severe. A plummet in China's stock and bond markets would send tremors across global markets.

Commodity prices are the intersection where trade and financial channels meet. With China the swing factor in demand for everything from soybeans to iron ore, a collapse in China's demand would trigger tumbling prices. Commodity exporters would suffer. Advanced economies that import commodities would benefit as prices fall—but not enough to offset the blow from falling exports and financial market contagion.

The Belt and Road Initiative got off to a slow start. Over time, however, China's investment in the rest of the world can only increase. A crisis in China, causing a sudden pullback of planned projects, would dent capital spending. The impact would be particularly marked for developing countries that rely on Chinese funding to get projects off the ground.

In 2015, China's economy came close—perhaps the closest it has come since 1989—to a hard landing. The combination of equity market crash, yuan slide, and massive capital outflows raised fears that the end was nigh. After the dust had settled, policymakers around the world decided it was time to take a long, hard look at exposure to China, and the potential for contagion from a China collapse.

The IMF devoted a chapter of its 2016 World Economic Outlook to "spillovers from China's transition." The European Central Bank pondered "the transition of China to sustainable growth—implications for the global economy and the euro area," a tactful euphemism for the real focus: what happens to Europe if China crashes?[11] The Bank of England weighed in, worrying that financial ties through Hong Kong, and the growing role of Chinese investors in the London real estate market, could amplify the blow to Britain if China stumbled.[12]

The headline conclusion from all that research: the impact of a China crash on the rest of the world would be big. The IMF estimates that a 1 percent drop in China's demand would result in a 0.25 percent drop in global GDP. Putting that together with Reinhard and Rogoff's conclusion that countries experiencing a banking crisis typically see a 9 percent drop in output, a crisis in China could knock 2.25 percent off global GDP, bringing the world to the brink of recession.

It's China's Asian neighbors that face the biggest risks. Economies like South Korea and Taiwan find themselves exposed to China both as a final source of demand for exports, and as a critical link in the supply chain that takes their products to consumers in the United States and Europe. In 2018, South Korea's exports to China were equal to close to 13 percent of GDP. That reflected a combination of final goods—like the dewy cosmetics coveted by China's fashionistas, and intermediate goods like the parts Samsung feeds into China's smartphone assembly plants. Based on estimates from the IMF, a 1 percent drop in China's demand would lower Korea's GDP by 0.35 percent. A crisis in China, with demand falling 9 percent, would plunge Korea and other Asian neighbors into recession.

Next in line are major commodity exporters. Economies like Australia, Brazil, and Saudi Arabia would suffer a double blow. First, they would suffer

11. Alastair Dieppe, Robert Gilhooly, Jenny Han, Iikka Korhonen, David Lodge, *The Transition of China to Sustainable Growth: Implications for the Global Economy and the Euro Area* (Frankfurt: European Central Bank, 2018).

12. Robert Gilhooly, Jen Han, Simon Lloyd, Niamh Reynolds and David Young, *From the Middle Kingdom to the United Kingdom: Spillovers from China* (London: Bank of England, 2018).

as China's crumpling investment hammered demand for commodities. In 2018, Australia's exports to China—mainly iron ore—were equal to almost 7 percent of GDP. For Saudi Arabia, oil exports to China were equal to almost 6 percent of GDP. Second, they would suffer as China's collapse hammered financial market confidence, resulting in plunging commodity prices. Australia faces the biggest risks, with a 1 percent drop in China's demand taking its GDP down by 0.2 percent, according to estimates from the IMF.

For major advanced economies the impacts would be smaller, with the blow from weaker exports and financial contagion offset in part by a boost from lower commodity prices. Germany and Japan stand out as exceptions. Japan, deeply enmeshed in Asia's electronics supply chain, would face a 0.2 percent blow to output if China slowed 1 percent. Germany, a major supplier of the engines, turbines, and other advanced manufacturing products required by China's industrial sector, would take a smaller but still significant hit.

For the United States, United Kingdom, and other European countries, the blow would not be as severe as that suffered by China's Asian neighbors or commodity exporters. Even so, it would be significant, and likely amplified by growing financial linkages. For the United States and the United Kingdom, the outsize role that financial markets play in the economy add downside risks. In August 2015, as China's equity markets crashed, the S&P 500 fell 3.9 percent on a single day. If a China crash sent US markets into a tailspin, the blow to consumer confidence and corporate financing would amplify the impact of falling exports.

China's holdings of US Treasuries are a complicating factor in the relationship, but unlikely to be a critical factor in the event of a crisis. At the end of 2018 China held $1.1 trillion in US Treasury debt—slightly more if holdings stashed away in other financial centers are added to the total. China's position as one of the largest foreign holders of US debt (they jostle for first place with Japan) has been a perennial source of concern. Part of China's first bank bailout—ahead of the listing of the big-four state-owned banks—was financed with a sale of foreign-exchange reserves. What if a financial crisis forced China to recapitalize its banks on an even larger scale, and it raised the funds with a fire sale of its Treasury holdings? Would that trigger a financial meltdown, with the US dragging the rest of the world down with it?

Maybe, and for that very reason, it's not likely to happen. Facing a crisis at home, China's leaders would hope for strong global demand to lift the economy out of its slump. A fire sale of Treasury holdings, triggering a crisis in the United States and potentially the rest of the world, would be counterproductive in the extreme. Back in 2007, Larry Summers coined the term "balance of financial terror," neatly encapsulating the idea that China had to keep lending to the United States, because if they didn't, the resulting crisis would sweep them away too. China has stopped adding to its Treasury holdings, which have been roughly stable since the end of 2013. Still, the balance of financial terror remains in place. Even in a crisis, China would find other sources of funds rather than risking a meltdown of its biggest trading partner.

The further in the future a crisis occurs, the bigger the impact would be. In 1989, when China's economy experienced its first system-shaking shock, its GDP was just 2.3 percent of the global total. In 1998, when the Asian financial crisis hit, it was just 3.3 percent of the total. In 2015, when equity market collapse and capital outflows raised fears of a hard landing, it had risen to 15 percent. By 2024, it will be close to 19 percent. China's financial markets are expanding and opening at an even more rapid pace. Based on projections from Bloomberg Economics, from 2017 to 2025 China's bond market could double in size. An expanding Belt and Road Initiative will accelerate financial linkages, and create new dependencies on Chinese trade and investment. In a crisis, the bigger China's economy is, the larger the impact through the trade channel. The bigger and more open China's markets are, the greater the potential for financial contagion.

A financial crisis in China is possible. If it does occur, the consequences for China and the world would not be pretty. A crisis, however, is not the most likely scenario.

12

It's Never Too Late

To read the history of modern China is to read the history of China collapse theories. In 1978, as Deng Xiaoping announced that "practice would be the sole criterion of truth," few anticipated that he was opening the door to four decades of rapid growth. In 1991, as the Soviet Union fell, the read across to the situation in Red China appeared clear, and regime collapse was anticipated. As the Asian financial crisis swept away crony–capitalist regimes from Thailand to Korea, it seemed like the days for China's inefficient state firms and bad-loan-laden state banks must be numbered. In 2001, China's entry into the World Trade Organization (WTO) was seen as a win for the United States. "Who will defend the Party when workers lose their jobs in the WTO economy?" wondered one of the grizzlier of the China bears. "Will some economist from Beijing University explain trade deficits and the concept of comparative advantage to an angry mob as it marches on the Communist leadership compound in Zhongnanhai?"[1]

The rise of the middle class, and their demand for participation in the political process, was expected to sound the death knell for Communist Party rule. China was expected to languish in a middle-income trap, unable to transition from an economy based on cheap labor and brute investment to one driven by high skills and high productivity. The great financial crisis was expected to topple China's exports, driving

---

1. Gordon Chang, *The Coming Collapse of China* (New York: Random House, 2001).

unemployment higher and threatening regime stability. The transition from investment to consumption as a driver of growth was expected to be unmanageable. Ghost towns of empty property, local government debt, and shadow banking were all identified as triggers for a system-shaking crisis.

Collapse theories have been many and varied. So far, they have one thing in common: they have all been wrong.

Why so? One reason is that they're not wrong, they're just early. MIT economist Rudiger Dornbusch's famous line, "Crises take longer to arrive than you can possibly imagine, but when they do come, they happen faster than you can possibly imagine," will one day prove prescient in China, as it has in so many other countries.[2] Beyond that, there are four factors at work.

China has underappreciated sources of strength—substantial room for development, stable funding for the financial system, and a determinedly developmental state.

The tradeoff between policy choices is overstated, or—a different way of saying the same thing—the creativity of China's policymakers is underestimated.

As a single-minded, single-party state, China has unique resources it can bring to bear on dealing with problems.

For those looking in from outside, there's a combination of low transparency and high emotions, which make it more difficult to form an accurate and unbiased view.

"What can we make?" asked Chairman Mao, launching the first five-year plan back in 1953. "Tables, chairs, and teapots . . . we cannot make automobiles, airplanes, and tanks." China's history since then, and more successfully since the beginning of reform and opening under Deng Xiaoping, has been an attempt to rectify that problem, with industrial planners marshalling resources to move the economy up the development

2. Michael Pettis, *The Great Rebalancing* (Princeton, NJ: Princeton University Press, 2013).

ladder. One reason they've been successful: something economists call the "advantage of backwardness," a path to growth simply by following in the technology and management steps traced out by global leaders. In the early stages of the People's Republic, China had it in spades.

Even more than half a century after Mao's remarks, China still benefits from the advantages of backwardness. In 2018, GDP per capita measured in purchasing power parity terms was $16,000, less than 30 percent of the level in the United States. That's a fact often overlooked by global visitors. Flying into Beijing's ultra-modern airport, staying in the Ritz Carlton on the west side of town or the other Ritz Carlton on the east side, attending meetings in newly built office towers, watching smartly dressed young professionals ordering ride shares on their smartphones, it's easy to forget that China remains a developing country. Countries with development space have room to grow through financial problems that might stop a more advanced economy in its tracks.

On its own, backwardness isn't particularly advantageous. Many African countries are poor; that hasn't helped them. What's accelerated China up the developmental ladder is its 1.3 billion population and can-do government. The 1.3 billion population was important initially as a source of cheap labor, enticing foreign firms to set up production in factories up and down the east coast. That's one of the big reasons WTO entry didn't play out like the China bears anticipated. In the years that followed, as labor costs rose and consumer power increased, incentives tilted toward producing for China's massive domestic market. Either way, foreign firms were ready to strike a bargain—access to China's market in return for transfer of production technology and management know-how.

The earlier adventures of Japan, South Korea, and Taiwan provided a ready-to-go blueprint for how to manage the process. Just as China didn't have to reinvent the wheel on technology—instead copying what already existed in more advanced economies—so also they didn't have to reinvent the model of a developmental state, instead copying what had already worked so well for their East Asian neighbors. Surprisingly, given the poisonous historical relations between the two countries, in the early days of China's reform and opening Japan was generous in its provision of technical advice. Liu He, the chief economic advisor to Xi Jinping, is part of a school of Chinese economic planners trained in the Japanese approach.[3]

The combination of space for development, enormous size, access to foreign technology, and a ready-made blueprint for development gave China a major head start. On top of that, add a high savings rate, controlled capital account, and a state-owned banking system. As a nation, China saves almost half of its income; a controlled capital account means it's difficult to move those savings offshore. As a result, the vast majority ends up in the domestic banking system. That's important because it guarantees China's banks a steady flow of cheap funding. And with the banks state-owned, that means government planners have a constantly replenished piggy bank for funding priority projects.

Put those pieces together, and the result is a formidable engine of development. China had space to grow by catching up to the advanced productivity levels in the United States, Japan, and Germany; a 1.3 billion–strong population as a lure for foreign firms and their technology; a made-in-Japan blueprint on how to put all the pieces together; and a captive pool of savings to pay for it all. For evidence of how successful that has been, look no further than China's own development record. Close to four decades of growth, averaging 9.6 percent, and (leaving aside questions about the official data) never dropping below 3.9 percent. Only the East Asian tigers come close to matching that. The rest of the developing world isn't even close.

Despite those strong fundamental drivers, China has faced and continues to face very serious structural problems. Critics portray China's leaders as stuck between a rock and a hard place, confronted with a series of damned-if-you-do, damned-if-you-don't dilemmas:

Development means creation of a middle class. A middle class will demand political rights. The challenge to the Communist Party's

---

3. Sebastian Heilmann and Lea Shih, The Rise of Industrial Policy in China, 1978–2012, University of Trier, 2013.

authority will result in regime collapse. Failure to develop will
leave the population in poverty, undermining the legitimacy of a
government that promised continued improvements in quality of
life, causing regime collapse at an even earlier date.

The creaking state sector must be reformed if China is to avoid
stagnation. But the state sector is the lynchpin of China's
industrial planning and demand management, as well as
the basis of patronage networks for leaders. Without it, the
government will lose control.

Runaway real estate prices must be curbed, or would-be
homeowners will agitate against the political order. But taming
prices will prick the property bubble and crater the construction
boom that has been the biggest contributor to China's growth.

So far, none of those tradeoffs have bitten, or at least bitten hard
enough to dent China's development trajectory. The middle class has
acquiesced to single-party rule—as long as they keep getting richer. The
state sector is big and complex. Closing down some of it and striving
for efficiency gains in the rest enabled increased economic dynamism
without sacrificing control of the commanding heights. The real estate
boom turned out to be more durable—and policymakers' capacity to
deflate bubbles without puncturing the economy greater—than analysts
anticipated.

One reason China's policymakers are able to evade the lose–lose choice
the bears say they are confronted with is that they are more imaginative
and flexible than their critics give them credit for. Jiang Zemin's "three
represents"—which opened the Communist Party to membership by
entrepreneurs and other members of the bourgeoisie—is the outstanding
example. Instead of crumbling in the face of a rising private sector and
middle class, the Communist Party simply broadened its church to include their leading representatives. In 2017, Wang Huning - the political
theorist credited as one of the creators of the three represents, became a
member of the Standing Committee, China's highest level of leadership.
Jack Ma, founder of e-commerce giant Alibaba and one of the richest men

in the world, is a member of the Communist Party. Pony Ma, the founder of Tencent and also one of the richest men in the world, is a delegate to National People's Congress.

Management of the ups and downs of real estate illustrates the same creativity. China bears thought there were only two settings for the real estate sector—boom or bust. By developing a wide range of instruments, and the capacity to deploy them with varying degrees of intensity and differentiate on a city-by-city basis, policymakers demonstrated that there are multiple positions on the spectrum in between. Moving mortgage rates and down-payment requirements, and shifting administrative requirements on who can buy a home, proved an effective way of modulating demand. Setting different requirements for first-, second-, and third-homebuyers added to the flexibility. China's real estate sector has extreme cycles, but so far that refined set of instruments has enabled policymakers to avoid anything that looks like Japan's meltdown or the US subprime crisis.

Capital account opening is a third example. The received wisdom was that China faced a stark and unattractive choice. A closed capital account—blocking the flow of funds between the mainland and the rest of the world—would present a barrier to capital flight but doom China's economy to the inefficiencies of financial autarky. An open capital account would deliver greater efficiency but expose China to risks of an Asian financial crisis–style sudden stop. The son of one of China's top officials, himself a major player in the financial sector, said that opening the capital account was the equivalent of "seeking death." Despite that dire warning, China's policymakers found a middle path—opening the capital account to long-term, patient investors while keeping it closed to the destabilizing influence of short-term speculators.

If underlying strengths, energy, and imagination all fail, China's policymakers can also fall back on the unusual resources of a Leninist party state. Chief among these is the ability to shift policy decisively, comprehensively, and without regard to procedural or legal niceties. That was on display in the response to the great financial crisis. The 4-trillion-yuan stimulus—already effective in timing and size—was the tip of a spear that comprised monetary, fiscal, industrial, and financial regulation policies.

It was in evidence again during the 2015 stock market meltdown, which ultimately came to an end when trading in more than a thousand stocks was suspended by administrative fiat, locking unfortunate investors into losing positions.

The stock market collapse also showcased the state's ability to contain flows of information. Press, television, and online media all received instructions on how to report the market fall, with policymakers aiming to stem the panic by eliminating the bad news. One unfortunate reporter with *Caijing*, a leading Chinese finance magazine, founds himself detained for allegedly fabricating and spreading false information. In a televised confession, Wang Xiaolu admitted to causing "panic and disorder" and apologized for causing "the country and its investors such a big loss." Wang wasn't alone; nearly two hundred people were punished for online rumor-mongering.[4]

China's government only gets to pull those additional policy levers at a considerable cost. Doing away with due process in government and free debate in society risks missteps in both directions. Policymakers can overdo it—which is what happened with the 4-trillion-yuan stimulus. They can also leave problems to fester for too long, as with the one-child policy, a large-scale policy error and one that a government benefiting from democratic checks and balances would surely have avoided. In almost all cases, the short-term flexibility and resilience enjoyed by authoritarian regimes has proved a source of long-term rigidity and brittleness. Many analysts have argued that ultimately will be China's undoing. Someday, that call will put them on the right side of history. So far, it has put them on the wrong one.

Behind all the challenges in making the right call on China are two hard-to-acknowledge truths. First, it is genuinely difficult understanding what is going on. For many foreigners, language is a barrier. Even for native speakers, or the few foreigners who have devoted the thousands of hours required to attain fluency, barriers remain. Policy statements are

---

4. Patti Waldmeir, "China Reporter Confesses to Stoking Market 'Panic and Disorder,'" *Financial Times*, August 31, 2015.

long on boilerplate platitudes, short on substance. Official data is patchy in coverage, flaky in quality at the best of times, and sometimes fabricated for political purposes. Officials are in no hurry to meet with inquiring outsiders. With government propaganda warning about spies on every corner, even previously forthcoming academics and think tank policy analysts have clammed up. A plucky band of investigative journalists, many of them working for the foreign press, do a great job under the most difficult of circumstances. Under the watchful eye of the propaganda police, there are fewer and fewer local reporters competing to splash scoops on the front page.

It is also genuinely difficult to come at the China question with an open mind. China is a single-party state with a history of scant regard for individual liberty. The state dominates the economy, with the biggest banks and industrial firms following the directives of industrial planners more than shareholders, and regulators intervening in markets before breakfast, lunch, and dinner. China is already disrupting US military supremacy in the Asia Pacific, and in the next decade will likely do so on a global scale. Looking through all these emotive issues, it's hard not to see China through a red mist. Dispassionate judgments are hard to come by.

Criticism of the different leadership styles of Hu Jintao and Xi Jinping illustrate the point. Hu operated through consensus, attempting to get agreement between all stakeholders before moving ahead. That had its advantages; policymaking was deliberative and thorough. But it was also slow-moving and, by attempting to placate all interests, ended up avoiding difficult decisions. Foreign analysts concluded that Hu was ineffectual, and that China needed a strong-man leader to bang heads together and get things done.

Xi adopted a diametrically different approach. Consensus discussion was out; unilateral decisions were in. "The Chairman of Everything," he was called ("Xi Who Must Be Obeyed" was the wisecrack). Following criticism of Hu for his wobbling prevarication, analysts might have been expected to embrace Xi's muscular decisiveness. They did not. Xi was cast in the role of a twenty-first-century Mao. A commentariat that until Xi's arrival had been calling for decisive leadership now took the view that this particular decisive leader was not what China needed. If dispassionate observation is pushed aside by perennial criticism, forming an accurate view of China's politics, economy, and finances, is harder to do.

THE END OF THE FOURTH CYCLE

Reform-era China has been through three cycles. The first started with Deng Xiaoping's decision to break with the ideological extremities of Maoism and ended with the student protests and conservative crackdown. The second started with Deng's southern tour and ended with the Asian financial crisis. The third started with Zhu Rongji's reform of the state sector and China's entry into the WTO, and ended with the great financial crisis. In each case, a successful policy generated a decade of growth but ultimately ran into its limits. In each case, the cycle ended in crisis, but that crisis proved a trigger for far-reaching reforms that—combined with the economy's underlying strengths—catalyzed the next decade of growth.

A decade after the great financial crisis triggered the 4-trillion-yuan stimulus, China is at the end of the fourth cycle. The surge in lending that started at the end of 2008 buoyed the economy through the global slowdown but ran too strong for too long. A decade on, banks are overextended on their lending and vulnerable on their funding. Industrial firms, real estate developers, and local governments have borrowed too much. Funds frittered away in wasteful projects compound the difficulty in repayment. The inertial weight of high debt and inefficient capital allocation mean that a rapid pivot to a new growth cycle is hard to envisage. A more hostile world—with the United States viewing China more as threat than opportunity—adds to the difficulties. So does a shrinking working-age population.

That doesn't mean a crisis is imminent. To begin the fifth cycle, China needs to engineer a series of interlinked and mutually reinforcing transitions:

On the supply side of the economy, a transition from capital-heavy, labor-light industrial firms to capital-light, labor-intensive services.

Within industry and services, a shift from inefficient state-owned enterprises to a dynamic, productive private-sector.

On the demand side of the economy, a move from exhausted exports and overdone investment to household consumption as the main driver.

In banking, a restoration of the relationship between credit expansion and economic output, enabling deleveraging to take place without hammering growth.

In different ways, those transitions are either already underway, or—given other changes taking place—could be soon.

In 2000, industry accounted for 46 percent of total output and services just 39 percent. Fast-forward to mid-2019, and industry's share has fallen to 40 percent with services rising to 53 percent. The share of investment in GDP peaked at 48 percent in 2011, and by 2018 had edged down to 44 percent. Over the same period, the share of household consumption rose from 36 percent toward 40 percent. In 2018, consumption contributed close to 80 percent of growth—indicating that the handoff from capital spending is accelerating. It's possible the official data are understating the pace of change. Analysis of China's GDP numbers by academics at the Chinese University of Hong Kong and University of Chicago suggested growth was exaggerated, and the main channel for exaggeration was investment.[5] China's economy may be smaller than the National Bureau of Statistics reports, but it may also be less unbalanced than China bears believe.

A larger role for services firms, higher income for households, and rebalancing from investment to consumption are mutually reinforcing trends. The services sector is more labor-intensive than industry: a restaurant or hospital has a lot of employees and not much physical capital,

5. Wei Chen, Xilu Chen, Chang-Tai Hseih, and Zheng (Michael) Song, "A Forensic Examination of China's National Accounts," Brookings Papers on Economic Activity, 2019.

while a steel mill or cement kiln has a lot of physical capital but not many employees. More labor-intensive production drives higher demand for workers. The pass-through from higher demand for workers to higher wages isn't straightforward. Many services jobs are low-skill, and workers have less bargaining power than they did on the factory floor. Still, all else being equal, more demand for workers pushes wages higher. As incomes rise, households consume more, and a larger share of incremental spending goes on services. As demand for services increases, employment rises and the virtuous circle begins again.

On the shift from inefficient state firms to dynamic private firms, progress is harder to see. Indeed, viewed from a certain perspective, the movement is in the wrong direction. In 2014, the share of state firms in industrial assets ended a decades-long decline and started rising again. The supply-side reform agenda privileged state firms over private competitors, many of whom faced shotgun mergers or bankruptcy. Major private and foreign firms discovered that the Communist Party committee was eager to play an expanded role in their operations.

Viewed from a different perspective, however, the picture is not so bleak. The state sector might be growing as a share of traditional industry, but traditional industry is shrinking as a share of GDP. Private steel mills and coal mines are going under. But steel and coal are China's past, not its future. In the industries of the future—e-commerce, electric vehicles, robotics, artificial intelligence—private firms are at the fore. Go back to 2007, and China's top-twenty listed firms were all state-owned, with the biggest banks, oil companies, telecoms, and industrial and infrastructure firms all represented. Fast-forward to 2019, and a number of private firms—Tencent, Alibaba, home appliance maker Gree Electric—have muscled into the top ranks. If they have any sense, Communist Party cells in foreign and private firms will focus on defending the Party's political bottom line, not calling the shots on business strategy.

On deleveraging, progress has been halting, but the structural features of the financial system mean policymakers have time on their side. A refrain running through this book is that financial crises do not start on the asset side of a bank's balance sheet; they start on the liability side. In

China, the high savings rate and controlled capital account mean a continual buildup of new deposits in the banking system, locking in a cheap and stable source of funding. State ownership of big and small banks means policymakers have unusual resources to manage liquidity within the system. Control of the media is not a positive for China. It does mean they are unlikely to face a downward spiral of market shock, amplifying press reports, and crumbling confidence.

With breathing room to manage down financial risks and drive efficiency gains in the real economy, China has made some smart and significant moves. The deleveraging and supply-side reform agendas took aim at the biggest problems, and registered immediate results. Shadow lending, clocking an annual 73 percent gain at the start of 2016, ended 2018 in contraction. Banks' reliance on expensive short-term funding from wealth management products followed the same trajectory. Forced rehousing of 8 million families a year absorbed overcapacity in real estate. The broader point is not that the supply-side reform and deleveraging agendas completely solved Chinese problems. Clearly, they did not. It's that they showcased the ability of policymakers to take extreme measures to shift the economic aggregates in the right direction.

Building an innovative economy is a longer-term process, and may have hit a major obstacle as the United States shifts toward viewing China as a strategic threat, imposing sanctions on major Chinese technology companies. Set against that impediment are two significant positives.

First, China's enormous size. As long ago as 1776, Adam Smith—the father of classical economics—wrote that "the great extent of the Empire of China [and] the vast multitude of its inhabitants . . . render the home market of that country of so great extent, as to be alone sufficient to support very great manufactures." Prescient in this as in so many other things, Smith said all China needed to take off was a little commerce with the rest of the world. Trade would enable them to "learn for themselves the art of using and constructing . . . all the different machines made use of in other countries." It took more than two-hundred years, but China's combination of vast domestic market and rapid learning from abroad mean that Smith's "very great manufactures" are now a reality. Even if relations with the United States stay frosty, the vast domestic market will remain a lure for foreign firms and their technology.

Second, no government anywhere in the world is making such strenuous, sustained, and well-funded efforts to move their economy up the development ladder. State-driven initiatives to move the economy toward the global technology frontier have been clumsy and wasteful. They have also been noticeably successful. In telecom equipment, high-speed trains, nuclear power, and sustainable energy, Chinese firms are either world leaders or jostling toward that position. In the next ten years it is entirely plausible that they will make similar strides in electric vehicles, industrial robots, and artificial intelligence.

Starting with the high savings rate, the fundamental forces that drive China's imbalances are starting to unwind. The generation born in the affluence of the reform era is more free-spending than their Mao-era parents and grandparents. The end of the one-child policy, aging of the population, buildout of the welfare state, and development of a more sophisticated financial system all pull in the same direction—increasing households' propensity to spend, reducing their propensity to save. There's a risk to lower saving; with less deposits flowing in, the funding base for banks will become less secure. But as less saving also means more consumption, there will be a parallel reduction in the need for bank-financed investment. As the imbalances caused by a high savings rate unwind, the need for a high savings rate to guard against the consequences of those imbalances is reduced.

Liberalization of interest rates and the exchange rate mean the price of money and the price of foreign goods are now being set by the market. The capital account is still managed, but with foreign investors now welcome in the bond and equity markets, cross-border capital flows are rising. A steady increase in defaults, including for state-owned borrowers, is starting to chip away at the problem of moral hazard. Taken together, those represent significant moves to increase the efficiency of capital allocation. That's a prerequisite if China is to restore the link between credit expansion and economic output—deleveraging without self-detonating.

China's policymakers are not all-knowing or all-powerful. They do, undeniably, get a lot done. Infrastructure building is overdone, but it has left major Chinese cities with world-class roads, railways, airports, power, and communications. Coverage of education and healthcare has expanded rapidly. Spending on research and development has accelerated. In the last twenty years China has faced down the Asian financial crisis and the Lehman shock, recapitalized and listed its major banks, halted two equity market routs, and stemmed capital outflows that threatened to trigger an old-school emerging-market crisis. If China's leaders appear confident in their abilities, there's a reason for that.

SEEING THE FUTURE IN A BOWL OF NOODLES

In the shadow of Beijing's financial district, a corner-hole noodle store does a lively trade. For 15 yuan ($2.20) hungry diners get a steaming bowl of homemade noodles swimming in a rich pork broth. For those with no afternoon appointments or disdain for high-falutin concerns about halitosis, cloves of raw garlic are available to nibble on. Vinegar from the owner's native Shanxi province and chili flakes are more universally accepted condiments. When I arrived in Beijing in 2008, cash was the only currency, and waitresses—most hailing from the same Shanxi village as the owner—shuttled back and forth carrying payment to a till at the front and change back to the customers. When I left in 2018 payment had shifted online, with customers using their smartphones to order and pay over the Alibaba or Tencent networks.

Over time, the explosive growth of mobile payments—on display not just at Beijing's noodle restaurants but in all kinds of transactions all over the country—could also be a game-changer. In 2011, the value of mobile payments was inconsequential. In 2018 it was 277.4 trillion yuan—more than three times larger than GDP. That's an important development for two reasons. First, it provides a means to integrate more entrepreneurs into the modern economy. There are more than 10 million small businesses operating on China's e-commerce platforms, accepting payments over the

Alibaba or Tencent systems. A disproportionately large share of them are located in the backward hinterland, where—absent the connections e-commerce provides—they would be unable to access the opportunities created by China's rapid development.

Second, the record of e-payment transactions forms a database that can be used for accurate credit scoring for even the smallest micro-business. "All their data is fake," said Mr. Li, the Wenzhou financial consultant, explaining why banks favored loans to big state-owned firms over providing credit to ambitious private startups. As of early 2019, Ant Financial—the banking arm of the Alibaba empire—had provided no-collateral loans to more than 8 million small businesses. In the future, the combination of credit scoring from the mobile payments network and lending from a major bank could provide financing for entrepreneurs on an even larger scale.[6]

Back in the early 1980s, at the start of the first cycle, the return of land to the tiller—the "household responsibility system" that drove a step change in agricultural productivity and fired the starting pistol on China's reforms—was not the result of a policy directive from Beijing. It started with the local initiative of farmers in Anhui province. In the early 2000s, the factories that seized the opportunity of China's entry into the WTO were not state-owned. They were owned and operated by entrepreneurs, driven by the desire to get rich first, and providing a path out of rural poverty for millions of migrant workers.

The narrow point, is that by creating a link to customers, a channel for payment, and access to loans, China's e-commerce and mobile payment revolution has the potential to empower a new generation of entrepreneurs to begin a new cycle of growth. The broad point is that the catalysts for China's past growth cycles have come from unexpected places. They could do so again. The digital economy is a potential game changer. So is China 2025—which could mean China owns the industries of the future. So is the Belt and Road Initiative—which could make half the world a welcoming market for Chinese firms. Bets against China ignore how good

6. Long Chen, *Digital Economy and Inclusive Growth* (Hangzhou: Luohan Academy, 2019).

the country has been at solving problems. They also ignore how successful it has been at creating and seizing opportunities.

It is the summer of 2017 and Hong Kong swelters in the heat. President Xi has just concluded the financial work conference. His announcement that financial stability is now the basis of national security fires the starting gun in the race to deleverage. Liu Mingkang, the former chair of the China Banking Regulatory Commission and one of the first to sound the alarm on risks from the excesses of local government borrowing, is addressing a room filled with Hong Kong's financial elite. Close to seventy years old, with an impeccable grasp of detail and meticulous English, Liu explains Xi's plan for stabilizing the financial sector. His presentation is drawing to a close. He pauses, gathering his thoughts for a resolution. The room is silent. "For an economy as big as China," he says, "it's never too late."

FURTHER READING

On the Deng Xiaoping Era

Growing Out of the Plan by Barry Naughton (Cambridge: Cambridge University Press, 1996)—a comprehensive and insightful treatment of China's early reforms.

Deng Xiaoping and the Transformation of China by Ezra Vogel (Cambridge, MA: The Belknap Press of Harvard University Press, 2013)—a magisterial biography of China's great reformer.

Burying Mao by Richard Baum (Princeton, NJ: Princeton University Press, 1996)—sets out a framework for understanding the cycles of liberalization and control that characterized the early reform period.

The Political Logic of Economic Reform in China by Susan Shirk (Berkeley: University of California Press, 1993)—a deeply researched treatment of reform in the 1980s.

On the Jiang Zemin Era

The Man Who Changed China: The Life and Legacy of Jiang Zemin by Robert Lawrence Kuhn (New York: Crown, 2005)—a comprehensive biography of Deng's successor.

Zhu Rongji Meets the Press by Zhu Rongji (Oxford: Oxford University Press, 2011) - a collection of speeches and interviews from China's hard-charging premier.

China's Unfinished Economic Revolution by Nicholas Lardy (Washington, DC: Brookings Institution Press, 1998)—a detailed examination of the challenges confronting China's reformers at the end of the 1990s.

Integrating China into the Global Economy, also by Nicholas Lardy (Washington, DC: Brookings Institution Press, 2001) - a contemporary view on China's entry into the World Trade Organization.

Back-Alley Banking: Private Entrepreneurs in China by Kellee S. Tsai (Ithaca, NY: Cornell University Press, 2004) - an early and insightful look at the shadow banking sector.

ON THE HU JINTAO ERA

Barry Naughton's regular quarterly essays in the *China Leadership Monitor* provide an analytic chronicle of China's economy, from Hu Jintao to Xi Jinping.

Privatizing China: Inside China's Stock Markets by Fraser Howie and Carl Walter (New York: Wiley, 2006) casts a world-weary eye over the partial privatization of the commanding heights of the economy.

Red Capitalism, also by Fraser Howie and Carl Walter (New York: Wiley, 2012)—the book that first fired investors' imagination on the risks lurking on China's bank balance sheets.

China's Trapped Transition by Minxin Pei (Cambridge, MA: Harvard University Press, 2008) sets out a framework for understanding the dynamic between reform and politics.

Factory Girls by Leslie Chang (New York: Spiegel and Grau, 2009) tells the little-told story of life for migrant workers.

Dealing with China by Henry Paulson (New York, Twelve, 2016)—an insider's account of China's bank privatizations and U.S.—China relations.

ON THE XI JINPING ERA

The Great Rebalancing by Michael Pettis (Princeton, NJ: Princeton University Press, 2013) sets out China's economic challenges at the start of the Xi era.

China's Economy: What Everyone Needs to Know by Arthur Kroeber (New York: Oxford University Press, 2016)—a comprehensive, insightful, and accessible guide.

Avoiding the Blind Alley: China's Economic Overhaul and Its Global Implications by Daniel Rosen (New York: Asia Society, 2014)—a detailed look at Xi Jinping's Third Plenum reforms.

Made in China 2025 by Jost Wübbeke (Berlin: Mercator Institute for China Studies 2016)—an early assessment of Xi-era industrial policy.

The Fat Tech Dragon by Scott Kennedy (Washington DC: Center for Strategic International Studies, 2017) dives into China's state-driven innovation strategy.

China's Great Wall of Debt by Dinny McMahon (Boston: Houghton Mifflin Harcourt, 2018) – on the ground reporting on China's financial risks.

Credit and Credibility by Logan Wright and Daniel Rosen (New York Rhodium Group, 2018) - a deep dive into the problems of the financial sector.

The State Strikes Back by Nicholas Lardy (Washington DC: Peterson Institute of International Economics, 2019) tracks the resurgence of state control.

Patriot Number One: American Dreams in Chinatown by Lauren Hilgers (New York, Crown, 2018) chronicles one village's struggle against government land grabs, as well as the experience of Chinese migrants to the US.

ON INTERNATIONAL EXPERIENCE

The Greatest-Ever Bank Robbery: The Collapse of the Savings and Loan Industry by Martin Mayer (New York: Scribner, 1990) – tells the story of the US savings and loan crisis.

Turning a Crisis into an Opportunity: The Political Economy of Korea's Financial Sector Reform by Wonhyuk Lim and Joon-Ho Hahm (Washington, DC: Brookings Institution, 2006) offers an insider's take on Korea's 1998 crisis.

The Chastening: Inside the Crisis That Rocked the Global Financial System and Humbled the IMF by Paul Blustein (New York: PublicAffairs, 2001) provides a detailed account of the Asian financial crisis.

"The Bubble Burst and Stagnation of Japan" by Etsuro Shioji (a chapter in *The Routledge Handbook of Major Events in Economic History*, edited by Randall E. Parker and Robert M. Whaples) sets out the factors at work in Japan's bubble economy.

The Holy Grail of Macro-Economics: Lessons from Japan's Great Recession by Richard Koo (New York: Wiley, 2009) uses Japan's experience as the basis for the theory of balance-sheet recessions.

This Time Is Different: Eight Centuries of Financial Folly by Carmen Reinhart and Kenneth Rogoff (Princeton, Princeton University Press, 2011) marshals a formidable array of data on the history of financial crisis.

Stabilizing an Unstable Economy by Hyman Minsky (New York, McGraw-Hill Education, 2008)—a prescient and challenging theoretical treatment of the causes of financial crises.

Manias, Panics, and Crashes: A History of Financial Crises by Charles Kindleberger, and Robert Aliber (London, Palgrave Macmillan, 2015) combines the theory of financial crises with a lively relation of the history.

Source acknowledgments

I would like to thank Dow Jones for permission to use sections from "How China Lost Its Mojo: One Town's Story" (*Wall Street Journal*, October 1, 2013), and "Tensions Mount as China Swaps Farms for Homes" (*Wall Street Journal*, February 14, 2013). I'd like to thank Bloomberg for permission to use material and charts from "Is Supply-Side Reform Momentum Ebbing? View from Guizhou" (Bloomberg, February 11, 2018); "How Slum Clearance Exorcised Fear of Ghost Towns" (Bloomberg, April 2, 2018); "What Ghost Town? How Zhengzhou Filled Up" (Bloomberg, November 6, 2017); "Winners and Losers from Made in China 2025" (Bloomberg, November 1, 2018); "China Shadow Banking Topic Primer" (Bloomberg, September 12, 2017); and "China Financial Risks Topic Primer" (Bloomberg, September 12, 2017).

For the benefit of digital users, indexed terms that span two pages (e.g., 52–53) may, on occasion, appear on only one of those pages.

WATCHING OVER THE WATCHER

SIMONE BEAUDELAIRE

Author's web site:

http://simonebeaudelaireauthor.weebly.com

Author's email:

simonebeaudelaireauthor@hotmail.com

ACKNOWLEDGMENTS

If it takes a village to raise a child, it takes a virtual village to grow a novel. Without the support of my friends in the online community, this novel would never have been made available. I would particularly like to thank my team of beta readers: Sandra Martinez, Nocomus Columbus, Jill Shannon, and Beary, and online mentor extraordinaire, R.C. Drake. I would also like to thank D.S. Williams, The Pedantic Punctuator, for her professional editing services.

This book is dedicated to first-time authors. It's a long, hard road, but you can do it. Learn, grow, and keep your vision alive.

CHAPTER 1

*S*elene Johansen bent over and scooped up a heavy cardboard box. Her long, white-blond braid slipped over her shoulder to dangle onto the carton, the end tracing squiggles in the thick dust. She hefted the box, and the unbalanced load inside shifted uncomfortably.

Thank goodness there are only a couple of boxes left.

Hoisting the burden, she made her way across the squeaky wooden floor towards the door of the compact pink and green bedroom. She had to step aside as her friend Maggie barreled in, black ponytail bouncing, intent on collecting another load.

Selene arrived made her way to the rusty white pickup and set the heavy box in the nearly-full bed. *Good thing we're about done here.*

She glanced around the small, tidy front yard. Neatly trimmed grass gave way to a row of carefully shaped shrubs along the front of the house. An aged oak shaded the windows of the front room, through which she could barely see the comfortable seating area. The clean, white-painted siding of the small one-story matched its larger neighbors for attractiveness, if not exactly for size. She smiled. *It looks like a baby house at play with older siblings.*

"Come on, Selene," Maggie called from the open doorway. "The day won't wait for us. Stop smelling the flowers and get to work."

Selene grinned at her friend's impatience. *Though Maggie's correct about one thing; the intoxicating fragrance of lilac is worth a moment's attention.*

As Selene headed back into the house, a brief blast of synthesized violin music from her pocket arrested her progress. She paused in the living room, fished out her cell phone and sank onto the sofa to answer the call.

"Don't you dare!" Maggie exclaimed, snatching the phone out of Selene's hand and making a swiping motion across the screen with her finger.

"Hey!" Selene protested, jumping to her feet. "That was probably work."

"And you're not on call," Maggie retorted, unperturbed. "The fate of the universe doesn't depend on you."

Selene shook her head. "I've told you before. You know how important it is for me to do what I do. Because of me, lives are saved that might otherwise be lost. I matter, Maggie."

"Yeah, I get that," Maggie replied, handing her back the phone, "but you're a person, too. You deserve a day off now and again, and you only have one weekend a month when you're not on call. Please, don't give it up because of a job. There are other cops, Selene. Give one of them a chance to shine." With that she flounced away.

Torn, Selene stared at the screen of her phone. *Maggie has a point*, a little voice in her head reminded her. *You've been working ten to twelve-hour shifts every day for the last three weeks.* Feeling suddenly determined, Selene tucked her phone back into her pocket and returned to the bedroom for another box.

Maggie squeezed past Selene carrying a box of…something with apparent ease. That didn't it was light. Maggie's job as a physical trainer left her amazingly strong. It showed in the slim, toned figure, the chiseled arms, and the perfectly flat stomach. Her face, of course, matched her figure. Her excellent conditioning made her impressive cheekbones and strong nose stand out in perfect relief. Her shining black hair, tied up today in a practical ponytail, hung neatly to her shoulders.

Selene returned to the bedroom and hefted the second-to-last box. Its staggering weight momentarily threw her off balance. *So that's where the Anatomy and Physiology textbooks Maggie kept after college ended up.*

"Remind me why we're doing this," she whined playfully to her friend as Maggie bounded into the room and scooped up the last box. "You always said it made sense for a single woman to live at home, especially since you wanted to keep your dad company."

Maggie shrugged. "I don't know," she replied. "I just felt like I needed a change. This seemed like a good time to do something different. Now shut up and move. This box is heavy."

Probably hand weights, Selene thought. Thankful for the hours of training she spent each week in the police department's gym, she moved the box to the back of Maggie's rusty old pickup, Maggie trailing behind her with the final carton.

"Ladies," a warm and friendly voice came from behind them, "before you drive away, would either of you like something to drink?"

Selene turned around. Maggie's father Brandon stood behind her holding out two glasses of what could only be his homemade lemonade.

"Thanks, Dad," Maggie said, grabbing one and downing it in three gulps.

"Yes, thank you," Selene echoed shyly. *I've always liked Maggie's dad, perhaps a little too much, but I've never felt entirely comfortable around him. I'm not sure whether he knows about my gift, but I hope he doesn't. I want at least one person to believe I'm normal, and if it could be Brandon Price, well, that would be just perfect.*

"I can't believe you're done already," he commented. "I was going to help."

"I guess you're slowing down in your old age, Dad. We young chicks are just too fast for you."

"Sorry, I got tied up."

"You know, Dad, you could have told Grandma you would call her back."

"Yeah right, Maggie. If I did that, I would hear about it for a month."

"You're right," Maggie grinned, "but it's okay, Dad. Selene and I got it taken care of."

Brandon's dark eyes met Selene's briefly.

She glanced away, studying the garden beds with great interest. To cover the nervous movement, she took a sip of the lemonade. *Mmmm. Perfect, like always. Tart and refreshing.* She swallowed another, deeper mouthful and peeked back at Brandon and Maggie, standing together on the driveway. The striking pair looked so much alike. Tall with glossy black hair, sculpted cheekbones, and warm dark eyes... *I wonder who my father was.*

Quick as a flash, she pushed away the errant thought.

There's no benefit in feeling sorry for yourself. Fate has decreed that you'll live without a family, and honestly, they'd a distraction from work. Mentally shaking her head, Selene tossed down the rest of her lemonade and handed the glass back to Brandon with a shy smile.

He smiled back, his white teeth flashing against the copper of his skin.

Selene felt a rush of heat to her face and hoped she wasn't blushing. She met his eyes again and he winked at her. *God, I'm hot. I must be blushing. Damn it.*

"Can I offer you ladies some dinner?" he suggested.

"No time, Dad," Maggie replied. "I still have to unload this stuff at the apartment."

Selene tried to squash down her disappointment. *After such a hard day's work, eating one of Brandon's delicious meals would have been the perfect reward.*

"Maybe Selene would like to eat with you though," Maggie continued, surprising Selene out of her contemplation.

"Don't you want my help at the other end?" she asked.

"Not really," Maggie replied with a sassy look. "I've already heard enough knowing sighs from you. I know where I want my things, and I don't want to spend the next six months looking for them because you had a 'better idea' about where they should go!" She planted her hands on her hips and smirked.

Selene smiled at the banter. "If you had any logic at all in that little pea brain of yours," she teased back, "you would realize I've put them in the best places and look for them there first."

Maggie shook her head. "You know, Selene, you would make a lousy roommate."

"Why do you think I live alone?" Selene replied. She wrinkled her nose at Maggie and giggled.

Maggie responded with a sort.

"So, Selene," Brandon said, drawing her eyes back to his face, "would you like to stay for dinner? I have a stuffed chicken breast with mushrooms calling your name."

Selene's mouth watered at the thought of food that didn't come frozen and sealed under cellophane. *You should really get home. You never know when they're going to call you into work. Still...this is Brandon.* "Sure," she told him, smiling again.

Maggie waved, hopped into her battered pickup and drove off, leaving Selene and Brandon to watch the precariously stacked boxes sway.

5

"Do you think she'll arrive with all her stuff intact?" Selene asked as she disappeared around the corner.

"She'll be lucky if it's all still in the truck," Brandon replied.

They both laughed, turning toward the house. He escorted her to the door and ushered her in with a hand on her back. As his pinky finger touched the centimeter of bare skin between Selene's shirt and jeans, his feelings washed over her. Sadness formed the largest part, but she could also detect some relief, and not over his daughter leaving, either. *I'm glad Selene is staying. I'm not ready to face dinner alone. I've been alone so long...*

She stepped away from him quickly, hating to intrude on the thoughts of innocent people. *I wish I could block this, shut it off except at appropriate times. Sadly, no such luck.* Any time a person's hand touched her bare skin, she knew exactly what that person was thinking. "I'm hardly fit company," she told him, looking down at her dirty clothing.

"Don't worry," Brandon said reassuringly, "I'm not likely to throw out a guest because of a little dust. Besides, it came from this house to begin with. Why don't you go wash up? I'll set the table."

Selene scuttled off to the bathroom. Standing in front of a mirrored pedestal with a scalloped sink, she brushed as much grime as she could off her oldest jeans and faded tee-shirt, hating the way it settled on the black and white tile floor. She washed her hands with a bar of fragrant soap. The aroma of herbs and prairie flowers wafted up, friendly, welcoming and homey. *I wonder where he finds this soap. It's not in any of the stores where I've looked for it.*

She splashed a little water on her dusty face. No makeup at all, and she looked like a teenager. The faint smattering of freckles she pretended didn't exist stood out against her skin, which seemed paler than usual. *I look a little sick.* She frowned at her reflection. *Well, I feel fine, and a little paleness is nothing to be too concerned about.*

Shrugging, Selene left the bathroom. Passing down the narrow hallway to the kitchen, she seated herself at the round wooden table in one corner. She glanced at Brandon, who stood with his back to her near the stainless steel six-burner stove, stirring something in a large pot. The cavernous work-space, crowned with shining gold and black granite, made an impressive showplace fit for Brandon's culinary prowess.

He approached her, carrying two plates and setting one in front of her, and then took a seat as she inhaled in apprecia-tion. The chicken breast had been stuffed with ricotta and spinach and served with a rich mushroom sauce, seasoned rice, and steamed asparagus.

She forked up a mouthful of the tender meat, closing her eyes to concentrate on its succulent flavor. *Delicious.* "You know," she told Brandon after several bites, "if you ever decide to give up being a career counselor, you could make a fortune working in a restaurant."

Brandon smiled, leaning his chin on his fist. "Thank you," he said. Then, more quietly, added, "I'm glad you stayed. It's always nicer to cook for someone else."

"I'm sure," Selene replied. "That's why I never bother. With no one else to feed, why go to all the trouble?"

He looked at her with his heart-melting brown eyes and said nothing, but his expression spoke volumes. She didn't need to be a powerful touch psychic to read that particular thought.

"It's hell being alone isn't it?" she asked softly.

He dipped his chin, acknowledging her comment. For the briefest of moments, his lip moved—almost a tremble—and then he bit down on it.

Selene laid her hand on the sleeve of his shirt, her way of giving a comforting touch while honoring his privacy.

He slid his arm out slowly from under her hand until his palm touched hers.

Selene tried to slip away, but he closed his fingers, encasing her in his emotions. "Please," she said softly, "you shouldn't do that."

"Don't you want to know?" he asked her.

Selene looked down at her napkin. *So, he knows I'm a freak.* "I'm trying to respect your privacy," she told him.

"I'm choosing to share."

"Are you sure… I wouldn't, I mean, I…"

"Unless you don't want me to…"

Not want to share thoughts with Brandon? Thoughts freely offered? "No. No, I'm glad. It's nice to feel normal emotions from someone for a change."

She laced her fingers through his and let his feelings wash over her. ***Sorrow, grief, loneliness and a little fear.***

He really doesn't want to be alone. She closed her eyes and then opened them to look deeply into his. The warm brown depths drew her like a magnet. She unconsciously leaned in, closer to him than she could ever remember being before.

God, he's handsome, and his lips are so close. I'd only have to move a couple of inches… She tried to remind herself that he just didn't want to be alone, that the circumstances, not her presence, made him vulnerable. *But I don't want to be alone either.* She moved forward, intentionally this time, but stopped, too shy to continue. Her attention focused on the sensations moving into her through their joined hands.

Disappointment.

Selene met Brandon's eyes in surprise.

He moved his chin down again, a slight nod. Subtle. Almost unnoticeable.

She noticed.

His free hand touched her chin and the double dose of sensation overwhelmed her. He lifted her face until her eyes met his again. She could feel the query pulse into her from both sides. ***Don't stop.***

He wants it too, but he can't hear my thoughts, she realized. *Goodness, how can people who aren't psychic communicate? Brandon won't know what I want unless I do or say something obvious.* The realization ignited her courage. Imitating his soft nod, she lowered her face into his hand and gently kissed the palm.

Oh, wow. His nerves fluttered into her, but he nonetheless moved toward her and pressed his lips lightly to hers. It was a soft touch, like the brush of a butterfly's wings. So gentle. She closed her eyes and lifted her face. He responded. Another brush, then another. She released his hand so both of hers could slide around his neck. His tongue swept her lips. She opened, letting him taste her.

Suddenly, Selene felt as though the lights had been turned off. Somewhere in the middle of that drugging kiss, he had released her face. The moment his hand left her skin so he could draw her to stand pressed against his body, she lost her sense of his feelings. Without that intoxicating but false intimacy, reality hit like icy rain.

What on earth am I doing kissing my best friend's father? Dear Lord, I'm nearly in his lap. She stepped back, breathing heavily.

"What?" Brandon asked. "What happened?"

"What are we doing?" she wheezed.

He blinked. The transition from passion to nervous questions had been too swift. "Commiserating," he finally said.

"That's all?" *Oh, God. It didn't mean anything.* She closed her eyes in disappointment and turned away.

His hand on her chin forced her eyes back to his. With the touch came a flash of something intense she didn't have time to interpret. Then his fingers withdrew. "If that's all you want it to be, but…"

"But?" She sucked in her breath.

He held out his hand. "I don't know the words."

She swallowed hard, realizing what she hadn't seen earlier. *He's using my gift to communicate with me. No one has ever done that before.* Nervous, about what, she wasn't sure, Selene touched his palm with her fingertips. A contact so light made his feelings more like an echo, but an audible one.

I've been interested for quite a while, attracted even. I like you. I didn't know how to begin, but sadness over Maggie moving out—along with your otherworldly empathy—overcame my restraint. I want your comfort, but I also want your company, and not because I'm lonely and you're convenient. I want you, Selene.

Selene exhaled a breath she hadn't known she was holding. *Brandon is interested in me? Oh, wow.* She let the realization wash over her, breathing in his scent even as her fingers captured his thoughts. It felt wonderful, like a hug, only better. Then reality intruded. *Wait, no, I can't just wallow in his feelings like a freak. We need to do this like normal people.* "Can we sit somewhere more comfortable and talk about this?" she suggested. "I mean, really talk with words."

"Of course." His fingers slid down her arm, but she dodged, not wanting to get sucked back into the irresistible vortex of Brandon's thoughts and emotions. He laid his hand on her back instead, and they walked into the living room and sat side by side on the western style sofa.

"I think you should back up and tell me what's going on here," Selene said, using the carefully neutral tone she often employed when interrogating suspects.

"There isn't much to tell," Brandon replied, his voice soft but intense. "Putting it into words would be like trying to explain the wind. I don't have the skill. Besides, you felt everything, right?"

"Yes, but that's not the point," she insisted. "This isn't how these things are supposed to work."

Brandon shrugged. "Who cares about supposed to? You're unique. Why shouldn't we begin in a unique way?"

Unique. Not weird, freakish, or odd. How nice it sounds. "Are we beginning something?" Her heart began hammering as she asked the question.

"We can if you want to," he said, and, after taking a deep breath, added, "I know I want to."

He wants to? Oh, how utterly and unexpectedly perfect. Have I ever had something I want simply handed to me? Could it be this easy? Again, the temptation to simply nestle into his thoughts and his waiting arms—crept over her... until reality intruded. "What about Maggie?"

A hint of a frown creased the little space between Brandon's eyebrows. "What about her? She's been after me for years to start dating again."

"I don't think I'm quite the person she had in mind," Selene pointed out.

One corner of his mouth turned up, acknowledging the awkwardness with a wry, humorless grin. "She'll adjust. Maggie is an adult now. She's moving on with her life. Why shouldn't I do the same?"

"But..."

"Listen," Brandon told her earnestly, laying a hand on her shoulder, "If you aren't interested, please just say so. I'd rather know than wonder."

"I didn't say I wasn't interested," Selene assured him. "I just didn't see this coming."

"Didn't you?" He traced a finger up her neck and over her cheek, sending her a quick flash of amusement. "Did I imagine all those shy smiles, the flirty looks? Was I dreaming your interest because it was what I wanted to see? That isn't what that kiss felt like."

Selene swallowed hard. "You weren't imagining it, but I never thought my childish crush would amount to anything. You were an attractive fantasy, something to keep me warm..." she choked and turned red, "when I'm lonely."

A look of masculine pride spread over Brandon's handsome face. "Why shouldn't your feelings amount to anything?" he asked, still trailing his fingers over her cheek.

She closed her eyes at the soothing touch. "They never have before," she said without emotion, not wanting to whine, but merely stating a fact, albeit one of the most discouraging facts of her life.

As though unable to restrain himself another moment, Brandon wrapped warm arms around Selene's slender frame. "The entire world must be populated with idiots. Will you take a chance on me, Selene? We'll go as slow as you want until you get comfortable with the idea. Will you give it a try?"

Selene thought for a moment. While every instinct she possessed—not to mention every nerve in her body—screamed at her to say yes, the analytical part of her mind that never really shut off reminded her of how much pressure her job placed on her, and how it devoured all her time. "I work a lot," she told him letting her regret show on her face. "Long hours, tons of over-time, and I'm on call nearly every evening and weekend. Being with me would still mean you'd be spending a lot of time alone."

He slowly shook his head, not accepting her words as the end of the conversation. "I've been alone for years. At least I could be with you sometimes."

He would accept even that? "I have very little to offer."

Incredulity and heat flared into her from his fingertips. "Let me be the judge of that," he said, his eyes boring into hers with passionate intensity.

She looked away. "Don't forget, Brandon, I'm a freak. I can read your mind. You'll never be able to keep a secret from me."

Can't have that. His words flared in her mind as he turned her to face him. "You're not a freak. You have a gift. If it can sometimes be uncomfortable, well, it has its uses too. It doesn't bother me. Say yes."

The heat in those eyes. The desire. No one has ever looked at me like this before. She could think of no other excuses, and really, she didn't want to try. The temptation overwhelmed her, and she couldn't withstand it. "All right then, Brandon. We'll try this and see where it leads." *I hope I sounded as nonchalant as I intended.*

He dazzled her with a white-toothed smile.

Selene badly wanted to pinch herself and see if she were dreaming. *No, I don't. If this is only a dream, I don't want to wake up yet. Kissing Brandon…I would never have imagined it outside of my wildest fantasies.* Even then, she rarely let herself indulge; it was so far beyond likelihood. *Oh, don't lie to yourself.* Alone, unable to sleep, she had sometimes succumbed to the temptation and imagined his arms around her, his firm full lips pressed to hers. The longing released by those fantasies had been excruciating. *And now you know your imagination fell utterly short of reality.*

Wishing she could communicate her own feelings without words, she gave Brandon a pleading look. He chuckled softly and pulled her against him in a tight hug. His mouth came down on hers. Instead of feather-light persuasions, this kiss smashed into the wall of her loneliness with the impact of a train. His hands did not touch her skin but rested gently on the back of her shirt. The only thoughts she heard were her own, a repetitive voice chanting, *Yes! Yes! Yes!* Her arms slipped around his neck, and she kissed him back with reckless abandon.

Time ceased to have any meaning as they explored each other's lips and mouths, and it could have been an hour later when they finally parted, panting.

Selene blinked a few times, startled by the intensity of desire and passion flooding through her. "Wow," she said softly. "That was…I don't even know how to describe it."

"Don't try," he urged. "The words don't exist."

He's got that right. This... whatever this is... is bigger than any word in any language. So big. So deep... it's a little scary.

"This is how hearts get broken," the voice of her insecurity whispered. "What are you planning to do, girl? Spend the night in his arms? And then, tomorrow, go back to work like nothing happened?"

She turned to the window, taking in a deep breath in an attempt to still her pounding heart. Darkness had fallen completely. *Wow. It's almost summer. Days are long. How long have we been sitting here?* "I should go home," she told him, hearing a hint of the regret she felt in her voice. "I don't want to ruin this by rushing it, and I have a lot to do tomorrow to be ready for my work week on Monday." *But I also really, really don't want this to end, just in case I wake up and find it was all a dream.*

"One more kiss, and then I'll take you home," he offered. His devilish grin flashing, making her heart increase its tempo yet again. Her belly fluttered with excitement.

She smiled, cheeks burning as she waited for him to reach for her, but he stayed where he was. *He wants me to initiate this kiss,* she realized. *Do I dare?* She licked her lips nervously and ran her fingers up his arm to his shoulder, around his neck, and finally pulled him towards her. Raising her face, she touched her lips softly to his. His fingers laced into her hair, stroking her sensitive scalp as she kissed him. Softly, shyly, she told him without words that she enthusiastically reciprocated his interest.

Several minutes passed while their mouths played and mated, arousing untapped desires, desires too long left dormant, too long denied. Finally, Selene ended the embrace. "Brandon," she said seriously, "it would be far too easy to rush this, to move too fast, and later have regrets. We could easily carry on all night, and then where would we be?"

Brandon gave her a wicked look. "Guess."

She blushed again, looking away.

"I'm kidding," he said, taking her hand so she could feel his sincerity. "It really is too soon for that, and the last thing I want to do is scare you off. I'll take you home now." He squeezed once and stood, still holding her hand to help her to her feet. She could feel his intense satisfaction washing over her in waves of soul-soothing joy.

CHAPTER 2

*S*elene released Brandon's hand and rose to her feet. Outside of her luscious embrace, the growing cool slipped past his defenses. *The early stages of a relationship have their downside. I'd much rather let this evening of cuddling lead to its natural conclusion, but that's going to be a long, long while, I suppose.*

She made her way through the kitchen to the connecting door of his garage, and then out to his truck. He followed, unabashedly admiring the roundness of her backside, the dip of her slender waist in her tight, faded jeans, and the line of her legs. *Pretty, sexy, smart and special... and she doesn't even know it.*

Brandon's silver pickup looked like a newer, cleaner version of Maggie's. He clicked the unlock button on the keychain. At the loud beep, Selene jumped, shook herself, and made an obvious effort to focus. She slid into the passenger side of the bench seat and fastened her seatbelt. Brandon climbed in beside her and started the motor. He pulled out of the driveway and turned left, his eyes on the road.

After a few minutes, Brandon glanced at Selene. *Daydreaming, I see, but the shy smile on her face tells me about what.* He couldn't resist laying his hand on hers, where it rested on the seat. He knew his intense attraction would be transmitted directly to her psyche. *While she might be uncomfortable with her gift, I'm glad of it. Instead of trying to express myself with words, which are often vague and open to interpretation, I can communicate my actual thoughts and feelings to her directly.*

∽

Selene jumped at the sudden contact, and then relaxed, allowing his fingers to lace through hers. *Holding hands is such a normal thing to do, but I never thought anyone would allow it. Not once they know what I can do. Who would have imagined, when I offered to help Maggie move, that my day would end like this? Finally, for the first time, I'm someone's girlfriend. No, not just someone's—Brandon's. How could such a perfect moment come to someone like me?*

Brandon's thoughts poured into her, filled with hope. ***Maybe this will work out. Maybe I won't be alone all the time anymore. Maybe I can finally…***

A fire engine shrieked behind them and Brandon thoughtfully pulled over, leaving room for the massive truck to slide past them. A few moments later another followed.

"Goodness," Selene commented, "there must be quite a fire burning somewhere."

Brandon nodded. He released her hand to grip the wheel.

As they approached Selene's neighborhood, the screaming of sirens and shouting of male voices penetrated the cab of the truck. Selene's heart began to beat faster. Fire engines blocked the street in front of her house. A hellish glow lit the tiny structure. Brandon pulled over a few houses down, and Selene scrambled out of the cab with shaking hands and trembling knees. Brandon followed.

She stopped dead and stared in dumb amazement at the

SIMONE BEAUDELAIRE

scene of desolation before her. Through the bay window to the left of the door, she could see orange and yellow flames greedily devouring her flowered sofa. Her breath caught as the curtains flared and then fell. Smoke belched from the edges of her garage door.

Oh no! The cats! Suddenly able to move, she advanced in rapid, uneven steps.

A uniformed police officer with a mop of curly brown hair blocked her path. "Stay back, ma'am," he told her brusquely, his eyes on the scene.

"Tony…" her voice wavered, almost inaudible in the din.

The cop looked at her sharply. "Selene? What are you doing here?"

She tried to speak, but her tight, tear-clogged throat prevented sound from escaping. She whimpered and tried again. This time, the words, "…my house…" carried through the commotion.

"Shit." The officer's gruff expression twisted into one of nauseous sympathy.

She tried to rush past him, but he moved in front of her. "You can't," he told her gruffly, gripping her upper arm, careful to keep his hand on her sleeve. "It's a total loss."

"No!" she cried. "Sammy and Margot are in there!"

She tried to pass him again, but Brandon grabbed her from behind. She fought him, desperate to get into the house, but he held her tight.

"Did she say there are people inside?" Tony asked Brandon. She heard the words, but dimly, as though the smoke of the fire affected her ears, not just her eyes.

"No," she heard Brandon tell the officer grimly as she turned in his arms and began to sob, "her cats."

With her face hidden against Brandon's chest, she could barely make out the crackle of a radio. "There are no people inside," Tony shouted. "I repeat; the owner is not inside. Get your asses out of there."

18

Selene clung to Brandon as she wept. *My home, all my earthly possessions, clothing, car—even my pets—will soon be reduced to ashes, and there's nothing anyone can do to stop it.*

"Ma'am," a hoarse voice broke through Selene's misery. She looked up, unconcerned with the tears streaming down her face. A filthy, soot-covered man in a flame-retardant coat stood in front of her. "I'm real sorry about your home," the firefighter said. Then he opened his coat and handed her an ashy bundle of gray fur. "Your big kitty didn't make it," he added in a gentle, gravelly voice, "but I think this little fella is going to be all right."

"Sammy!" Selene exclaimed, burying her face in his filthy gray fur. The kitten stared at her, the manic spark he usually had in his blue-gray eyes had gone blank, as though in shock. Letting out a tremendous sneeze, he dug his tiny, needle-like claws furiously into her shirt.

Brandon's arm remained around Selene, and he pressed gently against her shoulders, leading her away from the remains of her home. He lowered the tailgate of his truck and lifted her inside. She sat, dazed, cradling her cat against her shoulder with one arm as helpless tears streamed down her cheeks. Brandon sat beside her, his arm around her shoulders, stroking her cheek soothingly.

"Selene." She looked up to see that Tony had walked over to her.

Brandon tightened his grip protectively. His hand remained firmly pressed against her cheek, sending a wordless but comforting sensation directly into her.

Tony stared at them, jaw sagging slightly. Then he shuddered and cleared his throat. "I need to ask you some questions."

"Can't you see she's in shock?" Brandon scolded the officer. His voice, to her overwrought ears, sounded as though it came from inside a tunnel. "She's in no condition to talk right now."

"She should come down to the station," the policeman said firmly. "We can take care of her there."

"There's no need," Brandon replied. "She can stay with me until we straighten everything out." He slipped his hand into hers and sent images of warm hugs and safety to her over-wrought mind.

"Who are you?" Tony asked belligerently, gawking at their joined hands.

"Brandon Price," he introduced himself inattentively. His attention remained on her, not the policemen.

Selene fought her way up out of the fog as best she could. *I have to try and explain to Tony. I can't let him be aggressive with Brandon.* Her lips felt numb, but she reached out her hand. Tony flinched and dodged away. Then he frowned, steeled himself visibly, and went still. She laid her fingers on his shirtsleeve and forced herself to speak. "Brand is a friend," she told him softly.

"All right then," he grumbled, but she could hear that his tone had softened. "We'll need you to come down to the station as soon as possible and answer some questions. This fire was no accident." He turned to Brandon. "There's nothing the two of you can do but get in the way. Can you get her out of here?"

Brandon nodded. He helped Selene down from the bed of the truck and loaded her into the cab, fastening her seatbelt when her trembling fingers refused to perform the task. Silently, he drove her back to his house.

Once there, she sat forlornly on a kitchen chair, saying noth-ing, stroking Sammy with unsteady hands while Brandon dug a rusty cake pan from the back of his cupboard and filled it with kitty litter left over from last winter. He set it in the kitchen, along with a bowl of water. Lifting the grubby kitten from Selene's weak grasp, Brandon introduced him to his temporary accommodations. As soon as he was released, Sammy took a long drink of water then streaked away into the living room.

One unexpected guest dealt with, Brandon returned to Selene, who was shivering harder than ever. He scooped her off the couch and hugged her gently. Her skin felt icy, and she smelled strongly of smoke. Smudges marred her face and clothing, and ash from Sammy's fur stained her hands nearly black. She clung to him.

"Come on, sweetheart," he said soothingly, his hand circling on her back. "Let's get you into the shower."

Selene allowed herself to be led, like a sleepwalker, into the bathroom. Brandon turned on the shower, filling the room with steam.

"Will you be all right?" he asked her, but Selene didn't reply. She just stared at him blankly.

Brandon cursed. Striving to remain impersonal, he removed her clothing and loosened her braid. Then he quickly stripped off his clothes and escorted her into the shower. Praying she wouldn't notice his unwanted erection and become alarmed, he dipped her into the water, wetting her hair and rinsing the soot from her face. He poured shampoo into his hand and massaged it, gently but thoroughly, into every inch of those extra-long corn silk colored strands.

Once Selene was clean, and her skin warm to the touch, Brandon dried her with one of the large purple bath towels Maggie had given him as a joke. It seemed to swallow her up, she was so tiny. He wrapped his usual green one around his hips.

Well, Price, what the hell are you going to do now? Selene had no clothes except the filthy ones she had been wearing. Now she stood before him, naked under the towel and completely vulnerable. He wrapped her in a protective arm and walked her into his room, where he dug a tee shirt out of his drawer. He rarely wore it because it was so big on him, so on Selene's slight frame, it hung like a nightgown. *That will work for the moment.* Still she stood, frozen and unresponsive save for a slight trembling that set the tee-shirt fluttering. Reasoning that some sleep might help her, he led her to the bed and tucked her in.

Brandon had just turned to leave the room when he heard a soft, almost inaudible whisper.

"Don't go. Please, Brandon, don't leave." Selene had snapped out of her stupor and was watching him with desperation in her eyes.

"Okay, sweetheart, I won't go. Just give me a minute to put something on." He grabbed the first pair of clean boxers he found in the drawer and slid into the bed behind her, drawing her back against his chest and laying his arm across the narrow dip of her waist. She cuddled against him, and within moments her breathing became slower and more regular. Soon she dozed off.

Now what? It's only 9:20 and I'm not particularly tired, but I don't want to disturb Selene. So, he stayed, watching over her. It would be a lie to suggest he had never imagined this, holding her while she slept, but he certainly wouldn't have chosen these circumstances.

In his fantasy, of course, this would be the culmination of a night of fiery lovemaking. *Of course, if I'm not mistaken, Selene admitted earlier that she's never been in a relationship before. I could very well be dealing with a virgin. I'll have to take this slowly—which will be uncomfortable—but the potential reward is immense. Selene isn't a one-night stand or even a hot affair. She's the kind of woman a man wants to keep for life.*

Reminding himself he was getting way too far ahead, he kissed her softly on the cheek and closed his eyes. *She feels perfect in my arms.* Warm and content, Brandon fell asleep a few minutes later.

CHAPTER 3

*S*elene woke the next morning feeling groggy and disoriented. Without opening her eyes, she felt sure something was different. A warm lump of buzzing fur, which she recognized as Sammy, snuggled against her shoulder. *But where's Margot? And my sheets have never felt like this, nor do I remember owning a nightgown quite this baggy. Where am I?*

Her eyes snapped open and for a moment, she still didn't know. *This is not my bedroom. It isn't the lumpy sofa at the police station where I crash for an hour or so when I'm too tired to drive.*

Instead, she lay in a bedroom she'd never seen before. Three oversized windows framed in stained oak permitted bright sunlight to illuminate the room. The bedspread, decorated in colorful geometrics, did not resemble her sprays of lilacs. Every piece of furniture—from the bed to the dresser, to a chunky recliner in the corner—had clearly been built for someone much larger than her.

Then she remembered. *The fire. My house is gone. Margot's dead. My whole life in ashes. Shit.*

No! Don't cry again. You're alive, Sammy's alive, and you're not alone. She made herself remember she had friends, people who cared about her. She had money in the bank to buy new possessions. She had insurance on her car and home. Except for Margot, everything she had lost was replaceable.

And Brandon, dear, sweet Brandon, brought me home with him and cared for me. He washed me, she remembered, *dressed me in his shirt, and held me while I slept. What a hero.* At last, she remembered what had happened before the fire. Dinner, kisses, talking without words. It all seemed like a dream, except here she lay in his bed. In his bed, alone.

Wondering where he had gone, she got up, her legs still a little unsteady, and wobbled to the bathroom. A quick search of his medicine cabinet revealed a toothbrush, still in its package, which she appropriated. *One thing I'm not ready to do is face the man of my dreams with morning breath.* She also borrowed his hairbrush and tried to smooth the tangles left after a night of sleeping on her wet hair.

Moments later, she followed the intoxicating aroma of bacon and coffee out of the bathroom and into the kitchen, where she found Brandon, still wearing the boxers he had thrown on the previous night, scrambling eggs.

"Good morning," she said softly, and he turned. *Lord, he's glorious, all smooth tawny skin and slender, wiry muscle.* She'd never seen him so scantily dressed, and for a moment the sight took her breath away. Realizing her mouth was hanging open, she closed it with an embarrassingly audible click of teeth. Shaking her head, she attempted to pull herself together.

"Hi, Selene. You seem better this morning."

She hastened to reassure him with a playful answer. "Yes. I think I'll live."

"I'm glad. I was worried about you last night."

"I know. I was acting stupid, but I couldn't snap out of it," she murmured shyly, giving him a look that revealed her vulnerable feelings. "You were very sweet to take such good care of me,"

He removed the pan from the heat and laid it on an unlit

burner, then crossed the room, his long strides eating up the distance. He scooped her into a warm hug. Selene laid her cheek on his chest.

"I'm sorry about the fire," he said softly, "but taking care of you? That's just what a boyfriend does."

She smiled. "Boyfriend. I like the sound of that."

"I bet you'll like this too." He tilted her face up with one finger under her chin and kissed her softly, reminding her that yesterday had not been all bad.

Long moments later, they released each other. Sighing deeply, Selene moved to set the table with forks, coffee cups and juice glasses. She sat down in front of a plate of eggs and bacon. Brandon joined her.

"You know," she said, after crunching happily on a strip of bacon, "I don't think I'm doing too badly after all."

"What do you mean?" he asked, eyebrows drawing together. From this close, she could see small vertical lines between them.

He thinks I'm talking about the fire. No wonder he's confused. "Well, I've never had a boyfriend before," she explained, succumbing to the temptation to stroke her fingers down his arm, "but now, here I am, with you, and you're the man I've always dreamed of in secret but never thought I could have."

"You can have me as long as you want me," he rumbled tenderly.

"And if I decide never to let you go?" she whispered, daring to say what she had never admitted, even to herself.

"Sounds perfect."

Perfect? Is there a stronger word than that? Perfect isn't nearly enough. Selene squeezed his arm, but changed the subject, not wanting to overdo the intensity. "Once we're done here, I have to call my work. Tony said I needed to come in."

Brandon accepted the new topic with only a wry twist of his lips. "The chief called about an hour ago. I don't know how he found my cell number, but I told him I didn't want to wake you, and besides, you didn't have anything to put on. He agreed it was unrealistic to expect you at the station when you had nothing to wear. Once we get you some clothes, they want you to come in and make a statement. They think the fire was arson."

Suddenly, Selene's delicious breakfast tasted like ashes. *Ashes, like my life.*

No, she reminded herself, *my stuff is ashes. My life is actually not that bad.* "Why would someone burn my house on purpose? I don't know anyone well enough to have that kind of enemy."

Seeing her distress, Brandon took her hand in his, warming her fingers and sending her his strength. "I don't know," he replied, giving her a reassuring squeeze. "Maybe it was a pyromaniac. Maybe a police hater. Your friends can figure it out, it's their job. Meanwhile, you can stay with me as long as you like. I'm here for you, Selene." **You won't have to face this alone,** his thoughts pulsed into her.

Who would have guessed I had such a source of support right at my fingertips? "Thank you, Brandon. But staying here? Are you sure it's a good idea?"

"I'd like it if you would stay. That way I know you're safe." His fingers tightened gently on hers.

She stroked her thumb over his. A sizzle shot through her, and she took a deep breath. "Don't you think it would be…a little much?"

An image flashed into her mind of their naked bodies twined together. He acknowledged his unruly thought with a wry expression but offered no apology. "I can't imagine having too much of you. I understand you want to take this slow. I can make up the guest room if you want, but I don't like the idea of you being on your own when someone dangerous may be after you."

A guest room…in the house but not in his bedroom. Rationally, it's the best solution.

She opened her mouth to agree when in opposition to the logical thought, Selene's intuition jangled. The timing of the fire seemed almost too coincidental, like a message from fate. She had just begun a relationship with the man for whom she had harbored a desperate, secret crush for years. She had felt she ought to take it slowly, had tried to slow down, and then her house had burned leaving her stranded. The meaning became clear. Slowing down wasn't part of the plan.

Maybe it doesn't need to be. What's the reason for taking a new relationship slowly? To get to know the person? I know Brandon well, have known him for years. I know he's an honorable man who takes his responsibilities seriously. He's fun and charming, but definitely not a player. He's a great father to his daughter. It wouldn't be so bad to move this forward quickly.

"If you want me in a guest room, Brandon," Selene said, her shyness creeping into her voice, "then that's fine, but I slept really well last night, much better than I usually do. If it's not too much trouble for you...I enjoyed sharing your bed." She could feel the heat rising in her cheeks again.

He gave her a long, speaking look, his dark eyes glowing like coals. "Selene, I would like nothing better, but you have to understand where that's going to lead." That image played in her mind again, this time not quickly suppressed. Brandon let her see what he wanted to do to her, in all its enticing foreignness, making no secret of his desire.

"Yes, I know." She blushed even more deeply, her skin tingling with heat. Her breathing became ragged and shallow. "I would appreciate not going there...right away, but isn't that kind of the expected outcome? I mean, why else are we doing this?"

"Honestly?"

She nodded.

"Yes, I want to make love with you, though that's certainly not something I want to rush you into. You're sexy, pretty, smart, driven. I just find you...intoxicating. I think it's possible you might be the woman for me…for life. If I didn't think so, I wouldn't be here. I'm not interested in one-night stands. Sorry if that's too much. And to answer your question, I don't *expect* you to let me make love to you, but I'm hoping you will want me to, eventually."

His words and the accompanying images and feelings caused a swirl of confused, contradictory sensations in her. "I do, and I don't. It's strange."

"Level with me, Selene. You hinted very strongly last night that you're a virgin. Is that true?"

"Yes." She met his eyes, and then glanced away, face burning.

He nodded. "Well, then, I'm not surprised you find the idea of intimacy a little scary. I promise I'll let you set the pace."

Let me *set the pace? I'd be afraid to ask for more than a kiss!* "It may not be the best idea, letting my nerves decide what to do and when. We'll never get anywhere that way."

"Do you need to be pushed a little?" Eagerness pulsed in him.

The truth refused to pass her lips, so she settled for, "Maybe," while breaking eye contact.

He placed his free hand under her chin and lifted her head back up. His gaze was filled with desire, but also with tenderness. "Well, if we're sharing a bed, things are probably going to progress pretty quickly. I don't know if I'm strong enough to sleep beside you and keep my hands to myself for very long."

I know that. It's obvious. But she could feel his uncertainty, so she reassured him, forcing the words past the burning, choking sensation of her embarrassment. "Maybe I don't want you to. I mean, the reason I'm here is that I'm pretty sure you're the man for me too. I don't want us to regret anything, and that includes waiting so long that our relationship fizzles."

"I won't fizzle, Selene. I want you too much."

He pulled gently on her hand, lifting her to her feet and guiding her onto his lap so she straddled him. The kitchen chair was just wide enough for her to plant one knee on each side of his thighs. His hands slid up her arms to the back of her neck. Easing her down until her lips lay against his, he kissed her deeply. He skimmed his fingers down her back, gathering up the folds of fabric and sliding his hand under the tee-shirt. He caressed her bare back. *Just a little push,* he thought as he caressed her. *Don't scare her but let her know how much she's desired.*

Brandon's arousal seared Selene's senses. She made a quiet sound of pleasure against his lips.

After a long, heated moment, he pulled back, his fingers still on her skin. "I hope you're serious about everything you said. I don't know how long I can wait for you."

"Just a little while, Brand. Let me get used to the idea." She brushed his full lower lip with the tip of her thumb, feeling the wetness of their kiss still lingering there.

"Okay. I'll try." He sounded both encouraged and hopeful.

She touched her mouth softly to his and then slid off his lap. "Now, I need to figure out how to get to the store and buy some clothes without being arrested," she quipped, trying to lessen the intensity between them just a bit.

He took the subtle withdrawal graciously, sitting back in the chair and regarding her with an understanding expression. "I called Maggie while you were sleeping. She stopped by on her way to work and brought you some things. I think they're hers, so I don't know if they'll fit well, but they should be enough for decency. The bag is in the living room."

"Bless you, Brandon. Oh, and I stole your toothbrush, the one that was still in the package."

"Sure, no problem." One corner of his mouth quirked into a smile.

She smiled back and wandered into the living room. Sure

enough, on the sofa lay a white plastic grocery bag. She scooped it up and padded across the carpet to the wooden floor of the hallway, and then to the bathroom, where she washed her face before pulling out the clothing.

Maggie had, as expected, brought a black tee shirt featuring a band Selene had never heard of and a pair of black yoga pants. *Looks like they'll fit in the waist, but I bet they're too long.* Reaching into the bag again, she pulled out a new package of underwear. The bra she had been wearing was still relatively clean, so she retrieved it and dressed. Instantly she felt better, more in control. *Although, if Brandon's right about where this is headed, I'll soon be wearing even less for him.* The idea both terrified and excited her.

Deciding to think about it another time, she returned to Brandon and together they walked hand in hand to the garage. He helped her up into his truck and then circled around to hop into the driver's seat, firing the ignition.

"Selene, this shopping is going to be a strain," he reminded her. "You have to take it easy. You haven't been looking like your usual strong self lately, and that was before all this happened. Do you want to go to the mall?"

Ugh, never. "No, just the department store. Everything I need will be right there."

"Isn't it ironic," Selene commented idly as they drove to the police station, the backseat of the truck piled with new business and casual wear, pajamas, undergarments and makeup, "that a place most people would gladly never go inside feels like home to me?"

"It is. You know, the only time I've ever been inside a police station was when I was fingerprinted for my background check. I don't think I've ever been that uncomfortable in my life. Everyone was looking at me like I was some kind of drug dealer." He shut his mouth abruptly, cutting off his runaway words.

Parking carefully between the sun-faded lines, trying to avoid a deep pothole that had not been repaired after the spring thaw, he turned off the ignition. Selene hopped out of the truck before he could open the door for her, hurrying into the station.

The vestibule consisted of a bare, white-tiled, white-walled room with a single service window blocked off in Plexiglas. The opening was only large enough to admit an object the size of a credit card. The officer inside the little booth looked about bored enough to fall asleep right there.

"Hey, Jack." Selene knocked on the glass, making the young man jump. "Buzz me in. I don't have my key."

"Right away, Selene." The man pushed a button, and a door swung open. Selene led the way through, clutching Brandon's fingers.

They entered a large open space that matched the waiting room in color but was filled with rows of cubicles. The consensus seemed to be for disorder; most workspaces over-flowed with jumbles of paper. Doors around the perimeter were labeled: FINGERPRINTING, POLYGRAPH, INTERRO-GATION, LAB. To one side an office, separated from the rest of the room by a wall of glass had been labeled JAMES BRADY, CHIEF OF POLICE.

Despite being Sunday morning, the station teemed with activity. Cops, both in and out of uniform, escorted people from the reception area, through the workspace, and into one or another of the rooms. Other officers stood around, chatting and drinking coffee.

The moment Selene walked in, a mob of her co-workers descended on her; hugging her, patting her back, and gener-ally repeating to her how sorry they were about the fire. Tony —the police officer Brandon recalled from the fire—hugged her hardest. Slinging a muscular arm tattooed with an anchor casually around her shoulders, he led Selene away to take a statement. Brandon was left standing awkwardly in a room full of cops he didn't know. He would rather have waited outside.

His discomfort turned to alarm when the chief beckoned to him from inside the glass office. *I've never gotten so much as a parking ticket, but there are plenty of folks who will take one look at me and assume that any Indian is up to no good. I hope this Chief Brady isn't one of them.* He entered with more than a little trepidation.

The police chief, middle-aged but slim, had keen, dark eyes and a face like granite. Brandon swallowed hard.

"Are you the Brandon Price I spoke to on the phone this morning?" Brady asked in a tone that was curt to the point of unfriendliness.

"Yes, sir," he replied politely.

"Tony tells me you took Selene away from the fire. Is that right?"

His disapproving tone unnerved Brandon, which, in turn, made him feel a little angry. He crossed his arms over his chest and felt his expression harden. "Yes." No *sir* this time.

"Who are you, anyway?" Brady's eyes narrowed suspiciously.

"I'm her boyfriend." Brandon could hear defiance in his voice. *I'm not looking for trouble, but I'm no doormat.*

To his astonishment, a broad grin broke over Brady's stern features. "Ah, I wondered. Good for her. Everyone will be delighted to hear she has someone to look out for her. She does a terrible job taking care of herself."

Brandon didn't know what to make of the abrupt shift. He spoke without reflection. "Well, that's true. Of course, if her employer didn't insist she spend so much time at work…"

The chief gave Brandon a hard look.

Brandon's temper peaked. "Seriously, don't you think she's overdoing it? She's terribly thin and pale, and I've never

32

seen her so exhausted. She isn't sleeping well either. She's worn out. What are you going to do if she has a nervous breakdown?"

"Simmer down," Brady growled, a hint of humor sparking in his steely eyes. "No one insists. She can always refuse to come in when she's not on duty. She just never does."

"She sees this job as her reason for existing," Brandon explained.

"I don't blame her. She's excellent at what she does."

"Which is what exactly?"

"That's classified."

Funny. He didn't say that as firmly as I expected. Brandon decided to press a little. Placing both hands on the desk, he leaned forward and told Brady earnestly, "I'm the closest thing to family she has. I won't spill your department secrets, I swear, but how can I take care of her if I don't even know what she's doing?"

The look on Brady's face suggested he was suppressing a grin. "So, you're her protector as well. She needs that. Fine, come over here."

He motioned Brandon around his desk to look at the computer monitor. A couple clicks of the mouse brought up a video feed from an interrogation.

"You know about Selene's…gift?" Brady asked.

"Yes," Brandon replied.

Brady nodded. "Her job is to interrogate suspects. Most of the time she clears them instantly of guilt and saves us the headache of following up on details for weeks. Sometimes, she determines they're guilty, and she's incredibly skilled at asking the right questions to get them to confess, or at least to slip up enough so we can move forward with the case. Of course, this is not open for discussion with *anyone*. No one can know what she does or every interview she has conducted would become inadmissible. You understand?

33

Murderers would go free." His commanding expression no longer seemed amused.

Brandon nodded.

"This video is one of her most memorable achievements. The suspect here was brought in for questioning on a minor hit and run that damaged a parked car. Watch."

The video showed a small room in which a young man sat, visibly sweating and nervous. Selene entered, dressed in a black suit with her pale golden hair pulled back into a bun.

"Good afternoon, sir," she said politely. "I'm Officer Johansen. I need to ask you a couple of questions." She held out her hand.

She's offering contact to a stranger? That's what she does? Whoa!

The young man grasped her fingers gently. Instantly, Selene's whole face changed. Her eyes narrowed, her jaw clenched. She looked mad as hell. "What did you do with the body?" she gritted out between her teeth.

The suspect gaped.

"Did you think we wouldn't find out? That you could just hide what you did forever?"

He shot her a panicky look. "She…she deserved it."

"Deserved to be murdered?" Selene demanded.

"No, it was an accident," he whined, eyes shifting from side to side.

"Maybe her death was, but you slapped her, knocked her down so she hit her head, and that's how she died. It's manslaughter at the very least. And what about her poor family? Do they deserve to spend years wondering what happened to her? Is that right?"

"How did you know?" the suspect whimpered.

"We know all kinds of things about you. You can't hide. Tell us where she is, and we'll go easy on you, but if you don't confess right now, it's a murder charge."

"She's…buried in the sandpit, north of town. I swear I didn't mean to kill her." He burst into noisy sobs.

The chief pressed a button, and the video stopped. "We didn't even realize a crime had been committed. That young man pleaded guilty to manslaughter and a few other charges and was sentenced to a few years in prison. Without Selene, we might never have made the conviction."

Of course, she can do it well, intuitive as she is. After all, it had been his professional suggestion she go into law enforcement, but until today he'd had no idea just how good she was at it. *The hard-eyed professional on the screen bears little resemblance to the shy lady I kissed this morning at the breakfast table. She looked so fragile and vulnerable then.* Which brought him back to his original point. "Why was she questioning someone about a hit and run? Couldn't regular officers deal with the mundane stuff and save her the time and trouble? Keep her in reserve for the big cases so she doesn't have to spend her life at work? She's completely out of balance."

Brady agreed with a curt nod. "You're right, she is. I suspect she never had a reason to want to head home. Maybe it's up to you to give her that reason."

"So, if you call and she's not available?" Brandon pressed.

"She's not available," the chief conceded without rancor, "unless it's an emergency."

"Well, she's a cop. That's to be expected."

Brady gave Brandon a considering look. "Price, take good care of our girl. She's a treasure. All the guys love her. I've been worried about her myself. She seems very on-edge right now. This fire won't help."

"Of course, I'll take care of her," Brandon agreed, "but I do want to know one thing. Why is it that she's surrounded by guys who, as you say, love her, and I'm her first boyfriend? What's wrong with them? They can't all be married. Selene's looks alone ought to be enough to tempt someone."

"They're scared of her." Brady shrugged, dismissing the

answer as obvious. "She intimidates everyone. No one wants to be with a girl who can read minds. Doesn't it worry you?"

Brandon had considered that question ages ago and knew his answer. "No. She's more than her gift. She's also a warm, caring person who deserves to be loved."

"Well, *you* love her then," Brady replied, a hint of a grin lingering around his mouth again... or was it a smirk? "Maybe you're the only one who can, at least the way you're talking about. But be sure you treat her right because she has about a dozen big brothers here who will not be pleased if you hurt her."

"I promise."

The chief returned to his work, and Brandon walked out of the office, looking for Selene. He approached Brady's thickset secretary, with her long graying hair and a hint of a mustache. "Do you know—?"

Without looking up, she extended one arm, pointing him in the direction of the interrogation room.

"Thanks," he muttered, heading towards Tony, who stood outside the door, observing through the one-way glass.

"You're a cop?" a surprised male voice emerged through the speakers.

"I know I don't look like one," Selene replied wearily. "Anyway, do you know this woman?"

"Oh no, it's Carly!" The voice turned frantic. "Is she all right? What happened?"

"She was...hurt." Even through the speakers, Brandon could hear how carefully Selene chose her words. "She's in the hospital. We're trying to find out what happened, so we're checking with all her friends. Were you with Carly last night?"

Brandon turned to Tony in disbelief. "You're making her work? What the hell is wrong with you?"

The cop gave Brandon a clueless look, clearly oblivious to Selene's fragile state. Brandon wanted to shake some sense into him when he said, "She wanted to. It's a bad rape case. She insisted on getting right to it."

"Her house burned down last night. She's in no condition to interrogate suspects." Brandon shook his head. *I'm going to have to talk to Selene about setting boundaries at work.*

She left the room a moment later. "He's clean," she said wearily. "He was worried about running a stop sign until he saw the pictures." She swayed.

Brandon wrapped his arm around her waist. "Come on, sweetheart. You've had enough for one day. Let's get out of here."

Tony looked askance at the embrace but said nothing.

Brandon led her to the door. Outside, by his truck, he pulled Selene close and hugged her. She laid her cheek against his chest and he petted her hair. "Are you all right?"

"Yes," she answered automatically, but her slender body trembled in his embrace and she leaned on him heavily.

"No, you're not," Brandon insisted. "You're shaking. Why were you working?"

"That poor woman," she said by way of an answer, her tone mingling rage and sorrow. "You wouldn't believe what some bastard did to her. I have to help."

He put one hand under her chin and lifted her face, so he could give her a serious look. "How can you help if you don't take care of yourself, Selene? I'm not kidding. You're on the brink. You can't save the whole world alone. No one can. And don't forget that you've just gone through a hard time yourself. You have to take it easy. Come on, let's go home."

Back at the house, Selene looked ready to drop. "You'd better lie down," he urged, escorting her toward the bed.

"I never sleep during the day," she protested. "Even

sleeping at night is a struggle." A huge yawn forced its way up out of her.

"Just rest your body," Brandon suggested, lying down and tugging her with him. He settled her in front of him, so his arm rested on the dip of her waist and her bottom compressed his crotch. His penis reacted instantly to her proximity. *Down, boy. This is not the moment.*

Selene seemed not to notice. "You're so warm," she murmured before another yawn overcame her. A soft inhalation told him she'd gone out like a light.

While Selene slept, Brandon slipped out of the bed and ran her new clothes through the wash, thankful she'd purchased stuff that didn't require special handling.

It's nice living with a woman again. It will be even nicer when we used to it, he thought. *Right now, she looks ready to jump out of her skin. I wonder if she was serious when she said I was her fantasy, her crush. Imagine, all that time and I didn't have a clue until recently.*

Once the dryer finished spinning, he hung her work clothes next to his in the closet and shoved over a pile of socks in his drawer to make room for her new underwear and pajamas. The fabric slid silkily through his fingers, reminding him of Selene's hair. *This is going to be amazing.* He felt a thrill of anticipation and had to remind himself it might be a while yet.

Chores completed, he checked the clock. *About an hour since Selene fell asleep. I don't want her internal clock to get too far out of whack.* Brandon kissed her awake and took her out to dinner.

"What's the name of that burger?" Selene asked, as Brandon carefully parallel-parked along the curb outside alongside Max's, a famous dive.

"The Juicy Lucy," he replied. "There are a couple of places that have them, but this is my favorite."

"That's such an odd name," she said, laughing. "Why do they call it that?"

"You see," Brandon explained, "it's two patties smashed together with cheese inside, so when the whole thing cooks, it gets really, well, juicy. There's no such thing as a dry one."

He hopped out of the cab and walked around to open the door for her. Instead of just offering a hand to help her out of the cab, Brandon slid his arms around Selene's waist and lifted her down, letting her body slide against the length of his, and pulling her close for a hug. She wrapped her arms around his neck and enjoyed a brief cuddle before closing the door of the truck.

Brandon clicked the lock button on his keychain and escorted her into the dim interior. They found two empty stools at the bar, and they quickly claimed them. An old-fashioned black menu board—the kind with white letters that slid into place—had been mounted on the wall, and Selene scanned it.

"That's not necessary, you know," Brandon told her. "Just get the special."

She glanced down the bar where several patrons were devouring massive sandwiches, dripping with grease and melted cheese. "That's too big for me. I think I just want a plain hamburger."

"You're going to eat at a famous dive and *not* get the signature sandwich?" He looked dismayed. "Why?"

"It's too much food," she insisted. "If I eat all that, I'll get sick."

He shook his head as the bartender approached. As he ordered the two burgers, a cherry Coke for Selene and an iced tea for himself, Brandon slipped his hand into hers again. She turned to meet his eyes. He conspicuously scanned the room. No one was looking, so he pressed a quick kiss to her mouth. She beamed, glowing with joy from the inside out.

A few minutes later, the food arrived. Selene picked at her hamburger while Brandon piled into the legendary sandwich.

After swallowing a mouthful, he extended the molten, dripping mass to her. "You have to at least taste it," he insisted.

She nibbled and closed her eyes, enjoying the astonishing flavor. "Amazing," she told him softly.

Half an hour later, despite Brandon's urging, Selene had consumed only about two-thirds of her burger. He'd had no trouble polishing off his.

"How would you feel," he suggested, "about going for a walk? I'm a little overstuffed. I'd like to move around a bit."

"Sure," she agreed easily. "Where?"

"How about Lake Calhoun? They have a great walking path. We should have enough time. That storm isn't predicted to hit until later."

"Perfect." She flashed him a grin.

Brandon paid the bill, and they headed out to the truck to drive to the nearby waterfront. In the distance, the IDS Tower loomed blue and shiny above the Minneapolis city skyline's multiple skyscrapers. Vibrant green trees crowded close, as though standing guard between the marina and the sleeping giants.

A gentle breeze stirred the boats and sent the water lapping over the shore in soft soothing splashes, barely audible over a hundred conversations. Selene let Brandon help her down from the pickup once again and clung to his fingers as he led her to the cement walkway. They strolled hand in hand, drinking in the sunset over the water while skateboarders, bicyclists and dog walkers flowed around them.

Selene also drank in Brandon's contentment. *I'm so happy*

to be here with her, he thought. It warmed her more than the spring sunshine.

"Look," he said, pointing in the direction of what appeared to be an oversized, chrome-sided camper.

"What?" Selene asked, squinting against the scarlet sunset light as it reflected painfully off the vehicle.

"It's a food truck. Ice cream. Let's get some."

She started to shake her head, but he dragged her forward anyway.

"I'm full," she protested.

"You're never too full for ice cream on a warm day," he replied, dodging an overly excited Labrador retriever, who tried to tangle them up in his trailing leash. A boy with a red baseball cap perched sideways on his golden hair chased panting after the escaped dog. "This is some of the best in the city. It would be a shame for us not to have some since they're here."

Unable to summon a sufficient argument against his logic, Selene allowed herself to be escorted to the truck. Once they passed out of the blinding sun under the shade of several towering maples whose branches laced together to form a natural bower, she was able to read the sign hanging over the service window. *Hot Ice.*

"What kind of name is that?" she asked under her breath.

"They specialize in adult flavor combinations," he replied. "You know, hot like sexy?"

Selene rolled her eyes but peered at a second sign that seemed to show the flavors. *Hmmm. Cinnamon. Chocolate strawberry. Chile cocoa. Interesting.* "Glad they don't have oyster flavor," she quipped.

Brandon snorted. "What a strange thought. Do you know what you want?"

She shrugged. "I'll wing it."

A lady with dozens of blond braids hanging down around

her shoulders leaned out. A silver loop in her left nostril flashed. "Can I help you?"

"I'd like a two-scoop waffle cone," Brandon requested. "One scoop of Apple of Eden, one of Cinnamon Seduction." He grinned, and the woman's expression melted into a dopey smile.

Selene scowled. "I'll have a chocolate-dipped strawberry temptation," she said.

The woman seemed reluctant to turn her direction and then frowned at the sight of their joined hands. Then her unhappy look lifted into a sheepish smile. "Coming right up," she said, ducking back inside.

"Did I miss something?" Brandon asked.

"No," Selene replied, but she couldn't help wondering how long Brandon would remain interested in the face of so much obvious flirtation. *Having a super-hot boyfriend may not be all sunshine and roses. Still, any time I get to spend with Brandon is a blessing.*

On the ride back, Selene began to feel nervous. *Brandon said he was willing to wait, but we're planning to sleep together in the same bed.* Last night had not been premeditated, but tonight they had chosen a path that had a predictable ending. Though both of them wanted it, it was still life-altering, and therefore a little scary. She spent the rest of the drive vacillating between fretting and bubbling with excitement, so that, by the time Brandon pulled the pickup into the garage, she felt nearly ill.

Hopping down without waiting for his help, she bolted into the house. Sammy greeted her at the door with a flurry of wailing complaints and a tickly brush of his fluffy gray tail against her leg. She scooped the kitten into her arms. "Hello, baby."

He stopped squalling and began to purr. She scratched behind his ears.

"You okay, babe?" Brandon asked, stepping into the mudroom.

"Sure, fine," she replied. Tucking Sammy against her shoulder with one hand, she reached past Brandon to turn on the alarm.

"I can still make up the guest room if you want."

She shook her head. "No, it's not that. Remember, we're not letting my nerves make any important decisions. My intuition and logic say that we care for each other, can't keep our hands off each other, and we live together."

"And even then, if you're not ready, separate beds are fine. Take your time, Selene. Don't push yourself."

Selene considered the offer and shook her head. "No. No, I want to be with you. The guest room sounds worse."

"All right. Let's get ready for bed then. You go first. I want to run the dishwasher."

Grateful for the reprieve of at least not washing her face and brushing her teeth next to him, she made her way to the bathroom.

She brushed her teeth and braided her hair to keep it from tangling so badly in the night. Then tugged her new pajama set's baby blue tee-shirt over her head. She gulped to see just how much her nipples had hardened. *Nothing to the imagination there.* Shaking her head, she stepped into the soft blue striped shorts and made her way down the hall to the master bedroom.

She stared at the bed for long moments while Brandon brushed his teeth, and finally made herself get under the sheets, just as the promised storm arrived with a crash of thunder and a shower of heavy rain. The sounds of loud splashing on the bedroom windows enveloped the house as though in a blanket, shutting out the world and ensuring the privacy of a couple on the brink of intimacy.

Brandon joined Selene a moment later, wearing only boxers again. His coppery skin contrasted with the white bedding. *Also, with my own pale coloring*, she realized, as his arm snaked around her waist.

"Well," she asked, "now what?"

"I don't know. Normally when a man and woman go to bed together, it's for sex. Tell me, Selene, do you want to be pushed a little tonight, or just go to sleep?"

"Um, that's a tricky question." She blushed with embarrassment. *How does a woman ask a man to touch her? I have no idea. Even admitting to desiring it seems monumental.*

"Not really." He shrugged. "Just say what you want."

Easy for you to say. She prevaricated again. "If we…play around, won't that be uncomfortable for you?"

"What I have in mind for tonight won't be too bad," he said. "Later, there may come a time when, if you're not ready for intercourse, I'll have you help me…relieve the pressure."

She thought about what that might mean, and then quickly stopped herself. *Take it one step at a time, Selene.* "Oh, okay. Yes, I think I would like to…explore a little."

His lips curved into a wicked and beautiful grin, and her heart started to pound as he pulled her close and kissed her deeply with seductive thrusts of his tongue. *Lord, if this is what he means by not too bad, I'm afraid of what comes next.*

Thinking it wise to begin with familiar territory, Brandon reached under Selene's shirt to caress her silky back. He could feel her fingers twining in his hair.

Now, for just a little more. He removed his hands from inside her clothing and slid around her body to caress her breast through the tee. It was a lovely handful. Maybe not the biggest ever, but soft and round, with a sharply jutting nipple in the center. He shaped and fondled the dainty globe with increasing intimacy, finally grasping the peak through the fabric and rolling it gently between his fingers. Selene gasped against his mouth, and he could feel the tension in her thighs slackening as her pleasure increased.

He transferred his attention to the other breast, treating it to the same caressing. She again responded eagerly. *Oh, this is very good.* Brandon reached for the hem of her shirt and began to lift it, wondering when she would stop him. She didn't, so he stopped himself. *No rush.* He leaned down and kissed her belly before lowering her shirt back into place. Selene looked up at him, a little surprised.

"Why did you stop?" she asked after drawing a shaky breath.

"That's enough for tonight." He kissed her once more, sweetly. A telling mixture of relief and disappointment flashed in her eyes. She turned and snuggled close so her back pressed against his chest. His arms tightened around her. He kissed her temple and smiled as he closed his eyes.

CHAPTER 4

*S*ome sort of internal awareness brought Selene up out of the most peaceful slumber she could recall in years. She opened her eyes to find herself warmly embraced by a pair of strong, masculine arms. *Oh, that feels nice.* The clock on the bedside table read 4:48.

Ugh. That means it's time to wake up and get moving. I don't want to. She snuggled deeper into Brandon's embrace. His breath moved the hairs on the back of her neck, inciting tingles that radiated out along her entire body. *The days may be warm, but the nights are still chilly. I can feel the cold in the room.* Her eyelids fluttered, and sleep crept upward, threatening to drag her back down again.

If you don't move, the alarm is going to go off in twelve minutes and scare the bejeebers out of you. Come on, Johansen. Get moving. Life goes on. Reluctantly wriggling out from under Brandon's arm, she shuffled to the kitchen to brew coffee, warmed herself in a quick shower, and tossed on one of her brand-new work outfits.

Then, after combing out her long, white-blond hair, she settled down at the kitchen table a bowl of cereal and a cup of java, a novel cradled in one hand.

A few moments later, Brandon staggered out of the bedroom, looking sleepy, his short black hair ruffled. He kissed her forehead without a word and headed into the shower himself. She grinned. *He's so cute when he's sleepy, and I never even noticed. The intimacy of living together goes far beyond stroking each other in bed. Even beyond the sex we eventually plan to have. It's the day-to-day things no one else knows. Small things, perhaps not even noticeable, that sink into our being and bind us together on a subconscious level.*

Less than twenty minutes later, while Selene was tucking her dishes into the dishwasher, he entered, his wet hair combed into place, wearing black slacks and a white button-up shirt, with a colorful tie. The transformation into businessman left Selene blinking. She had rarely seen him dressed for work. *He looks nice, but not as nice as when he only wears a pair of shorts.* She handed him a cup of coffee, which he sipped gratefully, sinking onto the chair beside her. She poured herself a second cup and sat next to him, marveling that she could reach out one hand and grasp his, with the expectation that he would take the offer. He did, and a wave of unfocused affection radiated into her. *That feels awfully nice.* She squeezed his fingers gently. "Brandon, I need to be at work by seven, but my Mazda was totaled in the fire. Can you give me a ride, or should I call a patrol car to pick me up? Man, it's weird not to have a car."

"Are you sure you want to go to work today?" he asked, worry creating that tiny eleven between his eyes that she'd noticed before. Grooves appeared around his mouth.

All that for me? Wow. Selene smiled. *Admit it, girl. You're digging being babied.* But all she said was, "Completely. You're going to be gone, and there's nothing I can do here that I can't do from the station. I really want to get going on the rape case, so no one else has to suffer like that poor lady did. She's still in the hospital."

"I understand," he replied, not giving an inch, "but are

you sure you're up to it?"

I should be exasperated by his pestering, but I'm not. "Yes. I can't remember ever feeling so well-rested and happy. It should help balance the stress of the job. You're good for me, Brand."

He kissed her temple. "Don't call for a ride. I'll drive you. I have a client coming in at eight, so that will give me a few minutes to get ready. What are your hours today?"

"I'm fortunate to have a pretty regular schedule of seven to four," she said. "Unless there's an emergency."

His look told her he understood just how often emergencies popped up. "I'm done at five. Would it make sense for me to pick you up on the way home?"

She grinned wryly. *He knows me far too well.* "Only an hour late? How novel. Let's try it. If I have to stay later, I'll call you."

"Don't stay later," he urged. "You need to have a life outside of work, you know."

My goodness, that outside life has suddenly gotten a lot more interesting. Instead of filing paperwork long into the evening, I could be at home kissing my boyfriend, and... She gulped, realizing what the night would bring. With burning cheeks, she said, "I'll try."

Brandon helped himself to a bowl of cereal, and when he finished, Selene washed the dishes while he contemplated the contents of the freezer, eventually unwrapping some thin-cut pork chops and leaving them in the fridge to thaw. Then they climbed into Brandon's pickup and drove to the station.

"What time is it?" Selene asked, popping her seatbelt and sliding along the bench seat to Brandon, curling her arms around his waist.

"Six fifty," he replied, turning and cupping her face in one hand. He drew her toward him. Her belly fluttered in anticipation moments before his warm lips captured hers. Selene felt as though she were melting. The heat of her own desire, coupled with Brandon's pouring through his fingertips into her skin, warmed her from the inside out.

"Hmmmm," she hummed, shimmying closer. She released his lips, backed up and stared in wordless wonder into Brandon's deep, dark eyes.

"Pretty lady," he murmured.

Selene smiled. As one they moved back toward each other for another luscious embrace.

The seconds ticked away unnoticed, until Selene drew back with a gasp, whipping her head to the side to see the clock. "Crap. I have to go."

"Remember. Five, Selene. Don't be late," he urged as she yanked the door open and jumped to the asphalt.

Pain radiated up her legs as the sensible ballet flats compressed against the hard surface. She rubbed one knee. *Two minutes. Move your ass, Selene.* Wasting not another minute, she hustled into the police station and managed to slip through the open door behind a coworker who had already been buzzed in. Selene power walked to the time clock, but she could feel the eyes on her from all around the room.

She punched in with only seconds to spare. *This many years, and I've never been late. What a morning.* Still feeling the warmth of Brandon's lips on hers, a goofy smile spread across her face.

"Woo-hoo," a male voice called. "What have you been up to, little sister?"

She turned and tried to glare at Tony, but before she could speak, another cop called out, "I think she's been making out. We gonna have to kick someone's ass?"

"Nah, let the girl have her fling. She deserves it."

"What if it's not a fling? I think Selene's in looooove."

"Okay," Selene said loudly, "I'm only going to say this once. The man who brought me here yesterday is my boyfriend. His name is Brandon. I'm crazy about him, so

please, no more comments. I'll answer any legitimate questions later. Right now, I have a lot to do."

*It's astonishing how much paperwork piles up over the weekend
when you're not on call,* she thought, eying the messy mountain
of sheets threatening to overflow her inbox. Then she clicked
on her computer and sighed. Over a dozen interdepartmental
emails. Selene banished the novelty of her new relationship
and got right to work.

After a little while, Tony drifted over. "Hey, girl. Are you
sure you want to be here today?"

Selene looked up in an email haze. "Of course. Why
wouldn't I?"

"Well, I mean, I saw you at the fire, and yesterday…"

"I'm fine," she assured him. *Goodness, the men in my life are
intent on pestering me.*

"But what about your boyfriend?"

She shot Tony a puzzled glance. "What about him? He's at
work."

"He works?" Tony's bushy eyebrows drew together, his
forehead knotting in confusion.

"Are you serious, Tony?" Selene shot back, startled. "What
kind of question is that? Of course, he works."

"I don't know, I just thought…" he stammered to a halt, a
sheepish look on his face.

Oh, I know where he's going with that, Selene realized, her
rarely-incited temper flaring to life. "What, because he's
Native American?" she snapped.

Tony's face went pale. His mouth opened and then closed

Selene gave him no chance to defend himself. "Don't even
think such things," she snarled, chopping the air beside him
with the side of her hand.

Tony shied away from the gesture as it neared the forearm
he'd left bare when he'd rolled up his shirtsleeve.

Ignoring his discomfort, she continued her tirade in a
rage-filled hiss. "Brand has a good job. He owns a home. He's

as middle class as they come, and even if he didn't, even if he was unemployed and in poverty, would that make him less human? Less a man? How can someone who spends his days off volunteering at the homeless shelter even think such bullshit? Because you're my friend, I'm going to pretend—once—you didn't say that, but for heaven's sake don't do it again. Fast forward to the 21st century, please. Just because someone isn't a WASP doesn't make them some kind of vagrant. And let's not forget what people used to say about Italians not that many years ago. Are you in the mob, Tony? No? Then shut the hell up about Brandon."

They looked at each other in silence, and Selene could feel the heat creeping over her face as she realized what she'd just said to her friend. *I'm not sorry. It's not like me to be so harsh, but it's important I stand up for what's right.*

Tony's face turned sheepish in. "Delete comment. My bad. Let me try again. What does he do?"

She accepted the apology with a nod. "He's a career counselor. When I realized that I wasn't cut out for counseling myself, he's the one who gave me a personality assessment and suggested I try law enforcement."

Tony's eyes widened. "You've known him a while, haven't you?"

"My whole adult life. Longer than I've known you."

"And wanted him the whole time, huh?" Tony's tone and expression had turned sympathetic, not teasing.

Selene sighed. "Yes. The whole time."

"Well, then, good for you, girl." He balled up a fist and pressed it gently against the sleeve of her blouse. "It's great when your dreams come true. You deserve it. He'd better be good to you, though, or he's going to answer to an awful lot of people."

"He treats me like a queen," she replied, letting her mind wander for a brief moment to the astonishing sensation of being held close in Brandon's arms.

Tony caught the flash of dreamy contentment, and his teasing grin returned.

Knowing she needed to change the subject quickly, Selene said, "Are there any new suspects on that rape case?"

～

"What do you want to go with this pork chops," Brandon called in through the window from the backyard.

A waft of succulent smoke set Selene's mouth watering. "Salad would be nice," she replied. "Do you mind if I make it?"

"Sure you're up to it?" he asked. "I'm used to making whole meals on my own."

"I know," she called back, "but I don't mind. If you don't either—if you're not too territorial about the kitchen—I'd like to move dinner along. Honestly, I'm starving." *Hmmm. Starving? How long has it been since I can recall feeling hungry, rather than just being aware that it's time to eat?*

"Make yourself at home, Selene," Brandon replied. In the background, his oversized metal spatula scraped on the grates of the grill.

Selene got right to work hunting down a cutting board and retrieving a head of lettuce from the refrigerator. *Looks perfect. Paired with cucumber, tomato and a bottle of vinaigrette, they should go a long way to cut the richness of the pork.*

A few minutes later, just as she was grating carrot into a bowl, Brandon bustled into the kitchen, a plate balanced on one hand.

"That was quick," Selene commented.

"The chops are thin," he replied. He set the plate on the counter and started digging in the cabinet below, eventually producing a box of foil, which he used to wrap the plate. "These need to rest a few minutes," he informed her. "Can you pop that salad in the fridge?"

Selene complied, though the aroma of grilled meat tortured her. "Can we get out of here? It smells too good."

"Sure," he agreed. Casually grabbing her hand, he led her through the door into the living room and urged her to a seat on the couch, where he laced his fingers through hers and set them on his knee. "How does it work?" he asked.

"What?" Selene asked, distracted by the intense, surprising attraction she could still feel pouring into her.

"Your gift. I know it has something to do with touch, but what, specifically? Do you see people's thoughts anytime there's skin-to-skin contact?"

"Oh, that. I haven't explained this to anyone in years." She grinned. *Makes sense to do it now though. He needs to know.* "It's not any touch. Only if your hands touch my skin. When we… when we kiss, I don't see anything. If your elbow or knee touched mine, nothing would happen. I have no idea why the hands matter, but they do."

"Hmmm," he replied, clearly pondering. Then, he took his free hand and cupped her cheek.

Can you feel this? Can you hear it? he thought.

"Clear as day," she replied.

And now? He captured her lips in a tender kiss, all while pouring an intense… something into her with both hands.

"Oh, yes," she breathed." Leaning in, she captured his lips again.

The wordless sensation, whatever it was, had such power, Selene forgot her hunger. Forgot the constant litany of chatter that normally ran unchecked in the back of her mind. As his tongue slid against hers, she even forgot to feel startled or insecure. In the heat of Brandon's desire, something frozen in Selene's heart began to thaw.

"Dad?" The front door banged open and Maggie bustled in, carrying a large white box. "Selene, are you still here? I brought you some…oh *shit!*"

"Actually, Maggie," Brandon replied mildly, still clutching

Selene, "I don't intend to let her go anywhere." *Ever again*, his mind added.

Selene gasped, both from the surprise of the interruption and from the unexpected declaration.

Maggie blinked a couple of times. "This is a joke, right?"

"No, Maggie, it's not," Selene said softly.

"But…no, it can't be," Maggie stuttered. "Dad, you're supposed to go out with someone your own age, not one of my friends! Selene is too young for you. You can't be together, not the two of you. No way. What the hell are you thinking?" Her words grew louder and faster with each passing second.

"She's not as young as you are, Maggie," Brandon pointed out.

Maggie was having none of it. She nailed her father and best friend with a furious glare. "She's still too young for you! This must be some kind of sick trophy thing."

"That's not true," Selene said. Her stomach fluttered, and her face burned. "I'm no trophy. We… we care for each other, Maggie. Don't you want that for your dad? For me?"

After an internal battle for calm raged across Maggie's face, she responded with, "Well, yes, but not with each other. This freaking sucks. I don't believe it. I just don't believe it. How could you two do this to me?" Her voice broke.

Selene's heart clenched.

"Maggie," Brandon said, "we're not doing anything to you. This really doesn't have anything to do with you." He sounded surprisingly calm amid the turmoil.

"Nothing to do with me? I catch my dad making out with my best friend, and you say it has nothing to do with me?" she shrieked.

"Maggie please, can't you try to accept this? You know how much he means to me." Selene left the warmth of Brandon's embrace to touch her friend's sleeve.

Maggie jerked away. "You must just be sooooo happy,

Selene. You've wanted him for years. How can you be so self-ish?" Her eyes narrowed. "Did you sleep with him?"

Oh, Lord, not that question. "What do you mean by sleep with?" Selene stalled.

"Don't be stupid, Selene. Did you fuck my dad?"

"Maggie Elizabeth!" Brandon scolded.

"Answer the question," she demanded, unmoved by her father's stern tone.

"No, Maggie, I'm didn't," Selene said, her voice barely above a whisper. "Not yet."

"Yet?"

"I don't think it will be long." Selene blushed and looked away. "And I did sleep with him—in the same bed—last night."

"Well, this is just lovely." Maggie turned to Brandon. "I can't believe you would choose her over me!"

"That's not true. I haven't chosen anyone over you. You're my daughter. You always will be. Selene is my girlfriend. There isn't an either-or here."

Tears prickled in the corners of Selene's eyes. Ragged breaths clawed at her chest. *How can he still be so calm, so reasonable?*

"Yes, there is! If you're seeing HER," Maggie stabbed an angry finger in Selene's direction, "You sure won't be seeing much of me. And you, Selene." She turned on her friend with a glower so aggressive, Selene felt it like a physical blow. She stepped back involuntarily as Maggie continued. "I thought you were my friend! Turns out you were just after my dad."

"Maggie, that's enough," Brandon snapped. "You're way out of line, young lady."

"I'm not twelve, Dad," Maggie sneered. Maggie's biceps flexed, making the bag she was holding crackle. "Are you going to send me to my room next, so you can be alone with her?"

"No," Selene protested, not wanting to hear what either of them might come up with next. "No…"

"Selene." Brandon squeezed her hand, noticing her distress. "Selene, it's okay."

"It's not okay," Maggie shouted. "I came to see if you were recovering after the fire, and to offer my apartment until you can get back on your feet, and this is what I find? No, just no."

"Maggie, calm down," Brandon snapped.

"Calm down, he says. Calm down. I'll give you calm." She dropped a grocery bag to the floor. A boar bristle hairbrush, a bunch of scrunchies and a pretty headband spilled out. "You know what? Since you found what you needed to replace me, have fun. I'll be around… or not." She wheeled and darted out of the door, slamming it with such force, the window vibrated.

"Oh, God. What have we done?" Selene whispered.

"Nothing," Brandon replied. "We haven't done anything, Selene. She'll get over it. She always did want to direct my life, and it annoys her that she can't."

"Brand, she's legitimately upset," Selene pointed out to him.

"That may be, but she's also being ridiculous. I think, once she settles down, she'll see that us being together actually makes it easier for her. Now, listen," he lifted his hand and ran his fingers through her hair, making her tingle all over, "let's try to let this go. We haven't harmed my daughter. All we did was discover an important truth about ourselves. She may not like it, but she doesn't get a vote. She's grown and living her life. I finally get to do the same. She'll come around and all will be well. You'll see."

Selene bit her lip, her eager appetite banished by the emotional scene. "I hope you're right," she told him. "I wouldn't want to lose you… but I don't want to lose her either."

CHAPTER 5

Over the next several weeks, Selene and Brandon grew used to living together. They continued sharing a bed each night, making love, though stopping short of intercourse. Brandon eventually taught Selene to accept even the most intimate touches, his hands sliding inside her pajamas to bring her to culmination. He showed her how to return the favor, to use her hands and mouth on him, which made the waiting much easier to endure.

He also taught her how to say no to a call from work on her days off. As her life became more balanced, her sleep improved, and with Brandon's delicious cooking, so did her nutrition. She no longer looked pale and ill but developed a healthy pink glow.

One evening in June, Selene rested on her back on the sofa, her head pillowed in Brandon's lap. He idly stroked his fingers through her hair, his eyes fixed on a baseball game.

"Honey?" Selene spoke, interrupting a car insurance commercial.

"Hmmm?" His gaze left the screen and locked with hers.

"Isn't your birthday coming up?"

His fingers paused against her scalp. The diffused pleasure he'd been sending her evaporated. *Oh boy,* she felt him think. "Yes, I suppose so, but I hadn't planned on celebrating this year."

"Why not?" Selene wanted to know.

"Oh, well…" He resumed stroking, causing a tingling sensation to chase down her spine, but his unformed thought had an uncomfortable feel to it. "Um, it's my fortieth. I'm not sure that's something I want to commemorate."

"Forty isn't old, Brandon," Selene pointed out. "That's when men finally reach their prime. Besides, birthdays are a celebration of you, not of your age. I, for one, am very glad you came into the world. Would you mind if I planned something?"

"What did you have in mind?" he asked, eyes narrowing so the corners crinkled. "I don't want any wild parties."

"How would I even begin to plan a wild party?" she asked. "I don't know enough people unless I invite the police. They can definitely get crazy, but they're not your friends, they're mine. No, I just thought… a few loved ones, something good to eat. Some cake."

"Hmmm," he hummed again. The game resumed, and Brandon returned his attention to the television. He slipped his fingers away from her scalp, instead toying with the ends of her hair.

By the next commercial, it seemed he had made up his mind. "If you really think a party is necessary, then I think family only would be okay. Let's invite Maggie and my parents. It would be a good time to let them know about us anyway."

Selene blinked. "Okay, we can do that."

"Oh, but let's specify no gifts," he added. "I don't need anything. I have everything I want already."

Selene struggled upright and laid a soft kiss on his lips. A torrent of emotion tried to batter its way out of her, but she held it in. *When he says things like that, I don't know what to think except that this is too good to be true.*

The day before the party—a Friday—Selene sat at her desk in the police station, frowning at a pile of reports, when an urgent request from her bladder reminded her of the coffee she'd been drinking all day. Rising, she passed by the chief's office on the way to the bathroom and stuck her head in the door.

"Knock, knock," she said, attracting Brady's attention away from his computer.

"What's up, Johansen?" he barked gruffly.

Remember, don't take it personally, she told herself for the thousandth time. *It's just the way he talks, he does it to everyone, and it honestly doesn't mean a thing.* "Um, I can't be on call this weekend," she said. "I hope that's okay."

"No problem." He returned his attention to his work.

Puzzled, she made her way to the restroom, deep in thought. *They always call me in. Always. I've been on call three weekends a month for the last two years. Now I say I can't come in, and it's no big deal. Has it always been no big deal? Have I put extra work on myself? Brandon and Maggie both say I do. Wouldn't she love knowing I finally admitted she's right?*

Thinking of Maggie made Selene sad. *I haven't seen her since... that day. She says she's coming to the party, even that she'll bring cake, but she sounds so tense and awkward. Have I truly lost my best friend... just because I fell in love? That's not fair.*

Selene regarded herself in the bathroom mirror as she washed her hands. The pallor she had noticed the night of the fire had long since darkened to a slight tan from so many evenings spent outside in Brandon's backyard and her cheeks glowed with good health. She smiled. *Being in love suits me.*

And it really is love. I've always loved Brandon. Knowing what a magnificent boyfriend he is has only strengthened it.

She pushed through the door, her eyes skating over the bustling cubicles. Tony met her eyes and winked. She waved as she made her way back to her desk. *I wonder if I should say something to Brandon yet. No, probably too soon. We've only been together a month. I don't want to jinx it. And what if he doesn't reciprocate?* The thought produced a frown, one that deepened into confusion when she noticed an envelope on the keyboard of her computer.

It hadn't been there when she left, less than ten minutes before. *I wonder if this is some kind of prank, like the time they Saran Wrapped my car or the time they put pepper sauce in my coffee.* She grabbed the envelope and ripped it open. A type-written scrap of paper fell out.

Selene Johansen, I know what you did, bitch. You perse-cute innocent people. You will die.

Selene dropped the paper with a start. *This is not the kind of prank the other cops play. This is serious.* She scooped up a pair of gloves and an evidence bag and collected both the note and the envelope. Shaken, she took the bag to Chief Brady.

"What the hell?" He looked up from the note with a thun-derous, puzzled expression on his face.

This time, already shaken by the note, his temper got to her. She hunched her shoulders and tried to look smaller. "It was on my keyboard. You see, it has my name on it." Her voice sounded unsteady. *And why not? I feel unsteady.*

"Someone walked into *my* station and threatened one of *my* officers?" he bellowed.

"Yes sir," she replied, in a barely audible murmur. *Oh, grow up. He's not mad at you.* Forcing herself to use a normal volume she continued, "Do you think it might be related to the arson?"

Brady took a deep breath and relaxed his posture. When

he answered, his voice was calmer. "Seems unlikely you would have two crazies after you."

"But why me? I'm not a beat cop. I'm never out of the station and I don't even wear a uniform. Why would I be a target?"

"Who knows?" He shrugged. "These kooks are hard to explain. Ask Tony to pull the surveillance video and we'll see what's what."

Unfortunately, the video showed a number of unidentified people walking through the station in the vicinity of Selene's desk during the time when the letter appeared, but no one could be seen directly touching her desk. Nor could the people be readily identified. It was a dead end, so they sent the envelope and letter to evidence processing, hoping to find fingerprints or DNA.

"Maybe you should stay here," Brady told her seriously. "If there's some loon after you, you might not be safe."

"It's Brandon's birthday tomorrow. I have stuff to get ready." Selene could hear the stubbornness in her voice but refused to back down. *Brandon will be getting his birthday party, no matter what. I have plans for that man, and I refuse to let them be interrupted.*

"He wouldn't want you to get hurt either," Brady insisted. "I've talked to him. He's a good guy."

Selene drew herself up to her full height and lifted her chin to look directly into the chief's face. "Sir, I'm a police officer. Just because I'm not out patrolling in a squad car doesn't mean I'm a wuss. I can shoot a gun or Taser with good accuracy, and I know a lot of fighting techniques. I'm not helpless."

He looked startled at the strength of her reply. *And no wonder. Four weeks ago, I would have waffled under his stern stare,* she realized with a start. *The last month has changed me in a good way.* One corner of her mouth turned upward in an involuntary grin.

"You have to sleep sometimes," Brady pressed.

"We have an alarm system," she countered.

"Do you arm it?"

Selene rolled her eyes. *Good grief. Another pestering man who thinks I'm a child.* "Every night like clockwork."

Brady gave up. "Fine, but be extra careful, Selene. I really don't want to have to replace you, and not just because finding someone who can do what you do would be a pain in the ass."

"I love you too, sir," Selene said, understanding his meaning. She walked out of his office.

For all her brave words, Selene still felt distinctly unsettled. *Someone knows where I work, which desk is mine and walked right up to it—right into my space. I don't like it one bit.* She took out her little-used gun and strapped it to her hip, which settled her somewhat. Still, she couldn't shake the feeling that someone was watching her. She scanned the room, scrutinizing each face. *No one except my friends, police officers I've known for years and would trust with my life.* The letter writer had gone, but his creepy presence remained. Selene shuddered.

At five she clocked out and waited in the lobby, in full view of the receptionist's window, until Brandon's pickup arrived. She moved through the parking lot quickly, scanning in all directions as though she were going into a combat situation. Pulling open the door before Brandon could even get out, much less open it for her, she scrambled into the truck.

He gave her a startled look. "What's wrong, baby?"

"Something weird happened at work today," she replied. "I'll tell you all about it, but can we please get out of here?"

"Sure." He shifted the pickup into gear and drove out of the parking lot. "What happened?"

"Some creep left a threatening note on my desk. We're investigating it. The chief thinks it might be related to the arson."

"Holy shit! Someone's stalking you?" he demanded, appalled.

"Looks like it. Of course, a crime has already been committed, so if we can catch the guy, we can put him in prison. Most likely he's targeting my work because he doesn't know where I'm staying now." Then her businesslike tone fractured as she admitted, "I'm a little freaked out."

"Me too," he agreed. "Are you sure you're okay, Selene? Do you want to go right home?"

She shook her head. "No, I need to pick out a new car. I've put it off long enough, especially since the insurance money came in weeks ago."

"Have you decided what you're going to do with your property?" he asked, accepting her change of subject, though a tension in the corners of his mouth and eyes revealed he hadn't dropped the idea of a stalker so quickly.

And neither have I. Damn it, this was supposed to be a good weekend. Now I'm going to spend the whole time worrying. "Sell it," she replied, trying to focus on the conversation. "The lot is pretty big, and it's in a good neighborhood. Now that all the rubble is cleared away, it would be a great location to build one of those big family houses." She glanced at him. His eyes were flicking between the road and the rearview mirror. "Unless you think I should keep it?"

"What for?" He sounded distracted, and she noticed the reflection of a small blue Miata lingering far too close to the pickup's rear bumper.

"Well, in case you get tired of me crashing with you. I might be able to rebuild." Her fragile confidence undermined by the spooky letter, Selene revealed more of her internal anxiety than she had intended.

Brandon noticed immediately. "Selene, stop it," he told her gruffly, turning his attention away from the tailgater. "You're not crashing with me. You're not a guest. We're a couple. It's your home now too."

"Oh, well I wasn't sure." *You're starting to sound like the old, insecure Selene again. Stop acting that way!* But it was no use, not where Brandon was concerned. *This all still feels like a fairy tale, as though I'll wake up in my little house and find it was all a dream.*

"Be sure," he told her in his most serious voice. "I want you there. I don't see us living together as temporary, do you?"

"I don't want to, but I also don't want to assume anything." Afraid of the intensity of their conversation, she looked out the window at the large and shabby century-old homes that had been subdivided into fourplexes. The trash-cans sat full on the street, and she could just imagine how they must reek in the heat of the sun. *This is a crummy neighborhood.*

"What do you mean?" Brandon asked, refusing to be dissuaded by her feigned inattentiveness.

"Well, it's just that," she twirled a loose strand of hair around her finger, "you know, I still have a hard time believing this could really be happening."

Brandon relaxed. She glanced in the mirror as the Miata turned onto a side street. In profile, she could see the driver's door of the little car bore a deep dent.

"Selene," he told her, gently, "I know you're nervous about this relationship, but please try to relax with me. I want to be with you. I *always* want to be with you. It kind of annoys me when you act like I'm going to get tired of you and kick you out. I won't do that, you know. Not ever."

The soft words struck at her heart. *Oh, no. Could I be upsetting him? Could he really care enough for that?* Though it seemed unlikely, the evidence in his voice and expression could not be doubted. "I'm sorry, Brandon. I want to be with you. I love living with you. If you feel the same way, then I'm doubly lucky. I don't mean to be a pain. I'm afraid I don't know much about normal relationships."

He fell silent for the space of a couple of heartbeats as they drove under the shadow of three towering maples whose leafy branches stretched across the roadway and intertwined, blocking out the view of the sky.

At last, he responded. "Well, you're not the first shy lady to have a hard time adapting to a relationship. But there's more to it, isn't there? You're not just shy. You really believe you're not good enough, that your gift is the only part of you that has value. Selene, that's just not the case. Why don't you believe in yourself?"

Now it was Selene's turn to pause and think. Another large maple loomed ahead, and as she watched, a helicopter seed fell, spinning around and around like the blades of its namesake, until it disappeared onto the sidewalk.

Still looking out the window, she spoke. "As long as I can remember, people have shied away from me. Only total strangers will touch my hand, and when I was in school, the kids used to…say things. They called me a freak." *Lord, that was hard to say.* "Even my aunt and uncle basically kept their hands off me once I entered junior high and my gift became impossible to ignore. I guess I just figured I would be alone for the rest of my life. Touching me is too much of a risk, and until now, no one was willing, not if they knew what I can do."

This time Brandon needed no time to consider his words. "Well, I'm not afraid of your gift—I like it—but, Selene, you are more than your ability. You're also a person, a woman, and that part of you is just like everyone else. You have the same needs and desires as any other woman, and it's a shame everyone was so busy protecting themselves from you that they forgot you were a person too. I won't do that. Now, as for those kids, try not to take what they said personally. Everyone gets teased in school. It's part of growing up."

"Really?" She turned and looked at him. They stopped at a red light, allowing him to meet her eyes. She drowned for a moment in those warm brown depths. *What is it about a man with dark eyes? Like he knows all the secrets.*

"Of course," he replied. "People who are different always get it the worst."

"Even you?" Her eyes widened.

A car behind them honked. Seeing that the light had changed, Brandon waved an apology and turned right as he continued. "Selene, I'm Indian. When I was in eighth grade, my class read Tom Sawyer. For the rest of the year, kids called me Injun Joe, and ran away screaming, 'He's gonna scalp me!'"

Selene winced. *I can just imagine it. Poor Brandon.*

He continued. "It wasn't right, but kids can be little shits sometimes. That's all it was. If I'd had freckles, or been fat or had a mother with tattoos, they would have gone after that. Anything that marks a person as different is fair game. So, after a while—and I mean a long while. It did hurt like hell at the time—I realized it was something messed up inside them, not me. Either they had a bad family, or they were bullied themselves, or they grew up listening to racist adults. Their teasing didn't mean there was anything wrong with me." He paused as though in thought and then continued. "Try to think of it that way. Being teased doesn't mean you're wrong or bad. Does it bother you when your police friends tease you?"

"Kind of, but I know they don't mean anything by it." *And you have to remind yourself of that every time, don't you?* She acknowledged the thought with a rueful pursing of the lips.

"Baby, I wish you could see your own value. You're a wonderful person." He extended his hand to her, the way he always did when he wanted her to understand without the risk of words.

She laced her fingers through his without hesitation. *Oh, it's deep, what he's feeling!* Desire, affection, amused irritation. A complex swirl of indefinable emotions welled up into a pool of…something strong and sweet and fierce she didn't dare name. *It's enough for a lifetime.* Selene relaxed her tense shoulders and brought Brandon's fingers to her mouth kissing each one. *Enough dallying. I need to commit to this man, this relationship before my dithering ruins everything. I was strong with Chief Brady, and I can be strong with myself. Brandon deserves it.* "Brand." She nibbled daintily on one fingertip and then kissed it again.

"Yes?" He rubbed his thumb across her lower lip.

"I'm sorry. The truth is, I care so much about you that it scares me."

"These things are always scary. I'm here with you though. It's a relationship, not just a crush anymore." He lowered their hands away from her face and stroked her wrist, making her shiver pleasantly.

"I know. It means the world to me. You mean the world to me. You may already know this, but I need to say it."

"Say what?"

Selene took a deep breath. "I love you, Brandon." *Will he be surprised?* She listened to the thoughts coming to her from him.

Wow, she actually said it right out, and just as calm and confident as can be. I didn't even know she realized it yet. He squeezed her hand.

Now what? Selene wondered.

Brandon didn't speak. Instead, he sent a targeted thought, loud and true, straight into her mind. *I love you, Selene. You are so much more than you realize, and I will never let you go. I love you.*

She closed her eyes, letting the sensation of his love wash over her the rest of the way to the dealership.

≈

"Party time," Selene sang tunelessly, shaking her hips from side to side as she sliced pickles. She piled them onto the plate beside her and grabbed a tomato.

"Not yet," Brandon called through the screen. The scent of glowing coals and grilling beef floated in the window.

"That smells amazing, babe," she called back. "You're the grill king, aren't you?"

"Maybe, maybe," he replied with a chuckle.

"Are you sure it's okay with you that you're cooking your own birthday dinner?"

"It's not a birthday dinner. It's just dinner," he replied. "That this happens to be my birthday is irrelevant."

"Okay," she replied, laughing. "It's just dinner… with cake… and guests."

"Family members aren't guests," he reminded her. "Everyone who will be there has a designated bedroom in this house."

Family. Yikes. Are you sure your parents will like me?" She stacked the tomatoes next to the pickles and then retrieved a block of asiago from the refrigerator. *Fancy cheese. Wow. I would have unwrapped processed slices. Maybe the reason I didn't used to eat much is that I didn't buy tasty enough food.*

"They'll love you, honey. They want me to be happy," he reminded her.

"And you're sure I should… you know, shake hands? That's an intrusion. At school, they always told us not to touch without permission."

"Do you want to explain why?" the question carried in the window. Outside, the burgers hissed and sizzled as their juices dripped onto the coals.

Explain to Brandon's very ordinary parents that if I touch them, I'll know what they're thinking? "Yeah, not so much," she replied.

"I don't see any reason to open that particular can of

worms with them either," he agreed. "So just shake. It'll be one second. Even if you see something—"

"I will," she reminded him. "I always do."

"If you do, it will be their first impression of you. Look, honey. I know you and I know my parents. They'll probably just be thinking you're pretty or hoping *you* like *them*. If it's anything else, we can talk about it later, okay?"

Selene's cheeks warmed. "Okay."

She carried the plate to the table, where she found Sammy, sitting on a chair, his tail wrapped around his feet.

"Keep out of this cheese," she warned her kitten sternly. "It's not for you. It's for the guests."

Sammy yawned hugely.

"Thank you for your cooperation," she said, raising one eyebrow. Shaking her head, she returned to the fridge, glancing at the clock on the stove. *Five minutes until they're supposed to arrive. I guess I can get out the rest.* She retrieved the ketchup, mustard and mayonnaise, tucking them under her arm, and then a chilled bowl of potato salad.

"This is not for you either," she told her cat. He jumped down from the chair and sauntered away, puffy silver tail twitching. "Sorry if I offended you," she commented dryly.

Shaking her head, she meandered through the door into the living room, moved aside a yellow brocade curtain and peeked out.

"Nervous?" Brandon asked, wrapping his arms around her waist. "Don't be." He laid a luscious kiss on her lips. As usual, one kiss led to another and then another as they soaked in each other's love and affection.

"Dad?" Maggie peeked her head in the door. "Oh, no. Not again. Can't you two keep it under control for two seconds? Is this all you do? Make out like a couple of horny teens?"

"Do you blame me?" Brandon asked, nonchalant as ever in the face of his daughter's fury.

I don't know how he does that. I can feel her emotions from across the room, which is unusual. She's so angry—and so hurt.

"Knock it *off*," Maggie snapped. "It's a lot, asking me to spend time with you guys, knowing… what I know. Then you have to go make it more awkward by hanging all over each other. What the hell?"

"And again, I say, calm down. This isn't something you get to dictate to me, to us," Brandon reminded her, starting to sound irritated.

A buzzing sensation from his fingertips into Selene's elbow confirmed it.

"I can't tell you what to do," Maggie agreed in an icy hiss, "but I can decide not to come around if you're going to be all lovey-dovey gross."

"There's nothing gross going on," Brandon said, still more irritated than angry. "Loving someone isn't gross and you know it. Your discomfort with our relationship is something you need to work on. It's not rational."

Maggie snarled.

You can't let this go on, Selene realized. *Do something. They're going to hurt their relationship.* "Stop," she said with the authoritative tone of her profession.

Brandon and Maggie both turned her way.

"I'm not going to be in the middle of this anymore. What do you need me to do to correct the problem? Do I walk away from this relationship right now?"

"Selene, what?"

She turned to Brandon and saw the stunned disbelief on his handsome face. *He's upset over what I said, and I don't need to touch his hand to confirm it.*

She struggled to explain. "Listen to me, both of you. I will not be the cause of a fight or an estrangement between you. I never had a father, Maggie. I won't separate you from yours. If it means that much to you, I'll leave now." Her voice wavered, but she was determined to make them understand, so she swallowed hard and continued. "Don't mistake me, it will break my heart. Brandon will be hurt too, but you're too important to him—and to me—for me to let this happen. What do you want me to do, Maggie?" She gave her friend a level look and bit the corner of her lower lip to keep it from trembling.

"Selene," Brandon demanded, "how can you talk about leaving?" His low, beautiful voice, thick with hurt, slashed into her soul.

She wanted nothing more than to snuggle up against Brandon and make the world go away, to protect him from ever hurting again, but she was the one who had caused it. *And he loves you, you twit. Of course you hurt him. Well done. Can't you do anything right?*

She turned and walked back towards him, her emotions welling up. She was quickly losing the battle to suppress them. "Because I love you too much to come between you and your daughter." A tear slid down Selene's cheek, and she reached out to caress Brandon's face with her fingertips. "And Maggie is my friend. Your relationship is more important than me. You two are family. What right do I have to get in the way?"

His expression told her he disagreed. He slid his arms around her waist and crushed her close to him, looking down into her upturned face with an expression of wounded tenderness.

They turned as one to look at Maggie. Her eyes moved from Selene to Brandon and back, as though not sure what to make of them. She took several deep breaths. "Oh hell," she said, her voice suddenly neutral. "No, Selene, don't leave. Far be it for me to interfere in your love life. I still don't like it, though." She stomped down the hall to her old bedroom. The door slammed loudly.

Brandon's arms tightened. "Selene, don't ever talk about leaving again. I can't stand it."

Selene bit her lip. "I'm sorry. I hate that this upsets her so."

"I understand that, but these are her feelings to deal with, not ours to fix. We're not doing anything wrong. Now, listen," he lifted his hand and ran his fingers through her hair, making her tingle all over, "my parents will be here any minute, and it's the beautiful, smiling Selene I want them to meet." He kissed her once, softly, controlling his desire.

"Yes, I want to meet them," Selene replied. Her voice sounded calmer in her ears as the hammering of her heart began to slow, "but I need to talk to Maggie first."

"I think you should leave her alone for a while."

I've left her alone for a month, and it didn't help. Enough is enough. Selene pressed her lips to his cheek. "My intuition tells me otherwise."

"Suit yourself, but don't be manipulated into leaving. Remember that I love you and you love me. We're great together. None of which hurts Maggie in any way."

"You're right. I'll be back."

Selene knocked on the bedroom door and opened it before Maggie could reply. The younger woman sat on the bed, her face in her hands, her shoulders shaking. Selene walked up beside her and gathered her into a fierce hug. This time Maggie didn't push her away.

"I'm sorry you're upset," Selene said as she squeezed her friend's shoulders.

"But not for the reason behind it?" Maggie retorted in a flat, watery-sounding voice. She shook Selene off and looked her in the eyes with a challenging glare.

"No." Selene met the challenge without fighting or backing down. She chose to give Maggie the deepest, most honest answer she had in her. "I love him. The amazing thing is that he loves me too. Why would I be sorry about that?"

Maggie searched her eyes and sighed. "This is hard, Selene. I guess there's no reason why you shouldn't be together. He is a little old for you, but otherwise, I mean, I can see why you like him, and why he likes you. I'm too close to be able to look at this objectively. Really, for Dad's sake, I don't care. I know you'll be good for him. God knows you've been crazy about him long enough. But on your side, I still don't like it."

"Maggie, he's been amazing to me," Selene protested.

Maggie gave a curt nod. "Yeah, and he will be. He's a great person. But here's the thing; are you sure he's not just looking for someone to take care of now that I've moved out?"

Selene shook her head, her lips twisting into a secret smile. "He's not using me to replace you. Believe me, there's nothing paternal about his attention."

Maggie blushed. "Ugh, please, no more. That's one thing I'm pissed about. I always imagined you falling in love, maybe with one of your police friends, and we could have girl talk and drink wine and giggle and overshare. Now, I don't want to know the details, because if you're sleeping with someone, it's my dad, and that's gross. Part of our friendship has been taken away."

"But Maggie, it's a very small part. I still love you very much. That won't change," she insisted.

"Won't it? And what about when you two get married? You won't be my stepmother, you know. I won't have it. You're not old enough."

This time heat spread across Selene's cheeks. "We haven't even talked about getting married."

"You'll do it though. I've never seen Dad look at anyone the way he just looked at you." Her voice wavered. "Not even Mom. He's never going to let you go."

Selene shook her head, not ready to deal with the idea. "Your grandparents will be here soon."

Maggie gave Selene a measured look, as though debating what to say next. "They'll like you, I think."

In spite of everything, she chose to say something nice. I'm amazed. "Thank you, Maggie. And you? Do you still like me?" she added hesitantly.

"Of course. I'll just repeat what you said to Dad and me. I love you both too much to be responsible for coming between you. If what you need is each other, I'll work on being okay with it. Just don't expect me to get over it today. It'll take time."

That's fair, Selene acknowledged, *and yet...* "Are we still friends?"

"Yes," Maggie rasped, tears streaming again. She yanked Selene close, nearly knocking her over, and squashed her in a hard, tight hug. Selene could feel her arms trembling.

"Selene? Maggie?" Brandon called.

"You'd better splash some water on your face," Selene observed.

Maggie nodded. Releasing Selene, she hauled herself to her feet and trudged down the hall, ducking into the bathroom.

Selene returned to Brandon in the living room. Standing with him was an older couple who could only be his parents. *Oh, wow. They're as pale as me. Brandon has Caucasian parents? I didn't know he was adopted.* She filed that piece of information away to consider at another time.

"Ah, here she is," Brandon said, putting his hand possessively on the small of Selene's back. "Mom, Dad, this is my girlfriend, Selene Johansen. Selene, these are my parents, Richard and Elizabeth Price."

Selene smiled nervously and extended her hand.

Richard stepped forward first. A thin and dapper gentleman of about seventy he had a straight and upright figure and silver hair, neatly slicked back with pomade. He carried himself like a soldier. His palm touched Selene's for a moment, and she could hear him thinking, ***Now that's a tasty creature. I hope she's as nice as he says.***

"Pleased to meet you, Mr. Price," Selene said quietly, releasing his hand.

"You can call me Richard," he said.

"Richard then." She gave him a shy smile and turned towards his wife. Elizabeth, small and round with dimples in both cheeks, exuded an air of friendliness. When Selene touched her hand, though, what she heard was, **What a baby. I hope she's able to take good care of my boy.**

"I'm so glad to meet you both," Selene said by way of greeting.

Neither responded. She could feel their eyes fixed on her. *I wonder if they think I'm weird… or if they're thinking about the age difference… or what.*

"Well, Mom, Dad, the food is ready. Shall we eat?" Brandon suggested.

"Very well," Elizabeth agreed reluctantly, "but isn't Maggie going to be here?"

"Hi, Grandma, Grandpa. I'm here." Maggie emerged from the bathroom, the tear stains washed from her face and a charming smile fixed firmly in place. "Are the introductions over? I'm starving."

She hugged her grandparents and ushered everyone to the table. Brandon brought out pitchers of tea and water and everyone sat down to eat. Elizabeth seated herself next to Selene, and the interrogation began almost immediately.

"So, Selene, have you and Brandon known each other long?"

"Yes ma'am, about seven years," Selene replied. She smeared mayo on her bun, snagged a tomato, and assembled her burger.

Elizabeth regarded her with confusion, a forkful of potato salad poised over her plate. "How can you have? You're so young. Aren't you Maggie's friend?"

"Well, yes, but I'm not as young as Maggie. I'm almost thirty. I was an adult when Brandon and I met." *Well,*

ALMOST almost thirty, she thought, suppressing a smile at the idea of pretending to be older.

"Ah, you look younger than you are," Elizabeth said. She maneuvered the bite into her mouth and closed her eyes, savoring the rich flavor.

"Thank you," Selene replied. "I do hope we can become friends. I care for Brandon so much. I want him to be happy. He wouldn't like it if there's conflict between me and his family."

"I'm willing to give you a chance," Elizabeth said after she swallowed. "He certainly hasn't shown interest in anyone in ages." Seeming satisfied, Elizabeth returned to her dinner.

Selene nibbled her cheeseburger, though she had little appetite after her confrontation with her friend. Covering her shaky reaction with bravado, she plastered a gentle smile on her lips, refusing to let her lingering worry ruin the evening. *This is for Brandon and he deserves it. Hold it together.*

After the meal, Selene and Maggie carried the cake into the kitchen and lit a few sparkling candles. They started singing as they walked into the dining room.

Brandon closed his eyes for a moment and then attempted to blow out the candles. They relit instantly, so he tried again, but it was no use. The flames flared each time he extinguished them. Finally, laughing, he pulled them out of the cake and dunked them in his water glass.

"What did you wish?" Selene asked.

"I didn't blow out the candles, so it doesn't matter, but I couldn't think of a wish. I have everything I need right here. He squeezed Maggie's hand gently, wrapping his other arm around Selene's waist.

Selene leaned over and kissed his cheek. "Happy birthday, Brand."

"Happy birthday," the guests echoed.

After eating cake, they retired to the living room for an evening of lively conversation.

Selene sat quietly and observed, content to be included, especially since Brandon's arm rested around her shoulders. The evening grew quite late as chatter swirled shifted and broke into laughter. Shortly after eleven, Brandon's mother failed to suppress a huge yawn.

"Well, my loves, it was good to see you, but I'm done in, and we still have a long drive back to the suburbs, so we'd better call it a night before my dear husband falls asleep at the wheel."

"I'm perfectly fi i aaaah." Richard's protest dissolved into a yawn. He crimped his lips. "Never mind. Have a good evening." He levered himself to his feet with a groan and a loud pop from his left kneecap.

"Good night," Selene said, rising to see them to the door. "It was wonderful to meet you both."

"Likewise," Elizabeth said. "Now that Brandon isn't hiding you away anymore, I look forward to getting to know you better."

"That sounds good," Selene agreed, smiling.

She reached out her hand and Elizabeth clasped it, sending a not-quite-fully formed mixture of thoughts—hope and doubt, mostly—to Selene.

Maggie trailed up behind them. "See you later, Dad, Selene." Though the words sounded polite, her expression still held a hint of the hurt that had nearly wrecked the entire evening only a few hours before.

Somehow, we have to fix this, Selene thought. *Time will probably help, but I don't want to lose Maggie to awkwardness or discomfort. She means too much to me.*

The door clicked shut and Selene turned the deadbolt to the rumbling roar of Maggie's ancient pickup and the Prices' quieter minivan.

"Well, I'm hitting the shower," Brandon said. "I smell like I sat in a smoker all week." He pulled his tee-shirt away from his chest.

Selene nodded, kissed him once on the lips and drifted to the kitchen. Her mind wandered as she put dishes in the dishwasher and armed the alarm. Then she took her turn in the bathroom, releasing her hair from the ponytail she'd worn that day, brushing her teeth thoroughly and changing into the nightgown she'd purchased.

The black slip had lacy spaghetti straps that fell only to the middle of her thighs. It was also cut low in front, with a tiny bit of lace that teasingly revealed more than it concealed. This garment had only one purpose...to drive a man wild with desire.

Looking into the mirror, Selene felt a little silly. *Who am I fooling? I'm no temptress.* She considered touching up her makeup but decided against it. *This moment is about intimacy, not seduction. I'm giving Brandon my virginity tonight, but I'll do it looking like myself.*

She washed the remnants of the day's makeup from her eyes and lips and looked again. *This is the real Selene, with no barriers, nothing held back.* Slipping on the robe that matched her nightgown, she opened the door and walked into the bedroom.

Brandon was sitting in bed, propped up on pillows, leafing through a magazine. When he heard the door open, he glanced up, and the psychology journal slipped from his fingers. "Wow, babe, you look amazing."

"Thank you." She walked towards him, feeling a little unsteady, and untied the belt of her robe. The satiny fabric made a soft swishing noise as it slithered to the floor. Brandon swallowed hard, his eyes widening at the sight of Selene dressed so blatantly. In their weeks of passionate exploration, he had certainly seen plenty of her body, but they had always held back from full nudity.

"I hope you had a good birthday," Selene said, sliding one strap off her shoulder.

It took Brandon a moment to process the comment. "Yes,

very nice, thank you." His breath caught as she released the other strap. The nightgown slithered down around her slender body and puddled on the floor. "What are you doing, Selene?" he asked, his voice husky.

"What do you think? It's time, Brandon. I'm ready." Selene knelt on the bed beside him.

"Are you sure, baby?"

"Yes." She trailed her fingertips down his arm. "The longer we wait, the more nervous I get. Besides, it's not like we've just met and have to get to know each other. I've been waiting for this for a really long time. Tonight, it's your birthday, and I want to give you a present."

He swallowed hard, his throat working visibly. "That's one hell of a present, Selene."

"It's mine to give."

Brandon rose on his knees beside her and cupped her chin in his hand.

Gratitude, excitement, and overwhelmingly tender passion flowed over Selene, telling her she had made the right decision.

Brandon lowered his mouth gently to Selene's. Then he pulled back and looked her over. Years of physical training had left her body sweetly honed. While still a bit too thin, she had put on a little weight in the last month. He drank in the sight of her… silky, white-blond hair spilling to her waist, a lovely face with piercing green eyes, a small freckled nose, and dainty rosebud lips. She had a slender neck, shoulders, and arms, and shapely breasts large enough to be lovely without overwhelming her slim frame, crowned with delicate pink nipples. Her waist was narrow, her hips round. Lower, between her thighs, he admired a thatch of golden curls that held all the secrets he wanted to discover.

Selene's cheeks turned a bewitching pink, as Brandon deliberately looked her up and down. "You're so beautiful," he said, gathering her up into a crushing embrace. Kissing her hard, he drove his tongue into her mouth. She opened her lips for him, her arms around his neck, her breasts mashed against his smooth chest.

As he surfaced for air, panting, he realized he wasn't doing this well. *Selene's virginity is a precious gift, and needs to be savored, not devoured.* He planned to spend the rest of his life making love to Selene, and this introduction needed to be just right. He didn't want to hurt her or make her afraid of the next time. *Oh yes, you need to handle this very carefully.*

Forcing himself to slow down, he lowered her onto the bed, lying beside her, and gathered her into his arms again. Deliberately thinking about how much he loved her, he stroked his hand over her bare back while he kissed her thoroughly.

Although still nervous, Selene began to relax under the familiar warmth of Brandon's hands and mouth. *Don't be scared. He's made every other part good. He'll do the same with this.* His emotions washed over her. Love blended with the swelling desire. *Swelling is right.* She could feel his discomfort as his straining erection struggled with the waistband of his boxers.

Selene sensed his need and slid her hands into his garment, carefully lowering it so he could slide it off. *Now we're naked together.* She felt no fear of that swollen sex. She had handled it many times, caressing and tasting him, bringing him fulfillment that way. *But not tonight. Tonight, we're going to finish the process.*

Brandon made the first move towards intimacy by cupping Selene's breasts, shaping the dainty globes the way he'd learned she liked, gently and gradually, avoiding the nipples altogether at first, then skimming them lightly, and finally grasping them between his fingers, rolling them, which made her squirm with delight. He leaned down and took one in his mouth while he continued tormenting the other. Selene gasped, clearly loving the stimulation.

After thoroughly tasting both her nipples until they stood glistening and erect and she was panting with arousal, he rolled her onto her back and kissed his way down her belly. Her thighs parted for him, allowing him free access to her womanhood. He kissed the top of her mound before parting the outer lips and taking his first good look at the flesh he had spent so many nights caressing. She was lovely, pink, and so very wet. *She really does want this.*

He caressed the dainty folds and she shivered. Sliding one finger down to her opening, he pressed gently inside, feeling the stretch of untried flesh as he penetrated her. Her hymen provided a thin, insubstantial barrier, partially obstructing his progress and reminding him of his responsibilities. He had never been with a virgin. Not until now. *It's right. Selene is mine, and I'll never have to share her with memories of others, but she's small. I hate that this is likely to hurt her, even for a moment. So I guess I'll have to be sure she's ready.*

He began to caress her in the most sensitive of places with his thumb, driving her pleasure to a feverish pitch while he worked carefully on preparing her to accommodate him. It took some effort, but he managed to slide two fingers into her while he brought her closer to her climax. As he spread and stretched the resisting flesh, Selene came nearer to the brink. *Any moment now…any moment. Yes!* Her body arched up off the bed with the force of it. Her whimpers of ecstasy had to be the sweetest sound he'd ever heard.

Brandon trapped her hips with one arm and, while she

was still lost in spasms of delight, quickly pushed the tip of his sex inside her. Her eyes flew open, and she looked at him. He looked back, feeding another inch of himself inside that tiny passage and reaching the blockage he'd been dreading.

It was excruciating to stop with her wet sex caressing him so sweetly, but before he could continue, he had to be certain. "Baby, are you sure you want this?"

"What?" She blinked, clearly confused.

"This this the point of no return," he explained. "Once I press through, that's it. Or I can pull out right now, and you'll still be a virgin."

"Why would I want that?"

"I have to know you're really ready."

"Brandon." She caressed his face. "Brand, I want you. I want you now. I realize what this moment means, and there's no one but you that I would choose to share it with. What purpose would it serve to wait until another day? No, baby. Finish. Take me. Let's get this part over with so we can really be together."

She pulled him down for a tender kiss and twined her legs around his.

He swallowed hard and pulled back, so only the head of his sex remained inside her. They stared into each other's eyes for a long moment.

"I love you," he told her. Then he thrust forward. The barrier that had so concerned him turned out to be insubstantial. His momentum brought him past it without resistance until he rested deep inside her, deeper than he'd intended, and he found himself suddenly buried to the hilt, every inch of him embraced by the sweetest clinging wetness.

Well, the dreaded moment wasn't so bad, she thought. There had been a quick burning sensation, and now she felt uncomfortably full, but otherwise unharmed. *It doesn't hurt, not really.*

"Are you all right?" he asked softly.

"Yes, Brand. It wasn't bad."

"Am I hurting you?"

She looked into his eyes and saw the tender regret at war with aching eagerness. "No. It doesn't hurt anymore. It only hurt for a second. I'm fine."

"I'm glad. Would it be all right if I…move a little?"

Ah, yes, now the real lovemaking will begin. "Yes, darling, you can move."

He sighed deeply—almost a groan—and pulled back just a little, before pressing forward into her. Pulled back, pushed. Selene caressed his back as he sought to maintain his control so he could take her gently.

This movement feels interesting, she thought. *It has…potential. It makes me tingle.* Before she could decide where the tingle was headed, Brandon moaned softly as he climaxed inside her for the first time.

After such an intense moment, any words would have been a letdown. Brandon withdrew, cuddled her against him, and petted her hair until she fell asleep.

CHAPTER 6

The next morning, Selene woke up far earlier than she'd planned, her mind racing. Unable to go back to sleep, she slipped out of Brandon's embrace and pulled on her nightgown and robe before heading to the kitchen to brew some coffee.

She had never in her life experienced such a deluge of contradictory emotions. She wanted to laugh and cry at the same time, and she couldn't get her swirling thoughts to settle long enough to process any one of them.

Instead, she sat on a kitchen chair and sipped the strong black brew as she contemplated the strange experience of her deflowering. *At first, it was wonderful, all that intimate caressing, and a powerful, earth-shattering orgasm. Lovely. But then, the penetration was both more and less than I expected.*

The pain was minimal. I'm not even sore this morning, although I can still feel the internal stretching. I'm not sure what I thought intercourse would feel like, but I'm quite sure what I felt was not what I expected. Not certain what to make of it all, Selene took another swallow of her coffee with an appearance of outward calm, but inside she was roiling.

Of course, now that Brandon and I have finally had sex, he's going to want it again… often. I'm not sure if I can feel enthusiasm about the idea.

I wish there was a woman I could talk to, who could tell me if this typhoon of sensations is a normal part of becoming sexually active, but there's no one.

This is not the kind of conversation to have with a mother, so Auntie Karen is out. The obvious choice would be Maggie, but last night she posted a clear 'keep out' sign when it came to discussing sex if it involved her father, and rightly so. There are other women on the police force, but I'm not close to any of them.

I suppose I could ask Brandon, but what if I would hurt his feelings by admitting the night was…somewhat less than magical for me.

Shaking her head to try and clear it, Selene realized one thing. She couldn't sit on this chair and think about it another moment. Panic loomed dangerously close. Writing a note for Brandon, she crept back into the bedroom.

Her stomach clenched as she caught a glimpse of Brandon's gorgeous face, looking young and relaxed against the pillow. *He's at peace with the world. Lucky.*

She tossed on her jeans and tank top and slipped away through the kitchen, into the mudroom, where she stepped into a pair of sneakers. Then she made her way out to her car.

For a while, she drove around aimlessly, but all her random left and right turns eventually took her to the police station. *Perhaps I can lose myself in some paperwork and clear my head for a while.*

Though Sunday and still early, police stations are never really quiet or empty. Still, Selene managed to slip to her desk without being spotted.

She quickly realized working on reports was going to be extremely difficult because she felt so distracted and exposed, like a specimen on a slide. *If any of these guys knew what I did last night…*acute embarrassment set her cheeks on fire. She felt so clearly stamped with Brandon's lovemaking, as though a sign had been hung around her neck. *This is no help.*

At just that moment, Tony sidled over to Selene. "Hey, girl. What are you doing here so bright and early on your day off? I thought you'd still be sleeping," he said in his most trouble-making voice.

Wonderful. That's all I need. Tony the Terrible Tease. Be cool, Selene. Don't act weird. "I couldn't sleep," Selene muttered, not looking up, hoping he would take a hint and leave, but Tony had all the subtlety of a two-by-four.

"Why? What's wrong?" he pressed. "Did you have a fight with that lover-boy of yours?"

Selene raised her head and took in his scruffy, unshaven cheeks and tousled black curls. "Keep your voice down, Tony. I don't want to be stared at this morning. No, Brandon and I did not have a fight. Quite the opposite. Yesterday was his birthday."

"Oh yeah, I knew that. So, if it was his birthday, I really don't get why you're here. The morning after a birthday is a great time to get in some extra…cuddling if you know what I mean." He nudged her with his elbow.

Selene's cheeks flamed a brilliant, almost painful scarlet. Her whole face burned with embarrassment.

"Woo-hoo," Tony said, his voice pitched thankfully low. "What a night you must have had."

"Please just go away, Tony. I don't want to talk about it."

He somehow caught the acute discomfort in Selene's voice and dropped his teasing demeanor. Grabbing a chair from a nearby cubicle, he turned it around backward, straddling the seat. "I can see you're not okay about something. All joking aside, do you need to talk to someone?"

She looked away. "I can't talk about this with you. You're not a woman."

"No, but I'm your friend, Selene," he reminded her.

She considered for a moment. "Well, if I don't talk this out

WATCHING OVER THE WATCHER

with someone, I think I'm going to explode, but I swear, Tony, if you breathe one word of this to *anyone*, I'll tase you."

He took a step back at her semi-serious words. "Whoa, what happened? You seem messed up. Did he hurt you or something?"

As if Brandon ever would. "Of course not! It's just…I've never done it before, and I don't know what to think."

"Done what? Something kinky?" He waggled his eyebrows.

Selene lowered her gaze. "Hardly."

"Well, then I can't imagine what's twisting your tail," he exclaimed in quiet exasperation. "You're acting like you've just lost your virg…" Her face must have revealed something more than she'd intended because he interrupted his tirade with, "Oh shit. Seriously? You've been living together for a month!"

"I wanted to wait until the time was right," she muttered.

"Selene, you're twenty-eight. You're a virgin?" His volume was rising.

She shushed him with a finger to her lips. "Not anymore," she reminded him.

"Oh wow," he said, mercifully softer this time. "Why did you wait so long?"

"Why do you think, Tony?" she asked. "You should know. No one can stand to get near me, not even you, not even to shake my hand. I've got to be the most touch-deprived person on the planet."

He acknowledged her words with a nod. "You can hardly blame anyone for that."

"I don't," she replied. She reached out and laid her hand on his bicep, on top of his shirt, "but it doesn't provide many opportunities for intimacy, does it?"

He visibly flinched, then relaxed when he realized she was aiming for fabric. Noticing his reaction, he made an apologetic face before continuing. "Except for Brandon?"

"Right. He's completely comfortable with what I do. He uses it to tell me what he's thinking when he finds the words difficult."

His expression changed from incredulity to understanding. "Then he's your perfect match, isn't he?" the young cop said softly.

How interesting to see Tony react to the idea that someone might touch me on purpose, knowing what will happen. "Yes. That's why I wanted so much to be with him, and now…" She pulled back, folding her hands and looking out the window across the room. Outside, the edge of the rising sun barely illuminated the brilliant green of two juvenile oak trees growing on the edge of the parking lot, obscuring the building next door.

"Now?" Tony pressed.

"Well," Selene's face grew even hotter than before, "it wasn't like what I thought. I don't know what I was expecting, but…it was strange, and I feel strange about it, like everyone who looks at me will know, and…I don't know."

Tony shook his head. "Selene, listen. No one will know exactly what you did last night, but everyone knows you two are intimate, not because it's stamped on your face, but because we know you're in love with Brandon, and that you live with him. And you know what? No one cares. They're glad you have someone, finally. Everyone's happy for you. He's a good guy. As I see it, there's nothing wrong. You love him, you live with him, and you gave him a big gift last night. Good for you, and him. Don't ruin it by overthinking."

"But I feel so weird," she burst out.

Tony shrugged and rose, pushing the chair away with one foot. He perched his butt on the edge of her desk, one long leg dangling, the other planted on the floor. "Let me give you the male perspective, okay? For some reason, some women think they have to be embarrassed about sex, but you don't. It's not shameful, and when you love someone, it's really special. Sleeping with Brandon doesn't make you a slut or a whore.

You're a good girl in a good relationship. Try to be okay with it."

And here I thought I was the intuitive one. Boy does that hit it right on the head. But the problem remained. "I don't know how."

He crossed his arms over his chest and looked down on her with a stern stare. "Try, Selene, try really hard. Because here's a secret, okay? Men aren't very complicated. If you want your man to know you love him, it's really easy. Give him a ton of sex. He'll know what that means. And don't just put up with it, be eager, start it sometimes. Participate actively. Make sure he knows it's not a chore for you. If you do that, Brandon will always know he's loved."

"But I feel so…awkward," she argued. *As much with this conversation as the event itself.*

"Well, naturally," he replied, and there was a hint of *duh* in his voice. Selene scowled at him, but he ignored her displeasure. "The first time is always the hardest, but if you build it up in your mind into something scary or bad, it will be. Just remind yourself that new experiences are always uncomfortable, but the way to get comfortable is practice. Feeling strange doesn't mean you're doing it wrong. It just means you have to get used to it, and the way to get used to it is to do it again and again until it's normal. Make yourself believe that."

That's what any man would want, isn't it? An eager woman. Why am I angry about that? Is it wrong to long for intimacy with the person you love? Selene shook her head, trying to clear her rambling thoughts. *It's not wrong. And you wanted it just as bad yesterday. What changed?* "It's not that easy."

"Yes, it is," he dismissed her words instantly. "Just do it. Do you love Brandon?"

She closed her eyes and could still see Brandon's, the way he looked last night, his beautiful dark eyes boring into her soul with tender passion. "He's my whole world."

"Do you want him to be happy?"

"Of course."

"Then you know what to do."

"But…"

"No buts, Selene." He cut off her argument with a slash of his hand. "If you aren't willing to do this for him, break up with him."

She blinked in surprise.

"No, I'm not kidding," he responded to her expression. "This is fundamental. He won't feel like a real man unless he can please his woman in bed. If you refuse to allow yourself to enjoy it, you'll hurt him. It will destroy your relationship. It really is that important. Is Brandon worth more to you than your awkward feelings?"

The only man who has ever been willing to take me on? The man who tells me every day that he loves me? Is there any question? "Yes."

"Then let it go." Tony enunciated the words slowly, in a softly authoritative voice. "I suggest you get back in the saddle again as soon as possible before you can tie yourself into knots about it. Believe me, Brandon will appreciate it."

I hate it when Tony makes sense. "Okay. I'll try."

"Good. Now go home. You shouldn't be here." He hopped off her desk and gestured toward the door. Then he stalked away.

Selene grabbed her purse from the back of her chair. "You're right," she said to his retreating back. "Oh, and Tony?"

He paused and turned. "Yeah?"

"Thanks."

"Hey, no problem," he replied, with a smile and a wave. "Glad I could help."

And that was that. Selene gave up pretending to work and drove home. *There's nothing else to be done. I simply have to follow Tony's advice and practice intimacy until it's normal. I kind of figured that this was the case, but talking it out, humiliating though it was, helped a lot. I have to decide whether to let awkwardness or love guide my actions. I choose love.*

I'll go home right now and let Brandon know how much I still desire him; how much I want to keep learning about lovemaking. So, I'll exaggerate… hopefully only for a short time.

She parked, kicked off her shoes in the mudroom, and entered the kitchen. *More coffee to fortify myself,* she thought, pouring a cup.

Then she made her way through the door into the living room, to find Brandon on the sofa in his boxers, drinking coffee. It was such a normal, everyday thing to see. *He hasn't changed. Neither have I and really, neither has our relationship. We're simply discovering a new way to express our love to each other.*

"Hey, babe, did you have a good drive?" he asked, giving her a lopsided, white-toothed grin that made her heart turn over.

"Yes, I did, thank you." She joined Brandon on the couch and laced the fingers of her free hand through his.

"How are you today?" he said, and concern for her well-being filtered through their twining fingers.

"Fine," she replied cheerfully, lifting their joined hands so she could kiss the tip of his thumb.

"Sore?" ***Stupid question. Of course, she's sore.***

He's worried, she realized. At least she could answer honestly. "Nope."

I hope she's not mad. The thought pulsed through Selene's fingers.

"What's wrong?"

"What do you mean?" His Adam's apple worked painfully, reinforcing the worry she felt through his fingertips. Crinkles at the corners of his eyes showed his tension.

"I can read your mind, Brandon." Selene reminded him dryly. "Why would I be mad?"

"Last night." A jumble of images swirled in her head.

Somehow the tender interlude had transformed itself in his mind into something a lot more forceful and…*What's that? Selfish on his part? As though it wasn't my idea to begin with. Silly man.* "It was fine, honey. It was…easier than I expected."

"But it wasn't…all that it could be, all I had hoped."

"What do you mean? I had a really good time. It was very nice." She made her voice slow and soft, lingering sensually over the words.

"The beginning was good, but the end came…too fast, or rather I did." ***And for a man of my age and experience, there's no excuse for that.***

Puzzled by his feelings, Selene could only ask, "Too fast?"

"I wanted you to come too, baby."

"I did." *What on earth is he getting at?*

"I mean with me inside you. It's been so long since I've been with anyone, and it's you, and you were so beautiful and tight, and…I just couldn't wait."

"Oh." *Oh, wow! Tony was so right. Brandon is sensitive to my pleasure. He doesn't like the thought that I was left unsatisfied.* Determined to reassure him, Selene shrugged. "It's okay. Next time. Don't beat yourself up about it, Brand. It was really good. Since it was the first time, there's no way it could also be the best ever. We have to practice a bit more. We're going to be amazing together, but for an initiation, it was excellent. I really enjoyed making love with you."

"You did?" Uncertainty filtered through his words and his fingers.

Okay, enough talking. I'll show him. "Yes. Very much."

She placed her cup on the coffee table and took Brandon's from him, setting it aside as well. Swinging her leg over him, she straddled his lap. Selene coiled her arms around his neck, and brought her mouth down hard on his, snaking her tongue between his lips. She wantonly rubbed her chest against him. Pulling back a fraction of an inch, she looked at him with sultry green eyes and whispered, "Let's do it again."

"You're certain you aren't too sore?"

"Not a bit. Don't fret. I'm not a child. I know what I can handle."

"Believe me, Selene; I know you're not a child." He began to mold her breasts in his hands. She made a soft sound as the pleasure of his eager touch obliterated any lingering nerves.

He lifted the hem of her tank top. Pressing her back against the arm he had anchored behind her, he kissed her belly as he revealed it, kiss after kiss, tickling her with teasing swipes of his tongue. Warmth and moisture pooled between her thighs, and a kind of soft buzzing inside her head pushed her thoughts, and even his, to the background. The pleasure of his touch took center stage in her awareness, preparing her to receive what she'd asked for.

Eventually, he lifted her upright. She took hold of her top with both hands and removed it, tossing it aside. Then she leaned forward to continue exploring Brand's mouth with wet, passionate kisses. He unhooked her bra from behind with practiced fingers and let it slide down into her lap. She brushed it aside. Cuddling close again, she teased his chest with her nipples, liking the stimulation of his skin against hers. His chest was smooth and muscular, but with almost no hair, and Selene caressed it with her hands and her breasts.

"Oh, baby," Brandon groaned, "Stand up a minute. Let's get out of these clothes."

"Should we go back to bed?" she suggested.

"No. Right here." Brandon shucked his boxers and resumed his seat, sliding just a little towards the middle of the sofa.

"Here? Okay, if you say so." *Something different. Interesting.*

"Yes, you're going to like this, I think. Unbutton those pretty jeans and let me see what's underneath."

Selene's cheeks burned, but she removed her jeans as instructed, revealing black lace panties. She reached for the waistband.

"Hold on. Turn around once, slowly. I want to see."

She turned, showing him the full view, glancing over her shoulder to see him devouring her with naked hunger. *Has anyone ever wanted another person as badly as this? And it's all mine. He's all mine. How did I get this lucky?*

He reached out for her, drawing her towards him until she stood between his thighs. Brandon leaned forward and caught the fabric, pulling it down to reveal everything. Past the curve of her hips, the underwear lost its grip and fluttered to the floor.

Oh, God. Selene stepped out of them unsteadily; her feet no longer under her full control.

"Now then, let's see what we have here," Brandon said, cupping her mound. He pressed inward. She was still wet from the previous night's sex, and new moisture had been added in the last few minutes. He slid his fingers in deep, and Selene moaned softly. "I can't believe it. You're ready. Come sit on my lap, Selene."

She straddled him again.

He parted her gently. "Do you want me, baby?"

"Oh yes, please," she begged, suddenly aching with the desire to be filled with him again.

"Put me inside you."

She took his thick sex in her hand, stroking it for a moment, and then positioned it at her opening, sliding the head in.

He took hold of her hip and pressed her down on him. Inch by inch, with many pauses, he penetrated her, and all the while he caressed her clitoris with his free hand.

Today, it feels sooooo different, she realized. Every time he surged forward, pressing deeper into her, her pleasure built higher. Every stroke of his fingers on her heated flesh intensified it more.

"Do you want the rest?" he asked.

"Oh yes," she moaned.

He thrust once and filled her completely, his fingers still working her most sensitive spot.

"Ooooh," Selene breathed. "That's so hot. Oh, Brandon." She began to rock her hips restlessly.

"And now, I think, you're getting very close. Come hard for me, baby. Let me feel how much you like it."

Selene's breath caught in soft little gasping pants. *Aaaaaah…almost there…* "YES!" her head fell back, long hair sweeping Brandon's legs as she spasmed, trembling, her sex squeezing him hard.

He prolonged the moment, continuing his intimate caresses until Selene brushed his fingers away. "No more, baby. Oh, that was amazing."

"It was," he agreed. "And you look so pretty when you come."

She leaned her forehead on his shoulder and began to rock again, wanting to give him what he had given her.

"Yes, that's it," Brandon encouraged. "Ride me."

She did. She rode him with sweet abandon, driving him wild with pleasure until finally, ecstasy overwhelmed him, and he let go. His chiseled face turned harsh as he climaxed in her.

As passion ebbed away, Brandon and Selene kissed.

"Oh, Brandon," she said softly, "that was so good. I loved it." *It's not an exaggeration after all.* This time, Selene felt completely satisfied with her sexual experience, and somehow, her shyness about the act seemed to have melted away. *After all, pretty much everyone has sex. Why should I be different? I'm just lucky. I found the love of my life on the first try.*

After a long moment, they disengaged. Selene grabbed her clothes and walked to the bathroom to clean herself up and dress. When she emerged, she found Brandon, back in his boxers, waiting for her.

He hugged her tight.

"I love you," she said softly, "and I never imagined a feeling like that existed. You're so good to me, Brandon."

He smiled. "I'm glad. I love you too, Selene. Why don't you have some breakfast, okay?"

"I'm not hungry," she protested, not wanting to leave his company for a second.

"You need to eat something." His hand slipped under her shirt and pressed against her bare back*. Why won't you eat? You're still so thin, and with all the energy we just expended, you're going to make yourself sick if you don't watch it.*

"Please, honey. Don't be such a mother hen. I can take care of myself," she said, half joking, half exasperated.

"I know you can, but I worry about you, you know? Just have a little something, for me?"

Selene sighed, walking past him into the kitchen, where she poured herself a small bowl of granola. *He wasn't wrong to encourage me to eat,* she realized. *We* did *expend a lot of energy between last night and this morning.* The thought made her cheeks redden slightly, not with embarrassment exactly, but with a kind of shy satisfaction and anticipation. *I could definitely get used to this kind of treatment, which is good because I'm going to have to.* Her desire, ignited in his arms this morning, was not yet completely satisfied. *I think I'm going to need a little more pretty soon, but I'm sure Brandon won't object.*

She finished her cereal, put the bowl in the sink, and then went to find her lover. He still sat on the couch, watching the news.

"Sorry to have to tell you such a graphic story, folks," the young blonde on the screen said, her face appropriately sad, "but the Minneapolis police department is asking for your assistance. If you know anything, even if you're not sure whether it's relevant, please call the number on the screen…"

Selene sank onto the sofa with a sigh.

Brandon turned to her. "This is what you've been investigating?"

She leaned her head on his shoulder. "Unfortunately, yes. That poor lady. She's been in the hospital for a month, recovering from what he did to her, and we still don't have a suspect. All her friends and family are innocent, and it looks like a random crime. We may never catch the bastard. There are no new leads. If he picked her at random, then he's a serial rapist and could do this again. As violent as the assault was, he could kill next time."

"Oh, Lord. What a tragedy." Brandon pulled Selene down next to him and put his arm around her shoulders. "No wonder you've been so stressed out. If anyone can catch this guy, it's you."

"I don't catch the suspects. I only question them," she reminded him. "It's scary, you know? This girl was not a hooker—not that that's an excuse. She was just out with her friends at a club and had a little too much to drink. They were good friends, so they called her a cab. Next morning, she was found beaten, bloody and semiconscious in a ditch seven miles from town."

"Have you questioned the cab driver?"

"No one can find him," she said, shaking her head in helpless agitation. "Brandon, this could happen to anyone."

"I know," he said grimly. "Her friends must be devastated."

"They are. They all feel responsible. I do too. We need to put this monster away."

He soothed her with stroking fingers and calming thoughts. "But her friends aren't responsible. Neither are you. He is. Catch him, baby, if you can, but don't make yourself crazy. You didn't cause this situation. You're going to fix it."

"Even if we catch the guy, nothing can fix it," she said bleakly. "She has scars, physical and emotional, that will never go away. Some of the damage is permanent. It breaks my heart." She looked down at the floor as tears stung her eyes. *It's a job, Selene. Don't get emotional. Stay professional.*

Brandon cuddled her closer. "I know, baby. You're such a good police officer. You'll find a way to get justice for her." He clicked off the television. "One way to make sure you do your job well is not to dwell on it in the meanwhile. You can't be your best when you're obsessing. No more talking about work for the rest of the weekend. Come on."

"Where are we going?"

"To the shower." His soothing demeanor gave way to a naughty grin as he took her hand and pulled her to her feet.

Selene's eyes widened. "Together?"

"Yes." He turned back and winked at her.

"I've read about this in novels…does it really work?"

He tugged her through the bathroom door saying, "Oh, I don't know. I don't plan to do it in the shower. That's just the warm-up. Afterwards…well, we'll see where it leads."

"As if there's any doubt."

He winked at her again, making her laugh.

Oh, I can't wait. This is going to be phenomenal.

As the water heated, they undressed each other. "Do you remember the last time we did this?" Brandon asked as he led her into the tub.

"The night of the fire? Yes. I was awfully embarrassed." Her cheeks burned now, but with anticipation, not shame.

"You were so pretty. I felt bad because you were having a terrible time, but I couldn't stop wanting you." He cupped her cheeks in his hands and ravaged her mouth with a passionate kiss. "Selene, I'm so glad you decided to stay with me."

"As if there were any other options. Let's see…move in with the love of my life, or go to a hotel alone? Nope, no question what I was going to do. Now hand me that shampoo bottle."

And so, they washed each other. Selene taught Brandon the proper care of extra-long hair, to prevent a tangled mess afterward. Brandon taught Selene the potential associated with soap covered hands. They lingered over wonderfully sensitive, intimate places, kissing in the stream of warm water.

Selene pulled back with a gasp, nearly slipping on the slick floor, she was so focused on the overwhelming sensations of Brandon's tongue deep inside her mouth, one hand plucking her nipple while the other clutched her bottom, grinding her belly against his thick erection. "If we're not doing it in the shower, we'd better move. I can't wait much longer."

He grinned at her. "Shall we adjourn to the boudoir, milady?" Raw desire pulsed into her.

She nodded. He shut off the water and the sudden blast of chilly morning air stole her voice away, so only a startled croak emerged. The overpowering passion retreated. She stepped out onto a forest green bathmat and grabbed the purple towel Brandon had used on her the night of the fire.

Quickly patting the water from her body, she turned to the mirror and grabbed her wide-toothed comb.

"I don't think so," Brandon murmured, retrieving the comb from her hands and working it through the tangles himself, gently. She watched the darker skin of his hands moving over the pale strands and was struck by the contrast between them.

"Look at us, Brandon. See how good we look together?"

"Hmm, you're right. Picture perfect." He dropped the comb on the counter and ran his hands up her torso, cupping her breasts.

She sighed softly at the pleasurable sensation and the lovely sight. "Take me to the bed, love," she told him firmly. "I need you right now."

Brandon scooped Selene off her feet, draping her over his shoulder. She laughed as he carried her into the bedroom. "How very alpha male of you," she giggled.

"That's right, baby." He spilled her onto the bed and knelt between her thighs, on hand resting on her skin.

Brandon shook his head, and his unguarded thoughts poured into her. *This is what angels look like. Ethereal. Her hair looks almost golden against the pillowcase. Her body against the sheets is white on white, with flashes of color: eyes, lips, nipples, the golden curls here.* His hand slid up to rest on her mound. *How can anyone be so lovely? And she's all mine.*

His thoughts warmed her to her core.

She planted her heels on the bed, letting him view her most intimate place. *Look at that. She's drenched, of course, and from the previous two rounds of loving, her vagina is a little open. Looks like an invitation.*

Her cheeks burned at his frankness, but she couldn't hold in a pleasured moan when he took the invitation, sliding fingers into the tiny portal. She could feel his desire to give her more pleasure, and he lowered his mouth to her, licking the sensitive folds.

Selene grabbed handfuls of the sheets as intense pleasure shot through her. Moaning and whimpering, she tossed her head from side to side. *Oh, he's so good! This is going to be the biggest orgasm to date. No wonder it's called 'little death'. It's almost scary.* She squirmed away from the intense stimulation, but there was no escape, and the explosion proved every bit as intense as she'd expected.

She screamed as pleasure overwhelmed her every sense, and her body lifted involuntarily from the bed. *Oh God, oh God, oh God.* The senseless litany played in her head while wordless whimpers escaped her mouth.

Finally, she collapsed, utterly sated. She panted as Brandon positioned himself between her legs and plunged deep in one sure stroke. Selene lay passive against the invasion, letting herself be plundered with hard thrusts as her lover pleasured himself inside her body.

Eventually, her arousal renewed, and she reached a second, softer peak from the intense stimulation. She made a quiet sound as her body clenched, and the extra tightness wrung his orgasm from him.

"Oh, baby," he said softly, when he had recovered a bit, "are you sure you were a virgin yesterday?"

"You were there," she reminded him. "I just love you so much, I don't want to hold back."

"Never hold back. You were born for this." He cradled the back of her neck in one hand and kissed her forehead.

"I think you must be right."

They lay together a long time, nude, enjoying the intimacy of complete satisfaction. Selene cuddled against Brandon's side, her head pillowed on his shoulder, and he petted her, caressing her skin lightly so that she could hear him echoing her contentment with his own.

After a while, a question that had been hovering in the back of Selene's mind surfaced. Idly tracing her fingertips over Brandon's chest, she asked, "How is it that I've known you all these years, but I never knew your parents were white?"

"Hmm. Not sure," he replied. "I guess it never came up. I don't really think about it. They're just...my parents, you know? Obviously, I was adopted."

"Yes, I can see that," she agreed. Her hand flattened on his belly. "Here I imagined you growing up in a Native American community."

He chuckled making her fingers bounce. "Nope, I grew up in the suburbs. It was a little tough since I was the only Indian kid in my class until Claudia moved to town. Some people thought they knew something about me because of that."

"Let me guess. Lazy? Alcoholic? Addict? All the ugly stereotypes?" She softened the words with a light caress of his abdominal muscles.

"Right. It shocked the hell out of my classmates—and

some of the teachers—when I graduated in the top ten percent of my class. And then there were others, mostly silly girls, who thought I was terribly romantic. They must have read too many romance novels. It was a grave disappointment to them when I turned out to be just another teenager with a darker complexion."

"So, what's your story, love?" she asked. "Do you know anything about your background or your birth parents?"

"Not much," he admitted. "My natural father is a complete mystery. The story, which my mom told me— and which the hospital nurses confirmed when I asked them—is that a very young Indian girl arrived in full labor, giving only her first name; Angela. She needed to get to the delivery room right away, so there was no time for paperwork. I was born about a half hour later. By the time the nurses brought the papers for her to sign, she was gone, leaving me in a bassinet. I can't imagine what kind of desperate situation she was in to make such a decision, but I've always wished her well. I'm not sorry she gave me up. My parents are great."

He squeezed her shoulder and continued. "My story was featured on the news, and my parents, who had recently learned they would never have children on their own, stepped up to adopt me. So, I'm fully Indian, as far as I know, but I was brought up by white, Lutheran parents. The only downside is that I can't connect with my heritage. I guess I'm probably either Ojibwa or Lakota since those are the largest nations around here, but there's no way to know. Angela could even have been from out of town. If I could document my lineage, I could join a community. But I can't prove a thing, so all I can do is observe like any other tourist."

"Wow. How dramatic," she said, repositioning her head more comfortably against his shoulder.

"Not really," he replied, running softly tickling fingers down her side.

She squeaked and gave him a mock glower.

He grinned unrepentantly. "I was a baby when most of this happened. By the time I was aware of what was going on, I was already established with my family. It's just a story."

"Do you want to know something eerie?"

"What?" He tugged the ends of her hair, making her shiver.

"My story isn't all that different from yours."

His playful fingers stilled. "How so?"

"Well, my mom was also really young when she had me, only fifteen. Of course, I know who she was; Christine Johansen. She seems to have been the spontaneous origin of the psychic gift. She had it, but no one else in the family does. She didn't cope well with it and was rather depressed and unstable from early childhood. No one was surprised when she got pregnant. My aunt says Christine would have done anything to feel normal. Having a baby in high school did not help. Apparently, she couldn't handle the pressure of mother-hood, and she killed herself when I was a week old."

"Oh Selene, that's terrible." He gave her a little hug. "Were you also put up for adoption?"

"No. My grandparents wanted to, but my Aunt Karen refused. She said I was family, and she requested to be my legal guardian. The judge said no at first since she was only eighteen and single. So, she quickly married her boyfriend and absolutely insisted on keeping me. I was raised by my aunt and uncle. I also have three cousins. No one else can do what I do though.

"When I started middle school, Auntie Karen realized I was going to have a lot of trouble. Not as much as Mom, because Karen's a much better parent than hers were, and so is Uncle Paul, and I've always known they loved me, even if they didn't understand me very well. So, Karen searched until she found a boarding school for...children like me. It was there, among my peers, that I developed my gift, learned to respect the privacy of others, and learned to use what I do to help people. They thought I would be a natural at counseling, so I tried it. Maggie was my first and only client, and you know the rest."

"Well, there is a certain symmetry between us isn't there?" he said.

How much do you like knowing you have something in common with him? "Maybe that's why we're so compatible. It's that deep understanding that comes from knowing our most fundamental relationships were broken. Fathers unknown, abandoned by our mothers, and we both had to learn to love someone else as parents."

"I can see that. We have something else in common."

"What's that?" she asked.

"The sense of being…other…different."

What an insightful man. "You're right. Even among the gifted, I'm unusual. I've never met anyone else who can do what I do. Among the mundane, I'm a mystery and a threat. And you…"

"I have a foot in two worlds," he finished for her. "I'm not white, but I'm not really Indian either. Who am I?"

"I know who you are," Selene murmured, cuddling against him. "You're mine."

"Now that's a title I can live with." He kissed her tenderly. "Okay, sweetheart, let's get dressed and go enjoy the summer sunshine."

"Can't we just lie here all day?" Selene pleaded.

"Nope, let's move." He tugged her to her feet. "I want to show off my beautiful girlfriend to the whole world."

How can I resist such a charming invitation? "Okay."

CHAPTER 7

*J*une 20th, Selene thought as she punched her timecard. *Almost another month has gone by, and everything is going so well. I don't think I've ever been this happy.*

"Morning, Selene," Tony called from the break room. "Memos in the mailboxes."

"Budget cuts again?" she guessed, joining him and pouring herself a cup of the station's miserable, flavorless coffee.

"Yep. No overtime this month."

She sighed, sipped and frowned at the offending cup. "I'm going to have to take off early today then. I've questioned a lot of people this month."

"Early release on a Friday," Tony replied. "Lucky you… or is it?"

She shrugged. "It's nothing to get excited about. Brandon has clients all afternoon, so I guess it'll be talk show Friday for me."

"How is old lover boy anyway?" Tony asked.

Where once the indiscreet question would have embarrassed Selene, today she just rolled her eyes. "What are you, twelve? Grow up, Guido. He's fine, thank you. We're planning to visit his parents for the 4th and go to the lake. One of his great aunts has a homestead up near Brainerd."

"Wow. Holiday plans not involving the police station? You've changed, Selene. I hardly know you anymore."

"Yeah, I have a life now. Isn't that something?"

He pressed his fist lightly against the sleeve of her blouse. "Bout freaking time. I thought I was going to have to start taking bids, just so you could go on a date, get laid and cheer up your grumpy ass."

She grinned. "You're full of shit, you know that?"

Tony tutted, twisting his face into an expression of exaggerated offense.

"I think you really are twelve," she added. "Now, do you have anything constructive to add? If not, I'm going to see how much paperwork I can fill out in the next three hours."

He chuckled, refilled his cup, and wandered away.

It was just before noon when she arrived at the house. "Now what?" she asked Sammy, as she punched the keypad to arm the alarm. "I usually work late on Fridays, trying to get ahead before the weekend. I'm going to have such a pile of work on Monday, it will be like shoveling snow to get out from underneath it.

The kitten regarded her from his usual perch on the dining chair with bored blue-gray eyes and yawned hugely.

"I see my worries don't matter to you at all. Thanks for the support, little buddy. Why don't you give me suggestions of something to do? I'm already bored and it's not even afternoon yet."

Sammy wandered over and stared at his empty food dish.

"No, you don't, greedy boy," Selene admonished. "Not until supper time. You're getting too fat already."

Offended, Sammy stalked out of the room.

Hmmm. Supper. Maybe I could make food for Brandon for a change. I don't know if he realizes I can cook… but what to make?

She glanced at the counter and found the vast assortment of summer vegetables they had bought at the farmer's market the previous weekend: tomatoes, summer squash, fennel and pearl onions. In the fridge, she found freshly-picked carrots and bunches of parsley and basil. After most of a week, they were all starting to get a little wrinkly and sad.

Looks like soup to me. She dug a can of white beans and a bag of pasta wheels out of the pantry. *I haven't made minestrone in ages. With that loaf of artisanal bread we picked up on Sunday when we went downtown, it'll be a perfect light summer meal.*

She gathered her ingredients and regarded how they filled the counter.

This is way too much food for two. We'll get sick of the leftovers long before they run out, which defeats the purpose. Hmmm. I wonder if Maggie would join us. We haven't talked much since Brandon's birthday party. I miss her, and a dinner invitation might be a good way to break the ice again.

She quickly chopped the vegetables and set them to simmer in a pot of broth before dialing the familiar phone number.

"Hi, Selene," Maggie said, her voice wary, "what's up?"

Her tone stung, but Selene answered without rancor, "Just wondering what you're up to. I have the afternoon off, and, well, I miss you."

"Is my dad there?" Maggie asked.

"No, he's still at work," Selene said mildly, refusing to react to Maggie's tone. "What about you?"

"I have a bunch of aerobics classes to lead tomorrow, so I'm off today."

"Hey, do you want to come over?" Selene asked, pretending it was a spur of the moment decision.

"I guess," Maggie replied, sounding utterly unmoved by the invitation.

"I'm underwhelmed," Selene teased, covering her hurt with a joke. "Never mind this big pot of soup simmering here. I guess Brandon and I will have to eat it alone."

"Your homemade minestrone?" Now Maggie sounded eager. "Okay, I'm in."

"Maggie, you're a soup hussy."

"Yup," she agreed with a dry chuckle. "I'll be there in ten minutes."

Though glad Maggie was coming, Selene also felt a sizzle of nervousness. She couldn't bear for her friend to quiz her about her relationship with Brandon. *I hope Maggie truly doesn't want the details. It's too intimate, too special, to be put under a magnifying glass.*

When Maggie arrived a few minutes later, Selene noticed that her friend seemed tired and a little depressed. "Hi, Selene," she said listlessly, "you look happy."

"I am happy," Selene replied honestly, as she stirred the soup.

"It suits you." Maggie sighed deeply and sank into a chair.

"What's wrong, hon?"

"Nothing," Maggie shrugged. "Man trouble."

"What trouble?"

She made a face. "My new boyfriend isn't working out well. He's kind of an asshole."

"Dump him," Selene said bluntly. "You don't need that."

Maggie put her hands over her face. "I know, but I've slept with him, and now I feel weird about just taking off. Slutty. Damn, what a stupid mistake."

"Sorry." Selene winced. A sudden thought occurred to her and she spoke without thinking. "Hey, whatever happened to that Swedish guy you liked so much?"

"Jan?" Maggie's face grew even sadder. "He had to go back to Sweden. I miss him."

"Didn't he ask you to go with him?"

"Well yeah, but my life is here. Plus, I wasn't ready for that kind of commitment."

I'd love to grab her hand right now and find out if she still feels that way. "Do you ever hear from him?"

"He emails me a lot," Maggie explained. "I don't think he'd take me back though, not after I had sex with Jason."

I remember how Jan looked at her. I think he'd forgive a lot if she just asked. "Why don't you just try? He may be more willing than you think, especially if he loves you. One thing's for sure though. You need to unload Jason. If he's an asshole, and you still want to be with someone else, there's no hope for it."

Maggie smiled without the faintest touch of humor, more a grimace than a grin. "You're right. How did you get to be such an expert on complicated relationships?"

"Observation," Selene replied, raising one eyebrow. "You know it's not experience."

"What about you and Dad?"

Oh please, let's not head down that path! "There's nothing complicated about what we have. We just love each other. Simple."

"Simple sounds good," Maggie replied, accepting the unelaborated response.

"I might be wrong," Selene said hesitantly, "but it seems to me, if a relationship is complicated, that's not a good sign."

"Probably not. Just a minute."

Maggie left the kitchen and turned down the hallway. As she passed the master bedroom, which was barely visible from where Selene stood, she glanced through the open door. Selene winced.

Hopefully, Maggie didn't notice the unmade bed, still rumpled from last night's lovemaking. Heat prickled in her cheeks, though not as strongly as it would have a few weeks ago.

As she cleared away the carrot peels and tomato cores, she thought back to the previous evening. Brandon had wanted to try something new. Selene was always willing to let him experiment since the results were so delicious. He had piled up pillows and laid her over them, face down, so he could take her from behind. There hadn't been much leverage for exaggerated thrusting, but the deep nudges had been just as satisfying as something wilder would have been.

A few minutes later, Maggie came into the kitchen, her eyes red. "Okay, that was unpleasant. Do you have anything in here that could help?"

Selene opened the fridge. "What do you have in mind? Chocolate or booze?"

"Do you have booze?" Maggie raised her eyebrows.

"Just a few beers," Selene replied. "You know your dad doesn't drink much. Neither do I."

Maggie acknowledged the comment with a nod. "Well, I don't know if Jason is worth chocolate therapy, but I'll take a beer."

Selene pulled two cans out of the fridge and handed one to her friend. "To dumping Jason," she said.

"To the future," Maggie replied. They clinked cans. "Now if Jan won't have me back, that will require chocolate."

"Damn this day," Brandon grumbled as he wrestled open the door connecting the garage to the house. The keys promptly fell to the floor. "Damn it, damn it, damn it!" He yanked the keys off the floor and hung them on their designated hook.

He leaned down to remove one of his loafers, and nearly tipped over. "Argh," he snarled.

"Honey, is that you?" Selene's voice filtered through the kitchen door into the mudroom.

"Selene!" Maggie whined.

Maggie's here? Crap. I really don't need her drama right now.

"I'm here," he replied, throwing his shoe against the wall.

"Alarm, please," she said.

Annoyed at being reminded to do something he never forgot, he punched the buttons hard. One knuckle cracked. The soft beeping of the keypad sounded distressed. *Like an erratic heartbeat monitor.*

"Stop thinking like that," he ordered himself. Kicking off his other shoe, he hung up his suit coat. Opening the door into the kitchen with more attention and finesse, he noticed an enticing aroma of veggies simmered in fennel and tomato broth. He found his daughter, sitting at the kitchen table, laughing her head off while Selene, giggling, slid a foil-wrapped loaf of bread into the oven to warm.

"Hello, ladies," he said forcing his voice to mildness, "how's it going? What smells so good?"

"Hi, Dad," Maggie gushed. "Oh, are you ever in luck. Selene made soup."

Brandon turned to his girlfriend, who was leaning against the oven door, giving him a hungry look. "I didn't realize you knew how to make soup, honey," he said mildly, not wanting to show how raw his emotions were. *Not in front of Maggie. My daughter's presence messed up my plans something fierce.*

Selene accepted the light tone. "Oh, sure. I'm not a bad cook. My aunt would never have allowed that. Plus, I took two years of culinary arts in high school. I just never bothered much recently because I lived alone."

"Selene is too modest," Maggie countered. "She's a great cook. Almost as good as you. You're in for a treat."

"I can't wait." He paused. "Culinary arts class in psychic boarding school?" he asked as he crossed the room to her.

"Yes. We had all the normal classes, honey."

"Oh." He kissed Selene gently on the lips, trailing his fingers over her cheek. When he pulled back, her eyes had widened, showing she had felt the tension radiating from him. *She probably didn't need to be psychic to feel it.*

"Ewww. You two!"

"Shut up, Maggie," Brandon said gently. "I'm going to take a shower and change."

"Don't be too long," Selene urged. "This food will be ready as soon as the noodles cook. Should only be about fifteen minutes."

"I can manage fifteen." He kissed her again, hugged Maggie as he went by, and headed out of the room.

Selene dragged her eyes away from Brandon's retreating backside to see Maggie shaking her head. "You know," her friend said, "part of me still hates that you two are together, but I'm starting to feel bad about it. You both seem so happy. How can I not like something that makes the two most important people in my life so happy?"

"I wish you could be happy for us," Selene told her friend, a frown creasing her lips.

"I guess I am. It's just…kind of awkward, you know?"

I understand. I feel as awkward thinking about her reaction. "Thank you for trying," Selene said in her gentlest voice, "it means a lot."

A short time later Brandon emerged from the shower, his hair still wet, dressed in jeans and a black tee-shirt. By then, Selene had ladled the minestrone into bowls while Maggie had sliced and buttered the hot bread and poured the drinks.

"Now, isn't this nice?" he quipped, sitting down at his seat. He picked up his spoon and took a sip of the soup. His eyes widened. He swallowed, considered, and spooned up another bite. "Oh wow, that's delicious."

"Thank you," Selene said, lowering her head, but her cheeks glowed with pleasure at his compliment. He took her hand in his and kissed the knuckles. Something dark pulsed through her from his fingertips.

"Okay, Dad, enough with the lovey-dovey stuff. Save it for when you're alone," Maggie urged. "Just eat."

After dinner, Maggie didn't leave right away, much to Brandon's frustration. He clung to her fingers, sending waves of raw, wordless anguish into Selene's fingers; a flood of pain on which rode a litany of verbalized complaints. *Why does Maggie have to be here today? Why won't she go home? I'm glad to hear she broke up with that Jason dude. He rubbed me the wrong way. Arrogant ass. She must have gotten with him to protest our relationship, but she seems to have accepted us now. That's good. I've missed her. But it's late now and I need Selene. Please go home, Maggie.*

This constant internal monologue interfered terribly with Selene's ability to concentrate on the conversation. More than once she caught herself listening to Brandon's roiling thoughts and not what was being said.

Around 10:30, Maggie finally rose to leave. *At last. I can't wait another minute!* The wild need pouring onto Selene from her lover's hand made it impossible to utter more than the simplest goodbye. The second the battered pickup clattered away, he scooped her into his arms and carried her to the bedroom.

"Goodness, Brandon, what's going on?" she asked, not letting her surprise distract her from the pleasure of his strong embrace.

"I want you. I want you so bad." He began removing his shirt.

"Yes, this I can see," she commented dryly.

"Don't you want me?"

What's with the hesitant little boy voice? "Of course, I want you. See how much?" She shed her clothing willingly and walked into his embrace. He was already nude, and he lifted her. Bracing her back against the wall, he drove deep inside her. *Oof. What's going on? What happened to my tender, gentle lover?*

His hands clutched her thighs. Internal, barely-coherent words poured into her. *Yes, oh yes!* he thought while his emotions raged.

I'll find out later. She slipped her arms around his neck and clung to his hips with her legs.

He drew back and surged forward, claiming her to her fullest depth. A soft distressed sound escaped her. *It's too much. Yikes.* She opened her mouth to stop him when he thrust again. This time, the friction set her whole-body tingling. Her protest died. She gripped his shoulders, holding him close instead of pushing him away. The next thrust felt no less frantic, but she found herself able to appreciate its wildness. Selene relaxed into the lovemaking as he settled into a pattern of deep, hard thrusting.

Oh, my. This is… wow. I never imagined. He must really need me. Capturing his mouth, she told him with her kisses that she accepted their coupling gladly.

She gave herself over to the moment, and the more she relaxed, the more pleasure she took from it until passion peaked in a fierce climax that left her gasping, beyond even the ability to scream.

Panting, Brandon drove deep and growled, giving her his orgasm. She petted his back as he slowly calmed. Disengaging himself, he lowered her to the floor. Her legs wobbled. *Yikes. Gotta sit down… or better, lie down.* Leaning against his strength, she tugged in the direction of the bed and stretched out on it. He joined her, snuggling close.

"Are you okay, baby?" he asked, touching his lips to her forehead.

"Completely." She gave a sexy little wiggle in his arms. "Hmmm, it was so hot. Now, Mister, would you mind telling me what that was about?"

He closed his eyes for a moment, gathering himself, and when he opened them, they were suspiciously shiny. "One of my clients died." A wave of sorrow flowed from his hand into her back.

Selene instantly dropped her coy flirtation and wrapped her lover in a tight hug. "Oh, Brandon, I'm sorry. What happened?"

Brandon gulped and said, "I've been working with Miranda for a few years. She moved here to get away from a guy who was bothering her down south. She hadn't finished school, so I helped her find a program to pay the rest of her college tuition. In the last couple of weeks, I've been helping her look for a job. They told me today that the guy found her here and came after her. They're not sure yet if her death was a suicide, a murder, or an accident."

"That's terrible." Selene had a flash of insight. "Was she Native American too?"

He nodded. "Hopi. She had so much potential. She had recently become a registered nurse. She wanted to find a reservation school to work at. We just about had a position locked up in South Dakota. I had to call the school and tell them she wouldn't be coming because… she's dead."

His breathing had grown shallow and ragged. Selene wished she could comfort him with loving thoughts the way he did for her. Instead, she gently stroked him, trying to soothe as best she could. "You know I'll be on this, baby. I won't let it go."

"Find out what happened, Selene," he urged in a harsh, unsteady voice. "Make that bastard pay."

His grief tore into her and she snuggled close to him. "I will. I promise. I bet they'll have me interrogate him tomorrow, overtime be damned. For this, I'll work for free if I have to."

He said nothing more, just burrowed into her embrace, hiding his face against the soft place where her shoulder met her chest. She petted his back.

Eventually, her soft caresses soothed him to sleep, but

Selene had a hard time relaxing. *When such wonderful love as ours exists in the world, why does it so often go wrong? Why are there stalkers, rapists, and just plain jerks messing things up for everyone? All those women, their lives shaken, shattered, or even ended. It's why I do what I do. I can't prevent these things from happening, but I can help punish the perpetrators.*

"So, what you're saying, Mr. Jackson, is that you wouldn't take no for an answer?" Selene clarified, staring in narrow-eyed contempt at the greasy-haired specimen who sat across the table from her.

"Why would I?" he shot back, unmoved. His bloodshot blue eyes scanned Selene's slender frame with insulting interest. "I was nice to her. Bought her a drink, didn't I? How was I supposed to know she wasn't interested? She was at a *bar.*"

"Oh, I don't know," Selene replied. "Perhaps the fact that she refused the drink, declined to allow you to join her, and left when you sat down anyway?"

"Nah," he said with a laugh, blowing tobacco-scented breath across the table at Selene. "She was just playing hard to get. It's the chase, you know?"

Not likely, Selene thought, shuddering at the rank stench of the man. "You know, just because someone is present at the bar, it doesn't automatically follow that they're available for sex with any man who turns up."

He drew together light brown eyebrows in confusion.

The entitlement is strong with this one, Selene thought grimly. *I don't think I'll be able to help him realign his thinking, but it should be a piece of cake to get him to incriminate himself.*

"So, what you're saying then, is that you 'chased' her across Santa Fe for a year, getting in the way of her attending her classes, bothering her when she spent time with her friends and sitting in your pickup truck outside her parents' house?"

"Yep," he agreed easily. "She never went on any dates, so I know she was available. No reason for her to get her nose out of joint. I mean, I bought her flowers. Expensive ones, not from the grocery store."

Yikes. No wonder she was terrified. "Just because someone isn't in a relationship, it doesn't obligate them to accept advances, you know," Selene pointed out. "No is a perfectly okay answer."

Again, the confused face.

Shit. A redneck narcissist. Lovely.

"And then," Selene continued enumerating the timeline, "she left, moved all the way to Minnesota so she could finish school without being distracted by your 'chase.' Is that right?"

"I guess," he replied. "Maybe she got distracted. I mean, she probably thought school was important or something. Maybe I was too much man for her."

"Did you ever assault her?" Selene asked blandly.

"Hell naw!" he protested. "I would never. I only kissed her a couple of times. Boy did she get off on it. Squealing and wriggling, but then she'd get nervous and run away. I tried to tell her I would still respect her, but she wasn't ready, I guess. Some women really wanna be sure of a man before they give it up. It's wild from an Indian. They're usually up for anything, but I knew she was special."

"How many Native American women have you met?" Selene demanded. *Why did you ask that? It's not relevant, dummy.* But her relationship with Brandon had sensitized her to this sort of prejudice, and she felt helpless against the desire to confront it.

"There was this whore I knew, back in Odessa. Comanche, I think, or Apache. She told me once, but I forgot. Anyway, when I moved to New Mexico, there were so many, but

117

they're all full of themselves, won't give a fella the time of day. All but Randi. She wanted me, deep down. I could see it in her eyes."

That was probably the desire to vomit. Selene barely managed to suppress the words, knowing they would jeopardize the interrogation.

"Besides, my daddy told me all women want it. You just have to get past their defenses. They don't want to look like sluts. Want you to think you're the only one."

"Okay, enough of that," Selene urged. *If I have to listen to his chauvinist bullshit another minute, I might barf.* "How did you find out where she went?"

"Internet," he replied with a smirk. "Saw her graduation announcement on the university's website. Thought I'd surprise her, come up to congratulate her."

Oh, ish. No wonder. "You came up to congratulate her and what did you do?"

"Well, she wasn't home, so I had my cousin—he studies computers, you know? He got into her GPS and found her at the mall. So I went and found her in the parking lot. Told her I was proud of her finishing school and that now, we could be together. She jumped into her car and ran like hell. It was just like old times. Only this time, I knew she wanted me to catch her. Like you said, she must not have wanted to get distracted with school. But she's graduated now, so it's finally our time. I caught up to her at a red light, and when it changed, she peeled out fast. I stayed with her though."

"You chased her in your car?"

He nodded, pride creasing his dirty face.

"What happened then?"

He shrugged. "She musta gone too fast. Hit a curb. Flipped the car. Damned shame."

"You know she died in that accident, right?" Selene said.

"Yeah, I heard." His lips turned down. "Too bad I never had a chance to get with her. I'da made her real happy."

"Sure, you would." Selene couldn't keep the sarcasm from her voice.

"So, can I go now?" he asked.

She rose to her feet. "I don't think so. You won't be going anywhere for a long, long time. Excuse me, Mr. Jackson. I'm going to call the public defender's office now."

"What for," he asked, bewildered.

"For a lawyer. You're going to need one." Without another word, she stalked from the room, shutting the door behind her

"What a dink."

Selene jumped, startled by Tony's unexpected comment. "What are you doing?" she demanded, scowling at her friend.

"Listening in," he replied. "Always looking for new inter-rogation tips."

"Dink doesn't even come close," Selene replied wearily. "This is the kind that gives men everywhere a bad name."

"Hey, watch it," Tony protested. "He doesn't qualify as a man. Pig is too good a name for this dude."

"Agreed." Selene heaved a huge sigh. "I need to sit down… or maybe take a long, hot shower. I feel contaminated." She brushed past Tony and made her way to the desk, sinking into the chair.

In her exhaustion, it took Selene several minutes to see the envelope propped on her keyboard. Her eyes narrowed. Swallowing hard, she put on a pair of gloves and opened it. Inside she found another typewritten note, this one far worse than the first.

That was a nice show you and your Indian put on last night, slut—up against the wall. I should sell the pictures to a magazine.

Selene tried hard to keep breathing. Black spots swam before her eyes. Clutching the letter in one gloved hand and the envelope in the other, she walked unsteadily towards Chief Brady's office, grateful to find him in.

"Oh shit, Selene, not another one," he snarled. His voice hit her like a hammer blow.

She extended the letter. He took both documents with a glove, setting them on his desk.

After reading the brief message, he closed his eyes. Disgusted, he looked back up at Selene. She was swaying. "Sit down," he barked, "before you pass out."

She slumped into the chair gratefully.

"Is he guessing, trying to scare you?" he suggested.

She shook her head, breathing slowly. "Too much detail."

Brady looked a little startled at this information. It clearly didn't fit his image of something Selene would do. "How could he have known?"

"The blinds were open."

"Why?" he demanded, one eyebrow shooting towards his hairline.

"The windows in our bedroom face the backyard. We have a privacy fence," she explained, her shaky breaths sounding increasingly like sobs.

"So, the only way he could have known was if…"

"He was in our yard. He was watching us through the window." A sob climbed up Selene's throat. Desperately she fought to hold it in, but over and over the image rose in her mind to torture her. The special moment she'd shared with the man she loved, observed and sneered over by some malevolent presence. Her attempts to control herself utterly failed, and hysteria tugged at the edges of her mind.

A rough embrace shook her back to reality, and she opened watery eyes, shocked to realize it was Chief Brady holding her. He regarded her with alarm on his craggy face.

"Tony!" Brady shouted.

The officer wandered into the room. "Yes, boss…what the hell?"

"Call Brandon," Brady ordered. "Tell him to get his ass down here right now."

"Yes, sir." Tony dialed. Over the quiet sound of Selene's crying, the chief could hear both sides of the conversation.

"Hello?"

"This is Tony; I work with Selene."

"Yes, I remember you."

"We need you down here right away. There's been an incident."

"Is Selene all right? What happened?"

"She's not hurt. Just get here." He hung up.

"Take her." The chief passed Selene to her friend, who hugged her tight.

"What happened?" Tony asked softly.

Grimly the chief held out the letter.

"Oh shit. I'm so sorry, Selene." He patted her back.

Selene didn't calm down before Brandon arrived. He walked into the chief's office and was alarmed to see his beloved weeping in the arms of her friend. Tony surrendered her to Brandon gratefully. Wet spots soaked his shirt in the vicinity of where her face had been.

"What happened?" he demanded.

"I'll explain in a moment," Brady said. "Try to calm her down first, would you?"

Brandon concentrated hard on calm, soothing thoughts. He placed his palm against her cheek, giving her all the love he had. His other hand slid under her shirt to press against her bare back. While he held her, he murmured, "It's okay, baby. I'm here. You're okay." He kissed her gently on the cheeks, forehead, lips; sweet, soft kisses.

Much to the relief of the two officers, Selene began to calm under Brandon's soothing touch. Her sobs slowed to sniffles, and her breathing became a little easier.

Once she was under control, the chief took charge again. "Tony, you and Selene go look at the video feeds. Compare today to the last time this happened and see if you can find out who's doing this. I need to talk to Brandon alone."

Tony led Selene into the other room. Brandon watched as they sat together at Tony's desk. Then he turned back to Brady. "What the hell is going on?"

"Sorry," Brady replied. "I didn't mean to alarm you. We couldn't calm her. It's bad, Brandon. There's a real serious situation here."

"What?"

"Take a seat." The chief laid out the note on the desk in front of him.

As he read it, the heat drained from Brandon's face. His lips felt numb as he asked, "How could anyone have known?"

"He must have been in your backyard looking in the window. And there's more. I didn't want Selene to see it, or to tell you while you were touching her."

He pulled a second sheet out of the envelope, one Selene had not noticed. The paper held three pictures, all of them taken at close range through the bedroom window.

The first showed Brandon and Selene naked in bed with her on top of him, her long hair hanging down, her head thrown back in ecstasy.

In the second, she was in profile, draped over a mound of pillows with Brandon behind her, covering her body with his. He had laced his hand tenderly through hers.

Finally, the one mentioned in the note, with Brandon pressing Selene against the bedroom wall, her legs wrapped around his waist, her arms clinging to his shoulders, their mouths fused in a scorching kiss.

In all his life, Brandon had never felt such rage. *To think that our private moments were observed and recorded by a stranger. I could kill*. His fists clenched. "These are from three different nights," he said inanely, so stunned that his mouth no longer seemed connected to his brain.

"I guessed as much," Brady replied, wincing in sympathy. "I'm very sorry, but you had to know. You're both in danger. If this loon can take pictures of you, he can easily shoot you."

"What can we do?"

"I'm not sure. We'll have to think on it."

Another thought occurred to Brandon. "Who will need to see the pictures? Selene won't like that."

A new expression of discomfort crossed Brady's grim face. "I promise to keep it to a minimum. I know how much she values her privacy. But I swear, no one will tease her over this. It's too ugly, you know? It's a violation."

"Well, I certainly feel violated," Brandon drawled.

"You have been, and there's no doubt about it," Brady agreed.

"You'd better catch this guy." Brandon could hardly form the words, his jaw clenched so tightly.

"We'll do everything we can," Brady reassured him.

Tony came back into the room, looking from one to the other as though not sure where to start.

"Did you find anything?" the chief asked him.

"Maybe," Tony replied, raking his already messy curls with his fingers. "Selene's taking a closer look. We don't have a shot of his face though. We're pulling surveillance from other parts of the building."

"You left her alone?" Brandon nailed Tony with a disapproving glare. *Does no one but me realize how fragile Selene is?*

"She's fine. Look." Tony gestured.

Brandon turned to see Selene engrossed in the monitor.

Tony walked over to the desk where the pictures still lay. Horror bloomed on his face and he quickly averted his eyes at the sight of his friend, naked and entwined with her lover. "Oh shit! She didn't see these, did she?"

"No." The chief carefully folded the paper and set it aside.

"How the hell did someone as sweet as Selene end up the target of this guy?" Tony demanded.

"I don't know," Brady replied thoughtfully.

"It must be personal," Brandon said. "Someone thinks she's wronged him somehow. What did the first note say?"

"It said I persecute innocent people. Persecute, not prosecute. Isn't that interesting?" Selene spoke from the doorway. Her face was ravaged by tears, but her voice, at last, sounded steady.

"Who would say that?" Brandon asked. "Someone you questioned?"

"I doubt it," she replied. "Those who were innocent were released quickly and without fuss. Anyone I questioned who was guilty knew they were guilty. That's how I catch them. They're thinking about what they've done. My guess would be a disgruntled family member who feels the confession was coerced. I don't know how they got my name though."

"You're on the website." Tony reminded her.

She scrubbed at her forehead with one hand. "Right."

"Did you find anything?" Brady asked.

"No. He has a distinctive hairstyle with a big swoop in the front. I saw this guy in both feeds, and he stopped near my desk both times, though I can't quite guarantee he touched it. Subtle, you know? Still, no one else behaves this way in both videos, so he has to be the one. He kept his face turned away from the cameras, and we didn't get a good shot. He seems to be of average height, with dark hair and dark clothing. In short, it could be anyone, except for the hairdo."

"Well, hell," Brady said. "You guys have an alarm?"

"Yes," Selene replied, giving him a pointed look, which he ignored.

"Keep it on all the time."

"Right." They both nodded.

Brady continued barking orders. "Check the batteries on your smoke detector. This guy has already started one fire. Keep your cell phone at hand at all times. Lock the doors and windows, and for heaven's sake, shut the blinds. We'll patrol your neighborhood regularly."

"I have some suggestions too," Tony said. "Put something unpleasant, like a thorny bush or some rusty metal just inside the fence and put motion sensor lights in your backyard. You know what? I'm coming with you to find out how he got into your yard."

The instructions over, Brandon wrapped one arm around Selene's waist and walked her out towards the parking lot.

"Babe," Selene said, "I don't think I should drive."

He regarded her pale, shocky-looking face. *It's so rare for her to request help, she must be doing even worse than I thought. She must be holding on by a thread.*

"Okay," he said. "Get in the truck. I'll drive you back to the station to get your car later." He pressed the button on his keychain and handed her up into the cab. A squad car pulled in behind them, and for once Brandon didn't suffer the almost nauseous nervousness of having a cop on his bumper.

Back at the house, Tony parked prominently on the street and walked inside carrying a large kit in one hand. Brandon escorted Selene with a hand on her back.

They headed directly to the backyard. Outside the bedroom window, they found several pairs of sneaker impressions. Tony began by taking plaster casts of them for evidence. The footprints led to a spot in the fence where mud had been smeared on the boards. Just behind the fence in the alley was a dumpster.

"So that's how he got in," Tony said.

Selene cursed softly, but with great feeling and fluency.

"I'll call the city and get the dumpster moved away from

your fence. It won't stop him if he's really determined, but it might buy us some time to catch him."

"I'll call my security company and see about motion detectors for the backyard," Brandon added.

"I'll keep my Beretta in the bedroom," Selene said, "and I'm going to check out the inside right now, just to be sure." She walked away. A moment later the open blinds on the bedroom window jerked shut.

"Tony," Brandon said, "how pissed at me is everyone going to be?"

Tony turned dark, puzzled eyes on Brandon. "At the stalker, plenty. At you? What did you do?"

"I'm sleeping with Selene. Doesn't it bother all these guys who think they're her brothers? You, for instance?"

Understanding bloomed on Tony's face, and he clapped Brandon on the shoulder. "It's not a secret. Everyone kind of guessed when you two moved in together. Anyway, it's okay. You're really good for her. We've never seen Selene so happy, so no. No one's mad."

"Thank you, Tony," Brandon said.

"How the hell are you going to keep her from finding out about the pictures?" Tony asked. "The next time you touch her, she'll know."

"Oh shit," Brandon growled, raking both hands through his hair. "You're right. I guess there's nothing I can do about it."

"It must be hard having a psychic girlfriend," Tony commented.

"Not really," Brandon retorted.

"I was amazed by what you did. I've never touched Selene's bare skin in my life, not even to shake her hand. I never would. You put your hand right on her face. She knew exactly what you were thinking. It would have bothered the hell out of me." Tony shuddered.

Brandon gave him a look. "That's why I'm with her and

you're not. I'm not afraid of her gift. I like it; at least, until today. Poor baby. She's not going to take this well."

"That's for sure. Of course, she's tougher than she looks."

Brandon shook his head. *I swear they think she's some kind of interrogation machine, sometimes.* "She's still human, you know."

"I know. I'm so glad you're here to take care of her. She needs you."

"Yes," Brandon snapped, hands fisting to knuckle-whitening pressure, his jaw aching from being so tightly clenched, "look at all the good I've done for her. If she weren't with me, those pictures wouldn't have been possible."

Tony held up his hands, palms toward Brandon, urging calm. "I'm not kidding, man. If she hadn't been with you the night of the fire, she'd probably be dead. The pictures are embarrassing, but they're not deadly."

Brandon took a deep breath, trying to control his anger. *It's not Tony's fault,* he reminded himself. "I'm sorry to be short with you."

"No worries. I'd be pissed too if it was me and my girlfriend."

"Believe me, pissed doesn't even come close."

Tony pulled out a tiny notepad from his pocket and scribbled on it with the stub of a pencil. "Here, this is my cell number. If anything happens, if you hear a noise, anything, call me. I will get here no matter what. I can be at your place at a moment's notice. Don't hesitate to call."

"Thanks, Tony." Brandon took the slip, grateful for the promise of backup. *This is so damned unnerving.*

Something must have showed in Brandon's face, because Tony asked, "Do you want me to stay awhile?"

"No, that's okay. I have some work to do."

"Right. Remember, call me," the officer insisted.

"I will."

Brandon immediately got on the phone with his security

company, and two hours later a technician was installing motion sensor lights.

That night, Selene looked into the master bedroom and shook her head. "Can we sleep somewhere else tonight, please? I'll never be able to rest in here. It feels like someone's watching."

"Sure." He led her to the guest room, which was made up for when his parents stayed over. He had kept his hands off Selene all day, but he had to stop avoiding her now. *If I don't touch her at bedtime, she's sure to notice, and getting caught trying to hide something would be worse than just telling her.*

He tucked her into bed and snuggled her close. *This is the hardest part, trying to relax, knowing someone violated our privacy in such a terrible way.*

"I have to tell you something, baby," he murmured into her hair.

"Something bad?"

"Yes." He stroked her braid.

"Tell me."

Brandon swallowed hard. "He didn't just look. He took photos."

"What?" Selene's head shot up. "How bad?"

"Very bad."

Selene bit her lip before asking, her voice sounding small and vulnerable, "Did you see them?"

"Yes," he admitted.

"What did they show?"

"Everything. They showed us making love. They were very graphic."

"Shit." The curse sounded like a whimper.

"It's a funny thing," Brandon said, not thinking, just letting words roll off his tongue, "the pictures are actually kind of pretty. If we had taken them ourselves, they would be great, but since we didn't…"

Selene started to cry, not hysterically like before, but with great misery.

Brandon could do nothing for her, so he just held her while she cried herself to sleep.

He stayed awake all night waiting for the motion lights to come on.

They didn't.

CHAPTER 8

$\mathcal{I}$n the morning, Brandon's resolve had settled on several things. Getting up early, he brewed coffee and woke Selene.

Seated on the couch beside him, she yawned sleepily over a steaming cup. "What's wrong, honey?" she asked. "You look tired."

"I didn't sleep well."

She lowered her head in groggy acknowledgment. A few sips of caffeine and awareness began to dawn in her sleepy eyes. "I forgot to tell you. Yesterday we picked up Miranda's stalker. I questioned him. He was responsible for that poor woman's death, and he confessed. He's going to prison for a long time."

"Did he kill her?" Brandon demanded.

"Not intentionally. He was chasing her in her car, and she wrecked."

His insides clenched at the thought. *Poor Miranda. She must have been terrified.* "I hope they nail his ass to the wall."

"They will. I made sure of it. Vehicular homicide if I had my guess."

"Good girl. Listen, I don't want to hang around the house

today." Brandon shuddered. "My parents have invited us for lunch and to spend the afternoon. Want to go?"

She gave him a wan grin. "Sure. I'm game. I'd like to spend more time with your parents."

He acknowledged her with a dip of the chin and then continued. "But this morning, I'd like us to go to church. I want to pray. We need God's help with this mess."

Selene tensed at the word church as though Brandon had suggested a firing squad. "I can't do that." Her jaw locked, and she forced out the words through angry clenched teeth. "I won't."

Brandon blinked, taken aback by her vehemence. "Why not?"

She shook her head vigorously from side to side all the while her words tumbled from her. "I never go to church. When I was a kid, my auntie's pastor told me I was possessed by demons. He said that was why I could read people's minds. Brandon, I never asked for this gift. Certainly not from demons."

He gave her hand a little squeeze. "Of course not. He must have been out of his mind."

"But what if it's true? What if this *is* demonic? What if God hates me?"

No wonder she worries so much. "No, Selene. There's no way. You only use your gift to do good and help people. God doesn't hate you. He made you this way. Remember, it's a gift, not a curse."

"But what pastor will believe that?" she demanded, starting to sound hysterical.

"I know this guy," Brandon replied in a quiet, soothing tone. "He helped me out a lot after Claudia died. He won't do anything bad to you. Please, baby, this is important."

She turned away from him, looking out the open window where the sun had risen enough to make the neighborhood trees seem to glow. "You don't know what you're asking."

"Are you a demon?" he asked.

"Of course not."

He cupped her cheek, turning her back to face him. "Then what are you worried about? One bigoted pastor doesn't amount to much. He was probably afraid of you."

Selene considered Brandon's words and his expression. The intensity revealed how important this was to him. *Okay, Selene. He's not asking that much. The pastor won't know what you can do unless you tell him. Be brave.* "Okay, Brandon, I'll do it." Her belly clenched as she voiced the words.

"Thank you. We need all the help we can get."

"That's for sure."

Though the prospect of church twisted Selene's stomach more than the harrowing experiences of the previous day, she honored Brandon's request and pulled on some of her regular work clothes: a khaki skirt and a purple blouse. Then, she ran a brush through her hair and pulled the top back into an over-sized clip.

She was just brushing a sweep of orchid-colored shadow over her bloodshot eyes when Brandon knocked on the open bathroom door. "Ready, babe?" he asked.

"I guess," she replied. "Let me just get a cup of coffee to go. Is it far from here?"

"Few miles," he replied, slipping his hand into hers and lacing their fingers together. Through their joined hands, his tension radiated to her, echoing what she was already feeling. They paused in the kitchen to pour their beverages and then made their way through the mudroom, into the garage and out to the truck.

Selene sipped her drink in silence as Brandon drove. *Nothing to say. Nothing. Just watch the trees go by and try not to think. Summer is pretty in Minnesota. Look at the roses… and the daisies… who plants tomatoes in the front yard?*

"You okay?" he asked after a while.

"It's been a rough couple of days," she replied, "and to be honest, I still don't want to do this."

"Thank you for humoring me," he said softly. "I appreciate you taking the chance."

He took a sharp right turn into a parking lot beside a small but pretty building whose A-frame design and sun-faded stained-glass windows evoked a feeling of an earlier era.

Selene set her mug in the cup holder, but in her skirt, she wasn't able to jump from the cab unaided. Brandon circled the truck and lifted her to the ground. Taking her hand again, he led her into the back of the sanctuary.

Inside, gray heads bobbed and warbly voices sang, and the lovely organ music washed over Selene, soothing her nerves. *This isn't so bad*, she thought. *I guess I'll just see how it goes. Too bad I can't sing.*

After the service, the congregation filed out in search of coffee and donuts, but Brandon led Selene to the altar, where they both knelt.

"Hello, Brandon," Pastor Otten's mellow and well-modulated voice drifted over them. "It's been too long."

Selene regarded the man, who appeared to be in his mid-thirties, dressed in a clerical collar and a robe, but wearing a kind, mellow smile.

"You're right." Brandon stood, helping Selene to her feet. "This is my girlfriend, Selene."

"Pleased to meet you."

She nodded but ignored his offered hand.

The pastor raised one eyebrow but turned to Brandon without comment. "I'm glad to see you moving on, but I sense you are both deeply troubled."

"How do you know that?" Selene's eyes narrowed.

"When feelings are particularly intense, I can pick them up, like a radio frequency."

She blinked in surprise. "Are you gifted, then?" she demanded. "You, a pastor?"

"Yes," he replied, seeming a little startled by her aggressive tone. "How did you know about it?"

Taking a chance, she offered, "If your hands touch me, I'll know what you're thinking. That's why I don't shake."

"I see. Well, thank you for respecting my privacy."

She dipped her chin.

He continued. "I'm not able to prevent people's feelings from registering, but I can't see what causes them."

"We need prayer, Pastor," Brandon told him. "Someone is trying to harm us."

"Let's pray then." They remained kneeling for many long minutes until the shuffling of fabric alerted them to the arrival of worshipers awaiting the next service.

"Come back soon, friends," Pastor Otten urged.

"We will," Selene assured him. "I've never been to a church like this one. It's soothing here."

He smiled warmly and lifted a hand, as though waving and blessing them at the same time.

A sensation of warmth settled over the couple.

Summer heat touched their shoulders as they made their way across the crunchy gravel of the parking lot back to the truck.

A short drive later, and Selene joined Brandon in the living room. He stood by the window, looking over the vibrant green of the neighborhood's trees and lawns. He heard her approach and turned, his gaze sweeping the living room.

In the daylight, the house looked normal, but there was a creeping sense of eeriness. *Surely no one would be bold enough to invade the home of a police officer in broad daylight.* Still, Selene could feel the malevolent presence.

"Damn it," Brandon said furiously, "this is our home. I won't have it. I will not let this man destroy our peace!"

He drew Selene into his arms and kissed her hard, driving his tongue into her mouth and daring the darkness to touch them. She kissed him back. It was an act of defiance toward all that stood against them.

They stumbled to the couch, tearing at each other's clothing, wrenching open buttons and zippers until they could caress each other intimately. Brandon lifted Selene's skirt and ripped off her panties. Lowering his slacks to his knees, he mounted her and drove inside. She accepted him eagerly, seeking some normalcy. *If anyone's watching, let him watch. Our love will not be shaken.* They strained together, seeking and finding satisfaction in each other's arms.

It was madness as much as passion, and when they finished, panting, the house felt right again, and so did they. The danger remained, but they both dared to hope someday it might pass. Brandon helped Selene restore her clothing to order and they sat together in silence, holding each other.

"Baby," Brandon asked eventually, "what's it going to take to catch this guy?"

"I don't know," she told him honestly. Sammy meandered in and jumped onto her lap. She stroked his silky fur, letting his rumbling purrs soothe her. "If we can find him, it will be easy to convict. Arson is a felony, and there will be trespassing charges as well. If we can find him, the notes should be on his computer. Even if he erased them, the tech people will find them. Nothing's ever really gone from a computer. The pictures will be on his phone. But we have to have a name—or at least a face—so we can begin the process."

She hugged the kitten to her chest. He squirmed, and she set him on the floor. "Right now, I think they're going through my old cases to see who had distraught relatives that might seek revenge."

"Are there many?"

"Probably," she admitted sourly. "Most people, even the worst criminals, have a sibling, cousin, or best friend who swears they're as innocent as new-fallen snow. At least it will give us a place to start."

"Will you help?" Brandon wanted to know.

She shook her head. "I can't. I'm the victim of this crime. I can't help to process it. Anything I touch will be inadmissible. I'm going to have to focus my attention on the rape case. I know my friends will do everything they can."

Brandon squeezed her gently. "Of course, they will. They may not be willing to shake your hand, but they love you anyway."

"I know they do. They tease and butt in, but they have my best interests at heart. And when I need to be touched, I have you." She kissed his cheek. "Is it time to go?"

The clock on the DVD player read ten minutes after eleven.

"Yeah," Brandon replied. "It takes a while to get to the outer suburbs where my parents live. We'd better get started."

"Is Maggie coming too?"

"No, she has a spin class this afternoon. What did you tell her yesterday, by the way?"

"That some crazy person is stalking me and had been in the yard. The less she knows about this, the better."

"Agreed," Brandon said fervently, helping her to her feet.

CHAPTER 9

*B*randon's parents lived in a suburban neighborhood that felt almost rural, with pretty old homes set in large yards. Richard and Elizabeth owned a white two-story colonial with black shutters and huge sunflowers growing in the front yard.

At the sound of the doorbell, they both opened. "Brandon!" Elizabeth exclaimed, throwing her arms around her son.

"Hi, Mom," he said. His voice sounded normal.

So painfully normal it could shatter any moment, Selene thought. "Umph. Hello, ma'am," she said as Elizabeth released Brandon and hugged her. *I'm not used to being hugged by near-strangers, but how sweet of her to want me to feel like part of the family, and how nice that I don't have to shake hands.*

"Baseball?" Richard suggested as the older couple stepped aside to allow Brandon and Selene into a spacious, comfortable room decorated in Mission-style furniture. A big-screen television hung over the fireplace had already been tuned to the correct channel… as the white-clad figure high-tailing it toward first base demonstrated.

"Yes!" Brandon cheered, vaulting onto the sofa.

Selene made a face. *Well, no one said we had to like all of the same things, right?*

"Oh, poo on baseball," Elizabeth said. "Selene, do you want to watch the game? If not, I could use a hand in the kitchen."

"Kitchen it is," Selene agreed. "Anything's better than tele-vised sports—unless it's the Olympics."

"Figure skating?" Elizabeth asked, indicating an open doorway into the galley-style kitchen.

"Yes, and gymnastics in the summers," Selene concurred.

The women grinned at each other.

"Are you all right, my dear?" Elizabeth asked, washing her hands before crossing the huge black and white tiled room to the stove. "You seemed tense when you arrived.

Wow, she's intuitive for a mundane. I'll have to be careful what I say. "Yes, I'm fine," Selene replied, pulling her long hair into a ponytail to keep it out of the way. "I'm under a lot of pres-sure at work, that's all. How can I help?"

"Can you chop the tomato, lettuce, and cucumber for our salad, please?" She indicated a cutting board, knife, and bowl already set up with the pile of fresh-picked veggies beside them. "So, things are stressful at the police department?" she added as she moved to a large Dutch oven set over a low flame on the green vintage stove.

"Always," Selene replied, cursing her expressive face, "but right now it's particularly bad."

Elizabeth paused in her work. "It worries me a little, your job. I wouldn't want you to get hurt. It's dangerous being a big city police officer, isn't it?"

Selene couldn't help but smile. *Elizabeth is such a sweet woman.* She hastened to reassure her. "Not what I do. I'm not a beat cop. I interrogate suspects and shuffle papers mostly." Honesty forced her to add, "I love my job, but it isn't always easy."

"You must hear terrible things sometimes."

No point in denying the obvious. "Yes."

"How can you stand it?"

As she chopped a tomato for the salad, Selene contemplated her answer. "Someone has to. I'm always glad to help people." Then she considered another moment before adding, "For a long time now, I've let my life get out of balance. I was working too much. Brandon has reminded me I also need to relax and have fun. He's amazing."

"I'm glad he's found someone who loves him so much," Elizabeth commented with an accepting smile. "He needs that."

"Everyone needs that," Selene replied gently as she piled the chopped veggies in a bowl. "All done. What's next?"

"Could you please drain the beans, dear?"

"Of course." Selene took a set of potholders and poured the boiling string beans through a strainer into one side of the stainless-steel sink, then returned them to the pot with a generous pat of butter.

Soon a succulent beef roast was perfuming the house from the center of the dining table, surrounded by the beans, mashed potatoes, and gravy, salad and fresh, hot rolls.

Brandon opened the bottle of red wine he and Selene had brought and poured a glass for everyone. Then they sat down together to enjoy the family meal.

It didn't take Brandon long to notice his mother and Selene more at peace, and some of the strain around his lover's eyes was fading. The ladies chatted easily, like old friends.

Brandon's father leaned over to him and said softly, "She seems like a good girl."

"She's the best, Dad."

"So, you love her, really love her?"

"Yes." He couldn't help smiling as he said it.

Richard noticed his expression. "Good. You know we liked Claudia well enough. There was nothing wrong with her of course, but I always wanted you to have someone you loved, not just someone you tolerated."

"I learned to love Claudia, Dad," Brandon reminded him.

"I know you did. It's a credit to your character, but she wasn't the love of your life, was she?"

"No. I regret my actions where she was concerned. I stole her life." *That sorrow will never leave me.*

His father patted his shoulder. "I know she was content."

"But not happy, not really. That was my fault."

Richard shook his head. "You were seventeen years old. You made a mistake. It happens. Look at the good that came from it. You had a wonderful daughter both of you adored."

"That's true."

"And now you have a second chance. Do right by this one, would you?"

Brandon caught Selene's eye, and she gifted him with a shy smile. "Naturally."

The next morning, Selene considered calling in to work. She felt exhausted and slightly ill, but once she'd been fortified with coffee and homemade French toast, she decided she could face the day after all.

At the station, things seemed normal except for the occasional pitying glance from one of her coworkers.

Selene tracked down Tony in his cubicle. Her friend was scowling at a computer screen and poking at the keyboard with both index fingers.

"How many people have seen the pictures?" she demanded without preamble.

WATCHING OVER THE WATCHER

He glanced up and frowned in sympathy. "Not very many. Chief Brady, of course, Brandon, me, and Troy since we want our best photo tech to process them."

Selene swallowed. *My boss, my best friend and a random acquaintance now all know exactly how hot my sex life is... and what my boobs look like. Shit.* She took several deep breaths. *Still, only three.* "If no one else has seen them, why is everyone looking at me like that?" she asked.

He frowned. "Well, they've heard things. There are a lot of people working on the case. It's attempted murder you know, with the fire. Plus it's you and we... we're family, right?"

Ordinarily, the thought would have warmed her. Today, she was too on edge. "I want to see the pictures."

"No, you don't, Selene," Tony said, shaking his head so hard his messy curls bounced around his ears. "Trust me. They'll only upset you."

"I'm already upset. There are naked pictures of me in bed with my boyfriend circulating through this department and I've never seen them. I have to know, Tony."

He looked at her for a moment before agreeing. "I'll be right back."

He returned from the evidence lab moments later with a sheet of paper and a grim expression. Carefully opening it with gloved fingers, he showed her, averting his own eyes from the images.

Selene pressed her knuckles to her mouth and closed her eyes. Then she smiled a watery little smile. "Brandon was right. They are pretty. If only they hadn't been taken by some lunatic. God, we look so *happy*."

"You were. In all these pictures the two of you were so happy. This guy tried to steal that happiness away from you. Don't let him," Tony urged, folding away the humiliating images. "Keep on being happy."

"It's a little hard when you can't sleep for wondering

whether he's pressed his face against the window again." She wanted to weep. *Thank God my voice remained hard as I said it.*

"Be strong, Selene. We'll catch him, I promise. No one will rest until this guy is behind bars."

"Thank you, Tony. I trust you."

She kissed him on the cheek and returned to her desk.

CHAPTER 10

*T*hree weeks have gone by without incident, Selene thought as she flushed the toilet and made her way to the sink to wash her hands. *No progress made on my case. We're still on guard in our home, and I'm back to not being able to rest.*

She glanced in the mirror. Circles no amount of makeup could cover ringed her eyes.

I mean, I sleep—how can I not, warm and comfortable in bed with Brandon—but somehow, I never feel rested.

Sticking out her tongue at her reflection in the bathroom mirror, Selene stalked to the table where Brandon had made her yet another delicious dinner.

In spite of the constant tension, it has been a nice summer, she thought, recalling the Fourth of July at the lake with Maggie and Brandon's parents. *We all got sunburned and ate too much chicken, cherry pie, and ice cream. August will be a much less enjoyable month. I hate the heat and the stink of the lakes when they turn over and release all the rot from the bottom. I can't wait until fall.*

"This looks great," she said, admiring the colorful salad of greens, homegrown tomatoes and bites of grilled chicken. She inhaled. "Wow. What did you spice the meat with?"

"Cumin and coriander," he replied. "I felt like doing a Tex-Mex theme."

"Delicious." She squeezed his hand and took a bite. "Did you make the dressing too? It's lime, right?"

He nodded, but his eyes looked far away. "Baby," he said casually, "I want to ask you something." He slipped his free hand into hers, sending her the importance of the question.

She raised her eyebrows at him. "What is it?"

"There's a Lakota Wacipi in South Dakota this weekend," he explained. "Would you like to go? It's a bit of a drive, but we could use a getaway. If you left work a little early on Friday, we could get there in time to see the opening cere-monies and spend Saturday and part of Sunday there."

"Wa chee pee?" Selene raised one eyebrow. "Is that a Native American thing?"

"Lakota, in this case," he replied. "The Wacipi is a combi-nation of a tribal dance competition, rodeo, reservation fair, and so much more."

"How interesting. I've never been to anything like that before. What's it like?"

"It's amazing," he replied, his brown eyes lighting up. "There's music and dancing and regalia and food, and there's more that's impossible to describe. It's magical."

"Of course, I'll go, honey," she assured him with a sweet smile. "I know it's important to you, and it'll be interesting. Will you see people you know there?"

"Yes. I've been to this Wacipi several times. I kind of make a yearly event out of it. August is such a boring month; I look forward to the change of pace." He paused for a moment, and then continued, "You should know there's a woman who'll be there, Barbara. She's an event organizer. I used to go out with her."

A brief image flashed across Brandon's mind and into Selene's.

She colored. *It was exciting when he was thinking about me. I don't like this at all.* "Used to sleep with her too, I see."

"Yes, that too," he admitted uncomfortably. "It was about a year after Claudia died. I was really lonely. I helped her get financial aid to finish her degree and she…wanted more. So, we went out for…several months. Then she got the position in South Dakota and moved away. Our relationship wasn't deeply rooted, and we drifted apart. No drama, no hard feelings."

Well, at least he's honest. Of course, I knew him then… loved him then. There I was, wallowing in unrequited attraction and he was having a casual affair with someone else. "Were there other women after Claudia, besides this Barbara?" *What a stupid question. As if I actually want the answer!*

Brandon answered honestly again. "One other, about a year after Barbara moved. This one wasn't a client though. Just someone I met, and it only lasted a month. After that, I didn't feel like dating anymore. It was too hard on Maggie, and I sort of realized there was this pretty girl hanging around, someone I might like to be with someday."

Through their joined hands she could sense he was telling the absolute truth, that his interest in her had been building for at least four years. *It certainly isn't a bad thing, but it raises another question.* "If you've wanted me for so long, Brandon, why didn't you ever say anything?" *We could have been together for ages already.*

"I could ask you the same thing."

Selene blushed. "You know why. I didn't think you would be interested. I wanted to keep my attraction to you private, something I could cherish in secret because I knew that was all it could ever be. I've never been so glad to be wrong."

He acknowledged her ever-present insecurity with a rueful half smile. Then he answered her question. "Well, the reason I held back was...Maggie. When she graduated from high school, she went through another bad time, missing her mother."

"Yes, I remember that."

"She needed me to be there for her. She was a mess. It was all I could do to get her to go to class each day. She was convinced she would never be successful. I had to coax her through her entire kinesiology degree. It drove me nuts. Every time she invited you over, I wanted you, but she's my daughter. I had to take care of her first. I assumed one day it would be too late, and someone else would scoop you up, but no one ever did."

"That wouldn't have happened."

"I'm glad." He squeezed her fingers gently. A random thought crossed his mind, dancing lightly on the center of her palm. "Funny thing about Maggie. The only thing she liked, other than sports, was Swedish. I never understood why she took it as her minor when Lakota was available. *That* would have made more sense."

"You know why," she reminded him teasingly. "It was because of her boyfriend."

"Oh, that's right. She was talking about him the other day. They've been back in contact. I guess I never realized they were that serious. She mentioned him once or twice, but it sounded like a casual thing, more a study partner than anything else."

"No, Brandon. They were madly in love."

He took a few seconds to think about what she'd said. "Why did they break up?"

"His student visa expired, and he had to return to Sweden. He applied for a green card, but these things take time. He even asked her to go with him, but she refused."

"No wonder she's been so upset lately."

"Yes. She told me it broke her heart to end things with Jan, but she didn't want to leave you alone. He was her first, you know."

Brandon made a face. "Selene, that's not something I want to know about my daughter." He thought briefly before saying in a hesitant tone, "Do you think she'll get back together with him?"

"She might if he's willing."

On Friday, Brandon and Selene left around noon for the six-hour drive from their home to the reservation. Selene relaxed on the bench seat, admiring the intense greenery of an upper Midwestern summer. They passed farms and forests and eventually made their way into the sparse, rocky area around the Badlands. *Amazing that I've lived in Minnesota my whole life, but I've never come this direction.*

Finally, they arrived at the reservation. Selene jumped out of the truck without waiting for Brandon to open the door, eager to stretch her cramped legs. An incredible scene spread out across the rocky vista before them. Rows upon rows of vendor stalls, decked out in beautiful colors in honor of the festival, concealed the horizon. The smell of hot grease and seasoned meat wafted on the dry, dusty August breeze. In the center, a covered walkway surrounded a clearing.

Off to one side, a corral encircled by bleachers awaited tomorrow's rodeo. Brandon laid his arm across Selene's shoulders. "Well, here we are. What do you think?"

Though his words sounded ordinary, a note in his tone told Selene things he probably wasn't aware of himself. *This is his home, his place, and he'll never know it for sure. I could tell him, but it wouldn't matter. He's cut off from his roots.* "Words can't even express. Just like you said." Selene cuddled against his side, ignoring the heat. "What would you like to do first?"

"Let me show you around."

Without waiting for a response, he moved her toward the tents, many of them containing vendors selling items foreign to her experience, but no less beautiful in their unfamiliarity: earrings and tie clasps made of dyed porcupine quills and colorful blankets.

"This is so amazing," she said, running her fingers gently over a bone and bead choker.

"Are you hungry?" he asked. "The next stall is an Indian taco."

"What's that?"

"Something delicious," he explained. "Interested?"

She glanced into the next booth and raised her eyebrows. "I'll share one with you. I'm not attempting that by myself."

"Deal." He laughed. Pulling out his wallet, he purchased a huge bowl made of fry bread, filled with ground meat, cheese, and lettuce, and dolloped with sour cream.

Selene eyed the treat. "How do you eat this? It's too messy to pick up."

Brandon quirked one eyebrow and gestured at her with two plastic forks.

She laughed at her lack of imagination. "Of course."

"Well come over, here, baby and have some." Brandon extended a fork and then jerked it away from her fingers.

"Hey!"

He forked up a big bite for himself, stepping back out of her reach. The aroma of the food teased her. "Give me a bite, Brandon," she pleaded.

"You'll have to earn it," he teased.

Selene drew close to him and rose on tiptoe to kiss him. "Ugh. Your lips are greasy." She wiped her mouth on the back of her hand.

Brandon forked up a bite and offered it. Selene opened her lips and waited to see if he would share or tease again. He tucked the food into her mouth. She chewed and closed her eyes. "Mmmm."

"Good?"

She nodded with a smile.

"Let's sit down and enjoy, then," he suggested, leading her to a picnic table.

Selene drank it all in. *It's been so long since I've done something this fun. Besides, this is part of Brandon. Deep in his soul, behind the good little Lutheran boy, is a Lakota man.* Again, she felt a deep sense of rightness about the place, as though her boyfriend belonged here. *It's intuition, and can never be proven, but I know Brandon is Lakota. For this reason, he chooses this event, out of all the possible tribal events around the country, to make into his annual pilgrimage.*

"Brandon," another man called, waving as he approached.

"Hi, Bill," Brandon replied, beaming. "This is my girlfriend, Selene."

The man raised eyebrows at the sight of the dainty white woman, but he smiled at Selene. "Pleased to meet you, ma'am."

"What's this ma'am business? Call me Selene, please."

"All right then," Bill agreed. "Are you two here for the whole weekend?"

"As always," Brandon replied. "I wanted to show my lady here what it means to be Lakota."

"It's great," Selene added, not sure what else to say.

"We're glad to have you both," Bill assured them. "Better go find a place to sit. The opening ceremony will begin soon. I have to go get on my regalia."

"Break a leg," Brandon told his friend.

"I'm looking forward to it," Selene added.

Bill walked away. Brandon hopped up from the bench, stalked to the trash can and tossed the forks and the paper bowl in which their snack had rested. "He's right, you know. The seats fill up pretty fast. We'd better go." He extended a hand and helped her to her feet.

149

SIMONE BEAUDELAIRE

Selene swayed and gripped him tight, taking in a flash of concern.

"Are you all right?"

"I think I got a bit much sun," Selene admitted. Can we sit in the shade?" she suggested.

"I'll see what I can find." Still holding tight to her hand, he led her toward a growing crowd.

A tall woman in her late thirties approached. She looked at Brandon with a possessive expression filled with intimate knowledge. Unfriendliness radiated from her towards Selene.

"Barbara," Brandon introduced his new lover to the old one with the casual manner of an old friend. "Long time. How are you? This is Selene, my girlfriend. Selene, this is Barbara, the old friend I told you about." He didn't seem to notice the tense undercurrents passing between the two women.

"Brandon," Barbara said in a seductive voice that set Selene's teeth on edge, "Why don't you go and scope out the best spot for Selene to see the show? I'll entertain your lady friend for a moment."

Not for the first time Selene wished she could project her thoughts to Brandon. *I don't want to be left alone with this catty creature.*

"Good idea," Brandon replied, still oblivious, and after giving Selene a brief kiss, he wandered away.

Selene squared her shoulders and drew herself up to her full height—a disappointing five foot two—which left the gorgeous Lakota woman towering over her. Selene felt small, pale and insignificant next to this amazing specimen of womanhood. *It's unthinkable that Brandon, having once had this woman in his bed, would now prefer me.* She tried to be nice. "It's good to meet you, Barbara. Brandon told me about you."

"I'm not going to shake hands with you," the other woman sneered, her friendly manner abandoned.

"Good thing I wasn't offering." Selene heard her voice harden.

"Listen, Blondie, I realize that someone as WASP-y as you must find Brandon an exotic treasure, like someone out of a romance novel, but you shouldn't be with him. He's Indian, and he should be with an Indian woman. You will never understand what it is to be Lakota, so you can never be the one for him."

Selene's eyes narrowed. *Oh, so we're going to be rude, are we? Honey, you have no clue how thick my skin is, after years of police work.* Schooling her voice to the icy calm she used with recalcitrant suspects, she said, "I concede your point, Barbara. I will never know what it is to be Lakota. I can't even conceptualize it, but don't forget, Brandon doesn't know either. He grew up more white than Indian, and because of the situation, he will never be part of this community. You grew up here, didn't you?"

"Yes," Barbara admitted, making a sour face.

"You grew up knowing what it was to be Indian. You had Lakota friends and a Lakota family. There have always been many terribly hard things about living in a place like this, but at least you had a sense of community, of who you are. Brandon has never known what it is to be one of his people. He was alone, the only Indian in a sea of white children, the child of white parents. That is something about him *you* will never understand. He has never known who or what he is. But I understand what it is to be alone, to be unique. Only *I* can connect to Brandon in that way."

She crossed her arms over her chest and continued. "I'm not with him because he's Indian and I think he's exotic. I don't think of him like that at all. I'm with him because we have a deep connection. I realize you must feel very sad to have lost him—he is one of the best men I've ever known—but rest assured. I will make sure that while he may not have a place in his community, he will always have a home."

Unable to find a suitable reply, Barbara turned and walked away.

Selene released a lungful of air, feeling satisfied. *I wasn't rude, only brutally honest. I think I handled it well, not letting her walk all over me, but not being ugly either.*

Brandon returned to her. "I found us a good place, but we'd better hurry or someone will nab it."

Taking his offered hand, Selene let Brandon walk her over to a seat near where the dancers would perform. They stood in silence, fingers entwined, savoring the anticipation.

The ceremony began with drums, like the heartbeat of the earth. Selene's pulse soon echoed them, pounding in rhythm. A chanting song rose among the gathered people. She didn't understand the words, but the melody moved through her. Her fingers clutched Brandon's, and for a dizzying moment, she wasn't sure which thoughts were his and which were hers. Then she realized they felt the same thing; moved by the music but not really part of it. It called to them.

The procession began. First came an elderly gentleman in a wheelchair, scarcely able to hold his head up under a massive feathered headdress.

Next followed a row of soldiers carrying American flags. Their uniforms were in perfect order, but they took an extra step for each forward movement. It looked like a slow and deliberate dance more than an orderly procession.

Women and children in white fabric tiaras and colorful skirts, from which dozens of bells jingled, joined the circle. They stomped their feet so their shrill tinkling added a soprano counterpoint to the bass beats of the drum.

Following them were men, also adorned with bells and sporting arrangements of eagle feathers ranging from one or two to enormous collections trailing down their backs.

They walked the same slow path, opening the ceremony with a spectacle Selene found so beautiful, tears of joy slid down her cheeks. Brandon noticed, of course, and slipped his arm around her, so their free hands remained locked. Together, they drank in the mutual desire to belong, the grief of realizing no such place existed, and the joy that came from knowing they belonged together at least.

It was late when they returned to the hotel room, but the pounding drums still rang in their ears and in their blood, and they made love fiercely, deep into the night.

The next morning, after a breakfast that probably should have been called lunch, they returned to the reservation. The heat of the day beat down on them uncomfortably. Selene wiped sweat off her forehead. "It's a scorcher," she commented.

"It is," Brandon agreed. "Don't you feel sorry for the people in the rodeo?" He indicated the ring where a bucking bronco attempted to dislodge a long-haired man in a fringed leather jacket.

"Yes. The horses too," Selene said, "but to be honest, I'm not much into rodeos, particularly not in the heat. Do you love them?"

He shrugged. "They're okay, I guess, but I wouldn't cross the street to watch one. Want to go to the visitor center? I think it's air-conditioned."

"I love you," Selene said fervently.

They stepped into an echoing but blessedly cool pole building, and Selene stared in fascination at the carefully preserved historical regalia displayed on dress forms along one wall.

"Excuse me, babe," Brandon said, kissing her temple. "Nature calls. I'll be right back."

Selene barely noticed. Drawing near a bright yellow, beaded leather vest and trousers displayed over a bone breastplate, she examined each detail. Then she turned her attention to the placard beside it, which listed the name, birth and death dates of the original owner, and the piece's cultural significance.

"Wow," she breathed.

An itchy feeling between Selene's shoulder blades made her aware of a presence beside her, and she turned to find Barbara.

Today, the woman's demeanor had noticeably altered. "I wasn't very nice to you yesterday. I'm sorry."

"Don't worry about it. I understood. Besides, you weren't wrong. There's no way I can relate to all of this," she gestured at the displays, "even though I like it very much. I only wish Brandon could be as much a part of it as he wants to be. I mean, I understand why he can't but… it's sad."

"He's really special, isn't he?" Barbara asked wistfully.

"Yes," Selene agreed.

"That's why I left, you know," the woman explained, tossing a strand of dark hair over her shoulder. "I knew he didn't love me, and I couldn't stand to be near him without having his heart."

"It's painful, I know," Selene agreed. "I was his friend for years before we moved in together. Friends without benefits. It was…difficult. I'm still pinching myself to see if this is real."

Barbara smiled sadly. "Ah, so you two live together. I suppose if he has you for a wife, it's all right."

"Wife?" Selene blinked, taken aback by the thought. "I'm not his wife. Just his girlfriend."

"In our culture, when a couple moves in together, it means they're married."

Does Brandon think that too? "Well, as you pointed out, I'm not part of your culture." Her words came out more sharply than she had intended.

"Did I upset you? I'm sorry again. I was trying to say I approve of you being with Brandon after all."

"Thank you, Barbara. I appreciate it," Selene said quietly.

The other woman walked away.

Selene turned back to the displays, distinctly unsettled by the conversation. *I want to be Brandon's wife someday—because we chose it together. Not just by happenstance. I would feel like I've missed out on so many things I never realized I wanted. But I won't say anything. Not yet. I want Brandon to enjoy his visit. Afterwards, we'll need to talk.*

Brandon spent the entire day with his hand in Selene's, and the contentment radiating from him as he partook deeply of his culture washed over her in drowning waves. *It's an honor to be here to share it. As long as Brandon and I remain together, I will do this with him each year.*

After lunch, several men from the village descended on Brandon, eager to catch up. Left out of a conversation amongst old friends, Selene scanned the surroundings. Nearby, an ancient Lakota woman sat on a colorful blanket. A crepe of crinkled skin lightly covered her chiseled features, and the color had bled from the irises of her eyes, splotching the whites with dark brown. She looked hard at Selene, and the summons crashed in the young woman's head like a gong. Slipping her hand free from Brandon's, she approached, crouching on the ground in front of the woman.

"Did you need me, ma'am?"

The woman tilted her head, indicating a lack of understanding and extended her hand. Selene shook her head. *To read the thoughts of this elder would be a terrible affront.* "No, you don't want me to do that."

The hand thrust forward insistently. Selene's eyes widened. *Can this woman actually see what I am?* She grasped the fingers gently.

A jumble of images encompassing almost a hundred years of living swirled dizzyingly and then settled into the desired sequence. A man. Younger than the woman but far from young. Selene recognized him as one of the elders who had greeted Brandon upon their arrival. Next to him, a young girl, very young, his daughter. Heavily pregnant. Barely a teenager… *One morning, we found the empty bed, no note. No idea where she had gone. The next day, she returned, her belly sagging from recent delivery. No baby, but blood, too much blood. She was hemorrhaging. A hospital emergency room where my granddaughter bled out until her brief life ended.*

"I shouldn't be seeing this." Selene tried to pull her hand away, but it was no use. She could not break the connection with the old woman's frail fingers.

I could never be sure **he** *was that baby, but…* Two faces appeared side by side, one the girl, the other Selene's lover. The similarity was uncanny.

Don't tell him. The command was no less firm for being utterly silent. *Don't tell him how she died. He'll blame himself. It was not his fault. It was her time. He's a good man. Take care of him.*

"I promise," Selene said aloud.

The woman let go of her hand. As the images faded, Selene closed her eyes, trying to clear her mind. When she opened them, she was alone. A single black feather floated to the ground.

On the long drive home, Selene posed a troubling question. "Brandon, is it true that if a Lakota couple moves in together, they're married?"

"Yes, I believe so. Why?"

"Barbara told me. She said I was your wife."

"Is that a problem?" he asked, one eyebrow lowering in confusion.

She tried to explain her concerns. "We've only been a couple for a few months. I want to be with you, Brandon, but I can't conceptualize a wedding without a ceremony. So, tell me this: are we married?"

"We're not a Lakota couple, Selene," he explained. "Yes, honestly, I see this relationship as permanent, but we aren't married yet. I'm hoping someday to have a wedding in a Lutheran church."

Reassured, she relaxed. "Oh, okay. I would like that, some-day. You know, though, we're half of a Lakota couple."

He glanced at her. "Why do you say so? I could be anything."

"No, you belonged there. I could feel it. You are Lakota. I'll never be able to prove it, but I know without a doubt. It's why you like to spend time with them. They're your people."

"I want to believe that. Thank you, Selene."

CHAPTER 11

The next morning, Selene woke up feeling like she hadn't closed her eyes in days. Her stomach churned with fatigue. It was all she could do to swallow her usual cup of coffee.

"You'd better stay home today, honey," Brandon told her seriously as he loaded the coffee cups into the dishwasher. "You look exhausted. I guess the weekend was too much for you."

Wow. I look so bad it shows. She shook her head. "I may come home early. They're expecting a break in the rape case. Someone spotted the taxi driver in Baxter, and they're going to try and bring him in for questioning. Once it's done, I'll probably come home. Jeez, I just got up and I already need a nap."

"Have you had any breakfast?"

Selene swallowed hard as the nausea peaked. "Ugh, I can't even think about food right now."

"Babe, you know how important it is for you to eat!"

"Brandon, please don't nag. I'm not feeling well."

Brandon dropped the subject and kissed her goodbye.

At the station, Selene found Chief Brady waiting near the

time clock. "Sir?"

"He's here. I need the best, Selene. Find out the truth."

"Yes, sir," she concurred. "Interrogation room two?"

"Two," he agreed. Turning on his heel, he stalked back to his office.

Selene punched in and made her way toward the bathroom first to check on her appearance. *Can't go in looking like a drowned rat.* Her belly swooped. *A sick drowned rat. Damn it, I can't get the flu now.* Swallowing hard, she glanced through the glass into the interrogation room as she passed it to see a thickset figure fiddling with a Styrofoam cup.

Ducking through the bathroom door, she stared into the mirror and shrugged, tucking an escaped strand behind her ear. *I look exhausted but professional. It will have to do. Showtime.*

As she headed towards her suspect, she took a sip of water at the fountain, hoping to calm her churning innards. *I hope I'm not going to get really sick.* The water didn't help at all. Steeling herself, she walked into the room.

The cab driver turned out to be a handsome, middle-aged man with salt and pepper hair and a small, neat mustache. He looked Selene over thoroughly as he stood and said, "My goodness, the police force gets prettier every year. I may have to join. May I ask what this is about, ma'am?"

"Of course, we'll get to that in a moment. My name is Officer Selene Johansen," she extended her hand.

He took it eagerly, grasping her small palm with two giant paws. A deluge of darkness swamped her, and with it, a wave of nausea she couldn't ignore. Taking a deep breath through her nose, she wrenched her hand from his and muttered, "Excuse me a moment," as she ran for the door.

She barely made it to the bathroom stall. Falling to her knees on the cold tile floor, she vomited violently. Several long minutes passed in helpless gagging. Finally, Kathleen, one of the dispatchers, came in and found her.

"My goodness, Selene, what's wrong?"

"Could you please get me some water?" Selene panted.

"Of course."

"And get Tony."

"I'll be right back."

Kathleen returned quickly with the water. Selene took a small sip and closed her eyes.

"I shouldn't have come in today," she muttered. Hoisting herself to her feet, she staggered to the door of the ladies' room. Tony, bless him, waited outside.

He took one glance at her and immediately grew alarmed. "What happened?"

"I'm sick," Selene said quietly, "but you have to arrest that guy. He's guilty as sin. He raped the girl, and she wasn't the first. Not all the others survived." She swallowed convulsively several times and took another sip of water. "He's a serial rapist and killer."

"Can't you go back in there, make him confess?"

Selene thought for a long moment. She shook her head. "If I look at him again, I'll throw up. You don't want to know what's inside that man's head. I wish I didn't. You're a good interrogator, Tony. Can't you please do it?"

"I've never known you to refuse an interrogation before. You must be really sick."

"I've never felt this bad in my life." The lights overhead seem to burn Selene's eyes and she rested her hand on her closed eyelids.

"Maybe you should go to the doctor."

"I might." She gagged and swallowed. *If I can get there.*

Tony put his hand on her shoulder. "Come on, Selene. Let's go tell the chief you're going home sick. I'll take on the interrogation, and don't worry. I'll get him."

"Thanks, Tony, you're my hero."

Tony wrapped his arm around Selene's waist and supported her across the room to the Chief's office.

Brady glanced up from his desk, at first barely taking her

in. Then her condition registered on him and he focused on her face. "Selene, why are you so green? Are you hungover?"

She tried to answer, but another retch attempted to escape. She clapped a hand over her mouth.

"She's sick," Tony explained. "Like, dog sick. Better send her home, boss. I'll take over the interrogation."

"Well, damn," Brady cursed. "I'd hoped for your special touch, Selene."

"Thanks, boss," Tony said dryly.

Brady frowned at him and he shut his mouth with a snap.

"He's guilty," Selene said softly. "Tony will get a confession. I know he will." She gagged and couldn't entirely suppress it.

"Get out of here, Johansen," Brady snapped, "before you hurl on the floor. Tony, hurry up and get the confession. Let's get this bastard off the streets."

"Do you need help getting to your car?" Tony asked as Selene staggered out of the office.

"I'll manage," she replied, relying on pure bravado. He took her words at face value and hot-footed it back to the interrogation room while Selene walked unsteadily out to her car and sagged into the seat.

Twice on the short drive from the police station to the house, she had to pull over and breathe deeply for several minutes to try and stave off another round of retching. The second time, she didn't succeed. Luckily, there was a large public trash can nearby. It was humiliating, but Selene was too sick to worry about it much.

She made it home, barely, and staggered to the bathroom. Despite her empty stomach, she dry-heaved for several agonizing minutes. Growing increasingly alarmed at her condition, since even water wouldn't stay in her protesting stomach, she sought help.

Brandon's secretary, Judy, answered the phone. "I'm sorry.

Mr. Price is in a meeting and can't be disturbed. May I take a message?"

"No, no message." Wanting to cry, Selene hung up. *No, don't. You'll never stop.* Steeling herself, she called Maggie.

"Selene, you sound awful," her friend said bluntly, in response to her weak and wavering greeting.

"I feel awful," Selene wailed. "I can't stop throwing up."

"Do you need me to come over?"

"Please."

"Can I bring you anything? What's wrong?"

"I don't know." She swallowed hard on another rising gag. "This is either food poisoning or the worst stomach bug ever."

"You only eat Dad's cooking, so you won't get food poisoning. Do you have any other symptoms? I'm at my computer right now. There are a lot of illnesses that cause vomiting."

Selene had to breathe slowly through her nose a couple of times before responding. "We've been eating out… at the Wacipi and on the way home. Food poisoning isn't impossible. I've also been exhausted for days and a little queasy, but this is way worse."

"Hmmm. Are your breasts sore?"

"What?" *She must be joking. What would that even mean?*

"Seriously."

Or maybe not. She pressed with her crossed arms and winced. "Yes, now that you mention it, they are a little."

"Okay, I'm going to be there as soon as I can, but I have to stop at the store along the way. Try to hang on, sweetie. I'm coming."

"Thank you."

Twenty minutes later, Maggie let herself into the house with a plastic grocery bag on one arm.

Selene sprawled on the couch in her pajamas, her head resting wearily on her arm. Sammy, alarmed by her illness, sat on her lap. She petted his soft fur.

"Can you please arm the alarm?" Selene asked her friend.

"I did on the way in. Haven't they caught your peeper yet?"

"Not yet. What was the idea you mentioned on the phone?"

"Right." Maggie rummaged inside the bag." Now, this is going to sound weird, but trust me, okay? Here. Take this box. Here's a Dixie cup. I need you to pee in it. The instructions for what to do next are on the box."

Selene looked at the pink box in her hand. She raised her eyes to her friend's. "Maggie, I'm not pregnant."

"Are you sure? Is it impossible?"

Color rose in Selene's clammy cheeks. "I guess not."

"That's what I thought. Just humor me, Selene. If it's negative, I'm taking you to the doctor."

Selene staggered into the bathroom. After a few quiet minutes, Maggie heard the unmistakable sound of something plastic clattering to the tile floor. She knocked and opened the door. Selene sat on the floor with her arms around her knees. The stick lay where she had dropped it, face up, displaying an unmistakable pink plus sign.

"I'm calling Dad," Maggie said firmly.

"He's in a meeting."

"He'll talk to me." Already dialing her cell phone, Maggie stepped out of the bathroom, closing the door behind her. Inside, she could hear Selene retching yet again.

"This is Maggie," she told Judy, "I need to talk to my dad. It's an emergency."

A moment later, Brandon was on the phone. "What's up, Maggie?"

"I'm with Selene. She's really sick. You need to come home right away."

"She looked pretty bad this morning," he admitted. "Is she at home now?"

Oblivious much? "Yes. She needs you. Please hurry."

"I'll be right there."

Maggie returned to the bathroom. Selene looked shaken and miserable. "Come on," she said, helping her friend up from the floor. "I read on the internet the best way to deal with morning sickness is to eat something."

Selene gagged. "I can't eat."

"You'll feel better if you do. They recommend crackers."

Selene shuddered at the thought.

"Well think then. What sounds good?"

She closed her eyes. "An apple?"

"Do you have some?"

"Yes."

Maggie escorted Selene into the kitchen and helped her into a chair before retrieving an apple from the refrigerator. "How about some peanut butter with it. You could probably use the protein."

"Yes, that sounds good."

A moment later, she had neatly sliced the apple and neatly placed it in a bowl with a little puddle of peanut butter to dip it in. Selene picked up a piece warily, but clearly, she found it appealing. She took a cautious bite, swallowed, and continued. Eventually, some color came back to her cheeks.

"So, I guess," Maggie said wryly, "you and Dad haven't been going to bed together just to sleep anymore."

"Obviously not," Selene replied, too pale even to blush.

"What happened? Did a condom break?"

Selene replied dully, "Condom? No, there were no condoms."

"The pill? gel? Anything?"

Selene shook her head.

"Good Lord. Nothing at all? And, you've been having sex for how long?"

Selene seemed to calculate mentally, her fingertips touching the tablecloth, one after the other. "About six weeks, since his birthday party."

"And you haven't used *any* birth control?" *I can't believe it. They must be crazy!*

"Honestly, it never crossed my mind," Selene admitted, her tired face showing signs of sheepishness.

"I don't suppose this was a rare occurrence, you know, making love?" *Maybe a one-time thing? Please let it be.*

"No. We do it constantly, just about daily."

Awkward! "Okay, don't tell me any more about that." Maggie longed to cover her ears and unhear the uncomfortable truth. "Just one more question. Have you had your period since you and Dad moved in together?"

"Yes."

"Before or after you became intimate?"

"Before."

Maggie shook her head. "You probably got pregnant right away. It would be consistent with how sick you are."

"You mean, all this time…"

"Yup. Looks that way."

Selene laid her arms on the table and hid her face in them. "Well, shit. What do I do now?"

"I don't know. You and Dad will have to decide. You could get rid of it."

"No." Selene shook her head against her arm.

I had a feeling. Maggie rubbed her back. "Okay, well then you'll have to talk it out, the two of you. Hey, now you've eaten that apple, do you feel better?"

"Yes. But I'm so tired."

"Go to bed. I'll talk to Dad when he gets home and explain the situation."

"Thanks, Maggie. You're a real friend." Selene hoisted

herself from the chair and walked unsteadily to the bedroom. Through the open door, Maggie could see she had crashed to sleep in about twenty seconds.

❧

Not long after, Brandon arrived home from work. *Are they still here? It's so quiet.* He moved from the garage into the kitchen and found his daughter sitting at the table, staring out the window, her expression far away.

"Maggie." he hugged his daughter. "Where's Selene? Is she all right?"

"No, she's not." Maggie rose and stalked to the bedroom, closing the door. She beckoned her dad into the living room, and he followed. She suddenly looked livid.

Uh oh. What happened?

"Dad, are you the stupidest man alive, or what?"

Unprepared for her attack, Brandon's blinked. "What do you mean?"

"Why did you and Mom get married, and don't say anything about love, because I know better."

"You know why, Maggie." Brandon sighed. *I wish she didn't know.*

Maggie shrugged. "Yeah, she was knocked up. Of course, you were teenagers then, but now you have no excuse. You're forty years old, for heaven's sake, widowed. You're not some horny teen. How the hell is it that you've been having sex with Selene constantly for *six weeks* and you've never once used protection? What did you think was going to happen?"

Brandon's shoulders sagged. "Are you saying she's…?"

"Pregnant?" Maggie asked, her voice dangerously soft. "Oh yes, she's pregnant. I saw the test myself."

He cursed.

"You know," Maggie continued, "she loves you. I swore to her, when you two got together, that you would take good care of her. I see what a great job you did. Look, I don't care anymore that you two are sleeping together. Whatever. But, Dad, unprotected sex didn't work well for you in high school, and it still doesn't. Were you trying to get her pregnant?"

The question gave Brandon pause. *Was I? Maggie's right— it was unbelievably stupid to forget something so obvious and fundamental, and I never have, not since high school. Maggie's conception knocked the carelessness right out of me... until now. Why is this different? What had happened to my sense?* "I don't think so."

"Are you sure, Dad? I know you used to wish you had other children, even though Mom was content with one."

"That's true," he admitted, "but I wouldn't have done this intentionally to Selene. I just didn't think of it. Neither did she." *It's not a lie, but subconsciously, who knows? I guess it's possible.*

"She was a virgin until you got ahold of her," Maggie reminded him, her eyes narrow and her mouth tight. "It was your responsibility. You were supposed to protect her."

"I forgot."

"That's no excuse."

Brandon sighed. "You're right. It's not. How is she?"

"How the hell do you think?" Maggie burst out. "She's messed up, freaked out. I found her rocking on the bathroom floor. She's also sick as a dog and miserable."

"Did you get her to eat anything?"

"Yes."

Brandon sank heavily onto the couch, his face in his hands. *This is one piece of history I don't want to repeat.* He remembered Claudia's frantic voice on the phone, telling him she needed to talk to him. Her terrified face. They had married, but not because they loved each other. In fact, they had been little more than casual friends, apart from one date that had gotten out of hand. They'd married right after graduation, so Maggie could have a family. He'd turned eighteen just before the wedding. Claudia had still been seventeen. *Now it's all happening again. There is one difference, though.* "I love Selene." He said out loud.

Maggie didn't give an inch. "Is this how you show your love then?"

He held up one hand. "It was wrong, I concede the point, but this is not like before. I love Selene. We'll get through this."

Maggie sat down beside him on the couch. She leaned against him and he put his arm around her. "Daddy?"

"Yes, Maggie?"

"You're going to have another baby." She sounded vulnerable and worried.

"Yes, I know. There's only one Maggie though."

She hugged him.

CHAPTER 12

*S*elene woke up about an hour later feeling groggy and ravenous. *Something's ringing. My phone. Where is it? In my pants?* She groped her way to where she had left them and fished it out of the pocket.

"Hello?" she croaked.

"Selene, you sound like hell."

"Thanks, Tony," she mumbled. Her mouth felt like the Sahara and tasted like an old boot.

"The driver contradicted himself several times. Plus, a technician who just happened to be passing his car saw some suspicious stains. It was enough for probable cause. They found tape and a very curious flashlight in the trunk, along with hair and multiple blood and semen stains in the back-seat. We got him."

"Thank goodness."

"I just wanted to let you know. Go back to bed."

"Okay, thanks." She hung up but didn't want to go back to bed. Slowly she pulled on jeans and a tank top. *First a very long date with my toothbrush and then something to eat and drink.* She headed to the bathroom. After a few minutes of extended brushing, she stepped out. Immediately Brandon appeared and enfolded her in his arms.

Oh, that feels good.

"How are you, baby?" he asked tenderly in her ear.

"Hungry."

"That's a first." He kissed her temple. "Come on, let's get you something. What would you like?"

"Water," she answered, letting him lead her into the kitchen. "Also, some toast with butter and jam."

"Sure." He brought her a cup and she drank thirstily while he toasted some bread.

The food made her feel a little more awake. It must have shown because once the last crumb disappeared, he asked her, "Okay, how are you really doing?"

"Not well," she replied grimly.

"Do you still feel sick?"

"Not right now. Brandon, I'm pregnant." The words sounded strange in her ears.

"I know. Maggie told me. I'm sorry I wasn't more careful with you."

She shook her head. "I've been to health class. I've lived in the world. I know people are supposed to use condoms when they have sex. I forgot."

"I did too," he replied, his hand lingering on hers, and she could feel his calm and acceptance.

How is this not a crisis to you? "What are we going to do?" she asked, hating the whimper in her voice.

"What do you want to do?" Brandon asked.

"I don't know. Rewind? Try again?"

One corner of his mouth turned upward in a parody of a smile. "Unfortunately, time only moves forward. The baby is coming whether we're ready or not. Can you be okay about it?"

Okay? Are you joking? "I don't know. I feel kind of...overwhelmed. I don't know what to think." She pressed her fingertips to her forehead.

He laced his fingers through hers, sending the sense of calm even more deeply into her. "It's going to be fine, you know."

Selene shook her head, suddenly frantic. "I don't know that. Neither do you. What if I'm a terrible mother?"

"You won't be," he reassured her. *Calm down, baby. Relax*.

His mental urging only made her feel worse. "What if our baby is psychic? What then?"

The question gave him pause. "I don't know, Selene. But you're uniquely qualified to care for such a child if one arrives."

"No, I wouldn't wish this on anyone. It's no way to live, Brandon." She lifted her hand from his, shutting off his flow of thoughts to her mind.

"Hey," he said softly, "You're panicking. Calm down."

"Don't tell me to calm down," she snapped. "I can't deal with this. I have to get out of here."

"Get out? No, where will you go?" He sounded alarmed, but she was too overwrought to care.

"I'll go to…my Aunt Karen. That's where I'll go. She'll know what to do."

"Selene." Brandon took her hand again. *Please, baby. I'm here for you. Please try to listen*. "Will you come back?"

"I don't know. Let me go. I'm leaving."

Selene wrenched her hand out of his and ran to the bedroom, where she grabbed a change of clothes and to the bathroom for her toothbrush. Then she raced to her car and sped away. From the freeway, she dialed her aunt on her cell phone.

"Auntie Karen, this is Selene."

"Well hello, dear," replied the comforting voice on the

other side. "I haven't heard from you in so long. How are you?"

"I'm bad, really bad," Selene blurted. "Can I come and stay with you for a few days? I need you."

"Of course, you're always welcome. You know that."

Selene made the ninety-minute drive to her aunt's house in a little over an hour. Speeding through the countryside did calm her somewhat, but she remained in a terrible state. She had never been so scared in her life.

Her aunt met her at the door and hugged her hard. Selene immediately dissolved into tears at the sight of Karen's familiar iced tea colored hair, hanging in a curly mop to her chin, her soft brown eyes wreathed with smile lines, and her expression welcoming.

"Come on, honey," Karen said soothingly, "let me get you a cup of tea and you can tell me what's on your mind."

While the water heated, Karen urged Selene into an armchair and stood beside her, stroking her hair. It was a gesture she remembered from childhood, and it didn't fail to comfort now.

Selene couldn't stop crying, but she did find she was able to speak through it when Karen asked her, "Okay, what's going on?"

"I've just made the most horrible mess of my life. I don't know what I'm going to do now." She closed her eyes, focusing on the familiar scent of the home and her aunt's soothing touch.

"Okay, tell me more."

"I fell in love."

Karen chuckled. "Selene, it's okay to fall in love. Most everyone does. Don't assume you need to be more different than you already are. Is he a good boy?"

An image of her beautiful Brandon floated behind her closed eyes. "Yes. He's wonderful."

"Does he love you?"

Of the answer to that, she was absolutely certain. "Yes," she said unequivocally.

"And does he know about your gift?"

"Yes, he uses it to communicate with me."

Karen's grin looked wavery through Selene's tears. "Oh, that's very good. And he has a good job?"

"Uh-huh." Her stomach lurched again, and she closed her eyes.

"Well, dear, I'm having a hard time seeing the problem. He's not on drugs or anything is he?"

Selene's eyes snapped open at the surprising question. "No! No drugs, he doesn't smoke, and he rarely drinks."

"What's his name?"

She relaxed into the chair with a sigh. "Brandon. He's the love of my life. I think I've loved him forever."

"How long have you been together?"

"Since the beginning of May, about three months."

"That's a good start."

"Yes, but I've known him for over seven years. We've been friends a long time." She turned to face her aunt.

"That's good," Karen looked back, a little confused. "Can you please tell me the part where this is a problem?"

"We live together."

"Really?" Karen blinked at the unexpected turn.

She never was keen on cohabitation. "My house burned down. He let me stay with him. One thing led to another…"

Karen held up a hand to slow the gush of words. "I understand. But, Selene, your house wasn't that old. How did it burn down?"

"It was arson. Some crazy person tried to kill me. He's been stalking me. Oh, God, Auntie, he looked in our bedroom window. He took pictures."

"Pictures?" The timer beeped, and Karen brought a cup of tea, which Selene held carefully in trembling hands. "Pictures of what?"

This time, she could feel her face burning. "Pictures of Brandon and me…having sex. Terrible, intimate pictures. He left them on my desk at work, with threatening notes."

Karen's jaw dropped. Then she laid a comforting hand on the back of Selene's shirt. "Oh, my poor baby. No wonder you needed to get away. Why didn't you bring your boyfriend with you? I would like to meet him."

"I couldn't. I'm so messed up. I needed to get away from him… to think." Another lurch in her belly warned of imminent disaster. "Oh no!" Selene set the mug carefully on the coffee table and sprinted to the bathroom.

"Are you sick?" Karen asked when Selene emerged, wiping her mouth with a tissue.

"No. I'm pregnant."

It was to Karen's credit how quickly she assimilated this information. "Oh, dear. That all happened really fast, didn't it? You went from single to living with someone to pregnant in less than four months. It's no wonder you're upset. When did you find out?"

"Today. I feel terrible." Selene couldn't help moaning a little.

"I'll tell you what; let's see if Dr. Baker can fit you in this afternoon."

"What for?"

"A checkup, my dear, to see how you and the baby are doing. She might be able to offer advice about the morning sickness as well. Your mother had it pretty bad as I recall." Karen patted her shoulder.

"I'm scared, Auntie," Selene whimpered.

Karen moved her hand soothingly on her niece's back, keeping to the parts covered by her shirt and carefully avoiding touching the bare skin on her shoulder. "I know, Selene. I know you're scared, but it's going to be okay, I promise you. Now sit here and drink this while I call the doctor."

Selene sat and drank the tea. Her mind had finally gone blank.

Miraculously, the doctor had an opening in the afternoon schedule, and Karen loaded Selene into her minivan and drove her over. On the way, they continued talking.

"Don't you want a baby, Selene?" Karen asked, her voice filled with sympathy.

"I honestly never gave it a thought. I never expected to be in a relationship at all."

"There's no reason for you to think that way. There's nothing wrong with you." Karen reached over and squeezed the shoulder of her tank top.

"Thank you." Selene sighed deeply. "I don't know whether I want a baby or not. I'm still adjusting to the idea."

"Well, at this point it looks like your time to adjust to the idea has gone from infinite to about half a year."

Selene didn't reply.

Karen continued. "So, this Brandon, are you worried he won't be a good father?"

"No, he's a very good father," she insisted.

One eyebrow shot up. "He is? He has children?"

"One daughter, from his first marriage."

"First marriage?"

Sounds like Auntie Karen has misgivings. Selene hastened to explain. "Yes. His wife died of cancer about seven years ago. That was when we met. Remember how I thought I was going to be a counselor? Maggie was my first and only client."

"I remember, but I thought Maggie was a teenager then."

"She was fourteen. She's twenty-two now. She's a good friend."

"And exactly how old is Brandon?"

There's that doubting tone in Karen's voice again. "He just turned forty."

Karen glanced at Selene and quickly looked back at the road. "He was very young when his daughter was born."

"Barely eighteen."

"I see. He seems to have a history of this."

"It wasn't like that."

Karen seemed to realize expressing doubt about Brandon wasn't going to get her anywhere. "Don't be defensive, dear. I'll give him a chance. If you say he's a good man, I'll believe you."

They arrived at the doctor's office and a nurse quickly ushered them in, but not to see the doctor. There were a number of procedures needing to be done first, including a urine test and several blood tests as well as a lengthy questionnaire. Selene bore the indignity calmly, having long since cried herself out. Eventually, the doctor came in to see her.

Doctor Baker, a quiet and stately woman of about sixty, sat down on her stool and looked at Selene. "How are you, Selene? You're looking lovely as always. Why are you here to see me today?"

"I'm pregnant." The words still sounded bizarre.

The doctor glanced from Selene to the chart. "Why, yes you are. All right, I need to ask you a few questions. They may seem uncomfortable, but remember I have to ask everyone. They're not personal."

"Fine." Selene's crying fit had left her more exhausted than ever and she answered the doctor's questions in a drowsy monotone.

"When was your last period?"

"It was eight weeks ago."

"So that's about how far along you are..."

She shook her head. "No. It can't be more than six weeks."

"Why is that?"

Selene glanced at her aunt. "Because I lost my virginity six weeks ago."

The doctor raised one eyebrow, stole another look at the

chart, and then returned her eyes to Selene. "Ah, I see. Well, we measure pregnancy starting with the last period, not with the actual conception, so although you have probably been pregnant about six weeks, this is the eighth week."

Selene wrinkled her nose. "That doesn't make sense."

The doctor smiled. "You're right, but that's how it's done. When did you realize you were pregnant?"

"Today."

"Oh. No wonder you seem upset. How old are you?"

That isn't on that chart you keep studying? "Twenty-eight."

"Do you ever use illicit drugs, alcohol or tobacco?"

She rolled her eyes. "I've never used drugs or tobacco. I rarely drink."

"Have you had any alcohol since you became pregnant?"

A frisson of worry tightened Selene's belly, making her feel nauseous again. "Yes. I had half a beer once, and on a different day, one glass of wine. Will that hurt the baby?"

"Probably not." The doctor patted her leg. "You will have to stop now, of course."

Whew. "Yes, I know."

"The next question refers to the number of sexual partners in the last ten years. We need to be careful of undiagnosed STDs because they can affect the baby. However, in your case, may I assume one?"

At last, the burning in her cheeks revived Selene a bit. "Yes. I've only been with Brandon."

"Well, good. Tell me about Brandon. What is his ethnicity?"

"Native American."

The doctor's cheek quirked. "Does he use illicit drugs, tobacco, or alcohol?"

I don't like the juxtaposition of those questions… but I can't read anything into it. Just happenstance they're together on the chart—yeah right. "No to the drugs and tobacco, and he drinks less than I do."

"Sounds like a wise man. His age?"

"Forty."

The doctor blinked at such a significant age gap but didn't say anything. "What does he do for a living?"

"Why does that matter?" Selene demanded, finally giving in to irritation at the unnecessary questions.

"Well, if he's exposed to certain chemical or biological agents, it might harm the baby."

Selene rolled her eyes to the ceiling and counted the tiles. "Brandon is a career counselor. He works in an office. No chemicals."

"What about you?"

"I'm a police officer."

"Hmmm. That could pose a problem."

"Oh, I'm not on patrol," she quickly explained. "I interrogate suspects. I rarely leave the station. Not much danger there."

Karen's lips thinned but she didn't comment.

The doctor continued. "No, but I imagine there is a great deal of stress."

"Yes," Selene admitted.

"Well, be careful. It's not good to go through pregnancy stressed."

"I'll work on it."

"Now then, I assume this pregnancy wasn't planned?"

"No."

"Are you going to keep the baby, or give it up? I assume if you wanted an abortion, you would have asked for one by now."

Selene had been thinking about the idea of adoption, and one idea had come clear to her. "Both Brandon and I come from situations where our mothers abandoned us. I won't put my baby through the same thing. I won't give it up."

The doctor smiled at her fierceness. "You certainly don't have to, my dear. Ah, here are your test results. Everything looks normal. I'd like to order an ultrasound to confirm your due date. Otherwise, I think you're going to be fine. I'll write you a prescription for prenatal vitamins.

After the ultrasound, Selene's aunt drove her home. Selene sat in silence in the van. The doctor had seen something Selene couldn't understand in those shadowy images. *She said the baby would arrive in early March. Thank God she also added a prescription for anti-nausea medication along with the vitamins.*

"You know, Selene," Karen said as they left the pharmacy, "you're not so very unusual. You would hardly be the first woman to be blind-sided by a passionate romance and get in over her head. It's not bad, you know. It's not as though you've only known Brandon a few months. You've known him a long time. You know his character. Your relationship starts far before the first time you discussed your feelings."

Selene's eyes burned. "Thank you, Auntie."

"You are going back to him, aren't you?"

Surprise distracted Selene from her emotional reaction. "Of course! I told you he's the love of my life. It's just that when he's inside my head, I can't think for myself. I had to get a little distance so I could understand what *I* think and feel, not get trapped in his feelings."

"Oh, I see. Well, honey, does he know that?"

"What?" Lost in her own thoughts, Selene did not comprehend the question.

"That you're coming back?"

Huh? Not coming back never crossed my mind. "Of course, he does. We're in love, remember?"

"But when you left, did you tell him you would be back in a few days?"

"I can't remember, but he must know."

Karen gave her a stern look. "Selene, let me tell you something I learned from the other mothers of the gifted children you went to school with. Those with gifts are often lazy about expressing themselves. It's so easy for you to understand exactly what everyone is thinking, but don't forget others can't read *your* mind. If you didn't tell him you were coming back, he might not know it. I suggest you call him. You can't read his mind and be influenced by him over the phone, but he deserves to know you haven't taken off for good and taken his baby with you."

Selene's stomach clenched, and she had to spend a moment thinking about her breathing to settle it. The nausea faded to an uncomfortable churning. "Oh, do you think he might think that?"

"You never know. Better safe than sorry, especially when it's this important."

Selene pulled out her cell phone and hit the speed dial. It connected immediately.

"Selene?" Brandon's voice sounded wary.

Crap. Please, God, don't let me have ruined the best thing that's ever happened to me. "Yes, baby. I'm sorry about earlier. I was pretty freaked out."

"And now?" He didn't sound any more confident, and his flat, deadpan answers made her nervous as well.

"I'm a little better," she replied, trying to sound light and natural. "I've just come from the doctor. So far everything's okay. She gave me some medicine for the nausea. I hope it helps."

"Oh. That's good." The words were right, but his tone remained too flat, too controlled. "When are you coming home? I miss you."

And there's the hurt. He can't suppress it completely. Karen's right, he's worried. "I think the day after tomorrow. Tomorrow my aunt and cousins and I are going shopping. I'm going to need some maternity clothes for the fall and winter. Brandon, do you want to come up here tomorrow evening and meet my family?"

"Sure, baby. I'll come." He said it without hope or enthusiasm.

"Great. I love you."

On the other end of the line, Brandon drew in an unsteady breath. "I love you. Have a good time."

"Okay. Be safe."

"I will."

"You see, honey?" Karen said softly, as Selene hung up the phone.

"You were right. I feel terrible. He thought I was leaving him. Is it okay that I invited him?"

"Of course."

Next, Selene called Chief Brady. He agreed quickly that she should take two more days off work, to be sure she was feeling better. He had never seen her so ill.

When they arrived back at the house, Selene wanted nothing more than to take her new medication and sleep, but before she could move beyond the living room, two matching clouds of long blond hair converged, squealing and enfolded her in a tight hug.

"Selene! Selene! Where have you been? What have you been doing?"

The questions flew around her louder and faster until her head spun.

"Easy!" she urged, holding up her hands. "Hi, Cherie. Hi, Amy. I didn't expect to see you." *And that's silly. Why would two students not be home over the summer? Did you think the world stopped spinning because you moved away?*

"Come on!" Amy urged, laying a hand on the back of Selene's shirt and leading her into the den.

"Yes, I brought Chinese!" Cherie added. "Is ginger chicken still your favorite?"

Selene's mouth watered. "You'd better believe it. Where's Jake."

"He's gone canoeing with his friends," Amy explained. "If you called now and again, you'd know that he'd been planning this for months."

"Ouch. Yes, you're right. I should have called. I've been busy."

"Whatever." The twenty-year-old flipped her blond hair over her shoulder and stalked away.

Why did I stay away for so long? Why didn't I call? As a teen, I felt like I didn't fit in, but I think that might have come from me more than them. They don't touch me, but they're still family. I distanced myself from people who love me. All the loneliness I've suffered is my own fault. How silly.

A crackling noise drew Selene's attention to her younger cousin, who dug a white paper box out of a white plastic bag and carried it over to Selene. The intoxicating smell of spices wafted across the room.

"Can I get you a drink?" Cherie asked.

"Just water, please," Selene urged, sinking onto the sofa with her food. Amy claimed her favorite bean bag chair. Cherie returned with two glasses of water in her hands and a bottle of soda tucked under one arm. She handed Amy the bottle and Selene the glass before retrieving her dinner and joining her cousin on the sofa.

A few minutes later, Karen strolled into the room, arm in arm with Selene's uncle Paul. They plucked buckets of Chinese food from the bag and perched on matching recliners.

"So, as Amy pointed out, I've been a bit out of touch lately. What's everyone been up to?" Selene wanted to know.

"I start my last year of law school in the fall," Cherie said. "It's hard but so interesting."

Selene suppressed a shudder. "I'm glad you're enjoying it."

"And I've just finished a business degree," Amy piped up. "I'm hanging out this summer because I haven't decided whether to go to grad school or look for work."

"I've been promoted to vice principal," Paul said.

"That's great," Selene told him with a grin.

"Still teaching," Karen answered.

"What about you? How are you doing?" Amy asked, her voice losing its edge.

Guess she got over being upset. That's good. "I'm all right," Selene replied, after swallowing a mouthful of her chicken. "I met someone."

"Really?" Cherie raised her eyebrows.

"Well not exactly," Selene amended. "I didn't meet him. I moved in with him. He's been a friend for a long time."

Uncle Paul, from his seat on the leather recliner, grunted. His dark hair showed silver at the temples, but his eyes remained as shrewd as ever.

"Moved in?" Amy squealed. She glanced at her mother and then returned her attention to Selene, talking in a more subdued voice. "What's his name?"

"Brandon."

"Ooooh," Cherie sighed. "Sounds sexy."

"Very sexy," Selene agreed. "He's coming to meet you guys in a couple of days."

Feeling eyes on her, she turned to Paul, who was giving her a hard stare. "What's wrong?" she asked him.

"Why did you come without him?" he asked. "Is something wrong between you two?"

"Not wrong exactly. I, um…" she chewed another mouthful of food before finishing. "I'm pregnant. I got a little overwhelmed and wanted to spend some time with my family."

Now Paul's expression looked sour enough to curdle ice cream. "Pregnant? I don't like the sound of that. How irresponsible."

SIMONE BEAUDELAIRE

"It wasn't planned," Selene admitted, "but Brandon loves me. He's not going to take off or anything."

"I think it's great," Cherie said, staunchly defending her cousin. "Don't be so old-fashioned, Dad. Selene, congratulations."

"Thank you, Cherie."

They stayed up late talking and laughing; having a great time like they always had in the past. However, when Selene went to bed, she found sleep difficult. Used to Brandon's warmth beside her, the bed felt cold and empty, and she hated it. Eventually, she dozed, but fitfully.

In the morning, bleary-eyed and exhausted, she sipped coffee in silence while her cousins chattered around her. She made herself eat breakfast, chased down with her new vitamin and the vital nausea medication. *It doesn't exactly prevent the churning, but it does stop me from vomiting. That helps.*

At ten, the four women drove to the mall. Selene had never looked at maternity clothes before and didn't know what to do with them, but as her cousins cooed over the adorable styles, a clerk wandered over, her hands on her swollen belly.

"Hi, can you help me, please?" Selene begged. "I don't know how to do this."

"Oh, you're so tiny!" the clerk exclaimed. "I remember being tiny. I don't know if I'll ever get there again. Okay, here's what you do. The petites are over here. Find something you like and try on your regular size. That will get you most of the way through. At the end, you'll probably need to go up a size. When are you due?"

"March. And you?"

"November. I can't wait."

She escorted Selene over to the petites section and then sat down on a chair while her customer browsed among the racks. *Let me think. What will I need? It's hot now, in late August,*

184

but I'm not showing yet. Her summer work slacks and skirts still fit, so she concentrated on cooler weather clothing…a black pinstripe suit, khaki pants, some lacy stretchy camisoles in various colors, a couple of pairs of jeans with soft blue elastic instead of a waistband, and some warm sweaters. The clerk also insisted on some ridiculously larger bras. The cups opened with little clasps, for nursing the baby. This was a concept Selene had never considered before, but the more she thought about it the more appealing it seemed. She also hadn't realized the impact childbearing was going to have on the size of her breasts. *Oh well. Brandon should enjoy it.*

The purchases put a strain on Selene's credit card, but the lot where her house had once sat was in the final stages of being sold, so she had some money coming in soon. She planned on giving the rest to Brandon. It would be almost enough to pay off his mortgage. She wanted to be debt free before their baby arrived.

As she finished paying, her phone jangled. "Lo?" she said, propping it on her shoulder.

"Selene, it's me." Brandon's sexy voice washed over her.

She closed her eyes for a second. *I miss you, babe.* "What's up?"

"I decided to take off work an hour early today since my last client canceled. I should be able to get there by five-thirty if that's all right with everyone."

"That should be fine, honey," she said, mouthing 'thank you' to the clerk and tucking her credit card back into her purse.

"Um…" he broke off, cleared his throat, and tried again. "Do you think it would be all right if I spent the night? I don't like being separated from you. It feels wrong."

"I know what you mean," she told him fervently. "I don't think I slept a wink. I'll check, but unless you hear otherwise, assume that's the plan."

"Okay, great. Love you, Selene."

"Love you too." They hung up, and Selene continued on her shopping mall excursion, but the sadness in her beloved's voice took some of the sparkle out of the day. *I hate that I hurt him. I hope I can make it up to him soon.*

~

By midafternoon, exhaustion set in. Selene's aunt took one look at her pale face and drove them all home, where Selene napped for a couple of hours.

Waking alone again made her feel cross and grumpy. *I need Brandon. It was foolish to run off.* He wouldn't arrive for another hour or so, and Selene, not fit for human company, sequestered herself in the den, brainlessly flipping the television channels without really taking anything in. This freed her mind finally to address the issue she was facing. *Okay, I'm having Brandon's baby. I'm also twenty-eight years old and desperately in love with a wonderful man who loves me back. So why the hell did I freak out about it?* On the surface, one would think she should be delighted. *What about motherhood scares me so badly?*

Obviously, shock figured heavily into my reaction. She hadn't expected to find love, and thus she had never considered parenthood. This accounted for the panic attack… along with how sick she'd been, which had made her hysterical in its own right. Now, with the medicine calming her unsettled stomach, she became aware of a deeper antipathy fueling the nervous reaction. *Why does the very idea of motherhood make me cringe internally, to the extent that I still, to this day, call the only mother I've ever known Auntie and not Mom?*

She glanced across the room at the fireplace, her eyes flicking over the old family photos hung on the wall beside it. She'd spent years studying one in particular. The face looked like hers, but with dark brown eyes staring off into the distance. *Christine. The woman who gave birth to me and was driven to suicide within a week because of it.*

Selene clicked off the television and crossed the room, taking a closer look at the photos. *I was wrong to call Christine a woman. She was a child.* At fifteen, Selene had been in school, studying culinary arts and algebra and the ethics of psychic communication. She'd been surrounded by other children like herself. *It was a great blessing not to be alone at such an emotionally unstable time.* Christine's parents, as far as Selene knew, had encouraged her to bury and ignore her gift as if that were even possible. Denied the right to be herself, Christine had rebelled against her parents' expectations, which had led to her unplanned pregnancy.

Selene suddenly realized it wasn't motherhood that had driven Christine to suicide. Becoming a mother had only been the final nail in the coffin. She'd suffered so much from being different, from the pressure her family had placed on her, and from just being fifteen, which was hard on everyone. In fact, she'd been fifteen and pregnant. How difficult it must have been.

I'm different; healthier, stronger, and more mature than Christine. I conceived, not in an act of rebellion, but of love. I don't regret any part of my relationship with Brandon, not even this one. I can do this. Together we can and will be able to provide a loving and stable home for the child we made together. It will be all right.

Now that her sour mood had worn off, Selene began to feel excited about introducing Brandon to her family. *They'll like him. How can they not?*

Emerging from the den, she walked slowly through the house, feeling the weight of her history. *I was happy here once before I realized I was a freak, before that pastor called me a demon, and even sometimes after. In the future, I won't be such a stranger.*

Unable to remain inside despite the late summer heat, Selene pushed open the screen door and emerged onto the porch, where she took a seat on the top step. Karen and Paul soon joined her. Selene laid her head down on her aunt's knee, and Karen stroked her hair gently, letting the corn silk strands slide between her fingers.

Selene closed her eyes at the petting. "Auntie, I don't know if I ever thanked you."

"For what Selene?" Karen tucked a strand behind her niece's ear and Selene felt a quick flash of affection.

"For taking me in. You didn't have to. You had your whole life ahead of you. What must you have given up in order to become my mother?"

"Nothing of value. Not compared with what I've gained from having you."

Her kind words warmed her niece, and she continued. "And you, Uncle Paul, you had even less reason to take me on. Your girlfriend's abandoned baby niece. And you were always nice to me, even when I turned out to be so strange and difficult. You are truly a hero."

Paul colored a little. "You weren't difficult, you know. You're easy to love, Selene." He patted the back of her shirt.

"You were wonderful parents. I was lucky to have you."

"You'll be a wonderful parent too, honey," Karen reassured her.

"Auntie, what if my baby is gifted?" This last, lingering worry weighed on Selene's mind.

"Then you'll cope," Karen replied simply. "It's not easy, but it's not the worst thing ever. And parenthood in general isn't easy. You're gifted, but you're also a perfectly nice person, worth knowing. Besides, without your gift, the world would be a little sadder and darker, wouldn't it? Fewer criminals brought to justice. And your Brandon, could you relate to him so well, love him so well, if you couldn't do what you do? Imagine what you would lose if you didn't have it."

Selene blinked, considering the new concept. "I never thought of it like that."

"Well, if your baby is gifted, like you, then you'll still be a good mother, better than I was because you'll be able to relate."

Selene smiled. "That's what Brandon said."

"He's wise then," Karen said, and Selene's grin grew at her aunt's approval.

"I miss him."

"Well, I think he's here."

Sure enough, a silver pickup had arrived at the house. Selene jumped to her feet, the movement a little too quick for her overwhelmed senses, and she swayed. Uncle Paul anchored her with a hand on her arm. His pinky touched her skin, and she felt his concern for her. Once her balance stabilized, she hurried down the steps to Brandon as he climbed down from his truck.

He looked at her for a moment without moving. *He still isn't sure*, she realized, for once reading his expression instead of his touch. *My panic attack unnerved him*. Wanting to be at peace with him again, she threw herself at him, wrapping her arms around his neck and pulling him down for a kiss.

He enfolded her, and she closed her eyes. *How silly I was to look for answers away from this man. He's the answer to all my questions.* "I'm so glad you came. I've missed you, I love you so much," she babbled, pressing her lips over every inch of his face.

Brandon squeezed Selene a little tighter and then slid his hand down her arm to clasp her hand in his.

The complex swirl of emotions staggered her, but he didn't say a word. Through her palm, she could feel his distress and knew what it meant.

"Oh, Brandon, I'm so sorry, I just wanted to clear my head. I never meant you to think I was leaving for good. I got a little panicky about being pregnant, and I wanted to step out for a moment and think. I'm pretty sure I can't live without you."

"Good. That's the way it should be." He kissed her, hard, not caring that her aunt and uncle sat nearby, no doubt watching. She let him vent his confusing feelings without reservation on her lips and fingertips. Through this, she could sense their relationship stretching to new proportions.

"Okay, honey," Selene said after a moment. "We can continue this later. Right now, there are people I want you to meet."

"Okay." Brandon still smoldered into their joined hands, but he quickly suppressed it and walked with Selene to the front steps of her childhood home.

Karen and Paul turned out to be not much older than Brandon, certainly less than a decade. Karen greatly resembled Selene, to the extent that he could imagine what his girlfriend would look like in the future. *Pretty. Same petite stature, same kind expression.* Paul, tall and rather thickset in board shorts and a tee-shirt, ran his hand through salt-and-pepper hair and nailed Brandon with a stern but unreadable glare. *I can relate to these two. Like me, they were forced to step into parenthood when scarcely more than children. They seem happy and well adjusted.*

I wonder what they'll think about the girl they raised all grown up and bringing someone like me into their home. I hope they're not prejudiced.

"Auntie Karen, Uncle Paul, this is Brandon, my boyfriend," Selene said. Her smile shone brighter than the late summer sunset. "Brand, these are my aunt and uncle. They brought me up after my mother's…death."

Brandon shook hands with Selene's family, glad to know they didn't share her mind-reading ability.

"Pleased to meet you," Karen said warmly. "We're so happy Selene finally found someone who could accept her gift and see her for the wonderful woman she is."

Brandon smiled. "She's very special. I'm lucky to have her."

Paul looked less convinced. He scowled "I'm not sure I approve of you."

"Why is that?" Brandon said, hoping the reason was something that could be overcome, not just bigotry.

"Getting her pregnant is not the best way to begin a relationship." Paul steepled his fingers in front of his lips.

Ah, that makes sense. "You know, you're absolutely right. I do wish I had been more...careful. But she's irresistible, and I'm afraid I lost my head. I swear I'll do right by her, though."

"You'd better." Paul raised one dark eyebrow, his expression not softening one iota.

"Oh, stop growling, Uncle Paul," Selene said. "I did have some say in the matter."

The man glanced at his niece. She met his stare with a challenging expression. He sighed. "I suppose."

Just then two young women spilled out of the front door, eyeing Brandon and giggling. Rolling her eyes, Selene introduced her two cousins. "Brandon, these two airheads are Amy and Cherie."

They whined in protest, but Brandon only laughed, extending his hand to lovely young women who shared his beloved's pale coloring, though not her serene demeanor.

"Come on," Amy urged, grabbing Brandon by the arm. "We want to give you a tour." They pulled him into the house.

"Oh dear," Selene said as the door slammed shut behind them. "I'd better go rescue him."

"Wait a moment." Karen laid a restraining hand on her shirtsleeve. "They won't eat him."

"Are you sure?"

Karen ignored the quip. "Your Brandon, he's certainly not what I expected. He's very...beautiful though, isn't he?"

A dopey smile spread over Selene's face despite her desire to suppress it. "Yes. That's one thing about Brandon. He is beautiful. By the way, let's not have any talk of guest rooms or sleeping on the couch. Brandon stays with me. I can't sleep without him and I won't hear any objections on the subject." She gave her uncle a hard look.

He narrowed his eyes but remained silent.

"I can't imagine anyone would object too hard," Karen replied. "You two are a committed couple. You already act like you're married. You also have a baby on the way. What's left to protect you from?"

"You know, you're the second person in less than a week to suggest Brandon and I are already more or less married," Selene complained.

"Aren't you?" Karen pressed. "Mind you, I expect you to have a proper wedding ceremony eventually. But practically speaking, what's the difference?"

"None, really."

"I think you two might as well just get it over with," Paul groused. "There's no sense in waiting. Make it official."

"That's for Brandon to decide," Selene insisted. His first wife died, and it might be hard for him to commit to marriage again."

"You have a vote too," Paul pressed. "Men usually do what their women insist on."

"I'm lucky to have Brandon any way I can. I'm not going to put forth any ultimatums. Now if you'll excuse me, I need to see my man." She stalked through the door, her gait stiff with irritation.

"She's selling herself short," Paul observed, once Selene was out of earshot.

"I know," his wife replied, "but there's no way to tell her that. I suppose we should work on him instead."

"Do you want her to marry him?" Paul demanded.

"Is there any reason for her not to? She's an excellent judge of character," Karen reminded her husband.

"True. But I still don't like that she's already pregnant. It shows a certain lack of restraint." Paul frowned, worry about his niece creasing his features.

"They've known each other for several years," Karen pointed out. "Getting pregnant by someone you love, someone who's completely committed to you, isn't exactly a tragedy. Sometimes these things happen. It doesn't mean he'll be a bad husband."

Her husband raised one eyebrow. "We'll see."

"Watch it, Paul. It's her life. She's not a baby anymore."

CHAPTER 13

*A*fter dinner, washing the dishes, and extended conversations, Selene pleaded exhaustion and retired. Brandon intended to follow, but Karen stopped him. He felt no surprise that she and her husband wanted to talk to him alone.

"Well, Brandon," Karen said, her voice deceptively mild, "we have some questions for you."

He gave a humorless grimace. "Is this the speech about my intentions?"

"More or less," she concurred easily. "Because Selene always felt she was terribly different from everyone else, I don't think she was prepared for what a serious relationship might mean, and this one has progressed very rapidly, which is why she panicked so badly. Why are you rushing her?"

Rushing? Is that what they think? He exhaled heavily as he pondered his words. "Okay, that's a fair question. I'm not sure I intentionally rushed her, though. I've let her set the pace for the most part."

"Have you?" Karen continued. Her hazel eyes narrowed. "Remember, she knows what you're thinking. If she felt you wanted or needed something, she would probably try to give it to you, even if she wasn't ready. You're older than she is, and I imagine, capable of applying pressure so subtle she might not even realize it."

Ouch. Forcing down a wave of defensiveness so he could show he took their question seriously, Brandon carefully examined their relationship in silence. Then, he shook his head. "I realize what this must look like. Yes, I'm older than Selene, but she's no child. As for her being ready for a relationship, it was past time. She's been alone for far too long. I'm glad to be part of her life. I honestly don't think I'm putting any undue influences on her. I love her, and I want to be with her. She loves me, and she wants to be with me. It's as simple as that."

"So then, why aren't you engaged?" Karen demanded.

Brandon sighed, raking his fingers through his hair. "She's already overwhelmed. Won't proposing now be rushing?"

"The baby is on the way, Brandon," Paul pointed out. "She's already two months along. Did you know what she said, when we asked her the same question? She said she was waiting for you to be ready."

Brandon blinked in surprise. "Really? I didn't know that. I mean, I'm ready. I have a ring for her and everything. I was just waiting for some sign. Also, remember that we only found out about the baby yesterday."

Karen's face suddenly broke into a smile. "You already have a ring? Good. Consider this the sign."

Her apparent acceptance did not fool Brandon. *That's an order if I've ever heard one.* "Okay, I agree. I'll ask her right away. I wanted to anyway."

Eventually, Brandon managed to escape the harrowing conversation and find the bathroom. *It seems,* he thought as he brushed his teeth, *that I'll be welcomed into the family, but only if I make my relationship with Selene legal. Well, that's no problem.*

He had already talked to his parents, and while they expressed concern about him accidentally impregnating another girlfriend, they affirmed his desire to marry her. *Actually, they were delighted. Looks like Selene made a big impression on them.*

He flicked off the light and crossed the hall to the bedroom where the faint glow of a dim lamp set Selene's golden hair shining against a navy-blue sheet. He slipped into bed beside her, filling his arms with the warmth of her body. She cuddled against him.

"What's wrong, baby? Why are you awake?" he asked, touching his lips to her cheek.

"I can't sleep without you." She burrowed even closer. "Hmmm. My favorite place to be."

Brandon kissed her long and sweetly. She purred. He lowered his mouth again, this time passionately slipping his tongue between her lips. Selene felt more than ready to make love, her body heavy with desire, but Brandon pulled back. "I have to ask you something, baby."

She rubbed herself sinuously against him and reached for his hands, intending to place them where she wanted to be touched. He pulled back. "No, sweetheart, hold on. I need to do this the right way. Don't touch me for a second. I need to communicate with words."

"Okay. Talk away, but hurry, Brandon. I want you."

"Soon, real soon. Selene, I love you."

"I know you do. I love you too. Let me show you how much."

"Yes, but first let *me* show *you* how much."

Carefully sliding his hand close to hers, without letting even the tip of his finger brush her skin, he slid something onto her ring finger.

Selene stopped dead. Lifting her hand into the light from the lamp, she saw the fiery flash of a diamond; a good-sized solitaire circled all around with a band of glimmering emeralds.

"Oh, Brandon," she whispered, her eyes huge.

"Will you marry me?" he asked, his voice soft and tender.

"Is this because of the baby?"

He frowned and laid his hand on hers, sending irritation at her eternal lack of confidence. "No, Selene, because you're amazing. Because I love you. Because I've wanted to marry you all along. Remember the first morning after we got together? I told you that you were the woman I wanted for life. I meant it. For me, this relationship has never been about trying it out and seeing where it went. The reason we're together is because I wanted—intended—for you to be my wife. I tried to hold back on this last part because everything else came so quickly and I didn't want to overwhelm you. But I've been thinking about it, and really, I don't need to decide things for you. I'll just tell you what I want and let you choose what to do with it. If you don't want this Selene, tell me, I can take it. I would rather be your husband, but if that's not what you want, well, I'll take whatever I can get as long as I get to be part of your life."

"Brandon," Selene breathed, "how could I say anything but yes?"

Hope flared through her hand. "So, you'll marry me?"

"Yes. In a heartbeat."

"Because of the baby?" he quipped.

She giggled. "No, silly, because I love you too. We belong together. The only thing this baby changes is the timing, although honestly, you could have proposed the night of the fire, and I probably would have accepted."

"Really?"

"Really."

They sealed their betrothal with a kiss, and then another. The predictable ending was just as sweet as either of them could have imagined.

CHAPTER 14

*I*n the morning, Selene wanted to be radiant. She certainly felt happy enough, but her nausea rolled and churned so badly, she had to nibble a piece of bread to quiet her stomach enough to keep the medication down. As she waited on her first cup of coffee, Brandon walked into the kitchen and put his arms around her from behind. He laced the fingers of one hand through hers. His joy shimmered in her heart, echoing hers. She turned her head and kissed him deeply, over her shoulder. With her other hand, she caressed his cheek. The ring glittered in the morning sunlight.

"Look at them," Amy whispered from the living room doorway. "He's touching her. He seems totally okay with her reading his mind."

"Amy, stop staring," Karen scolded. "Of course, he must be at peace about her gift, otherwise they couldn't be together."

"Did you see her ring?"

"Yes, dear. It's lovely."

198

"I think Brandon is lovely." Amy smirked.

"Well, yes, perhaps he is."

Selene and Brandon each grabbed a cup of coffee and joined Amy and Karen in the living room, still holding hands.

"That's a great ring, Selene." Amy cooed.

"Thanks. Brandon has excellent taste."

"It matches her eyes." Brandon said, matter-of-factly, "and it reminded me of her. She's one of a kind."

She smiled crookedly. "Right now, I suppose the emeralds match my face as well."

"Yes, dear, you are a little green. Don't worry. The morning sickness doesn't last forever," Karen said soothingly.

"I would like it best if it didn't last another day," Selene complained.

"You'll survive. Have you two thought about a wedding date?"

Brandon looked at Selene but didn't say anything.

"What about mid-October?" Selene suggested. "I love the fall, and the leaves should be glorious."

"So soon?" Her aunt regarded her with wide eyes.

"Why wait? As everyone is so fond of pointing out, we're practically married already. And there's the question of fitting into a wedding dress. What do you think, honey?"

"Whatever you want is fine with me. I have no objection to October." Brandon sipped his coffee, tracing little patterns on Selene's hand with the tip of his thumb.

"Great." Selene beamed. "Brandon, do you think your pastor, the one I met the other day, would perform the ceremony?"

"I'm sure he would," he said, smiling a little distractedly. His expression had a hint of the *weddings are for women* air about it.

199

"Outside?" Selene pressed.

"Outside in October?" Amy asked, startled by the thought.

"Why not?"

"It might be cold." Karen pointed out gently.

"That's okay," Selene countered with a shrug. "I'm tired of the heat. An afternoon wedding outside in October should be nice. There's this place by the lake, where the trees meet overhead like a canopy. It's beautiful, and there's an open space nearby where we could put some chairs for the guests."

"I know where you mean," Brandon replied, a bit more attentively. "Are you sure it's big enough for a whole wedding?"

"How big a group are you thinking of?" Puzzled, she turned to meet his gaze.

"The police force is pretty big," he pointed out.

"Oh, I wouldn't invite everyone." Selene laughed, gesturing with her mostly empty cup. "Only the few closest to me. Chief Brady, Tony, a couple of the others. Oh, and you guys too, of course." She indicated her aunt and cousin. "I think I only have about ten people I would want to be there. Brandon, would it be weird if my attendant was a guy?"

"Tony?" Brandon guessed.

"Yeah, he's a really good friend," Selene confirmed.

"That's true. Well if Tony stands up with you, Maggie can stand up with me. And I would invite a couple of people from work, my parents, and a few friends from the reservation, so I think about ten also.

"Please, not Barbara." They both laughed.

Amy gave Selene a quizzical look, which she ignored.

"Oh," Selene added, setting her cup on the coffee table and toying with her ring. "Maggie's boyfriend is finally coming back from Sweden for a visit. I think he might be here right at that time."

"She hasn't really been happy since he left, has she?"

Brandon said, off-handedly, gulping the last of his tepid drink.

"No, I think she loves him."

"Who's Maggie?" Amy asked.

"My daughter," Brandon replied. "She's twenty-two."

Amy did a visible mental calculation and her eyes widened, but all she said was, "Me too. It's a good age."

"Auntie Karen," Selene returned to the pressing topic, "Do you think a wedding with twenty guests or so is weird?"

"If people can elope and have strangers as witnesses, then I don't see why a small guest list is wrong. Anyway, you'll save a fortune on food and cake and champagne."

"No champagne," Selene said firmly. "If I can't have any, no one else can either. We'll toast in sparkling cider."

"Maybe we should toast in mulled cider," Brandon suggested. "I'm sure the guests would appreciate a hot drink."

"What a great idea, honey."

They continued to chat, planning out their day. Selene could feel herself glowing. She had never been so happy.

CHAPTER 15

"*R*emind me why we're here," Selene whined, frowning at the stuffily decorated salon. From every corner, a dizzying number of white and ivory gowns hung in clear garment bags. Selene could see racks of lace and ruffles everywhere, like meringue piled on top of a pie, but nothing that would suit her.

"Because you're getting married in less than two months," Aunt Karen said dryly. "Are you planning to go naked?"

"I bet she'd go in a police uniform if she had one," Maggie suggested, wrinkling her nose at Selene.

"Why can't I just get a dress from the department store?" she suggested. "This place is so expensive, especially for a dress I'll only wear once!"

Cherie rolled her eyes. "A *discount* bridal store is too expensive? Just imagine what would happen if you went to a true boutique."

"My dear," Elizabeth said gently, "you and Brandon have planned a lovely, small wedding. You only have twenty guests, you're making your own snacks, and your family will be playing the music. Brandon even said one of your police friends will be taking the pictures. You can afford a nice, simple wedding dress. Why not treat yourself to something pretty?"

Thwarted, unwilling to argue with her future mother-in-law, Selene stuck her lips out and quit complaining. *I wish I could leave.*

"So, who's the bride here?" A woman of around fifty, with tightly curled hair and a brisk, competent air, drew close. Selene noticed that her nametag read 'Mary.' She regarded the group, nearly salivating at the sight of Maggie's tall, statuesque figure and dark good looks.

"I am." Selene stood.

"Oh." Mary blinked as though startled by the contrast. "Well yes, certainly. Hello, my dear. What is your name?"

"I'm Selene. This is my best friend Maggie, my Aunt Karen, and my future mother-in-law, Elizabeth."

"Pleased to meet you all," she said from a safe distance, not offering to shake hands. "So, Selene, tell me a little about your wedding," Mary requested, perching one fist on her hip.

"It's going to be very small. Only about twenty guests or so, outside under the trees. It's also in six weeks, so I don't have time to order anything."

The consultant's eyes widened. "Actually, if you choose one today, there should be just enough time for any alterations before the wedding, and I suspect you will need alterations."

Selene agreed. "There's no doubt about it. Okay, here's the thing. I don't wear dresses much. I'm a police officer, you know? So I'm not all that girly. I'm also short. Even in heels, I probably won't top 5'4. I don't want anything ruffled or puffy that will overwhelm me."

Maggie rolled her eyes at Selene's blunt assessment of herself.

Whatever, girl. You're so beautiful it hurts to look at you, Selene thought. *Not all of us are so blessed.*

"I can see that," Mary said, eyeing Selene's petite stature

with a considering air. "What about something fitted? Sheath dresses are very popular right now. The shape would suit you well."

"That might be tricky." Selene's cheeks prickled with embarrassed heat, but she pressed on. "I'll be about five months pregnant by the time we get married, and a sheath dress is unlikely to fit by then." She took a deep breath and continued. "I don't care if I look pregnant. Everyone who'll be there already knows. I just want to be sure, having spent the money on a dress, that I'll be able to fasten it on the day." Unconsciously, her hand went to her belly. Though invisible under clothes, she thought she could perceive a tiny change there. She met the consultant's eyes.

Mary seemed unfazed by the information. *As if she would be. I'm sure she's seen a pregnant bride before.* "Very understand-able," the woman said mildly. "And what is your budget?"

"I'd like to stay under five hundred dollars," Selene said.

Mary blinked. "Well, we can certainly accommodate your price range. The style however might be tricky. Let me think…" She tapped one pink, artificial nail on her front teeth. "Not full, not ruffled, not fitted. Give me a moment and I'll pull the dresses we have that might work, but there won't be many. If you don't like any of them, we may have to rethink one of the requirements. Oh, by the way, dear, white or ivory?"

"With my coloring? NOT white!" Selene exclaimed. "I'll disappear. Oh, but if there's some color on the dress, like an accent, that would be nice."

Mary nodded. "All right, come with me."

She led Selene into a fitting room and returned a short time later with three dresses. The first two Selene rejected out of hand. One featured heavy pleating, and she could just imagine how much like a beach ball she would look with her belly spreading out the folds. She shook her head. The other seemed more promising, although gleamed in a snowy white. She lifted the heavy satin in her arms and carried it towards the mirror. Glancing down at the garment made her stop dead in her tracks. *It's worse than I imagined. Instead of making me disappear, the fabric gives my skin a sickly yellow tone.*

"No, thank you," she said gently, handing Mary the dress. Their hands brushed accidentally beneath the fabric and Selene learned that Mary, far from offended, completely agreed with her assessment.

The third gown differed from the first two. Made of chiffon instead of satin, it draped over her body lightly. The bodice—adorned with sheer, full-length sleeves—formed a low square across her chest, but the best feature was the high waistline. It tightened just under her breasts with a band of golden flowers in what Mary called Empire style. Below the flowers, the dress flowed loosely to the floor in a soft spill that neither clung to her body nor floated away from it, instead resting lightly on each curve.

Selene looked at herself in the mirror and a slow smile spread across her face. "Yes, I like this. It feels right."

"Shall we show your group?" Mary suggested.

"Of course," Selene agreed, opening the fitting room door. Outside, she stood in front of her friends and family on the stage, surrounded by mirrors that shot her image in all directions.

"Well, what do you think?" Selene asked.

"You look comfortable in it," Maggie said.

"Yes, I am."

"It's very suitable for the kind of wedding you're planning, isn't it?" Elizabeth commented. "Especially those flowers. They match your color scheme very well."

"I like it," Karen said.

The dress turned out to be on clearance, a leftover from last summer, so even the price was perfect. *It's still a pinch to write a check for over three hundred dollars, but I'm satisfied. I want to be married to Brandon, and now I'm much closer to my dream.*

CHAPTER 16

*T*he clock on Brandon's bedside read one forty-five in the morning when the phone rang. Brandon and Selene lay sound asleep, Selene tucked like a spoon, as usual, in the curve of her lover's body.

"Hello?" he said sleepily.

Selene could hear Maggie's voice on the other end, slurred and semi-coherent.

"Sorry, Dad, didn't want to wake you. I've had waaaaay too much to drink. There's no way I can drive home. Could you please come and get me?"

"Yes, okay, Maggie… Where are you? …I'll be right there." He hung up the phone and touched Selene gently on the arm. "Come on, baby."

"I'm half-asleep, Brandon," Selene whined. "Do I have to go? Can't I go back to sleep? Just to make sure the alarm is armed before you leave."

"Are you sure, baby?"

"Yes."

"I'll be back as soon as I can." He kissed her and departed.

Selene drowsed a bit after Brandon left, but settling into a deep sleep proved impossible with the chilliness of the empty bed biting at her. The further they progressed into September, the colder it grew, especially at night, and the more she appreciated Brandon's cuddling. She was sleeping better overall, whether it was because she felt so comfortable with her life, or because she had finally passed into the second trimester of pregnancy, and was no longer sick all the time, she wasn't sure. Her body was starting to change though, which she found disconcerting. Her breasts had grown much bigger, which Brandon enjoyed this very much. Her waist was also thickening. Soon she would have to put away her normal-sized clothing. *I'm not sure, but I think I might be feeling the baby move a little sometimes. It tickles.*

She had just about decided to give up trying to sleep and turn on the lamp to read when the motion light in the backyard clicked on. Lying still in the bed, Selene stared at the blinds. Clearly outlined beyond the window stood the silhouette of a man. She could see the shadowy figure raise his arm to the level of the bed.

Moving as quietly as possible, Selene pulled the Beretta out of its holster on the headboard and slipped to the floor, taking the cell phone with her. As she crept through the open bedroom door, two shots rang out, striking the headboard right above where she'd been lying. She crawled to the guest bedroom, shut the door, and speed-dialed Tony's number.

"Guido," barked the gruff answer.

"Tony, it's Selene," she whispered. "He's back. He just fired a gun into my bedroom."

"Where are you?"

"In the guest room."

"Can you get outside? Go to the neighbors?"

"I don't know where he is." Even her whisper seemed to be whimpering. "What if he's outside?"

"I'm already on my way. I'll be there as fast as I can. Stay on the line."

"Okay."

The unmistakable sound of glass falling to the floor preceded the wail of the alarm. Selene's breathing quickened as she heard the thud of a heavy person landing in her bedroom.

"What's happening?" Tony demanded.

"He's inside the house," she breathed. "He broke the window."

"I'm on your street. I'm almost there. I'll find you."

"How will I know it's you? I don't want to shoot you by mistake!"

"You have your service weapon?"

"Yes," Selene whispered. The hand holding her gun shook.

"Good girl. When I open the door, I'll say 'Police'. If you don't hear it, shoot."

"Okay." Selene whimpered again. She crouched on the floor beside the guest room door, at an angle where she wouldn't be seen immediately if the door opened. With trembling hands, she aimed the weapon and waited. *At this rate, I'll never be able to shoot straight.*

Something soft brushed against her ankle and she started violently, but it was only Sammy. Somehow the little cat's presence soothed her. *I'm not a coward hiding in the corner. I'm a policewoman and I've been trained to deal with situations like this.* "Get a grip," she told herself silently, reaching out to run her fingers through Sammy's silky, silver-blue fur. The touch steadied her hands, and she resumed her defensive position.

"I know you're in here, bitch." A harsh voice rang through the house. "You can't hide forever." At the sound, Sammy streaked under the bed and hid.

Selene concentrated on breathing as silently as possible, but her heart pounded so hard, she wondered if the whole street could hear it.

The doorknob slowly rotated. Selene took a deep breath,

trying to steady her hands. The door opened. She waited a split second longer, but no identifying shout emerged. She could see, outlined in the darkness, the distinctive swooping hairstyle she had identified on the surveillance video.

Selene pulled the trigger.

From this angle, the shot appeared to hit the intruder directly in the hip. He groaned, going down hard. She jumped up and kicked the gun out of his hand.

The front door exploded inward as the call of "Police!" rang through the house. The intruder staggered to his feet, pushing Selene roughly to one side, and limped back towards the bedroom. She fired another round after him but couldn't tell in the dark whether she hit her target or not.

Lights flooded the house as Tony burst through, hitting switches as he went. He found Selene standing in the guest room doorway, aiming her gun down the hall, a puddle of blood at her feet. She could hear the assailant running, dragging his wounded leg with incredible speed across the wood floors. With a grunt that seemed to signify he had leaped out the window, the intruder fled.

Rather than pursue him, Tony grabbed Selene in a fierce hug. "Are you all right, girl? Is that blood yours?"

"No, I shot him. Get him, Tony, don't let him escape. I'm fine."

Tony raced after the suspect as more police, summoned by the alarm, burst into the room. Finding only one small, pregnant woman in her pajamas seemed to disappoint them, and several hurried out the back door to see if they could catch the perpetrator. Moments later, the cops returned to the house, led by Tony. All of them looked dejected.

"We didn't get him, Selene," her friend groused. "The bastard had a car in the alley. He must have stood on it to climb in. No plates. We're back at square one."

"It's okay, Tony. We have his blood everywhere. Now we can finally find out who he is."

"What if he's not in the system?"

"It doesn't matter," Selene retorted. "If it's this personal for him, he has to have a close relative who is."

"Selene, you can't be here while we process the scene," Tony pointed out. "You're too close. So am I for that matter. Let me take you back to the station. You can give a statement. Now could you please put down the gun?"

"Oh." She lowered the weapon.

Bubbling with adrenaline, Selene chattered inanely most of the way to work.

"It feels bizarre to be heading to the station in pajamas," she commented from the passenger seat of Tony's squad car.

"I'm sure." His eyes remained fixed on the road.

"Wish I'd had time to change… but wait, I couldn't, could I? My bedroom is a crime scene."

"That's right." They pulled into the parking lot. Selene attempted to jump out of the car, but her legs wobbled. Tony wrapped an arm around his waist. This close, she could hear his harsh respirations.

"Wouldn't want to be wading in blood and broken glass to get out some jeans and a tee-shirt." She giggled. *I need to stop babbling.* Her mouth refused to cooperate. "I don't think it would be possible to put any more of my fingerprints in there though."

"They'll eliminate yours," Tony pointed out as he dragged open the heavy glass door and ushered her inside.

I knew that. "Oh, yes, that's right."

"She all right?" Brady met them at the door.

"Yeah," Tony grunted in reply.

"You sure? There's blood on her."

Selene looked down at the fine mist splattered down the front of her tank top and shorts and began to giggle. The giggle rapidly transformed into a sob.

"She says she shot him," Tony explained, his arm tightening around her waist.

"Well, she's acting weird. Joe was a paramedic before he went into law enforcement. Get him over here, would you?"

"Sure thing, boss. Come on, Selene. Let's find you somewhere to sit."

CHAPTER 17

*M*aggie emerged from the bathroom, wiping her mouth. Brandon extended a cup of water and two aspirin. "How are you doing now?" he asked, one eyebrow stuck in an expression of ongoing disapproval.

"I feel like hell," she croaked.

"You deserve it," he replied bluntly. "You know better than to drink to excess. What on earth possessed you?"

Her eyes skated away from his, and then she groaned and laid a hand on her forehead. "Skip it, okay, Dad?" she asked.

"I don't think so. You know, I was worried about you. Alcohol poisoning can be deadly. I'm glad to hear you talking more or less normally. Still, you dragged me out of my warm bed, away from my warm fiancée, to pick up your drunk ass."

She rolled her eyes and then squeaked in pain. "Let's skip that too, okay? I still don't want the details."

Brandon ignored her request. "And then, I drove you from that seedy apartment back to your townhouse. You almost puked in my truck. You've been throwing up ever since. For *two hours*. Are you safe now? Can I go home? I have to work tomorrow."

"Call in," she suggested. "I plan to."

"You should go in, hangover and all," he suggested.

"Go to hell, Dad," Maggie snapped. "I'm going to bed."

"Keep your phone on the nightstand," he ordered. "Don't roll your eyes at me. You'll only give yourself a headache. And I'm not kidding. You're not out of the woods yet."

"I'm fine, Dad. Go home. Cuddle your woman." She pursed her lips, belched, and wiped her mouth again.

"With such a charming invitation, how can I do otherwise?" Brandon replied, scowling. "I'll see you later, Maggie." He turned to leave.

"Oh, Dad?"

He glanced over his shoulder.

"Thanks."

With a nod, Brandon exited the townhouse and hopped into his pickup.

He blinked hard as the road wavered and dimmed in front of him. *It's hell trying to stay awake and drive at almost four in the morning.* Only by visualizing Selene waiting in bed for him was he able to proceed safely.

Until he arrived to see his house surrounded by police cars, lights flashing, and the front door smashed open. He shook himself to be sure the image hadn't come from a half-drowsing nightmare, but the cars did not disappear. *Oh, Lord, what is this?* Brandon stepped out of his car numbly and staggered into the house.

He found two technicians collecting blood samples in the hallway. *Blood!* The sight obliterated his lingering exhaustion. "Oh, God, Selene! Selene, where are you?" he called, panic growing with each word, each step. The technician looked up. "What's going on?" he asked them sharply.

"Sir, you can't be in here," one of the technicians said, rising and blocking Brandon's approach into the bedroom.

"This is my house," he protested, still trying to progress past the young woman. "What's going on? Where's Selene?"

214

"Your wife? She's not here," the technician said. She squeezed his arm, trying to get his attention.

"Not here? Where? At the hospital? What's going on? Whose blood is that?" His words tumbled over each other. "Is she all right?"

"I don't know, sir, I'm sorry. I'm just collecting evidence," the woman said.

"Kelly, I have enough here," the other technician—older and male, with a puff of silver hair fluffing out the sides of his white plastic hood—offered. "Let me drive him to the station. He can find out what's going on there. Come on, sir."

In the police car, Brandon slumped limply against the passenger seat. *I shouldn't have left her. What if she's injured? Worse? I buried one woman I loved. Losing this woman will bury me.*

He had worked himself into a terrible state by the time they arrived at the station. He stared blankly at the plastic-guarded booth.

"I'll buzz you in, Mr. Price," the young man, whose name he could not remember, said gently.

The first person he saw was Tony, standing outside Chief Brady's office. Brady stood inside, his hair uncombed, shouting incoherently into the telephone. The whole station seemed in chaos, cops racing this way and that, phones ringing. Striding quickly through the room, he grabbed Tony hard by the arm. "Where's Selene?"

Tony jumped and then turned, surprise fading to understanding in his eyes. "Calm down, Brandon. She's fine."

"There was blood." His voice sounded like a lost child in his ears.

"The bastard came back. She shot him."

"Where is she?"

"She's in the break room. Come on." He led Brandon through the central room and an innocuous door labeled staff.

Inside Selene sat on a cheap-looking fake leather sofa, holding a Styrofoam coffee cup with shaking hands.

"The paramedics have checked her out and she's fine. He never even touched her."

Brandon walked slowly towards Selene, not quite believing she was alive, much less unharmed. "Baby?" he said softly.

Her head shot up. "Oh, Brandon! Oh, honey, you're here." The cup fell from her hand as she launched herself into his arms. He crushed her to him, unable to speak. She urged him down on the sofa and slithered into his lap. He rested his head on her chest, breathing hard and shaking.

She hugged him tight, stroking his hair and his back, trying to break through, but it was no use. So, she just held him and whispered, "It's okay, baby. I'm fine. I'm not hurt. It's okay. It's okay."

No one dared to tell them how inappropriate it was for her to be sitting on his lap in the police station, his head against her chest. All Selene's friends understood how close they had come to losing one another that night, and they all could relate to the imminent presence of death, and its impact on those who survive.

CHAPTER 18

*H*ours later, a quiet Chief Brady drove them home, furious the suspect had escaped but pleased so much physical evidence had been found. He dropped them off at around seven in the morning.

They stumbled in the door, adrenaline gone, and fatigue warring with a goodly bit of fear. The evidence had been collected, but nothing had been cleaned up.

Selene stared at the mess of blood and dirty footprints in the hallway and frowned. *The master bedroom must be a shambles—broken glass and bullet holes.* In her exhausted state, all she could think about was finding a clean bed to crash in. She stumbled on her way to the guest bedroom, Brandon trailing behind her like a sleepwalker. He ran into her back when she pulled up short, dismayed at the sight of a deep puddle of blood on the floor.

Where did he not go? The only room left was Maggie's old room, with its small bed and pink bedspread, but she didn't care. Dragging feet that no longer wanted to lift, she entered the room and heaved a huge sigh of relief that it looked clean and untouched. Swallowing hard, she tore off her bloody pajamas and hurled them in a heap on the floor. *How did this disaster become my life? Good God.* She sank to a seat on the edge of the bed. *Only a double but being close to Brandon will feel good.*

Brandon slowly dropped his jeans and tee-shirt to the floor, still looking a little out of it. Selene grasped his arm and drew him to the bed. "Sleep, honey. You'll feel better."

Brandon froze, staring into her eyes. His lethargy burned away, replaced by a manic fire. "No, not yet. Not yet. I need you."

"Okay," she agreed easily, his desire quickly igniting her own. *We're alive. We made it.* She lay back on the bed and he stretched out beside her. Hauling her tight against his body, Brandon claimed her lips with his. She caressed and fondled him, making him ready while he kissed and stroked her. Finally, she pulled him on top of her, feeding his sex into her body.

"Are you sure you're all right, baby?" he asked in that lost-sounding voice.

"Yes, I'm fine. Now love me, Brandon. Love me hard. I need you too."

He began to thrust deep, pounding into her. "God, I thought I had lost you."

"I know. I'm sorry, I didn't think."

"You shot him?" he pressed.

"Yes. I wish I'd killed him."

"Me too. Will this ever end?"

"We have his DNA. We can catch him now."

"Selene…"

"Stop talking and make love to me."

"I love you."

"I love you too."

For a long time, there was only the slap of flesh on flesh as they claimed each other hard and deep, reaffirming life in the face of terror. This time, when Selene came, she really did scream. Brandon groaned loudly in his climax. They fell asleep almost immediately afterward.

At around noon, the phone rang.

Selene fumbled on the floor until she found her purse and extracted it. Pressing the button, she groaned into the receiver. The person on the other end also emitted a pained exhalation.

"Maggie?" Selene asked, slowly. Her head swam, and she sank to the floor, leaning her back against the side rail of the bed. Brandon snored on, oblivious.

"Yeah. Shoot me now."

"You sick?"

Maggie groaned again, and the sound could have come from the pit of hell. "Hungover. I don't even know how much I had to drink. I'm sorry for inter... inter...the late-night call."

"It's okay." Selene pronounced each word carefully, not certain how effectively she'd be able to communicate. "Actually, it's good you did." Even as exhausted as Selene still felt, she knew that didn't sound right.

"What? Ooooh," Maggie's exclamation must have come too fast.

I bet her head is pounding. "Yeah, someone broke into the house and tried to shoot me. If you hadn't woken us up ahead of time, we'd probably both be dead."

"Oh, God," Maggie replied. Though her voice sounded like one long groan, she managed to focus on the conversation. "I'm glad you're okay. You are okay, right?"

"Yeah, no one's hurt. The place is a mess though."

"I'll be there as soon as I can."

About an hour later, wearing dark sunglasses, Maggie arrived to help sweep up the debris. Opening to her knock,

SIMONE BEAUDELAIRE

Selene grabbed her friend in a tight hug. The women squeezed each other for long moments.

"I'm so sorry this happened," Maggie told her.

"Hey, it's just stuff," Selene replied. "Everyone survived."

"Thank God."

"Does God use binges?" Selene quipped.

"God works in mysterious ways," Brandon called from the other room.

Maggie grinned, then winced, her arms crossing over her stomach. "My dad is amazing."

"I'm not going to argue with you. Um, not that I'm complaining, Maggie, but what on earth were you doing? You never get drunk."

"I called Jan. I asked if we could get back together, but I felt guilty about misleading him." Maggie sank onto the living room sofa, her head in her hands.

"Oh, Lord. And?"

"And I told him about Jason," she mumbled. "He's thinking about it. Did you expect him to be happy?"

"No. Oh, Maggie. I wish I could tell you it would all work out," Selene cried.

"I know." Maggie gingerly shook her head. "I knew I was risking everything when I told him, but I couldn't lie, so now I might lose the man I love for good. Everything's gone to shit."

"It has," Selene agreed.

They regarded each other in mute suffering for a long moment. Though each woman had ample cause to be unhappy, Selene could feel the frayed edges of their friendship knitting back together. "Well," Maggie said at last, "let's not sit around when there's work to be done."

"Right. Here's a dustpan. Let's get rid of that glass before someone gets cut."

Miraculously, Sammy hadn't escaped through the broken window. Brandon nailed up boards until a new one could be purchased. The headboard was destroyed, but at least there were no bullet holes in the wall. They got out rags and buckets and scrubbed the blood from the floor and walls. When they finished, Selene felt satisfied the house had become habitable again, but she knew none of them would feel comfortable until the stalker was captured.

CHAPTER 19

*T*he lab rushed the DNA evidence through the system and a short time later identified a suspect; a near relative of one James Flannery, recently released after serving time for manslaughter.

"*That* guy?" Selene exclaimed, stunned by the text she received during their wedding rehearsal dinner.

"What?" Brandon wanted to know, leaning over her arm to peer at the screen of her cell phone.

She showed him the message. "He was brought in for a hit and run but confessed to killing a woman accidentally. It was a really weird case."

Brandon lowered his eyebrows, concentrating. "You know, I think I saw the video of the interrogation. Brady showed it to me once. The guy was desperate to confess. He was just waiting for the opportunity. Someone thinks *that* confession was coerced?"

"The chief says it seems likely the stalker is his brother, William Flannery, called Billy. He's much younger than James. He attends college about three hours away, and he kind of hero-worships his brother. He's been in and out of town because he has to go back to attend classes and only comes here between terms, and sometimes on weekends. That's why so much time passed between incidents. He's also missing. Here's his picture." She swiped the screen until it showed an average-looking young man with dark hair gelled into a swooping style. She continued, "If the asshole has any sense, he's gone to Mexico and will never come back."

"I wouldn't count on it," Tony called from the next table. "He's been pretty determined so far."

Selene made a face. "True. Well, he'd better not turn up tomorrow. I have plans."

"And what would those be?" Brandon asked, teasing her, trying to recapture the joyous mood.

She smirked, accepting the distraction. "Oh, I'm getting married."

"Yeah, anyone I know?" He waggled his eyebrows.

"Just think of the most beautiful, kindhearted, courageous, loving Lakota man you can imagine."

Brandon grinned. "Funny thing, I'm getting married tomorrow too."

"Really?" Her eyes widened in feigned surprise.

"Yes. You see, I met this beautiful girl. She's got the courage of a lion. I don't think I could live without her, and I'm sure I don't want to try."

"You don't have to." She leaned over and kissed him as Tony and the other police officers hooted and catcalled. Since the incident, they had all unofficially adopted Brandon, and he suddenly found he had a bunch of new friends. *And I'm getting married tomorrow. If only they could catch Billy and lock him up, everything would be perfect.*

CHAPTER 20

*T*he next morning, Brandon's parents picked him up early and took him to their house, so he could get ready and leave Selene in peace.

Twenty minutes later, Maggie, Karen, Amy and Cherie arrived. They helped Selene into her dress and then Cherie twisted Selene's white-gold mane into a complicated braid down the back. She threaded with long-stemmed orange and gold mums.

Selene walked over to the mirror to put on her makeup. "Wow, this looks great. Thanks."

In the reflection, Cherie beamed. "Who knew a semester of high school cosmetology could come in so handy to a future lawyer?"

Selene giggled.

Now that the moment had arrived, she felt a little teary, but she held it together, even as she admired her reflection. The alterations on the gown had been finished exactly two days before the wedding, and it fit perfectly, just long enough to sweep the ground around her ballet flats. The bodice had been loosened quite a bit to accommodate her swelling breasts, and under the high waistband, the fabric draped flatteringly over the curve of her belly, not so much concealing as decorating the little bulge. *I look like a pregnant bride, but what does it matter? This kind of thing has been going on since the dawn of time.*

Leaving the bathroom, she dropped into a seat on the sofa beside her aunt. The baby squirmed, and Selene grabbed Karen's hand and pressed it to the spot. She could feel the awe in her aunt's thoughts and released her quickly, not wanting to intrude.

"You look beautiful, honey," Karen said. "Shall we get going?"

The ladies loaded the trays of finger sandwiches and several jugs of cider into Karen's minivan and drove down to the park. The sun shone, slanting golden beams down through the canopy of leaves as they placed gold and orange tablecloths on the tables in the pavilion and arranged the trays. Finally, it was nearly time to start, and Karen and her daughters went to tune their instruments. Selene waited in the pavilion with Tony and tried not to chew on her nails.

"Don't worry. He'll show," her friend said.

"Of course, he will." *I have no concern about that. Of course, he'll show up. He wants this as much as I do.*

"He loves you, you know."

Selene smiled. "I know."

"And he's a good guy. Aren't you glad you took my advice?" He winked.

"Yeah, look how well that worked." She indicated her swollen belly.

"I never told you to get knocked up, dummy."

Selene laughed, hitting him with her bouquet.

"Hey, take it easy on that thing. It won't hold."

"It'll hold long enough to thrash you." She couldn't stop smiling until her face hurt with it.

"Mr. Guido, it's time," Maggie said, interrupting their

banter. She looked regal in a scarlet dress, and she hugged Selene. "I'll be back for you in a minute."

Abruptly, Selene found herself alone. *Soon I'll never be alone again. I'll be part of a marriage, a family.* She ran her hand over her belly, thinking her life had never seemed so full before. *Oh, I was busy with work, to be sure, but busyness is not the same thing as fullness. It's hard to believe that only a few months ago, I only had one friend who wasn't a police officer and indulged in secret fantasies about that friend's father. Now I'm was about to marry him, and I'll soon bring his child into the world.* Selene closed her eyes and saw a vision of herself, sitting in a rocking chair, her belly large with child. She rocked gently, singing a quiet song to…another child. In her arms, she held a little boy, no more than two years old, with a shock of wild black hair and copper skin. He slept peacefully with his cheek on her shoulder, a thumb in his mouth. She rubbed his little back in soothing circles and finally kissed the top of his head. Hefting the toddler, she tucked him into a small bed with a red car on the blanket, patted herself on the belly, and left the room.

She knew instinctively that this vision was true. *So, I'll give Brandon two children, and the first at least—like his daughter—will wear their proud heritage for all to see. I have the privilege of bringing that beautiful little boy into the world.* Joy beyond anything she'd ever dared allowed herself to imagine welled up in her. She patted her belly gently. "Come on, little man," she whispered. "I have a date with your daddy, and I don't want to be late."

Maggie returned, beckoning to Selene. They walked together across the lawn to the rear edge of the golden yellow runner, which had been laid down between the two sections of seats. There, Uncle Paul waited to escort the bride. Selene's family picked up their instruments and began to play the Pachelbel Canon, and Maggie walked down the aisle, carrying a knot of golden mums. Instead of walking to the bride's side, she went to her father.

Tony already stood at the front, waiting to support Selene. Brandon looked gorgeous in his black slacks, white shirt, and blazer. In deference to his heritage, he wore a string tie with an elaborate, beaded clasp.

He's waiting for me. Waiting to become my husband.

The music didn't change as she took her uncle's arm and they walked slowly towards the moment she'd never dared dream about. At the altar, Paul kissed her on the cheek and handed her to Brandon, who took her arm. His hand covered hers, and while Pastor Otten began the wedding service, Brandon sent Selene a quick thought. ***I'm so glad this day has finally come.***

Her smile turned radiant. Time seemed to shift and fade around them so that seconds became hours, and yet Selene blinked in surprise when the time arrived to say their vows.

"I, Brandon David, take you, Selene Alexandra, to be my wedded wife…" She could hear the words with her ears and her heart.

"I, Selene Alexandra, take you, Brandon David, to be my husband…" the wonder of the moment shone through in her soft tone.

Off to the side, holding her violin, Auntie Karen wept into a handkerchief, as befitted her role as mother of the bride. Brandon's mother looked a little misty too.

"I now pronounce you husband and wife. You may kiss the bride."

Brandon touched his lips to Selene's in an embrace of aching tenderness as the trio struck up a wedding march by Mendelssohn, the traditional departure music. They walked back down the aisle together towards the new life that awaited them. *All is not perfect in our world, but at least we're married, and for today, it's enough.*

CHAPTER 21

"*D*o you think," Selene joked as she unbraided her hair, removing several wilting mums, "people might guess we've had sex before tonight?"

"Oh, I don't think so," Brandon replied, unbuttoning his shirt and hanging it up in their bedroom closet. "Everyone knows I'm a virgin."

Selene giggled. "Is that right? Well, I'm not. I guess it's up to me to be sure everything goes all right." Her dress slithered to the floor, followed quickly by her undergarments.

"Are you up to it?"

"I am. The question is, are *you* up to it?"

He looked down the midline of his body at the bulge straining his trousers and lied, laughing. "Sadly, no. But I know someone who can change that."

"Really?" She boldly unfastened his pants, letting them fall to the floor, and slid her hand into his underwear. "Who could that be?" She caressed his sex with expert care. It hardened further.

"Oh, Selene," he groaned. "Sweet wife. That feels amazing."

"It should. You taught me how to do it."

"Show me more."

She lowered his underwear to the floor and knelt before him, kissing the sensitive tip. He groaned with pleasure as she tasted and licked him. Then she opened her mouth wider and worked her way down from far as along the shaft as she could go without choking. She clutched his buttocks with both hands and squeezed gently, running her nails over his skin

He shivered, enjoying the stimulation for several minutes. "Please stop, baby," he said finally. "I don't want to finish this way tonight."

Selene let him go, smirking at how easily she could make this beautiful, mature, experienced man come to the brink of losing control.

"Now it's your turn." Brandon scooped her up and carried her to the bed, kissing her hard as he went, wetting her lips with his tongue and dipping teasingly inside. He dropped her on the mattress and crawled over her, tasting each nipple as he went before settling on top of her, supporting his weight with one arm to protect the baby.

He continued kissing her, caressing every inch of her body with exquisite attention to detail. He cupped first one swollen breast, and then the other, teasing her nipples between his clever fingers before stroking his way down over the swell of her belly, pausing as their little one rolled against his hand. Then he continued down, lower, between her thighs.

In pregnancy, Selene was wetter than ever, and he touched the slick folds expertly, making her writhe with pleasure and desire. At last, he rolled her on top of him, so she could slide him into her. They rocked together, drowning in their love and deliriously happy. They reached a glorious shining peak at the same moment. Then, overwhelmed by the day and the evening, they curled up and slept.

CHAPTER 22

*A*s autumn passed into winter, even Selene began to believe that Billy had perhaps been dissuaded against his ugly vendetta after receiving a bullet for his trouble. He hadn't been seen since the incident. Forbidden to have anything to do with the case, she was unable to pry information about his whereabouts from the brains of his friends and loved ones. *Perhaps it's just as well. It would be unethical.*

Instead, the newlyweds concentrated on decorating their home for Christmas. Brandon purchased a fresh pine tree, which they put up in the living room, festooned with lights and dripping with paper ornaments Maggie had made in Sunday School when she was very small. *Soon*, Selene thought with a smile, *new paper plate angels will join the old ones.*

One bitterly cold night in mid-December, Selene and her husband sat in their pajamas in front of the Christmas tree, admiring the lights and sipping hot cocoa as they snuggled together, sharing their warmth. *No heater on earth can truly compensate for an Upper Midwestern December*, Selene thought with a shiver.

Brandon took her empty mug and set it on the coffee table. "Are you cold, baby?" he asked.

"A little," she admitted.

He waggled his eyebrows. "Let's go to bed. I know a good way to keep you warm."

She grinned but offered a joking protest. "That again? How can you want to when I'm this big? I even look pregnant in this nightgown."

"You look pregnant out of that nightgown too," Brandon pointed out, playing along, "and since you are pregnant, I don't have a problem with that."

"But the question is, why do you want to make love to someone so swollen?"

"It's a good exercise for my creativity," he replied, helping her to her feet. "To what better use could I put it? Besides, I know you have a good time, don't you, baby?"

Selene stopped playing as anticipation welled up. "Oh yes. Each and every time."

Taking his wife by the hand, contentment radiating through them both, they meandered down the hall to the bathroom for a quick brushing of the teeth before they retired to the bed and snuggled up. They took long moments to kiss and taste each other. *No matter how many days pass, kissing never really gets old. Brandon's sweet mouth never fails to arouse me*. He began to touch her, caressing her breasts, lifting the hem of her nightgown.

Selene heard a strange shuffling sound. *Cat*, she thought, turning to look, but it was no cat. The one person they had hoped never to see again stood in their bedroom, glaring with bloodshot eyes. Selene shrank against Brandon as the intruder raised a handgun—Selene's own—and pointed it at them.

His hand shook badly, and his stance seemed awkward, as though his leg hurt.

Slow, deep breaths. Don't panic. Slow down and think. What do

I do? What do I observe that can help? He's a kid, young and scared. The realization spawned a wild plan. Sliding away from her husband, Selene rose from the bed. As she expected, Billy's attention followed her.

∾

Brandon longed to leap from the bed and protect his wife, but reality forced him to admit that she, not he, had the training to deal with this situation. He might, by jumping in, make everything worse.

"Billy Flannery," she scolded, her voice surprisingly calm, like a displeased schoolteacher, "what are you doing here? Don't you know it's rude to come into someone's home without being invited?"

"I'm going to kill you, bitch," Billy snarled.

Brandon stared at the boy, startled by how young he seemed. *He's scarcely more than a teenager.* Using the cover of the ongoing conversation between his wife and the youth, he sneaked his cell phone from the bedside table, hit the speed dial and then turned off the speaker.

"Yes, I gathered that, could you please explain *why*? No one can understand why an intelligent young man like you would behave in this way."

"I'll tell you why," the boy trembled in terror, but remained determined. "You put my brother in prison."

"I'm sorry, Billy, but that simply isn't true," Selene replied calmly. "I didn't put your brother in prison. He put himself in prison. But he's out now, isn't he?"

"Yes, but he's not the same. Bad things happened in there." The boy's face twisted.

She frowned. "I know, and that's very hard, but the truth is, he caused bad things to happen on the outside too. I'm sure what he went through was no worse than what he did to that poor woman and her family."

"Shut up!" Billy snarled. "He didn't do it."

"He told me he did," Selene refuted. "He said it was an accident, he didn't mean to kill her, and I believe him, which was why he was charged with manslaughter, not murder. If he had called 911, he might have gotten community service, but he hid her body, Billy. He hoped her family would never know. It wasn't right. You know he pleaded guilty."

"That was you!" Billy yelled, taking a threatening step forward. "You did something to him to make him confess, didn't you? You coerced him. I saw the video. It didn't make any sense. How did you get him to say he killed her?"

"He wanted to confess. He felt terrible. All I did was give him the push."

"But how did you know?" the boy wailed. "He was only brought in for denting a car!"

"I've been questioning suspects for a long time. I get a feeling about these things. Come on, now Billy. That's enough. You've scared us really bad, but isn't it time to stop?" She took a cautious step towards the boy.

His gaze hardened, and his hand steadied on the gun. "No. I'm going to shoot you."

She took another step towards him, and her nightgown swirled around her body.

"Oh shit, you're pregnant?"

She covered her belly protectively with one hand and gave the boy a wistful look. "Yes. I'm expecting a baby in just a few months. Billy, if you're going to shoot me, could you please not aim for my belly? Give my husband a chance to rescue our son, so he doesn't die too? Can you do that for me, Billy?"

Her words caused an unpleasant feeling to sweep through Brandon, so he didn't know if he wanted to hurl or cry. "No, Selene." Ring from the bed, he wrapped his arms around her, hugged her, and then pushed her behind him. "I won't raise a child without a mother again. He'll have to kill me to get to you."

Billy looked from one to the other, panicked, not sure what to do. "I'll do it." His voice sounded uncertain. "I'll kill you both."

"All three of us?" Selene stepped out from behind her husband, and ran her hand across her abdomen, drawing attention to the swollen bulge again. "I thought you only wanted me, not my husband, not my baby."

"It's your own fault! You shot me. I can't even go to the hospital to get it fixed. The infection nearly killed me. It never did heal right."

"What did you think I would do?" she demanded. "You tried to shoot me in my sleep. That wasn't nice either, Billy. When you have a disagreement with someone, you don't sneak around setting fires, taking pictures and shooting into dark bedrooms. You talk it out. It's what adults do."

She's distracting him again. Out of bed, Brandon realized how close to Billy he was standing, and how close to the gun. *If only I could grab it…* He took a slow step towards the boy. The muzzle swung in his direction and he froze.

"Billy Flannery, stop pointing that thing at my husband. Honestly, young man, where did you learn manners?" Selene's hand wrapped around a floor lamp, leaning on it as though for support. In a movement so quick the assailant had no time to react, she yanked the slender lamp off the floor and smashed it into Billy's damaged hip.

Brandon grabbed the wrist holding the gun and jerked the weapon away, tossing it to Selene. One hard punch to the gut, and the fight was over. Their tormentor lay on the floor.

Selene aimed the gun at the boy while Brandon scooped up the cell phone and turned the sound back on.

"Tony, are you there?" he said.

"I'm here. What happened?"

"He's down," Brandon explained. "Selene's got him covered. Where are you?"

"About two blocks away."

"Good. See you in a minute. Oh and, Tony, tell Chief Brady we'll come in and make a statement in the morning."

"Honey," Selene said as Brandon hung up the phone, "could you please open the front door? I don't want Tony to smash it down again. The neighbors won't like it, and it will let the cold in."

"Are you sure it's safe?" Brandon eyed the intruder and made no attempt to hide his anger.

"I have the gun now," Selene replied in a voice as cold as the winter wind swirling outside the window.

He gave the boy a dangerous look and left the room.

"Now you remember, Billy," Selene snarled, "if you give me any trouble, I'll shoot you. And I've already shot you once, so you know I mean it. Be still."

"Why?" he moaned. "Why didn't you just kill me?"

"Because I'm a good person," she replied. "Oh, I wanted to kill you, especially after those photographs, but I'm going to do something even worse. I'm going to forgive you. It may not be today, but someday soon, I will tell myself, "That Billy Flannery is not going to make me angry another moment. You see, my life is too valuable to waste it on hatred and murder. Yours is too. I'm giving you a second chance. Don't mistake me, you'll have to pay a heavy price for what you've done, just like your brother did, but use the opportunity to learn from your bad choices and make better ones in the future."

Billy didn't move a muscle until Brandon and Tony returned to the room. Tony handcuffed the stalker and hoisted him to his feet.

"Thanks," Selene said, hugging her friend around the shoulders. "We owe you one more. We'll have to name the baby after you. Caleb Anthony sounds just right, doesn't it, Brand?"

Brandon twisted his lips to the side but nodded.

"It's a deal." Tony grinned. "Thank God this is finally over."

"No kidding. Oh, and Tony, make sure he gets medical attention, would you? I don't think the bullet in his hip is doing him any good."

"Sure thing," he agreed, escorting the suspect out the door.

Climbing back into bed, Selene began trembling from both the cold and adrenaline.

Brandon hugged her. "It's over, baby. We got him. He can't hurt us anymore." He traced her face with his fingertips. Admiration trickled over her skin with the touch. "You were amazing. How did you stay so calm?"

She cuddled in his embrace, enjoying the soothing warmth. After a moment, she took a deep breath and answered. "I know my way around a suspect. He was shaking so hard; I knew he was scared to death. He never thought he would have to confront us directly, and he wasn't prepared for it. He was a pretty effective sneak, but in person, he's just a kid, not a hardened criminal. He didn't know what he was doing. I knew our only chance was to talk him down. But you? What a hero you are, taking on an armed man with your bare hands. I'm very impressed."

"Well, I had a little help," he said, petting her hair. His fingers grazed the back of her neck and she could feel a surge of masculine pride.

"Sure, we all need a little help. You taught me that. I was trying to save the world all alone, and never rely on anyone else for support. But what I didn't understand was that unless you have someone to love, saving the world has no point. Tonight, I realized what we have—our family—is so valuable, and I'm part of what gives it that value. Without me, the equation doesn't work, does it?"

"No," he agreed. "A family without a mother isn't the same. We both know that."

"We do. Of course, we also both have a rather broad definition of what constitutes a mother. I think it's made us better people, don't you?" she asked.

"Maybe," he replied, "but I also think it's good our son is going to have, not just a mother and father, but his own mother and father."

"Oh yes, that's the best part of all."

They held each other close for a tender kiss, each savoring the feeling of all that might have been lost. As one kiss led to another, and then another, peace like neither had ever known before enveloped them. Finally, Brandon and Selene found healing and wholeness for their wounded hearts in each other.

AFTERWORD

I hope you enjoyed spending time with Brandon and Selene. These two are old friends of mine, and writing their story was a blast. I would love to hear back from you about whether you liked this book, and whether you would be interested in reading more. Check out my website: http:// simonebeaudelaireauthor.weebly.com/ or email me at simonebeaudelaireauthor@hotmail.com.

If you would be inclined to head over to Amazon.com and write a review, I would very much appreciate it. Reviews are the means by which readers can give feedback to authors and help them hone their craft. They also give authors greater exposure. Writing a review for a book you enjoy can make a great deal of difference in the author's publishing career by letting other readers know what to expect in the book. And it isn't necessary to write a huge amount. A single paragraph giving your opinion will suffice. Thank you so much!

Sincerely,
   Simone Beaudelaire

Dear reader,

You can discover more books by Simone Beaudelaire at
https://www.nextchapter.pub/authors/simone-
beaudelaire-romance-author.

Want to know when one of our books is free or discounted for
Kindle? Join the newsletter at
http://eepurl.com/bqqB3H.

Best regards,
Next Chapter Team

You might also like:
Where The Wind Blows by Simone Beaudelaire

To read the first chapter for free, please head to:
https://www.nextchapter.pub/books/where-the-wind-blows.

NOTE

The Lakota people, part of the Sioux Nation, are one of the larger Native American groups in the United States. Many live in the area surrounding the Black Hills of South Dakota. I have tried very hard to represent their culture accurately and apologize for any mistakes I may have made. Like Selene, I'm not Lakota and cannot grasp what it must be like to be one, although I like them very much. If you are interested in the Lakota, there is a wealth of information available, the best of which is prepared by the people themselves. There are videos of Wacipis on YouTube, and if you are fortunate enough to live near a community, these events are often open to the public.

ABOUT THE AUTHOR

In the world of the written word, Simone Beaudelaire strives for technical excellence while advancing a worldview in which the sacred and the sensual blend into stories of people whose relationships are founded in faith but are no less passionate for it. Unapologetically explicit, yet undeniably classy, Beaudelaire's 20+ novels aim to make readers think, cry, pray... and get a little hot and bothered.

In real life, the author's alter-ego teaches composition at a community college in a small western Kansas town, where she lives with her four children, three cats, and husband—fellow author Edwin Stark.

As both romance writer and academic, Beaudelaire devotes herself to promoting the rhetorical value of the romance in hopes of overcoming the stigma associated with literature's biggest female-centered genre.

BOOKS BY SIMONE BEAUDELAIRE

When the Music Ends (The Hearts in Winter Chronicles Book 1)

When the Words are Spoken (The Hearts in Winter Chronicles Book 2)

When the Heart Heals (The Hearts in Winter Chronicles Book 3)

Caroline's Choice (The Hearts in Winter Chronicles Book 4)

The Naphil's Kiss

Blood Fever

Polar Heat

Xaman (with Edwin Stark)

Darkness Waits (with Edwin Stark)

Watching Over the Watcher

Baylee Breaking

Amor Maldito: Romantic Tragedies from Tejano Folklore

Keeping Katerina (The Victorians Book 1)

Devin's Dilemma (The Victorians Book 2)

Colin's Conundrum (The Victorians Book 3)

High Plains Holiday (Love on the High Plains Book 1)

High Plains Promise (Love on the High Plains Book 2)

High Plains Heartbreak (Love on the High Plains Book 3)

High Plains Passion (Love on the High Plains Book 4)

Devilfire (American Hauntings Book 1)

Saving Sam (The Wounded Warriors Book 1 with J.M. Northup)

Justifying Jack (The Wounded Warriors Book 2 with J.M. Northup)

Making Mike (The Wounded Warriors Book 3 with J.M Northup)

Lightning Source UK Ltd.
Milton Keynes UK
UKHW022019020221
378140UK00003B/306

9 781034 331162